LUMINOUS
EMPTINESS

LUMINOUS
EMPTINESS

Understanding the
Tibetan Book of the Dead

Francesca Fremantle

SHAMBHALA
Boston & London
2003

Shambhala Publications, Inc.
Horticultural Hall
300 Massachusetts Avenue
Boston, Massachusetts 02115
www.shambhala.com

10   9   8   7   6   5   4   3   2

Printed in the United States of America

⊚ This edition is printed on acid-free paper that meets the American National Standards Institute Z39.48 Standard.

Distributed in the United States by Random House, Inc., and in Canada by Random House of Canada Ltd

Book design by Judy Arisman, Arisman Design, Essex, MA

The Library of Congress catalogues the hardcover edition of this book as follows:

Fremantle, Francesca.
    Luminous emptiness : understanding the Tibetan book of the dead / by Francesca Fremantle.
        p.   cm.
    ISBN 1-57062-450-X (cloth)
    ISBN 1-57062-925-0 (pbk.)
        1. Karma-gliṅ-pa, 14th cent. Bar do thos grol.   2. Intermediate state—Buddhism.   3. Death—Religious aspects—Buddhism.   4. Funeral rites and ceremonies, Buddhist.   I. Karma-gliṅ-pa, 14th cent. Bar do thos grol.   II. Title.

BQ4490 .K3713   2001
294.3'423—dc21   2001040094

*This book is dedicated
to the memory of
the Vidyadhara, Chögyam Trungpa Rinpoche,
incomparable messenger of dharma
and to
Rigdzin Shikpo (Michael Hookham)
who continues his tradition*

Contents

Illustrations

Preface

Understanding little of my guru's teaching,
Even that little not put into practice,
How can I write as though it has entered my heart,
Like a dewdrop dreaming it can hold the sun?
Please grant your blessing so that beings such as I
May drink the nectar of the Ocean of Dharma.

THE TRUE FOUNT OF INSPIRATION behind the writing of this book is Chögyam Trungpa Rinpoche. It was he who introduced me to the *Tibetan Book of the Dead* and established my lifelong connection with it by asking me to translate it with him. It is he who is the source of whatever understanding I may have of it. To my deep regret, I was unable to fulfill his expectations and intentions for me while he was alive. This book is my offering to him. With it, I hope to share some of the riches I received from him and carry out at least a small part of his wishes.

Trungpa Rinpoche was probably born in 1940 and was recognized at an early age as a reincarnation in the lineage of the Trungpa Tulkus. He was the eleventh in a line of highly realized teachers, and abbot of the Surmang group of monasteries in eastern Tibet. *Tulku* means "emanation body," which we usually call an incarnation; *Trungpa* is the name of his lineage, meaning literally "one who is in the presence"; *Chögyam* is an abbreviation of one of the many names he received during his training, meaning "Ocean of Dharma"; and *Rinpoche* is a title meaning "precious jewel," generally used for all respected teachers.

Following the invasion of Tibet by China, he escaped to India in 1959 and came to England in 1963. While living in Oxford, he began teaching a few students, and then moved to Scotland where he founded Samye Ling, the first Tibetan Buddhist center in the United Kingdom. In 1970, he was invited to North America, where his teaching attracted a tremendous response. The United States and Canada remained the bases of his teaching activities until his death in 1987.

The Trungpa lineage belongs to the Kagyü school of Tibetan Buddhism, but many of Rinpoche's teachers were from the Nyingma school. In his own life and teaching, he combined the characteristic qualities of both traditions. However, for practical purposes, there are significant differences between the methods of the two schools. With his first students in England, he taught primarily from the Nyingma perspective, but after his move to America, he emphasized the Kagyü style of practice. In later years, he developed his own unique presentation, known as the Shambhala teachings, whose basic principles he discovered as "mind treasures" (*gongter*). The Shambhala teachings are drawn from ancient Tibetan and other Asian wisdom traditions, as well as Buddhism; they bring the sacred vision of the tantras into everyday life without the need for any religious affiliation or the use of specifically Buddhist terminology. Thus, three great rivers of his inspiration and blessings have flowed out to the world from the Ocean of Dharma.

I first met Trungpa Rinpoche in the spring of 1969. At the time, I was engaged in research for my doctoral thesis on the *Guhyasamaja Tantra* at the School of Oriental and African Studies in London. Feeling discouraged by difficulties with the text, I hoped that he might be able to help. I had begun studying Sanskrit in the early 1960s because of my love of Indian civilization and philosophy, and soon came across works on tantra in the university library. I felt an immediate attraction to it as a spiritual path that relied on direct experience rather than belief and that gave genuine respect and equality to women. It revealed a transforming vision of a sacred world not to be looked for elsewhere but to be discovered here and now, embracing the whole of life. As I had been brought up with the poetry of William Blake, tantra seemed to embody the philosophy of my favorite work of his, *The Marriage of Heaven and Hell*, especially its closing words: "For everything that lives is Holy."

As part of my undergraduate studies, I was fortunate enough to spend six months at the Government Sanskrit College in Calcutta. While in India, I met several remarkable Hindu teachers, but none with whom I felt a very strong personal connection. On gaining my degree, I planned to return to India to pursue my interest in Hindu tantra, but by auspicious coincidence, as Trungpa Rinpoche would have said, Professor David Snellgrove persuaded me that the Buddhist *Guhyasamaja Tantra* would be a suitable subject for my dissertation. This led to my learning Tibetan in addition to Sanskrit and becoming immersed in the classical world of vajrayana. However, I did not realize that there was any access to vajrayana as an authentic living tradition outside Tibet, where it was rapidly being destroyed. It was not until about halfway through my research that I learned of the existence of a genuine master living in my own country and decided to visit him.

My first glimpse of Trungpa Rinpoche was at early morning meditation at Samye Ling. The sun had not yet risen, and in the darkness, the room was lit only by candles on the shrine, above which hung a glowing gold and red thangka of Amitabha. As he walked into the room and prostrated three times in front of the shrine, his movements were filled with a grace, dignity, and awareness that were overwhelmingly impressive. He radiated a sense of profound stillness and presence that I had never seen in anyone else. During my visit, not only did he give me the help and inspiration to continue with my research, but somehow, without actually saying very much, he transmitted an insight into the real spiritual meaning of tantra.

About a year later, he moved to America, and in the following year I went there to join him. In 1971, he gave three seminars on subjects relating to the *Tibetan Book of the Dead*. One of these formed the basis for his commentary to our translation and the other two were later published in his book *Transcending Madness* (Shambhala, 1992). During these intensive periods, his teaching produced extraordinary effects on the participants. As he explained the inner meaning of the bardos and the six realms of existence, many of us experienced a roller-coaster ride through those various states of mind, as well as the flashes of openness that accompany their extremes of tension. The vivid emotions of the six realms, the enlightened qualities of the five buddha families, even the process of dissolution that leads to death and the experience of emptiness and luminosity became for that short time much more than beautiful and profound metaphors. It was both terrifying and wonderful—a glimpse into a totally new way of looking at life.

For the seminar most directly based on the text of the *Tibetan Book of the Dead*, Trungpa Rinpoche used a Tibetan blockprint while the audience tried to follow him in the only available English version, translated by Kazi Dawa-Samdup and edited by W. Y. Evans-Wentz. Although he had great respect and appreciation for their pioneering work in publishing this and other very important texts, he was less happy with the actual translation. That is why he suggested that we should produce a new version together, which was first published by Shambhala Publications in 1975.

When work on the translation was finished, I came back to England to live in London, fully intending to return frequently to the United States. But at that time I was not committed enough to be able to follow a single path, and too many other interests absorbed my attention; in particular, a deep karmic link with Bengal and Hindu tantra needed to be resolved. However, the connection with Rinpoche was never broken, so eventually, after a long, roundabout journey, I came back to the practice of vajrayana, thanks to the influence and example of my dharma brother, Rigdzin Shikpo.

As Michael Hookham, Rigdzin Shikpo was one of Trungpa Rinpoche's earliest Western students. He had already been practicing various types of Buddhist meditation for ten years when they met in 1965, so he was exceptionally well prepared. Rinpoche gave him the teachings and transmission of the Nyingma lineage and later authorized him to establish the Longchen Foundation, which at present is based in Oxford and North Wales. In 1993, Michael completed a three-year retreat under the direction of Khenpo Tsultrim Gyamtso Rinpoche and was given the name Rigdzin Shikpo, by which he is now known.

With a deep knowledge of Buddhism, he has an extraordinary gift for expressing it in vivid and poetic ways and for creating links with many aspects of Western culture. Above all, he has an attitude of complete devotion, so that his mind has become one with the mind of the guru. Listening to him talk about dharma, I often feel as though Trungpa Rinpoche is speaking through his voice. Without him, I would never have gained the experience or the confidence to write about these profound teachings. With regard to this book, he has answered my innumerable questions with endless patience and interest. I am particularly grateful to him for his help in understanding the practices and terminology of dzogchen, and especially for sharing the insights of his yogic experience.

The idea of writing such a book has been growing slowly for a long time. Ever since the publication of the *Tibetan Book of the Dead*, the same questions have been put to me again and again. These questions mainly concern the meaning of the visions of the deities that arise after death and the reason for such an elaborate system of symbolism. There are also many questions about reincarnation and the significance of the six realms of existence in which one may be reborn. My original idea was to produce a fairly short work centering on the iconography and symbolism of the deities, but it soon became apparent that, in order to do this properly, they would need to be related to the basic concepts of Buddhism.

One of the unique aspects of Trungpa Rinpoche's communicative skill was his ability to make connections across the whole range of teachings, which are traditionally kept in separate compartments. He not only linked the various components together, but also explained how each of them relates to everyday life in a very practical way. With this as my basic inspiration and guideline, I have tried to incorporate all the most relevant aspects of the teaching into the first part of *Luminous Emptiness* in a manner that will illuminate the text.

Coming to the text itself, I have retranslated all the excerpts that appear in the second part of this book. The revision is mostly a question of style, which has become rather more free and less literal, although I also discovered some mistakes that I have taken the opportunity to rectify. As the quotations included here are quite extensive, it is not really necessary to refer to a complete translation of the *Tibetan Book of the Dead*, but if readers wish to do so, it should not be difficult to follow the explanations with any of the current translations.

Trungpa Rinpoche was unusual among Tibetan lamas in speaking excellent English, and he greatly enjoyed the challenges of translation. He was very open to suggestions, but he also had firm views on certain issues. For example, he wanted to avoid any hint of theism or theosophy, and he was determined not to use words that suggested the sense of guilt and blame prevalent in much of conventional religion, whose effects he saw in his students. In fact, he originated many terms that were later adopted by other Buddhist teachers and have become part of dharma language, especially in America. However, those were very early days in the transmission of vajrayana to the West, and with hindsight I feel that not all of our decisions in the 1975 translation have stood the test of time. Especially in the area of dzogchen texts, there have been some excellent translations during the intervening years, through which several of its key terms have become widely accepted in English. Although in a certain sense all of Trungpa Rinpoche's teaching was imbued with the flavor of dzogchen, he did not go into many of its technical details at that time, and I did not possess enough knowledge to ask him the necessary questions while we were working together.

In common with many scholarly Tibetans, Trungpa Rinpoche had great respect for the Sanskrit language, and he often used Sanskrit as well as Tibetan words in his teaching when he could not find a suitable English equivalent. He always preferred to use the Sanskrit names of deities. In Tibet, the names of the more important and well-known deities—the five male and five female buddhas for example—are generally translated into Tibetan, although in some texts they are simply transliterated into Tibetan script. In this text, we find a combination of both methods, but I have kept to Trungpa Rinpoche's practice of rendering them in Sanskrit and giving English translations. A very few are referred to mainly by English names when the meaning is particularly relevant and the Sanskrit is particularly unwieldy.

Rinpoche was always concerned with how best to express the true spirit of Buddhism, and his interest extended into every area of its presentation. For instance, he had strong opinions about what he saw as the overuse of initial capital letters, which he related to an underlying theistic attitude. He felt that it produces a false impression by making too much of concepts that should be presented as simple, accessible, and unpretentious. He wanted to put across the idea that enlightenment is no big deal—it is our natural state. Readers who are not accustomed to his style may be surprised to find words such as *dharma* or *bodhisattva* not capitalized. Even *buddha* is lowercase, except with reference to a specific buddha, like Buddha Shakyamuni. (Neither the Sanskrit nor Tibetan script possesses capital letters, so it is often difficult to tell whether a word is a proper name, a title, or an epithet.) Words such as *Nyingma*, *Zen*, and so on are names of distinct schools or traditions, so they are treated as true proper nouns. But the three yanas, tantra, mahamudra, and dzogchen are stages on the path or styles of practice, so they are not capitalized. In this I have followed Trungpa Rinpoche's guidelines with a few exceptions. I have decided to use capitals for the names of the five families of buddhas (Buddha, Vajra, Ratna, Padma, and Karma), treating them just as if they were family names in English so as to avoid confusion with the alternative meanings of buddha, vajra, and karma. I am very much indebted to Larry Mermelstein, of the Nalanda Translation Committee, for clarifying these issues, drawing on his long experience of working with Trungpa Rinpoche in this field.

Apart from proper names, I have tried to reduce the use of Sanskrit and Tibetan in this book to a minimum. However, there are some examples of rather specialized terms that I felt I should keep, and I have explained the reasons where such terms first occur. There are also a few words that I do translate, but where an examination of the original Sanskrit, and sometimes the Tibetan as well, helps to illuminate their meaning. I have perhaps indulged my fascination with words and their meanings too much in these passages, but I hope that some readers may find these digressions interesting; those who do not may skip them without much loss.

As this is not an academic work, I decided rather regretfully not to use the accepted transliteration, with diacritics, of Sanskrit words. This system is obviously preferable for those who already know it and provides the only reliable guidance to correct pronunciation; but it can be a real barrier for those who do not understand it and requires quite an effort to do so. There is a different problem with Tibetan, because the correct transliteration generally creates even greater difficulties in pronunciation. Where Tibetan words occur in this book, I give approximate phonetic versions, with the full spelling in brackets or in the endnotes. As an aid to the pronunciation of Sanskrit words, it helps to imagine that one is speaking Italian rather than English, especially with regard to the vowels. Another point to note is that, in both Sanskrit and Tibetan, *th* is never pronounced as in "other," but as in "hothouse." Similarly, *ph* is not equivalent to *f*, but is an aspirated *p*, as in "uphold."

Perhaps I should explain a little about my own approach to translation. Since my introduction to Buddhism came about through Indian studies, I am always very much aware that Buddhism grew out of Indian thought and culture, and that its expression is very closely linked to the Sanskrit language. I feel it is absolutely essential to keep returning to the Sanskrit roots of Buddhist terminology. Some of the work that has been done purely from Tibetan sources, apparently without any reference to Sanskrit, seems to me to depart occasionally from the original meaning.

Translation of Buddhist texts into English presents entirely different problems than those faced by the early translators of Sanskrit into Tibetan. This is because our language has been formed by so many diverse influences. As a result, it contains a huge number of synonyms and many alternative ways of saying the same thing. With so much variety, our individual choice of words and expressions is extremely subjective. All translation is interpretation, and there is no perfect translation, least of all in this field. I sincerely hope there will never be a standardized code of translation for Buddhist literature. Any such attempt would have a deadening influence. Even though such a great variety of different versions may seem confusing to students of Buddhism, it can also be regarded as an opportunity. By comparing translations, those who do not know any Sanskrit or Tibetan may be able to look at these elusive concepts from different points of view and gain greater insight into them.

Westerners are at a disadvantage in that our whole background of philosophical and religious thought is very different from that of Buddhism. This means that certain English terms, which might at first appear suitable, are too heavily loaded with inappropriate implications. All the same, it is perhaps surprising that some translators are not content with the incredible richness of the language of Shakespeare and feel the need to invent even more new words or to hunt out obscure ones. In keeping with the Buddha's own attitude toward teaching, the great majority of dharma texts, whether in Sanskrit or Tibetan, use ordinary, everyday language. In the context of dharma, this simple language is used to express the most profound ideas and experiences, yet the Buddha and his successors did not choose to use complex or obscure words to express themselves, and I believe we should try to follow their example. An exception to this would be in the study of philosophy and logic, where technical terminology is entirely appropriate. However, this affects only a very small area; it does not apply in most cases, and especially not to tantric literature.

In any language, we can understand these ordinary words in a special way according to their context. If further explanation is required, it can be given in commentaries or notes, but I believe that it should not intrude into the translation itself. Some teachers say that because the experiential meaning of certain words such as *emptiness* or *compassion* changes at different stages of the path, especially in dzogchen, they should be translated differently. To me, the important thing is that those words were not changed. The great masters of long ago had plenty of choice, but they chose to retain the same terms. Part of their effectiveness is that they can be understood on many levels. It is for the reader to imbue them with meaning according to the context and in light of his or her own experience.

Above all, translation is an art. As translators, we must remember that the same words that give us so much trouble in trying to pin down their meaning are not just technical terms but are used in poetry, spontaneous songs, and liturgies whose purpose is to inspire and arouse the imagination. Sadly, it is sometimes impossible to find a solution that is both accurate and aesthetic, but we should try, as far as possible, to retain the spirit of the original. Beside the depth and beauty of texts such as the *Tibetan Book of the Dead*, I am only too aware that my own work is clumsy and confused, and I apologize for its defects. Nevertheless, I feel that I have been blessed with tremendous good fortune in being able to produce this book. It has given me great joy in the writing; may it bring joy and benefit to all who read it.

Acknowledgments

First and foremost, my profound thanks to the late Chögyam Trungpa and to Rigdzin Shikpo, to both of whom this book is dedicated; the parts they both played in its origination and its eventual completion are explained in the preface.

There are many other accomplished lamas, as well as teachers from other traditions, from whom I have received much help and kindness; in particular, I had the great privilege of meeting and receiving teaching from several of the exceptional Tibetan lamas of the older generation who are no longer with us in the same bodily form. To all of them, I am extremely grateful. I remember with deep gratitude the late Sochi Sen, my guide in the Shakta tradition, whose life exemplified the genuine spirit of tantra beyond sectarian differences. Thanks also to the many scholars and translators whose writings have been a source of both information and inspiration.

I would like to express my gratitude to my friends who read early drafts of the manuscript and made many valuable suggestions, especially Caroline Cupitt, David Hutchens, Barbara Wanklyn, and Kathleen Taylor; also to Larry Mermelstein, who greatly improved it in the final stages with his expert advice.

Thanks also to Gonkar Gyatso for his beautiful paintings, combining the ancient and the contemporary in timeless imagery.

Finally, at Shambhala Publications, I am most grateful to Samuel Bercholz, chairman and editor-in-chief, for his enthusiasm and encouragement; to my editor, Emily Bower, for her skill, patience, and understanding; as well as to everyone who worked on the book and contributed to making this dream a reality.

Part One

FOUNDATIONS

Homage

I bow down at the feet of my gurus:
May the power of their presence
Inspire and dwell within these words
So that their vision is fulfilled.

May the peaceful and wrathful devatas
Shine within our heart and mind
So that we may clearly know them
As our own awakened nature.

May the dakinis who dance
In the boundless sky of wisdom
Reveal the secret treasure
Of dharma profound and vast.

May the powerful dharmapalas
Protect the truth of the teachings,
Grind to dust all misconceptions,
And guide us always on the path.

Chapter One

A Book of the Living

THE BOOK THAT WE KNOW in the West as the *Tibetan Book of the Dead* is a most extraordinary and wonderful text. It was one of the first examples both of vajrayana literature and of Tibetan literature to be translated into a European language, and is probably still the best known among Buddhists and non-Buddhists alike. Although the choice may have been accidental, it is well deserving of its fame as a representative of Tibetan Buddhism. It bridges a wide range of interests, for on the one hand it is a very specialized teaching connected with advanced meditation practices, but on the other hand it is an expression of a universal truth, appealing to many people beyond the sphere of Buddhism. The purpose of *Luminous Emptiness* is to serve as a guide to understanding this classic text by interpreting in detail the concepts on which it is based, the terms it uses, and the imagery it contains. This book is addressed to everyone who feels attracted to the *Tibetan Book of the Dead*, whether they are Buddhist or not. I hope that non-Buddhists will not find it too full of technicalities, and especially that it will be helpful in illuminating the complex symbolism of vajrayana both to them and to Buddhists of other traditions who are unfamiliar with it.

The first question we must ask is whether it should really be called the *Tibetan Book of the Dead* at all. Probably most people who have read it, in any of its translations, are aware that this is not the original title, but a name given to it by W. Y. Evans-Wentz, the compiler and editor of its first translation into English.[1] This was chosen because of the text's apparent similarity in subject matter to the *Egyptian Book of the Dead*, which was very popular at the time. That title was also invented and had proved to be extremely effective from the point of view of publicity. It is human nature to feel a fascination with death and an intense curiosity about what will happen afterward, so a name like this is excellent for catching readers' attention. It is quite likely that if Evans-Wentz had introduced it to the Western world as the *Great Liberation through Hearing during the Intermediate State*, it would not have attracted so much interest. Trungpa Rinpoche did not particularly like the new title, but we continued to use it for our translation because it is so well known.

Calling it the *Tibetan Book of the Dead* is not entirely inappropriate; after all, the text is undeniably addressed to those who are close to death or who have just died, and it is read aloud to guide them. In another sense, we who think of ourselves as the living could really be called the dead. We are the unawakened, living our lives in a dream—a dream that will continue after death, then through life after life, until we truly awaken.

In this book, however, I shall refer to it by its short Tibetan title: *Liberation through Hearing*. This is because I also make use of some of the other texts associated with it, so it seems more consistent and appropriate to give it its real name alongside them. Also, my intention is not to treat it as a book of the dead in the usual sense of the word. Except incidentally, its application to the care of the dying and preparations for death, or its use in rituals for the dead, will not be discussed at any length.[2] Instead, it will be presented as a book of the living: a book *for* the living, about this life. The ideas, the visions, the insights it contains can have no genuine, effective significance for us if we approach them only as descriptions of what happens after death, and if we do not understand that they apply to us here and now in our everyday lives.

Trungpa Rinpoche, at the very beginning of his commentary to our translation, remarks that it could just as well be called the *Tibetan Book of Birth*.[3] He explains that it is a misunderstanding to treat it as part of the lore of death and compare it to the *Egyptian Book of the Dead* or to the death traditions of any other culture. "The book is not based on death as such, but on a completely different concept of death." Its whole point is "the fundamental principle of birth and death recurring constantly in this life." Wherever there is birth, there is death, and wherever there is death, there is birth. The book describes not only the process of dissolution, but also the process of coming into being, and these two processes are continually at work in every moment of life. According to the Buddhist view, nothing is permanent, fixed, or solid. The sense of self in each one of us, the "I," is being born and dying every moment. The whole of existence, the entire world of our experience, is appearing and disappearing every moment.

Whatever happens to us after death is simply a continuation of what is happening to us now in this life, even though it manifests in unfamiliar ways: as the text says, "samsara is reversed, and everything appears as lights and images." We are not catapulted into a completely different world, we just perceive the same world in a different way. Everything the text describes can be understood symbolically in terms of this life. Learning to perceive the world in this way is part of the transformational process of vajrayana Buddhism, and a practitioner who continues far enough along the path will be able to experience it all directly through meditation. But it is only in this life that we have the opportunity to prepare ourselves. After death, without the grounding influence of the physical body, events will overtake us with such speed and intensity that there will be no chance to stop and meditate. To be of use, meditation must become part of our innermost nature. That is why this is a book of the living as well as a book of the dead.

To treat it as a book of the living is not to deny that it is also literally about death nor to suggest that it cannot help the dead and dying. This interpretation does not in any way lessen the importance of contemplating the certainty of death or diminish its tremendous significance. Meditation on death, on the ephemeral nature of life, and on the inevitable consequences of our actions remains fundamental throughout the whole of the Buddhist path. There is no intention here to explain away rebirth in the six realms of samsara as an allegory or to reduce the visions of the deities, who are the living presence of the awakened state, to psychological archetypes. On the contrary, being able to see them all in terms of this life gives them an immediate relevance and rescues them from the danger of becoming mere fantasy.

Reading *Liberation through Hearing* with this attitude can provide tremendous motivation and inspiration for practice.

In it, the events that take place during the period between death and rebirth are described in a way that is, by any standards, extraordinary—extraordinary to many Asian Buddhists as well as to people who are neither Buddhist nor from an Asian culture. Buddhism is said to be a nontheistic religion, yet here we find visions of buddhas known as the peaceful and wrathful deities. These deities are awe-inspiring and frightening, even in their peaceful forms, and overwhelmingly terrifying in their wrathful manifestations. They may be multicolored, many-headed, many-armed, part animal or part bird, or they may appear as avenging demons who pursue the dead through surreal landscapes amid a bizarre cacophony of sounds. Then there are the six realms of existence into which the dead person may be reborn, perhaps as an animal or even as an otherworldly being such as a ghost or a god or goddess.

Sometimes people ask, "Do Buddhists really believe all this?" The immediate answer must be that only a small minority accepts the whole of this particular account, but that many more probably accept the principle behind it, if not all the details. The outline of the teachings concerning death—dissolution of the elements of the body followed by rebirth in accordance with one's previous actions—is accepted by all schools of Buddhism. But the existence of a period of transition between death and rebirth is not held by all, and there are different ideas about its nature. *Liberation through Hearing* presents us with very elaborate descriptions of all these processes, which are not found in such a complete form in any other tradition.

To answer the question in a more satisfactory manner, we must look at the nature of belief in Buddhism and at the place of *Liberation through Hearing* in its history. The Buddha did not teach a dogma; he offered a path based on understanding and personal experience rather than a creed. His own spiritual search was one of constant questioning and experimentation. The enlightenment he attained, the highest awakened state, cannot be expressed in ordinary human language. At first, he was extremely reluctant even to talk about it. Even after he was persuaded to teach, he never asked anyone to believe in what he said, but only to try it out for themselves. Words can only point to the truth; genuine knowledge must be experienced directly.

From the absolute point of view, to speak about truth is inevitably to lie, yet it is the very nature of truth to communicate itself. Once it is put into words, or even into images and symbols, it becomes subject to the limitations and distortions of human thought and language. The Buddha was very much aware of the limitations of human expression, and he knew that his teaching would be misunderstood. Frequently, he would remain silent when he was questioned about such things as the existence of the self or what happens to an enlightened person after death. At other times, he would allow the questioner to keep on suggesting alternatives, and to each one he would say no, it's not like that. Often his silence was an invitation to the questioner to look deeper into the preconceptions implicit in the question, which was based on false assumptions. Only a very few were able to understand his silence itself as an answer and to go away satisfied.

The Buddha certainly possessed that supreme gift of the greatest teachers to convey truth simply by his presence and to lift his disciples' minds into an intuitive state of awareness where doubts and questions become irrelevant. The warmth and radiance of his personality, which is clear from all the stories about his life, must have demonstrated better than any words his totally positive approach to the meaning of life and death. Unfortunately, his silence has left itself open to interpretation in rather negative ways, while his positive statements seem to have been ignored or glossed over, and Buddhism has sometimes falsely been presented as world-rejecting, agnostic, and even nihilistic. In contrast to this misleading impression of the original teaching, later forms of Buddhism may appear to go to the opposite extreme and are not accepted as genuine by followers of some Buddhist traditions.

Above all, Buddhism is a religion of practical methods for spiritual realization. Because of this, it contains many different views and formulations in response to people's needs and a huge variety of techniques to suit their inclinations and capabilities. Some of these may appear contradictory, yet they do not teach different truths; they present different points of view from which to approach the same truth. To distinguish the main movements, Buddhism is often described as consisting of the three yanas: hinayana, mahayana, and vajrayana. *Yana* is generally translated as "vehicle," but can also mean the path or the journey itself. The use of these three labels has become a rather sensitive issue, but they are very widely found, especially in the context of Tibetan Buddhism, so it is worthwhile to look into them a little.

In the most obvious sense, they correspond to phases in the historical development of Buddhism, represented by their characteristic scriptures. Hinayana, "the lesser way," is a retrospective label referring to the first period and is based on the actual words of the Buddha as reported by his disciples. The Buddha himself never attempted to codify his teachings into any kind of system. He taught in his local dialect rather than in Sanskrit, the language of orthodox religion. His disciples traveled far and wide, so that many different collections of his discourses, instructions, and rules for monastic life were handed down from memory in the various languages of India and the surrounding regions. According to tradition, eighteen separate monastic orders grew up during the centuries following the Buddha's death. Most of them died out or amalgamated, but four remained as distinct schools, which flourished alongside the later developments in the great monastic universities of India. Among these, the sarvastivada provided the monastic rule and basic philosophical analysis that were transmitted to Tibet. The descendent of only one of the four schools, the Theravada, still exists today as a fully independent tradition, thanks to its survival in Southeast Asia and Sri Lanka. Its collection of teachings was preserved in Pali, a dialect of western India, and provides the most complete record we have of early Buddhism.

By about the first century B.C., a new movement was developing, which began to produce its own distinctive scriptures, the sutras. Traditionally, they are believed to have been taught by the Buddha during his life, but since people were not yet ready to hear them, they were entrusted to the serpent-deities and other semidivine beings until the time was ripe. The followers of this movement referred to it as mahayana, "the great way." In contrast, they called the earlier tradition hinayana, which, it must be admitted, had the meaning of inferior. This discrimination rested mainly on their differing attitudes toward liberation. On the one hand, certain hinayana orders seem to have concentrated on a negative concept of nirvana as extinction, with the belief that it can only be attained by oneself and for oneself. On the other hand, the mahayana was based on a sense of the interrelationship of all existence and the aspiration to lead every single living being to enlightenment, seen as a very positive state. Many different traditions with widely divergent views and practices, from the devotion of the Pure Land school to the distinctive meditation of Zen, emerged from the spread of the mahayana throughout Asia.

The third phase is vajrayana, "the indestructible way." Its scriptures are the tantras, revealed by the Buddha not as a human being, but in his transcendent aspect. The dating of this movement is still very speculative. There appears to be no recorded evidence of Buddhist tantras in the monasteries until the second half of the seventh century A.D., but they may well have been practiced secretly in isolated places long before that time. Vajrayana is not considered separate from mahayana, but a special section within it. The *Guhyasamaja Tantra*, for instance, says that those who practice it will "succeed in this best of ways, the highest mahayana, this way of the buddhas, the great ocean of mahayana."[4] Vajrayana spread to the Far East in an incomplete form, and it was only Tibet that received and has preserved the complete heritage of Indian Buddhism, including all the levels of tantra.

That is the historical meaning of the three yanas, which cannot be totally disregarded, but which can be quite misleading. It is especially misleading if we try to label existing Buddhist schools, such as Zen, Theravada, or Tibetan Buddhism itself, as belonging to one or another yana on the basis of their historical origins. Contemporary Theravada practitioners understandably object to their path being considered inferior. Besides, hinayana contains all the fundamental teachings, and it is not possible that mahayana Buddhists intended to disparage the actual words of the Buddha! They were reacting only to what they perceived as a narrow-minded interpretation of his teachings on the part of certain groups at that time. If we look at those teachings as they are recorded in the Pali scriptures, we can find many passages to support the evolution leading to mahayana and vajrayana. In addition, the changes occurred very gradually and generally incorporated, rather than displaced, whatever existed already. In fact, all three yanas flourished together in India right up until the final destruction of the monasteries by Islamic invaders in the thirteenth century, as a result of which Buddhism was no longer able to survive in the land of its origin.

But there is another way of looking at the three yanas. The Buddhism of Tibet, although it is often referred to simply as tantric

Buddhism, actually contains all three yanas. Trungpa Rinpoche and other teachers in his tradition treat them as stages in spiritual progress: different psychological attitudes to the path, all equally valuable and necessary.

The journey begins with hinayana, which is not regarded as inferior, but as the preparation for and the foundation of the other yanas. Trungpa Rinpoche called it the narrow way. He described it as the path where we begin to make friends with ourselves and learn not to be a nuisance to ourselves and others. Here the emphasis is on working toward our own awakening, rather than that of all living beings. It is based on an attitude of honesty and humility. We realize that we need help and feel that we must do something about our own problems before we can even think about helping others. It is a path of simplicity and renunciation. At this stage, the attractions and temptations of worldly life are regarded as obstacles to be avoided, and there are many rules of conduct to help guide our behavior. As the basis of the entire path, it is never abandoned, but built upon like the foundation of a house. The meditation practices of this stage are those of tranquillity (Sanskrit *shamatha*), which is the practice of mindfulness to tame and calm the mind, and insight (Sanskrit *vipashyana*) into the nature of existence, which leads to the discovery of selflessness.

Practicing correctly with the simplicity of hinayana quite naturally results in a transformation of our relationship with the world. The narrow path leads into the open way, mahayana. The mahayana vision of the universe is a boundless web of interconnections embracing the whole of time and space. With this wider vision we realize that we are each part of the whole and that individual enlightenment attained in isolation is incomplete. With the feeling of space and relaxation that comes with selflessness, we begin to see that others are more important than ourselves. Compassion becomes the motivating force of practice. Training on this path is directed toward developing the six perfections, or transcendent virtues of generosity, morality, patience, energy, meditation, and wisdom.

Mahayana focuses not so much on the historical Shakyamuni Buddha, as on the principle of buddhahood manifesting in countless divine forms. The perfection of the spiritual realm is expressed in terms of all that is best in this world, and so the language of mahayana is filled with images of royal splendor, riches, sensual pleasures, and the beauty of nature. It emphasizes the ideal of the *bodhisattva*, an awakened person who chooses not to dwell in the peace of nirvana but to act for the benefit of all beings. At this stage, practitioners take the bodhisattva vow, a commitment to serve all beings and not to rest until every single one has awakened. We begin to realize that buddha-nature already exists within us, so it becomes possible to let go of spiritual ambition and the idea of attainment. Sensual pleasures are no longer regarded as hindrances in themselves; they can be purified and enjoyed by offering them to others. The path becomes a celebration, a great feast of joy to which we invite all living beings as our guests.

Vajrayana goes even further along the open way. No experience is rejected; everything is integrated into practice. Vajrayana is a path of spiritual alchemy, a path of transmutation. What is transmuted or transformed is our own experience: our perception of our own body and mind is transformed into divinity, the ordinary world is transformed into a sacred world, and the energy of negative emotions and destructive passions is transmuted into wisdom and enlightened action. A verse from the *Hevajra Tantra* expresses this principle very clearly:

> Those things by which the world is bound,
> By those very things may its bondage be released,
> But the world is deluded and knows not this truth,
> And without this truth will not attain perfection.[5]

The methods of vajrayana are based on identifying oneself and the whole of one's experience with the qualities of enlightenment, which are brought to life in the forms of all the peaceful and wrathful deities. The awakened state manifests everywhere, in every aspect of existence. This is the key to the language of vajrayana and the symbolism we find in *Liberation through Hearing*. The tantric path itself is divided into four or six stages, depending on which tradition one follows. At the final stage, the innermost essence of vajrayana, the very heart of tantra, lies the recognition that we have never been anything other than awakened. Here there is no longer any need for techniques, for symbolism, or for transformation. The practitioner who has accomplished the path lives in a condition of complete simplicity and direct experience of reality.

Although the development of the three yanas seems perfectly natural in retrospect (at least from the point of view of vajrayana), the texts contain stories that show how revolutionary some of these ideas were perceived to be. In the sutras, it is related that many hinayana disciples walked out of the assembly and refused to listen to mahayana teachings; and when vajrayana was expounded in the tantras, even the bodhisattvas fainted in fear and had to be revived by rays of light shining out from the hearts of all the buddhas.

From the vajrayana viewpoint, they are different aspects of the same, single path. The Buddha did not hold anything back in his teaching, but how those teachings were interpreted and applied by his later followers could vary greatly. It depended not only on their own understanding, but also on the spirit of the times. Changes in social conditions, as well as the intellectual and religious environment, affect people's receptivity to ideas and their ability to put them into practice. India was never isolated; it was open to many streams of influences, especially in the far northwestern regions where vajrayana flourished. This does not mean that anything essentially different from the Buddha's original message was introduced, nor does it imply that his enlightenment was surpassed. The sutras of mahayana and the tantras of vajrayana simply unfold in their own special ways a vision already inherent in the Buddha's own words. They drew out to the fullest extent various aspects of his teaching that had not been emphasized previously because they could not be understood completely in accordance with the prevailing circumstances and conditions.

In the vajrayana tradition, one of the ways of communication is through extremely vivid and dramatic imagery. This approach, like the silence of the Buddha, has dangers, but of a different kind. There is the possibility of becoming fascinated by tantric symbolism and misled by its ambiguous language. This may lead to a belief based on wishful thinking and to a practice without understanding. The human tendency to believe what someone else tells us rather than try to understand through our own experience can easily provoke the opposite reaction, complete rejection: they are two sides of the same coin. We might have a reaction of bewilderment, or even of fear and dislike, which would prevent us from going deeper. This is why it is important to look carefully into the genuine meaning and purpose of these images during life in order to appreciate their potential significance for us after death.

My intention in this book is to relate the symbolic world of vajrayana both to nontantric Buddhist teachings and to the experiences of everyday life.

Liberation through Hearing belongs to the highest stage of vajrayana, although it also speaks to a whole range of people of different capacities and levels of experience, taking for granted a familiarity with the entire Buddhist path. Inspiring as it is in its own right, its message is likely to be distorted without some understanding of the foundations on which vajrayana is built. It is impossible to understand tantric texts without a knowledge of these foundations and even more impossible to engage in tantric practices in any meaningful way without genuine experience of the basic principles of Buddhism, which are essentially the development of selflessness and compassion. As Trungpa Rinpoche said, "Trying to practise vajrayana without compassion is like swimming in molten lead—it is deadly."[6]

The first part of this book is intended to provide an infrastructure of basic information. It is not a comprehensive account of Buddhism, but only introduces those aspects that are particularly relevant as a guide for further exploration of *Liberation through Hearing*. On certain points there are doctrinal differences and disagreements, even among the Tibetan Buddhist traditions, but in such cases I have followed Trungpa Rinpoche's teaching to the best of my understanding. The second part of the book will go through the text itself, bringing these principles into relationship with it. Before that, however, let us look at its origin and authorship.

Liberation through Hearing came into existence in its present form in the fourteenth century, but its story goes back six hundred years before that. Buddhism had already entered Tibet[7] in various forms from India, central Asia, and China, perhaps sporadically even as early as the third century. It was given royal patronage by the seventh-century king Songtsen Gampo, who sent his most learned ministers to India to learn Sanskrit and to create a script for the Tibetan language. Then in the second half of the eighth century, his descendant, Trisong Detsen, invited several famous teachers from India and firmly established

Buddhism by founding Samye, the first monastery in Tibet. This is known as the earlier diffusion of dharma in Tibet.

Among these teachers was Padmakara, better known in the West as Padmasambhava. Both names mean "the Lotus-Born": literally, "he whose origin (*akara*) or birthplace (*sambhava*) is a lotus (*padma*)." In the tradition that he founded, Padmakara is the preferred name, and Trungpa Rinpoche hoped it would become more widely known and adopted, so I have decided to use it in this book. (Padmakara should be pronounced with an emphasis on the second syllable, which has a long "aa" sound; the others are short.) According to the legend of his miraculous birth, he was discovered as an eight-year-old child, sprung from the heart of a lotus in the center of Lake Dhanakosha in Uddiyana, now identified with the Swat Valley in northern Pakistan. He became renowned for his supernatural powers and was expressly invited to Tibet in order to overcome obstacles to the building of Samye and the spreading of Buddhism. Very little is known about him historically, but his spiritual influence was enormous, and in time he became revered as the most important figure in Tibetan Buddhism.[8] He is also known as Guru Rinpoche, "the Precious Teacher," and is regarded as the second Buddha, inseparable from the historical Buddha Shakyamuni himself, taking human form once more in order to teach the tantras. Through the work of Guru Rinpoche and his colleagues, Tibet received all the streams of Buddhism that existed in India: monastic, lay, philosophical, yogic, and magical.

During the following century, the line of kings descended from Songtsen Gampo died out, and the kingdom descended into political chaos. Buddhism was first suppressed and then neglected by the ruling families who had previously supported it. It survived in the border regions and continued to develop there, but almost a century and a half went by before it returned to the whole country in what has become known as the later diffusion of dharma. Gradually Tibetans, including Marpa, the guru of the great yogin and poet Milarepa, started traveling to India once again to receive teachings and take them back to Tibet. As a result of this revival, several distinct traditions developed, based on the work of certain renowned teachers and the particular practices they taught. Over the next few centuries, these "new schools" formed the three main traditions now known as Kagyü, Sakya, and Geluk. In contrast to them, the tradition that had survived from the old days became known as Nyingma, "the Ancient." (The suffix *pa* can be added to the names of the schools to form an adjective and also indicates their followers.)

Padmakara, with his overwhelming presence and spiritual power, is the central figure and inspiration of the Nyingma tradition. He realized that the Tibetans were not yet ready for many of the profound insights of tantra and foresaw that Buddhism would soon endure a period of great upheaval, and so he magically concealed a vast number of teachings for the future. He did this with the assistance of his consort, Yeshe Tsogyal, who embodies the feminine principle of inspiration and communication, which is of great importance in tantra. These hidden teachings are known as *terma*, "treasure." He prophesied that they would be rediscovered at the appropriate time by certain accomplished practitioners and gave many predictions about the places, times, and circumstances of their coming to light. A person who finds them is called a *tertön*, "revealer of treasure." All the tertöns have a particular connection to Padmakara, and in many cases are the reincarnations of his close disciples. The tradition of teachings being concealed until the appropriate time for their propagation is not confined to Tibet, but goes back to India, as we have already seen in the case of the mahayana sutras being guarded by the serpent-deities.

Termas are of two main kinds: earth treasures and intention, or mind treasures. A teaching concealed as an intention treasure appears directly within the mind of the tertön in the form of sounds or letters to fulfill the enlightened intention of Padmakara. Earth treasures include not only texts, but also sacred images, ritual instruments, and medicinal substances, and are found in many places: temples, monuments, statues, mountains, rocks, trees, lakes, and even the sky. In the case of texts, they are not, as one might imagine, ordinary books that can be read straightaway. Occasionally, full-length texts are found, but they are usually fragmentary, sometimes consisting of only a word or two, and they are encoded in symbolic script, which may change mysteriously and often disappears completely once it has been transcribed. They are simply the material supports that act as a trigger to help the tertön reach the subtle level of mind where the teaching has really been concealed. It is the tertön who actually composes and writes down the

resulting text, and so may be considered its author. Some recent translators of terma texts prefer to ascribe authorship directly to Padmakara,
but Trungpa Rinpoche emphasized the importance of the tertöns' role.
They are not just intermediaries, but great teachers who through their
own experience and realization bring "into living form" the practices
and teachings they discover.

The concept of terma may seem incredible to us now; like reincarnation, it presents a problem for many people because it seems to contradict science. But science is only beginning to probe the mysteries of
time and space and to consider the relationship between energy and
consciousness. We still know so little about the laws of nature, it is
surely best to keep an open mind. However, the extent to which we
literally interpret the concealment and rediscovery of these treasures
does not really affect our appreciation of them. If a material text is
found, its real function is as a key to unlock the treasure within the
tertön's mind. All genuine expressions of truth originate from the ultimate awakened state, which is always present. Padmakara, as its human
embodiment, acts as a focus by means of which human beings can relate
to that truth. The important point is that the tertön makes a direct
connection with Padmakara's eternally present nature and thus receives
his inspiration.

The discovery of the Nyingma termas began in the eleventh century, when conditions were favorable once again, and continues up to
the present day. It is an extremely important part of the Nyingma
tradition, enabling new, authentic lineages to arise. *Liberation through Hearing* is part of a large collection discovered by the tertön Karma Lingpa,
who lived during the second half of the fourteenth century. According
to his traditional biography, he was the reincarnation of Lui Gyaltsen
of Chogro, a great scholar, translator, and teacher who was one of
Padmakara's twenty-five chief disciples and who translated for him and
for many of the other Indian masters.[9] At the same time, Karma Lingpa
is regarded as one of eight bodhisattva emanations of Padmakara. He
was the eldest son of Nyinda Sangye, also a tertön, who discovered
texts concerned with the transference of consciousness at the time of
death. Their home was in Takpo in the southeastern part of central
Tibet.

Karma Lingpa was a devoted practitioner of the tantras, renowned for his spiritual and supernatural powers, and he evidently became a successful teacher with a large circle of students. He made his discoveries at the early age of fifteen in the mountain Gampodar, which is described as looking like a dancing deity. He brought two great cycles of teachings, as well as many other treasures, from the mountain. Both cycles are concerned with the peaceful and wrathful deities—the expressions of the awakened state whose visions lie at the heart of *Liberation through Hearing* itself. This particular terma was sealed with the condition that it should be transmitted only to a single person for three generations, so he gave it only to his son, Nyinda Chöje. Intriguingly, it is said that Karma Lingpa did not meet with the spiritual consort prophesied for him, and therefore he did not live long.

According to a tradition related by Trungpa Rinpoche, Karma Lingpa discovered these teachings after the death of his child, closely followed by the death of his wife.[10] This would fit in with the central point about terma teachings, that essentially they are drawn forth from the hearts of their discoverers under the influence of certain conditions. The time, place, and circumstances must be exactly right or the discovery cannot take place. Karma Lingpa was an accomplished meditator, and the double tragedy of losing his wife and child would no doubt have opened his mind to receive profound insights into death, which would prepare him perfectly for the discovery of these particular teachings.

One of the special requirements for the discovery of termas is the inspiration of the feminine principle, just as it was necessary for their concealment. The great majority of tertöns have been men, and generally they are accompanied by their wives or female companions (who need not necessarily have a sexual relationship with them). Alternatively, something representing the tertön's complementary energy, whether male or female, must be present. So it seems very probable that Karma Lingpa was married and that his wife was living at the time of his discoveries, even though they took place when he was so young.

On the other hand, termas are not always made public right away. The conditions may not be right; people may not yet be ready for them; and further instructions may need to be revealed to clarify their meaning. Often, the tertön himself has to practice them for many years. So it is also possible that the death of Karma Lingpa's wife and child occurred sometime after he had actually extracted the basic teachings from the mountain and provided the inspiration for him to interpret and complete them. According to yet another tradition, he had a son who died at about the age of fifteen.[11] Unfortunately, we have very little information to go on, so all this must remain pure speculation. At all events, he certainly had at least one surviving child, the son to whom he eventually entrusted the whole cycle. Presumably, the prophesied consort, had he met her, would have acted as his partner both in practices to prolong his life and in making further discoveries.

Nyinda Chöje passed on the teaching to one of his own disciples, who in turn passed it to Namkha Chökyi Gyatso, after which the restriction on its transmission no longer applied. *Liberation through Hearing* with its other associated texts then spread widely and has remained extremely popular in spite of its esoteric nature. While it is used and respected by all the schools of Tibetan Buddhism, it is especially strong in the Nyingma and Kagyü traditions, both of which were the heritage of Trungpa Rinpoche.

To return to the question put at the beginning of this chapter, there is in fact no single Tibetan title corresponding to the *Tibetan Book of the Dead*.[12] The overall name given to the whole terma cycle is *Profound Dharma of Self-liberation through the Intention of the Peaceful and Wrathful Ones*, and it is popularly known as *Karma Lingpa's Peaceful and Wrathful Ones*.[13] It has been handed down through the centuries in several versions containing varying numbers of sections and subsections, arranged in different orders, ranging from around ten to thirty-eight titles. These individual texts cover a wide range of subjects, including the dzogchen view (see chapter 10), meditation instructions, visualizations of deities, liturgies and prayers, lists of mantras, descriptions of the signs of death, and indications of future rebirth, as well as those that are actually concerned with the after-death state. The *Tibetan Book of the Dead* as we know it in English consists of two comparatively long texts on the bardo of dharmata (including the bardo of dying) and the bardo of existence. (See chapter 4 for explanations of the different bardos.) They are called *Great Liberation through Hearing: The Supplication of the Bardo of Dharmata* and *Great Liberation through Hearing: The Supplication Pointing Out the Bardo of Existence*.[14] Within the texts themselves, the two combined are referred to as *Liberation through Hearing in the Bardo, Great Liberation through Hearing*, or just *Liberation through Hearing*,[15] the title I shall use throughout this book.

Chapter Two

Liberation: Uncoiling
in Space

IN THIS AND THE NEXT TWO CHAPTERS, we shall look at the meaning and implications of the title *Great Liberation through Hearing in the Bardo*. This will give us the opportunity first to explore some of the most fundamental principles of Buddhism, and then to look at some aspects specifically related to vajrayana and the Nyingma tradition. The first key word in the title is *liberation*, and it takes us straight to the heart of the Buddha's teaching.

What is liberation? How is it accomplished? Who is liberated, and from what?

The state of liberation is the ultimate goal. It has been given many names and has been described in many different ways, although it is essentially inexpressible. It is our true, innate nature, our inalienable birthright, yet we do not recognize it. We seem to be imprisoned in a condition of unknowing. This unknowing, ignorance, or delusion is the cause of all evil and pain, but it is not intrinsic to our being; it is like clouds obscuring the clear sky or dust that has accumulated on a mirror. Instead of having a concept of original sin, Buddhism speaks of basic goodness, for buddha-nature dwells within us as our hidden essence. Liberation is synonymous with the Sanskrit word *bodhi*, which means awakening, understanding, or enlightenment, and with *nirvana*, which means blowing out or extinction: the extinction of illusion.

The Buddha said that his entire message was concerned with suffering and the ending of suffering. We suffer because we do not know the true nature of reality, and so we have a false idea of what we really are. Liberation is release from this condition of suffering, and the path to it leads us through the process of questioning and finding out "who" exactly is to be liberated. We shall discover that "who" and "from what" are really the same. All the philosophical developments within Buddhism, all the different methods of practice, and all the elaborate symbolism of vajrayana are concerned with these two basic principles: understanding the nature of suffering and becoming free from it. This is the message of *Liberation through Hearing*, just as it is of all Buddhist scriptures, and so to journey along the path of the bardos, we must begin with these fundamental teachings.

The foundation of Buddhism is the four noble truths proclaimed by Shakyamuni, the Buddha of this age, after his enlightenment: the truth of the existence of suffering, the truth of the origin of suffering, the truth of the ending of suffering, and the truth of the path that leads to its ending. Suffering in this case is not just ordinary pain as opposed to pleasure, but a deeper, more pervasive sense of lack and of unreality, which is inherent in worldly existence itself. Suffering is closely linked to the impermanence of everything in our lives. The Buddha described all worldly phenomena as having three characteristics: impermanence, suffering, and nonself. We suffer because we imagine what is not self to be self, what is impermanent to be permanent, and what from an ultimate viewpoint is pain to be pleasure.

Existence with these three characteristics is called *samsara*, which means continually flowing, moving on, from one moment to the next moment and from one life to the next life. Samsara is not the actual external world or life itself, but the way we interpret them. Samsara is life as we live it under the influence of ignorance, the subjective world each of us creates for ourselves. This world contains good and evil, joy and pain, but they are relative, not absolute; they can be defined only in relationship to each other and are continually changing into their opposites. Although samsara seems to be all-powerful and all-pervading, it is created by our own state of mind, like the world of a dream, and it can be dissolved into nothingness just like awakening from a dream. When someone awakens to reality, even for a moment, the world does not disappear but is experienced in its true nature: pure, brilliant, sacred, and indestructible.

The key to the Buddha's realization and teaching is the understanding of causality, because it is only when we know the cause of something that we can truly bring it to an end and prevent it from arising again in the future. In his search for the origin of suffering, he found that he had to go right back to the very beginning, to the very first flicker of individual self-awareness. In his spiritual practice, too, he always went further and further, never satisfied with the states of knowledge, peace, and bliss that he attained under the guidance of his teachers. He always wanted to know their cause and to see what lay beyond. In this way, he surpassed his teachers and eventually attained his great awakening.

He awoke to a state of perfect enlightenment, which he described as deathless, unborn, and unchanging. If it were not for that, he said, there could be no escape from birth and death, impermanence and suffering. There is indeed a condition of ultimate peace, bliss, knowledge, and freedom, but to reach it, we must first understand the cycle of conditioned existence in which we are imprisoned. Samsara is like a sickness; the Buddha, who was called the Great Physician, offers a cure, but the patient must recognize the illness, with its causes, its symptoms, and its effects, before the cure can begin.

The Buddha discovered the whole causal process of samsara, the complete cycle of the stages of cause and effect. According to tradition, he once described this process in a series of images, so that it could easily be sent in pictorial form to the king of a neighboring country who had inquired about his teaching. An artist drew the images according to the Buddha's instructions, illustrating the whole realm of samsaric existence from which we seek liberation. This picture is known as the wheel of life (plate 1) and is familiar throughout the Buddhist world. It springs from the same tradition of imagery that flowers so dramatically in vajrayana, but goes back to the beginnings of Buddhism, so in every way it provides an excellent introduction to the understanding of our text.

THE WHEEL OF LIFE

The outer rim of the wheel of life is divided into twelve sections, each containing a small picture. These represent the twelve links in the chain of cause and effect, known as dependent arising or, as Trungpa Rinpoche put it, the samsaric chain reaction. The twelve links can be seen as stages in the evolution of the individual human being (or any other living being), but at the same time they can be applied to one's states of mind, which are continuously arising, developing, and passing away. The Buddha was inspired to set out on his search when he saw a sick man, an old man, and a corpse being carried to the cremation ground, and he realized the inescapable, universal nature of suffering. He also saw a wandering ascetic, whose look of peacefulness and inner joy deeply impressed him: he had caught a glimpse of freedom and he determined to attain it. Starting from the same point of departure as the Buddha, we can trace back the causes of suffering to their root by means of the twelve links in the chain. They should all also be understood as taking place within us from moment to moment, so that as we go through this whole series of images, we are also observing the birth, life, and death of mental states.

1. Decay and Death

The iconography may vary slightly in different paintings, but somewhere on the rim, generally at the top left, we find a picture of a corpse being carried to the cremation ground: this is called decay and death. It is often translated as old age and death, but since many people die young and do not reach old age, here "age" really refers to the whole process of aging and decay, which actually begins as soon as we are born. All pain, whether it is physical or mental, arises from some aspect of loss, destruction, or decay, so this image represents all the sufferings of existence.

2. Birth

The real cause of decay and death is not our physical condition, not illness or accident, but life itself, the simple fact of having been born.

Moving counterclockwise around the circle, we come to the second picture, a mother giving birth to a child. Although this link in the chain is known as birth, it does not mean just the event of being born, but the life that has come into being; it encompasses the whole lifetime of that particular embodiment. It can refer to the birth of a living being or the physical appearance of something in the external world, or it may be interpreted as the arising of a thought or a mood in the mind.

3. Existence

The next picture, illustrating the cause leading to birth, is sometimes of a pregnant woman and sometimes of a man and woman in sexual union. Both these images suggest conception, the beginning of a new life. This link is called existence, life, or becoming—coming into existence. Existence means being in the state of samsara; outwardly subject to birth and death, inwardly under the influence of ignorance and confusion.

4. Grasping

Why do states of mind arise? Why do we continuously create our version of the world from moment to moment? Why does a living being enter a womb to be born? When we search for the cause of becoming, we find it in grasping. The word for this link in the chain literally means appropriation or taking to oneself, and it is symbolized by a figure picking fruit from a tree. Grasping is the opposite of giving and letting go. We hold on tight to our opinions, our views of life, and our ideas about ourselves; again and again we grasp at the next thought, the next emotion, the next experience; at the moment of death, we grasp at the next life.

5. Thirst

Grasping is based, in turn, on the fundamental instinct of needing, wanting, and longing called thirst. It is depicted by a person drinking or being offered a drink. This is the thirst for existence that makes us cling to life at all costs, and it is also the basic drive to experience pleasure and to be free from pain. Thirst can never be satisfied; even if we drink as much as we can, it will return sooner or later. It is inherent in our sense of self. This thirst, also translated as desire or craving, is often said to be the cause of suffering. It is not the ultimate cause, but it is the immediate and most obvious cause.

6. Sensation

Thirst for experience depends upon the possibility of feeling or sensation, symbolized by a man pierced in the eye by an arrow. This brutal image reminds us sharply that the whole series is intended to express the inescapable suffering of samsara. It is interesting to note that the Sanskrit word for feeling can specifically mean pain as well as sensation in general. This points to the truth that in samsara, from the absolute point of view, all feeling of any kind is essentially painful because it is related to our false idea of self. But in the awakened state, where there is no self-centered attachment or aversion, all feeling is experienced as "great bliss." Great bliss is not just increased pleasure, but a transcendent experience of sensitivity that can be aroused by means of any sensation whatsoever, not only through pleasure, but also through what we ordinarily think of as pain.

7. Contact

Sensation arises from contact or touch, illustrated by a man and woman embracing. This represents the contact between the senses and their objects. In the tantras, this powerful imagery is transformed into a passionate embrace of love, a magical dance of the awakened mind with the world perceived in its true, sacred nature. But here, while we are still concerned with very basic principles, it simply illustrates what happens whenever there is the experience of duality and a relationship exists between subject and object.

8. Six Senses

The embrace can only take place because of the existence of the six senses, depicted by a house with six windows. In Indian tradition, the mind is considered to be a sense organ that has as its objects all the perceptions, thoughts, feelings, and so on that arise within it. So in addition to the usual five senses of sight, hearing, touch, taste, and smell, the mental function is counted as the sixth.

9. Name and Form

If the six senses exist, there must be a particular living being to whom they belong. The next picture is of a boat filled with passengers, which is called name and form. Name and form together constitute the individual person. Form is the material aspect, the boat of the body, that carries us along the river of life, while name includes all the nonphysical aspects of our being (the passengers could be regarded as the different "personalities" within us). In many parts of the world, a person's name is considered to have magical significance. When we are given a name, we receive an identity; our name defines who we are. If we think of someone's name, we automatically remember his or her physical appearance and vice versa. Body cannot be separated from mind; the physical and nonphysical aspects of existence both arise from the same cause, and they reflect each other.

10. Consciousness

For a person to exist, individual consciousness is necessary. Consciousness functions through the six senses. It is what makes us aware of ourselves and divides the world into subject and object; it gives us the sense of being "I" as opposed to everything else that is not "I." Consciousness is appropriately pictured as a restless, inquisitive monkey leaping from object to object, never staying still. Sometimes the monkey is shown picking fruit from a tree, and sometimes peering out through the windows of a house—the house of the six senses.

11. Conditioning

Consciousness is not pure, direct awareness, but is produced and conditioned by the way the mind functions, so the next link in the chain is called conditioning (or formations). It refers to certain characteristic mental forces or patterns that motivate our thoughts, words, and deeds. It is here that the law of karma begins to operate.[1] The word karma literally means "action," but generally when we speak of the law of karma, it refers to both action and its result: the universal law of cause and effect on a personal level. Everything we think, speak, and do has an inevitable consequence. The Buddha taught that karma really refers to intentions, not just to actions in the literal sense. Our lives are shaped by our innermost thoughts and deepest motivations, including those on the most subtle and hidden level, which can only be discovered by profound meditation techniques. This link in the chain is symbolized by a potter making pots. In theistic religions, the image of the potter is sometimes used for God the creator, while in Buddhism the force of karma is continually creating the world anew for each living being at every moment.

12. Ignorance

But why does conditioning arise in the first place? How did the whole process ever start? The Buddha traced the root cause back to ignorance, the mind's ignorance of its own awakened nature—the final and original link in the chain. This is the farthest back we can go within the circle of samsara; this is where everything begins. Indeed, we can say that this whole cycle really has no beginning and no end, because our very notions of past, present, and future are part of samsara. Ignorance is symbolized by an old blind woman, tottering about with the aid of a stick. Trungpa Rinpoche referred to her as a blind grandmother. She has given birth to generations of samsaric existence, endlessly proliferating and reproducing. Ignorance means ignoring the truth of reality, shutting one's eyes to the awakened state. Although the light of reality is ever-present, ignorance chooses to remain blind. The nature of this blindness is to believe in the existence of a separate, independent self. Trungpa Rinpoche also used to say that ignorance is very intelligent. It is actually the intelligence of samsara, which is fighting a continual battle for survival and constantly looking for ways of keeping up its own illusion, its own self-deception.

Here we have traced each link in the chain backward to its cause, from the suffering of mortal life, culminating in death, all the way back to its ultimate origin, ignorance. The whole series of pictures can also be read in reverse order, from ignorance to death. If we do this, we can clearly see the inevitable development of the twelve stages: ignorance, conditioning, consciousness, name and form, the six senses, contact, sensation, thirst, grasping, existence, birth, and decay and death. The twelve links form an unending circle. At death we fall into a state of ignorance once more, and the cycle starts all over again. Samsara means going on and on, round and round, without beginning or end.

Inside the outer rim, occupying the main part of the wheel of life, are illustrations of the six realms of existence in samsara: the worlds of the gods, jealous gods, human beings, animals, hungry ghosts, and hell-beings. Very often only five divisions are shown, because the gods and the jealous gods are basically the same and can be classified together. The six realms are described in detail in a later chapter, so they are mentioned only briefly here. In the outer sense, they depict all the possible varieties of sentient life classified into these five or six main groups. They are all conditions of life into which we could be reborn. Except for those of animals and humans, the other realms are invisible to us, but they all coexist with us in an inconceivably vast, multidimensional universe.

In the inner sense, all these realms are found within our own minds. Although we have the form and psychology of human beings, we are continually going through states of mind that correspond to the other realms. In exactly the same way, gods, jealous gods, animals, hungry ghosts, and hell-beings all experience the states of mind of the other realms colored by their own dominant states. Also, within each of the six realms, every living being goes through the entire cycle of the twelve links of the samsaric chain reaction. The human realm is the most balanced and least extreme of the six, so it is easier for us to encompass the full spectrum of conditions within our experience, from the hells to the heavens. Of course, the entire wheel of life is necessarily described from the human point of view; nevertheless all life fundamentally shares the same buddha-nature and is conditioned by the same forces arising from ignorance.

In some depictions of the wheel of life, the figure of a buddha is shown in each realm. In the human realm, this is the human Buddha Shakyamuni; in each of the other realms, he appears in the form of one of its inhabitants. This indicates that the compassion of the awakened nature extends infinitely without obstructions and can manifest in any form in order to communicate with all the different types of existence, even in the extreme suffering of hell.

Moving further in toward the center of the wheel, the next section is divided into two parts: a light half in which human figures are climbing upward, and a dark half in which they are falling downward. This represents the last stage of the period between death and rebirth, during which the results of our previous actions draw us toward a higher or lower condition. The figures moving up, in the light semicircle, are on their way to taking rebirth as human beings, gods, or jealous gods; those moving down, in the dark semicircle, will be reborn among animals or hungry ghosts or in one of the hells.

At the center of the wheel lie the three roots of suffering: passion, aggression, and delusion, symbolized by a cock, a snake, and a pig, respectively. The Buddha called them the three fires with which the whole of samsara is ablaze. Nirvana is the blowing out of their flames, a blissful state of coolness and peace after the suffering they cause (the translation of *nirvana* into Tibetan literally means "passed beyond suffering"). They are also known as the three afflictions, defilements, or poisons. They pervade and influence the mechanism of samsaric existence from beginning to end; they keep the whole process of dualistic experience going. They are the three basic reactions that the "I" can have when it perceives something outside itself as "other." We can be attracted to that other, wish to possess it, control it, or take it over and make it part of ourselves: this is passion. We can reject it, push it away, or try to destroy it: this is aggression. Or we can ignore it and pretend it does not exist: this is delusion. At heart, all three reactions are attempts to overcome duality by making "I" the only thing that exists in the world, but instead they actually reinforce and perpetuate the split between "I" and "other."

The entire wheel is held in the clutches of a terrifying figure; this is Yama, the Lord of Death. His name literally means "restraint," since he is the ultimate restraint on the freedom of all living beings. He does not simply represent death in the ordinary sense, the end of life, but the very principle of mortality, which includes within itself birth and death, rebirth and re-death. Immortality, the birthless and deathless state of nirvana, lies beyond the cycle of the wheel of life.

THE THREE CHARACTERISTICS OF SAMSARA

Suffering

The wheel of life is a diagram of the whole of samsara, which, as the Buddha said, has the characteristics of impermanence, suffering, and

ree, suffering is the one that inspired the Buddha
h and that he proclaimed as the first noble truth.
ty of suffering, he was not being negative or
pessim... imself in that way because of his extremely
practical ... ality. He did not want to entice people
with beauti... enlightenment that would only fuel
dreams and fa... naterial for philosophical arguments.
He certainly did ...owers to exaggerate the misery in
their lives, but rath... to their present condition. Understanding the truth ...lly a matter of facing up to
reality, not attempting to ... from pain, but identifying
it and examining its cause ... it to an end. Deliberate
hardship, asceticism, and dwe... l aspects of life are not
recommended in Buddhism; aft... inspiration and goal
was the ultimate complete liberati... ...ing.

There are three levels of suffer... ...nere is suffering in the sense that we usually mean it—physi... ...ain or mental unhappiness, the kind of suffering that everyone knows about. These woes of life are often listed at great length in traditional texts, with the intention of persuading people to turn away from attachment to worldly existence. At the same time, human life is considered fortunate in containing a balance of pleasure and pain, which is conducive to spiritual aspiration and practice. Suffering can sometimes prove helpful by jolting us out of our habitual complacency and reminding us of the certainty of death. It can awaken feelings of sympathy and empathy toward others, and it can be dedicated to the welfare and happiness of all living beings. With the right attitude, it can become a powerful tool in cutting through illusion. In fact, there are many different ways, at all stages of the path, of making use of the inevitable troubles that life brings.

Behind the more obvious meaning of suffering lies the suffering that is inherent in change. Everything changes: we cannot hold on to happiness. Our loved ones may die, our health may fail, our possessions may be destroyed; ultimately there is nothing we can rely on in this world. There is an underlying sense of sadness in the fragility and impermanence of life that sometimes becomes overwhelmingly poignant. Change is another word for impermanence, and, as we have seen, impermanence leads inevitably to the first kind of suffering—to the mental pain of loss and the bodily pain of sickness and finally death.

But suffering has a deeper message still, it points to something more fundamental and subtle, beyond the contrast of pleasure and pain, behind everything we experience. This is the pain of the confused mind arising from ignorance, the profound sorrow of not knowing reality, of living a lie at the deepest level of our being. Some Buddhists prefer to use terms such as unease, frustration, or unsatisfactoriness instead of suffering, but to me this seems to water down its impact (besides not really being appropriate for the other two levels). When we wake up for a moment and catch a glimpse of what Trungpa Rinpoche called basic sanity, the comparison with our ordinary state of mind is extremely painful, and we realize that our usual condition of unawareness and confusion really is a state of suffering. Moreover, we realize that this is not just the suffering of one individual, but that it is shared by countless other sentient beings in all the possible realms of existence, and this realization arouses deep compassion. Within that pervasive suffering of ignorance, the pain of not being awake to reality, lie all our relative joys and sorrows, which come and go, arise and pass away.

Impermanence

Like suffering, impermanence is familiar to everyone; it has an obvious, everyday counterpart to its more profound meaning. Even on the purely material level, science has demonstrated that the physical world is continually in a state of flux and has no solid basis, that everything is utterly impermanent and insubstantial. Emotionally, too, we know in our hearts that nothing really lasts and that everything must come to an end. Yet we still feel and act as if both we and the world around us were real, solid, and permanent. We want things to be lasting, we become attached to them, and this inevitably leads to suffering in all kinds of ways. Impermanence and suffering are inseparable, because impermanence always results in change, decay, and loss. Meditation, together with the practice of mindfulness in daily life, can show us very clearly the momentariness of our experiences, our emotions, our thoughts, and even consciousness itself. They appear, they last only an instant, then they disappear. There is nothing permanent, nothing substantial, under-

lying them or running through them. Phenome⸱ ⸱nal or
external, have no real existence in any absolute se⸱

This lack of permanence and substantiality lea⸱ ⸱ar-
acteristic of samsara, the absence of any independe⸱ ⸱t
entity that can be regarded as the "self." It follows o⸱
from impermanence. Yet even when we see this clear⸱
experiences and in the world around us, we still have a de⸱
that there is something real and permanent within us, almos⸱
is someone inside our heads who is having all these thoughts
riences. It is not at all easy for us truly to understand the imp⸱
of impermanence and insubstantiality in relation to ourselve⸱
wheel of life shows that all phenomena are transient and interde⸱
dent: everything arises from a cause and in turn becomes a cause for
next appearance to arise. This means that nothing can exist in isolatio⸱
We ourselves are composed of extremely complex combinations of conditioned, momentary appearances. However hard we look for something that lasts and does not change, we shall not be able to find it,
either within ourselves or without.

Nonself

Nonself is the most difficult of the three characteristics to understand.
Unlike the other two, it is not obvious in daily life; indeed, it seems to
contradict our normal experience. But this is partly a problem of definition. First of all, it does not apply to the obvious, everyday use of the
word *self*. After all, the Buddha continued to use ordinary language; he
did not stop saying "I" and "you." He certainly did not deny personal
identity and individuality, which he referred to as the "person." There
is, in everyday experience, a quite neutral sense of being oneself, which
naturally goes along with the existence of body and mind, and is not
grasping, possessive, or divisive. In this sense, self is just a conventional
term, a label, like one's name. It is simply a reference to a person, with
no special emotional charge or philosophical significance, any more
than when we speak of a table or a chair.

The problem arises when we imply something more than this. We
feel, very deeply and instinctively, that there is a central core to our
being, something extremely precious and extremely vulnerable. Then
the reasoning mind reinforces this emotional conviction by asking,

"Who am I?" and concluding that there must be an essence that makes us unique and separate from all others. Not everyone would agree that they hold this view; many people are materialists who do not believe in any unifying central core. Recent thinking about the nature of the self has produced very interesting developments that seem, on the surface at least, quite close to the insights of Buddhism: they suggest that self is simply a narrative, a story we tell ourselves in order to make sense of our experience. Yet this kind of reasoning does not alter people's emotional attachment to the self; they still behave as though it were real. Samsaric life is based on self-centeredness, not as a moral judgment, but in the most literal sense of the word: relating everything back to oneself as the center of one's world. This is the self or ego of samsara. It is the constant feeling of "I, me, mine"—a centralizing, solidifying tendency.

As well as the self or ego, we have the slightly different concept of the soul or spirit. We cannot directly experience the soul, yet many people believe in it as a personal essence that survives death. From the Buddhist point of view, the logic behind both these ideas is the same. We feel that because we continue to exist as the same person from moment to moment and from day to day, there must be a permanent self; and by analogy with day-to-day life, we also assume that if we continue to exist after death, there must be an immortal soul. In Buddhism, the idea of a soul is considered merely an extension of the illusory, worldly self. Again, there are many people who do not believe in a soul or an afterlife, yet it does not make any real, practical difference to their attachment to self.

Just as the Buddha did not deny ordinary experience, he did not deny life after death. Instead, he suggested a different model of what life really is; he showed that the assumption of either a self or a soul is unnecessary and, in fact, only causes trouble. All the suffering that we endure and that we cause others arises from attachment to "I, me, mine." He never spoke in terms of searching for a true self or essence, because that very search reinforces attachment and carries egoistic grasping to more and more subtle levels.

A living being is a temporary combination of various elements, always changing, just as a river is composed of uncountable drops of water, never remaining static even for the smallest imaginable moment of time. The sense of continuity we have from day to day, which we experience as a static state of being, is really a dynamic process, a continuous flow. There is simply no need for a self, we function perfectly well without it. We *are* that flow, that dance of life, without fixation or solidity. We do not need to look for someone behind that.

At the same time, there is a profound truth in our search for an essence. Our essence is the potentiality for enlightenment, *tathagatagarbha* in Sanskrit, the buddha embryo, often called the buddha-nature. As this potentiality begins to manifest, it is known as *bodhichitta,* the awakening heart or mind. At first, as relative bodhichitta, it is the aspiration toward enlightenment for oneself and all beings; finally, as ultimate bodhichitta, it is the state of wakefulness itself, the awakened heart and mind. The whole of existence is really nothing other than all-pervading buddha-nature. Yet even to speak of buddha-nature, buddha mind, primordial buddha, and so on may once again give the impression of some kind of substance or entity, when in reality it is completely beyond all concepts and cannot be described by any analogy. It is the condition of being awake: buddhaness, awakeness, wakefulness. It cannot belong to anyone; it is not yours or mine, even though we do sometimes speak of it loosely in that way. It is realized by individual persons and it manifests through individual persons, yet it is not personal or individual. The difficulty is that we cannot help thinking of it as our own and thus completely distorting it. Here we come up against the practical and emotional aspect of what is meant by the self: it is not just an abstract principle, but something that touches us very deeply. We instinctively think "this is *my* buddha-nature" or "this is *my* true self" without having really let go of the limited, personal self.

Yet we are not just nothing. We do not disappear when we enter selflessness. To believe that would be nihilism, a view the Buddha condemned. He even said that nihilism was more difficult to overcome than the opposite extreme of belief in an eternal self. When self is transcended, being or presence is still there, the world is still there, and experience is still there. Someone has to be there to communicate the truth, to manifest love and compassion, and to perform enlightened activities. In some sutras and tantras, this state of transcendent being is called the great self. When a word is qualified as great, it often indicates that it transcends both its ordinary meaning and the opposite. So the great self transcends both self and its negation; it passes completely beyond the reach of our ordinary conceptions of self and nonself. It is a condition of total paradox, which the conceptual, dualistic mind cannot encompass.

The great self is not God. Just as there is no need for a self in everyday, individual existence, so there is no need for a centralizing principle on a cosmic scale. There is simply the experience of selfless presence, with no necessity to identify an ultimate owner, creator, or controller. When there is no fixed center or reference point, awareness becomes all-pervading, and whatever arises within it is recognized "just as it is": the awakened state of mind.

There appears to be nothing in Buddhism corresponding to the self of modern psychology, no concept of developing a mature, balanced, integrated self for its own sake, without reference to a spiritual goal. This idea is a comparatively recent development, even in Western thought, and it was not something the Buddha would have needed to address. So how can we relate it to the Buddhist approach? The qualities that produce a fully developed personality are fundamentally the same as those that are needed for successful meditation practice. Buddhism continually reminds us of the wonderful potential and unique opportunity we have as human beings, and that we should never denigrate human nature or feel ashamed of what we are. So the issue of self development versus spiritual development really depends on our attitude. The qualities and functions of the "psychological self" are neutral in themselves. If they are based on that centralizing tendency, which is actually considered quite normal in much of modern psychology, they belong to the realm of samsara. If, on the other hand, they flow spontaneously from a state of openness and awareness, then they are seen as aspects of bodhichitta. From the Buddhist point of view, a buddha is the only complete human being. The fullest possible realization of human potential is to awaken. The very same characteristics that we possess in the confused state are transformed into enlightened characteristics in the awakened state. Buddhas could not manifest at all without distinct qualities and individual personalities, yet at the same time they never depart from the absolute nature of oneness.

Several writers on early Buddhism have pointed out that the understanding of self or soul current in India at the time of the Buddha

was very different from our own. However, there is considerable dis-
agreement about exactly what it was: whether the Buddha was responding to the universal, impersonal self of the Upanishads or to a more
popular, even animistic concept. Fascinating though it would be to
know more about the exact context of the Buddha's discourses, I do
not think this problem affects the practical application of his teachings.
After all, Buddhism spread far beyond India and flourished in very
different civilizations, such as China and Japan, with different ideas
about self and soul, and it is still absolutely valid today in our own
culture.

Our contemporary concept of the self as a unified whole has actually proved very useful in the teaching of dharma, as it provides a
shorthand term that did not exist in the traditional Buddhist languages.
Consequently, Buddhist teachers nowadays talk about self and ego
much more frequently than we find equivalent expressions in the texts.
Traditionally, they might have referred to the five skandhas (see chapter
6) or the five poisons (see chapter 7); or they might have used the term
self-grasping, which means the belief in self, the concept of self, not as a
theory, but as a deeply felt, instinctive conviction. Trungpa Rinpoche
usually spoke of ego, contrasted with nonego or egolessness. This
makes it clear that he was not referring primarily to the philosophical
concept of a self or soul, but to the personal, experiential, egoistic self
of ordinary life, the material we have to work with here and now.

So when we ask who is liberated, it is not the self. Liberation is not *of*
the self, but *from* the self. If we keep on asking "Who?" we shall only
find another "self" who is released from "self." Whenever we try to
identify the final watcher, the ultimate experiencer, we are once again
creating an imaginary "I." This is why, when Trungpa Rinpoche taught
meditation, he always emphasized letting go rather than concentration.
We shall find that the attitude of letting go is also the basis of the
advice repeated over and over again in *Liberation through Hearing*. Letting
go means loosening the tightness of grasping and clinging, relaxing the
strain of continually holding on, when there is really nothing to hold
on to. Letting go is emptying out, emptying oneself of illusions, concepts, and imaginary constructs of all kinds. Eventually, through the

process of letting go, we arrive at the experience known as emptiness
(*shunyata*).

Emptiness is the heart of Buddhism. Like nonself, it indicates the
absence of solidity and fixation, and the lack of inherent, independent
existence in anything. Yet it is not negative. It is the creative source of
all apparent existence. It is the zero (*shunya*) dimension, from which
everything arises and into which everything dissolves. If it were not for
emptiness, nothing could appear at all. At the same time, if there were
no appearances, there could be no emptiness. Emptiness on its own has
no meaning; it would be utter nonexistence. Thinking about it purely
theoretically can easily lead to absurd conclusions. It is an inner experience, an understanding of how things really are, replacing our usual
fixed ideas about existence. But common sense does not have to fly out
the window! An awakened person still perceives the world just like
everyone else, but without the obscurations and distortions of false
concepts. Within emptiness, with emptiness as their essence, appearances continually arise. This inseparability of emptiness and appearance
avoids the two extreme beliefs of nihilism (or nonexistence) and eter-
nalism (or absolute existence).

From the point of view of ego, emptiness seems like annihilation,
because it is the actual experience of egolessness. To enter this state, we
have to take a leap into the dark and be willing to risk the feeling that
we may lose our whole existence. Letting go completely is like death,
and this is exactly what *Liberation through Hearing* is all about. Emptiness
is the experience of vast openness, spaciousness, and freedom. In it,
the limitations and complexities of individual existence fall away; the
boundaries between inside and outside dissolve; and everything is spontaneously present in its natural purity and perfection, free from the
duality of subject and object. The brilliance and clarity in which all
phenomena appear as they really are, yet are seen to be empty in essence,
is called luminosity. As we shall find later on, *luminosity* is a key term in
the *Tibetan Book of the Dead*.

There are several different views or ways of understanding emptiness among the Buddhist philosophical schools, and vast amounts have
been written about it. These views arise from increasingly subtle realizations of the nature of mind, which in turn produce more and more
profound and subtle experiences of emptiness, ranging from the basic

insight into nonself to resting in the luminous emptiness of the ultimate nature of mind. Emptiness is not simply a void that is left when illusions have been cleared away. Like the mind itself, it is a continuous process, the living essence of each moment of experience.

Wisdom, which is called the mother of the buddhas, is nothing other than the understanding of emptiness. This is the great secret of awakening. All the buddhas are born from this realization, for only the wisdom of emptiness can give birth to enlightenment. Wisdom is the direct, transformative experience of the reality of emptiness in our own lives. It is the living certainty that nothing exists as a separate entity in the way we normally believe. In the symbolism of vajrayana, as we see in part 2, emptiness and wisdom are regarded as the feminine principle of enlightenment, inseparably united with the masculine principle of compassion and skillful means or method.

Compassion is not just a feeling of pity and empathy, but an active force, a fundamental energy that is ceaselessly at work to remove the causes of suffering. It cannot help arising, because in the realization of emptiness there are no boundaries between oneself and others. Compassion is absolute sensitivity, unbiased love, and limitless concern for everything in existence. It is the natural outward expression of the bliss of enlightenment. Even in ordinary life, when we are happy and fulfilled, we feel more loving toward the world and we want to express that love. Skillful means is the application of compassion, the enlightened activity that strives to remove suffering and to lead all sentient beings toward supreme happiness.

Emptiness and compassion are completely intertwined. The relationship between them has been compared to that of a flame and its light or a tree and its leaves. Activity in the world is not truly enlightened unless it springs from the awareness that, in the absolute sense, nothing is being done or needs to be done. Yet at the same time, the awakened heart feels as its own the suffering of all who are not yet awakened. The bodhisattvas embody this activity for the welfare of all beings. Through wisdom the bodhisattva knows that samsara is illusion, and through compassion helps those who are under its spell. Both aspects go together all the way along the path. We cannot wait until we attain wisdom to manifest compassion. Simply being as compassionate and skillful as we can at every stage is what deepens our realization of emptiness. They grow together, they mutually inspire each other, they are the two indispensable elements of the awakened state.

Wakefulness, enlightenment, the state of total liberation, is inde-structible. It is symbolized by the *vajra* (or *dorje* in Tibetan), the ritual instrument that gave its name to vajrayana. *Vajra* is a Sanskrit word that means both "thunderbolt" and "diamond." As thunderbolt, it is an invincible divine weapon, combining irresistible strength, power, and energy. As diamond, it is brilliant, pure, sharp, and unbreakable; no other substance can cut it, but it can cut through everything. The icono-graphic form of the vajra is derived from the ancient thunderbolt weapon of Indra, the Vedic sky-god. It consists of a central sphere with a number of prongs, usually five or nine, emerging symmetrically in two opposite directions. These prongs originally represented lightning, but they could also suggest rays of light flashing out from a diamond; they also have various symbolic meanings according to their number and context. When there are five prongs at each end, they often symbolize the five male and female buddha principles, who spontaneously appear out of luminous emptiness as pure manifestations of wisdom and com-passion.

Looking into the significance of the word *liberation* has enabled us to explore many fundamental aspects of the Buddha's teaching. Libera-tion means release from samsara with its three characteristics of imper-manence, suffering, and nonself. It is the awakening from an illusion, in which we believe that we are separate, substantial, and independent. We are liberated from suffering into great bliss, from nonself into great self, and from impermanence into the indestructible reality of vajra nature.

Liberation is often referred to in these texts as "great liberation." Like the transcendent meaning of great self and great bliss, great libera-tion is not just freedom as opposed to bondage; it transcends the very concepts of freedom and bondage. In the light of ultimate truth, there has never been any illusion, so there is no need to awaken from it. Neither imprisonment nor freedom has ever really existed. This is also the underlying meaning of *self-liberation*, a term that is frequently used in Nyingma teachings. Ultimately, all liberation is self-liberation. As we have seen, the Buddhist path contains many different approaches and methods, all ways of liberation. These various approaches are not imposed upon us by any external authority; they correspond to our needs and capacities and develop naturally out of our own points of view and our own attitudes toward the path. Sometimes we seem to be going through a process of renunciation, at other times purification, at still others transmutation, and once in a while we may have flashes of direct recognition. Yet mind itself has always been pure, perfect, awake, and free. Self-liberation is the spontaneous realization that there has never really been anything else. Liberation is traditionally illustrated by the simile of a snake unwinding itself, naturally and effortlessly, from its tangled coils. In Trungpa Rinpoche's poetic words, "the snake-knot of conceptual mind uncoils in space."[2]

Chapter Three

Hearing: The Power of Transmission

THE SECOND KEY WORD in the title is *hearing*. We are assured that liberation can be accomplished through hearing these teachings during the bardo. How is it possible to be liberated just by hearing a text, and how can a dead person hear it being read?

We have seen that in the Buddhist view a living being consists of a continuous flow of moments of consciousness, and this flow continues on a subtle level after the death of the physical body. We have also seen, in the diagram of the wheel of life, that the physical and the nonphysical are inseparably intertwined: mind and matter originate from the same source. From the scientific viewpoint, consciousness depends on the existence of the brain and central nervous system. Some Western Buddhists are even beginning to question rebirth on these grounds. But such a view only takes into account the coarse or outward manifestation of body and mind (see chapter 9).[1] This is the only level of existence we normally encounter in ordinary life—its visible, tangible aspect. It is like the tip of an iceberg appearing above the surface of the ocean. If we have not actually experienced the reality of more subtle levels in meditation, we might indeed conclude that death must mean the total extinction of consciousness. Death is explained as the separation of the coarse and subtle levels. The subtle continuity of the mindstream carries with it the imprints of karma; that is to say, it carries the potential results of past actions, the seeds that will ripen and bear fruit in the form of a new body and mind when the right circumstances arise.

The law of karma is extremely important in understanding *Liberation through Hearing*. What happens to us after death is nothing to do with punishment, fate, or a higher power, but is entirely the result of our own actions. It is simply the application of universal law, universal justice. The Buddha said that if we want to understand our past lives, we only need to look at our present conditions, for they are the result of the past. If we want to know what our future life will be like, we should examine our present actions, for they are the cause of the future. This does not mean that we can draw up mechanical lists of causes and results; external factors and the actions of other people also play a large part in shaping our destiny, and there are far too many variables to make accurate predictions, especially about outer events and circumstances. But our reactions to those circumstances and what we make of them are entirely our own responsibility.

It is in the inner world of our thoughts, emotions, habits, and reactions that we can really observe the mechanism of cause and effect. Karma works from moment to moment, as well as over long stretches of time. Any thought or emotion that arises in the mind creates an effect; it leaves its trace there, and that trace can reproduce itself over and over again. Anger gives birth to more anger; wanting gives birth to more wanting. Whenever a certain negative reaction becomes habitual, it sets in motion an endless, circular process of a cause giving rise to an effect, then that effect becoming a similar cause in its turn, and so on, over and over again. What may seem at the time like very minor reactions of annoyance or resentment can end up poisoning the mind for hours or even days.

Fortunately, the force of karma is just as strong in positive directions. Happiness generates further happiness, both for ourselves and others. A feeling of sympathy or an act of kindness creates the conditions for greater and greater goodness to develop. Generally, it seems easiest to think of karma in terms of significant good or bad actions, impelling us toward fortunate or unfortunate future lives. But it is really the very ordinary, familiar, and almost unnoticed current of thoughts that is continually determining the pattern of our destiny. The day-dreaming and subconscious gossip, the habitual thoughts and worries that go through our minds all the time are continually creating karma, perpetuating our sense of self.

But it is possible to stop the karmic chain reaction and break the pattern. At any given moment, it is only that moment that matters. Even though we are pushed forward by a vast, cumulative weight of karmic force, and there are countless karmic seeds in the mindstream that must ripen sooner or later, still we can only deal with one moment at a time, one thought at a time. As the Chinese proverb says, a journey of a thousand days begins with a single step. Karma is a doctrine of total responsibility for ourselves. We may have to endure the results of our past mistakes, but we do not have to perpetuate them. Whatever may have happened in the past, the doctrine of karma gives us the certainty that right now, at this very moment, we can begin to change the future course of our existence.

Karma and self go together. From the ultimate viewpoint, karma is just as illusory as the self, but as long as we function from the deep-seated belief in self, we are subject to the laws of karma. Until a sentient being attains enlightenment, the sense of self is still there in the mind-stream, and so karma is produced. Karma, the chain of cause and effect, creates the link between past, present, and future and between the past life, this life, and the next life. Even after separating from the physical body, the attachment to self continues, so during the period after death, the departed consciousness still feels itself to be that same "I" as before. The important point to understand is that "I" is always imaginary, whether we are thinking of a past life, yesterday, now, tomorrow, the bardo state, or a future life. If we really grasp that point, the question of how the personality can exist after death, or who is reborn, may seem less problematic. One illusion gives place to another illusion. Does it really mean anything to ask whether they are the same? Can we really say that they are different? The only solution to all these enigmas of life and death is to dispel the illusion that created them in the first place.

There is no individual entity that continues from one life to an-other, but a continuous flow of change. The "I" that we imagine our-selves to be in this life is not the same as the "I" of the previous life or the "I" who will be born in the next life. Yet these past, present, and future "I"s are linked together by the illusion of self and the karmic imprints that sustain it from life to life. Someone will be born whose existence and character and destiny depend on our actions now. As long as we continue to believe in the self, karma and rebirth are real for us. The moment the self is seen not to exist, the chain is broken then and there.

It is perhaps rather ironic that many people enjoy reading the *Tibetan Book of the Dead* because it describes the amazing things that happen to us after death and it reassures us that we will have another chance in a future life, when really the purpose of these teachings is to help us escape from the whole cycle of birth and death. The very fact that someone is going through the bardo means that he or she has not yet attained liberation and is therefore still under the power of karma. In the bardo state, a sense of self arises, linked by the chain of cause and effect to the previous life. The subtle imprints or traces in the mind create the feeling of having a body like the old one, with all its senses intact, very similar to the sensation of a body we have when we are dreaming. In dreams we are not using our physical senses to see and hear, but we still seem to have the experience of seeing and hearing. The same kind of process takes place for beings in the bardo. Whatever kind of communication may reach them, they will interpret it in terms of seeing and hearing.

So the text describes how the consciousness of a recently deceased person remains in the vicinity for some time and is able to see and hear all that is going on. She or he will sense the atmosphere around the corpse, will still feel an attachment to it, and will be strongly affected by the attitude of the people who are gathered around it. At this time, it is especially important for the family and friends to remain calm. If they are frightened and overwhelmed by grief, quarrelling among themselves over their share of the inheritance, or if they perform the death rituals carelessly or hypocritically, all these negative emotions will be magnified in the perception of the dead person and will cause fear, anger, and confusion. But if the friends and relatives can provide an environment of calmness, warmth, and confidence, this will communicate itself and be of tremendous help. Trungpa Rinpoche emphasized that this is really the best gift we can give the dead.

Reading *Liberation through Hearing*, and especially reciting the verses connected with it, which contain its essence, can reassure and inspire the minds of the living at such an emotional time. This in itself will benefit the dead, even if one does not feel that one is making any real connection. Normally, in order to bring another person's consciousness into the state of emptiness and clarity, one must be able to enter and remain in it oneself. As the departed consciousness drifts farther and farther away from this life, only a highly accomplished practitioner would be able to reach out and guide it on its journey. Nevertheless, if the right circumstances come together, if the mind of the reader is stable enough and the mind of the dead person responsive enough, then the inherent power of the teaching itself may bring about liberation. It is said that the consciousness becomes immeasurably clearer when it is no longer confined by the coarse material body, so it will easily understand and remember the essential points of the instructions.

In several places, *Liberation through Hearing* states that it is a reminder of what we have already been shown by our teachers and experienced in meditation. It emphasizes very strongly the importance of practice during life and recommends reading and memorizing the text, so we become completely familiar with its contents. We should make it so thoroughly a part of ourselves that we would not forget it even if we were being chased by seven dogs or a hundred murderers!

As a reminder, the book reaches out to us on many different levels of understanding and realization. In a crisis, the mind returns to whatever practice has touched us most deeply and had the greatest effect on us; we cannot be sure in advance which one it will be. Throughout, there is the most simple and direct instruction: simply to recognize. This is the best, but also the hardest, path to follow. Those who were engaged in the practice of a deity are reminded to look upon whatever they see as the manifestation of that deity, which is in reality their own awakened state. Those who have not received the empowerment of any special deity are urged to have faith in Avalokiteshvara, the living presence of compassion. Again and again, the basic teachings of emptiness and compassion are found: Whatever appears, it has no real substance, so do not be either attracted by the visions or afraid of them. You are the natural form of emptiness, so nothing can hurt you; emptiness cannot harm emptiness. Dedicate all your thoughts and all your actions to the good of others, and resolve to become enlightened for the sake of all beings.

In this way, whatever one has practiced in the past is called to mind by the reading of the book. Yet it also states that it is "a teaching that enlightens without meditation, a teaching that liberates just by being heard." In his foreword to the *Tibetan Book of the Dead*, Trungpa Rinpoche wrote: "Liberation, in this case, means that whoever comes into contact with this teaching—even in the form of doubt, or with an open mind—receives a sudden glimpse of enlightenment through the power of the transmission contained in these treasures."[2]

Mention of the power of transmission introduces a very important principle in vajrayana. In this passage, Trungpa Rinpoche was referring to the Sanskrit *adhishthana*, which is often translated as "blessing." There is no really satisfactory equivalent in English, but analyzing the Sanskrit and Tibetan words can help to shed light on this mysterious but extremely powerful reality, which is a cornerstone of vajrayana practice. The Sanskrit word literally means "standing over" and conveys ideas of taking possession, dwelling within, presence, protection, and sovereignty. The Tibetan literally means "an engulfing wave or flood of splendor and power." Trungpa Rinpoche described it as creating an atmosphere that influences the environment, an intense experience of presence that overpowers and possesses us, and he compared it to the way young birds are covered and protected by their mother's wings. He also sometimes used the term *transmission* to refer to the Sanskrit *abhisheka*, the consecration or empowerment to do a tantric practice. Abhisheka is a specific, formal kind of adhishthana; the two are very close and are sometimes used synonymously in the tantras.

We can approach the idea of adhishthana through quite ordinary experience. In essence, it comes down to simple communication between two people, but that communication contains something more than is conveyed by the outer words or actions. As children, we receive everything from our parents or parental figures; they not only pass on to us the knowledge and skills that we need, they deeply influence our whole lives. In a way, they possess us and continue to live within us. Children are much more open than adults to absorbing influences, good or bad, but even as adults we are continually learning from others, being affected by others, and receiving adhishthana in all kinds of ways without realizing it. Excellent teachers instinctively convey the power of adhishthana when they pass on their knowledge and expertise. Lovers mutually exchange adhishthana when they share each other's interests and enthusiasms. In fact, every relationship contains an element of adhishthana in some sense, whether it is positive or negative.

But the adhishthana that is meant here is the transmission of the presence of the tantric guru. The whole idea of the guru-disciple relationship has had a very hard time in the West, which is not to say that it has always had an easy time in the East. In spite of the great potentiality that exists for misunderstanding and abuse on both sides, the essence of this relationship remains as true and profound as it has always been. It is not about control on the one side, nor is it about submission on the other. Essentially it is about adhishthana, which is called forth by devotion and longing and received with faith and an open heart. Adhishthana is the real business of the guru.

If enlightenment is our true nature, why do we need anyone's help to find it? It sounds very reasonable to say that no one can really give us anything, and that we should not call anyone our master. Yet the fact remains that although we are all buddhas, we still do not realize it. If we could attain liberation by ourselves, why have we not done so before now? Why is it so difficult? Why have we remained imprisoned by the power of illusion during all our lives, for countless ages?

Although enlightenment truly does dwell within us, it has to appear to come to us from outside because of our attachment to self. Ego cannot penetrate its own illusion, cannot dissolve itself. One of the difficulties that sometimes arises for Westerners in relation to vajrayana is the suspicion that secrets are being kept from us, that we are "not allowed" to do this or that. The real issue here is that certain meditation practices simply do not work if we try them out by ourselves, acting from our own will. They may have some effect and produce some kind of insight or even psychic power, but they will not be able to transmute confusion into wisdom, they will not open up a gap in the solidity of ego. It is not that we are forbidden to do anything, but that psychologically, in our own minds, we need to know that we have received authentic permission and correct instruction from a qualified person for the practice to be effective. There is a genuine transmission that takes place, and for that to happen, a relationship of trust must exist between teacher and student. Through the power of adhishthana, the guru gives us confidence on a very deep level. The greater the trust we have in him or her, the more our confidence will increase; it is really a continuous process of opening up more and more to our innate buddha-nature.

The guru is someone who has become transparent to the awakened state, who allows it to shine through unhindered. At the very moment of transmission, the mind of the guru and the mind of the student meet and become one. There is no longer any separation between guru and disciple. So it is said that the guru gives us back what has always been our own.

The power of adhishthana is inherent in *Liberation through Hearing* because it is a terma. The teaching comes directly from Guru Rinpoche (Padmakara) and is imbued with all the wisdom, compassion, and power of his living presence. The entire concentrated force of his intention and aspiration gives the termas their power to liberate sentient beings. It is as though he himself is present whenever the text is read. This sense of immediacy and freshness is an important reason for the terma tradition. Inevitably, teachings are lost over the centuries, their lineage of transmission may be interrupted, or corruptions may occur, but when a terma teaching is revealed, it comes straight from the ultimate source, the primordial awakened mind. The authority of a newly discovered terma is just as great as that of one discovered centuries ago.

Liberation through Hearing says of itself: "To meet with this is great good fortune. It is hard to meet, except for those who have purified the obscuring veils and developed goodness." This means that not just anyone can come across it. To hear it or read it at all implies that either in this life or in past lives we have made some connection with it. Even if we just happen to pick it up in a bookshop, this is not entirely by chance. The connections we have made during the whole measureless course of our existence are extremely significant. Through their power seeds are sown, and again through their power those seeds may ripen at any time. That is why Trungpa Rinpoche said that any form of contact with this teaching will confer a sudden glimpse of enlightenment; we need not believe in it, but something will definitely have entered our minds as a result. It does not mean that we become fully enlightened at that moment. Our confusion will probably prevent us from recognizing that sudden glimpse, but it will be reawakened at some time in the future. There is no doubt, as the tantras say.

Liberation through hearing is only one of six ways of liberation taught in the Nyingma tradition. The other five are liberation through sight, liberation through touch, liberation through taste, liberation through remembrance, and liberation through wearing. All these ways possess the same potential to arouse a flash of spontaneous self-liberation through the power of adhishthana, originating from Guru Rinpoche, who is the embodiment of all gurus.

Liberation through sight is brought about by seeing terma objects such as images, paintings, symbolic diagrams, or texts. The text of *Liberation through Hearing* belongs to this category as well as to the category of liberation through hearing, for, as it says of itself: "it is a profound instruction that liberates just by being seen or heard or read." Liberation through sight could also mean the sight of Guru Rinpoche in a dream or vision; it is said in Nyingma teachings that simply by seeing his face one is liberated.

Liberation through touch refers particularly to the tantric partner or consort. The consort embodies the sacredness of the objective world and the apparent "otherness" of inspiration. The relationship of lover and beloved becomes extremely important in the higher tantras to overcome the last traces of egoism in the notion of achieving one's own enlightenment by oneself. For a man, his partner is seen as a *dakini*, embodiment of feminine enlightened energy, while a woman's partner is looked upon as a *daka* or *heruka*, the corresponding male energy. Padmakara is described as always surrounded by dakinis. Sometimes he is called the teacher and tamer of dakinis, sometimes they are seen as his inspiration and helpers, and sometimes they appear spontaneously as manifestations of his wisdom energy. He and they are one, for although they appear in different forms, they are both manifestations of the one awakened state. So, whether male or female, if one is practicing in this tradition, the relationship with a consort creates a direct connection with Guru Rinpoche himself.

Liberation through taste is attained by eating special substances known as *amrita*, "ambrosia" or "nectar of immortality." These are often prepared in the form of pills by great lamas, who imbue them with the power of their adhishthana and give them to their disciples for use in serious illness or at the time of death. They also may be placed in the mouth of a corpse after death. Many amrita pills were prepared and hidden by Padmakara and rediscovered along with other treasures.

Liberation through remembrance refers to certain instructions that specifically relate to the time of death. They are intended to be learned during this life and practiced sufficiently to gain confidence in them, for the purpose of calling them to mind at death. Among them is the transference of consciousness. Karma Lingpa's father discovered termas on transference. This practice is discussed further in part 2, when we come to the text of *Liberation through Hearing*, where it is said that it "liberates spontaneously as soon as it is thought of."

Liberation through wearing indicates the wearing of *yantras*: diagrams, pictures, and written mantras that are generally kept in a pouch or amulet and worn next to the skin. As well as being worn during life, they are often attached to the corpse. Texts containing these mantras are included in Karma Lingpa's terma collection. It is recommended that they be read aloud together with *Liberation through Hearing*, "for the two combined are like a golden mandala inlaid with turquoise."

Chapter Four

Bardo: The Experience
of Nowness

THE FINAL KEY WORD in the title is *bardo*, the word that really defines these teachings and sets them apart. Trungpa Rinpoche and I chose to keep the Tibetan word in our translation because it was already so well known. For this book, I originally intended to translate it as "in-between state"; however, when I read that some newly discovered poems by Ted Hughes included one called "Crow in the Bardo," I felt that bardo had truly entered the English language and decided to return to it.[1]

I have two reservations about using the Tibetan word, which I mention in order to dispel possible misunderstanding. One is that it may associate these teachings on the after-death state exclusively with Tibet. It so happens that *Liberation through Hearing*, the most famous work on the subject, was written in Tibetan, but the ideas it contains originated in India and are thoroughly part of the Buddhism that was transmitted from India to Tibet. My other reservation is that it may suggest something strange and exotic, instead of being a tool that is practical and accessible. It is crucial to our understanding of *Liberation through Hearing* that the bardo not be seen as only a mystical experience or something that happens after death, but as part of everyday life.

Originally bardo referred only to the period between one life and

53

the next, and this is still its normal meaning when it is mentioned
without any qualification. There was considerable dispute over this theory during the early centuries of Buddhism, with one side arguing that
rebirth (or conception) follows immediately after death, and the other
saying that there must be an interval between the two. With the rise
of mahayana, belief in a transitional period prevailed. Later Buddhism
expanded the whole concept to distinguish six or more similar states,
covering the whole cycle of life, death, and rebirth. But it can also be
interpreted as any transitional experience, any state that lies between
two other states. Its original meaning, the experience of being between
death and rebirth, is the prototype of the bardo experience, while the
six traditional bardos show how the essential qualities of that experience
are also present in other transitional periods. By refining even further
the understanding of the essence of bardo, it can then be applied to
every moment of existence. The present moment, the now, is a continual bardo, always suspended between the past and the future.

Bardo can have many implications, depending on how one looks
at it. It is an interval, a hiatus, a gap. It can act as a boundary that
divides and separates, marking the end of one thing and the beginning
of another; but it can also be a link between the two—it can serve as a
bridge or a meeting place that brings together and unites. It is a crossing, a stepping-stone, a transition. It is a crossroads where one must
choose which path to take, and it is a no-man's-land belonging to
neither one side nor the other. It is a highlight or peak point of experience and at the same time a situation of extreme tension caught between
two opposites. It is an open space filled with an atmosphere of suspension and uncertainty, neither this nor that. In such a state, one may feel
confused and frightened, or one may feel surprisingly liberated and
open to new possibilities where anything might happen.

Such moments as these occur continuously in life, unrecognized;
this is the inner significance of the bardo states as Trungpa Rinpoche
taught. He spoke of them as periods of uncertainty between sanity and
insanity or between the confusion of samsara and the transformation
of confusion into wisdom. "They are the heightened qualities of different types of ego and the possibility of getting off ego. That's where
bardo starts—the peak experience in which there is the possibility of
losing the grip of ego and the possibility of being swallowed up in it."[2]

Wherever there is the death of one state of mind, there is the birth of another, and linking the two there is bardo. The past has gone and the future has not yet come; we cannot catch that in-between moment, yet it is really all there is. "In other words, it is present experience, the immediate experience of nowness—where you are, where you're at."[3]

According to this tradition, the six bardos are the bardo of this life (or birth), the bardo of dream, the bardo of meditation, the bardo of dying, the bardo of dharmata (or reality), and the bardo of existence (or becoming). Other traditions recognize some additional ones, but the principle is the same. The bardos are distinguished from each other in this way because they indicate different modes of consciousness, just as the waking consciousness differs from the dreaming consciousness. These states can last for a short or long period of time, as long as a whole lifetime in the case of the first one, yet they all share the mysterious and immensely powerful quality of "in-betweenness." Or we could say that, by learning to see these stages of our lives as bardos, we can gain access to that power, which is always present, unnoticed, in every moment of existence.

Another terma text in the same cycle gives detailed instructions for practice within the six bardos, and has been translated into English under the title of *Natural Liberation*.[4] These practices have many similarities with the more famous "six dharmas" of Naropa, better known as the "six yogas," which were originally called instructions for liberation in the bardos.[5] The instructions are very briefly summarized in *The Root Verses of the Six Bardos*,[6] which accompanies *Liberation through Hearing*. These verses describe very concisely the nature of each bardo and the means of awakening within it, so I will quote them here to introduce each of the six bardos.

THE BARDO OF THIS LIFE

Now when the bardo of this life is dawning upon me,
I will abandon laziness, for there is no time to waste in life,
Enter the undistracted path of hearing, thought, and meditation,

Making mind and appearances the path, I will manifest the
   trikaya.
Now that for once I have obtained a human body
This is no time to linger on diverting sidetracks.

Literally, this bardo is called the "place" or "state of birth," which does
not refer just to birth itself, but to its result, the condition of life into
which we are born. It can also be translated as "birth and remaining."
It means this particular birth, this life. Another name that is sometimes
used for it is the bardo of birth and death. Some traditions actually
interpret the birthplace as the womb and recognize a separate bardo of
gestation, but here, according to the verse, it clearly indicates this life.
It lasts from birth until death and covers the whole of our ordinary,
waking existence. We can also think of it as any moment or situation
that occurs during waking life or as the lifetime of any mental state,
however short or long it may be. Anything whatever, after it has arisen
and before it passes away, takes place within the bardo of this life,
appearing to exist and to be absolutely real.

   Trungpa Rinpoche said that this state is based on speed, the mo-
mentum of keeping things going. If a flaming torch is whirled around
fast enough in the air, it appears to be a solid circle of fire. If an airplane
loses its speed, it will stall and fall out of the sky. In this case, speed is
necessary to keep up the illusion of what we are; it keeps us believing
in the solidity and permanence of our individual existence and of the
external world. The essence or peak point of this bardo is when a gap
suddenly occurs; our speed falters for a moment and the continuity is
broken. At that very instant, there is a possibility of seeing through the
illusion, but this may well seem terrifying, like falling out of the sky
into empty space.

   The verse reminds us that birth as a human being is extremely rare
and precious, and that we should use this opportunity to follow a
spiritual path, which is the whole purpose of life. Hearing, thought (or
contemplation), and meditation are the three indispensable aspects of
the path in Buddhism. First, of course, one has to hear about it. In a
general sense, this means studying and learning about it from any
source, which may include reading books and watching films or videos.
But literally hearing, listening with an open mind to the words of a

living teacher, produces a very different effect. This is especially important in vajrayana, where the guru embodies the presence of the whole
tradition and transmits its energy and inspiration. We have already seen
how this power of transmission applies to the text of *Liberation through
Hearing*.

Second, one should think carefully about what one has heard, ask
questions about it to clarify its meaning, and test it against one's own
experience. Then one should reflect deeply on the teachings and recall
them as often as possible so they permeate one's whole mind. Buddhism
has great respect for the intellect and believes that it must be trained
and used in the proper way, as a tool for its own transcendence. The
various views put forward in Buddhist philosophy are never purely theoretical. They are meant to guide one's thought into the correct framework for the experience of meditation. All these teachings and practices
sometimes seem extremely complicated, but this is only because of the
complexity of our conditioned minds. For countless lives, we have been
living under the influence of ignorance, and so it is not easy to clear
away all the obstructions to understanding or to reach the deeply hidden layers of confusion. Through careful thought and reasoning, we
can become convinced of what is true and gain confidence in the path.

Finally, what has been heard and thought about must be put into
practice through meditation. This is much more than contemplation of
the teachings or understanding them intellectually. At this point, the
rational, conceptual aspect of the mind must let go, allowing a breakthrough into direct, intuitive experience. Meditation means working
directly with the mind and inner energies in accordance with whatever
technique one is following. By this process, delusions are cleared away,
the chain of karmic cause and effect is interrupted, and the mind is
transformed. It brings about an actual change in one's mode of consciousness, so it is counted as a bardo in its own right, the bardo of
meditation occurring within the bardo of this life.

In each of the bardos, the essence of the practice is to use the
particular circumstances of that state as a means of awakening. The
verse tells us to make mind and appearances into the path. *Appearances*
means everything that arises in the fields of the senses; appearances and
mind together constitute our whole experience. We take that experience
itself as a path so that it becomes the basis of our practice. External

appearances seem to be quite separate from the mind, because of our dualistic habit of dividing experience into subject and object, but gradually we come to see that they are indivisible and that all appearances are the spontaneous play of the mind. The guru reveals the true nature of the mind by a process of direct transmission, a meeting of minds that can most readily take place during this bardo, our present lifetime.

The *trikaya* literally means the "three bodies," the three dimensions of the awakened state: its absolute empty essence, the visionary expression of its luminous nature, and its actual appearance in this world. A fuller explanation of the trikaya and its connection with the path is found in chapter 9. By following the path, we come to realize that the true nature of both mind and appearances is the primordial state of buddhahood. We ourselves are intrinsically buddha, and therefore we naturally manifest the three aspects as the spontaneous expression of our own being.

The bardo of dream and the bardo of meditation both take place within the bardo of this life. Dreaming intensifies the illusory nature of life, whereas meditation presents a way of seeing life as it truly is. Here I am reversing the traditional order and taking the bardo of meditation first in order to introduce certain ideas that are also relevant to the bardo of dream.

THE BARDO OF MEDITATION

Now when the bardo of meditation dawns upon me,
I will abandon the crowd of distractions and confusions,
Rest in the boundless state without grasping or disturbance,
And gain stability in creation and completion.
At this time of meditation, one-pointed, free from activity,
Do not fall into the power of confused emotions!

Meditation is a state of mind with greater clarity and awareness, different from our ordinary condition of consciousness, a gap in the continual flow of confused thoughts and complete identification with ego. Here Trungpa Rinpoche interprets it not as formal meditation practice, but as a natural function of the mind, an innate intelligence that sees the clarity of things just as they are. Often, when people have such flashes of openness, they ignore them, try to suppress them, or even fear they may be going a little crazy. We have lost the tradition of valuing them, and unless one is following a spiritual path, there is no context in which to understand them; they seem disturbing and subversive, undermining the importance of the so-called real world. On the other hand, it is possible to become very attached to these natural meditative states, or indeed to any kind of meditation, whatever tradition it belongs to. Then it can become a trap and, instead of producing greater awareness, keep one firmly bound within samsara.

Experiences like these are brief glimpses of "the boundless state." This is the true nature of the mind, but we are continually distracted from it and confused by the disturbed emotions arising from ignorance. In order to rest in it and gain stability, it is necessary to train the mind in a more structured manner. The verse itself specifically mentions the method of meditation used in vajrayana, consisting of the two stages of creation and completion. This method is called deity yoga, the practice of union with the deity.

The meaning of the deities in vajrayana will become clearer over the course of the following chapters, and especially in part 2. It is a little confusing because the same word, from the Sanskrit *deva* (masculine) and *devi* (feminine), is used to mean both the deities of samsara and the deities of the awakened state. The deities of samsara are the gods and goddesses who can be found in all ancient religions of the world: Indian, Far Eastern, Greek, Roman, Celtic, and so on. What characterizes them as belonging to samsara rather than to enlightenment is simply that they are believed in as real, external beings; in other words, there is no understanding of ultimate emptiness and nonself. The monotheistic religions of Judaism, Christianity, and Islam replaced these deities with one supreme God, but as we have seen (see chapter 2), Buddhism regards this as still being a response to the sense of self. The deities of the awakened state are synonymous with buddhas; they are the living presence of enlightenment in all its various aspects and functions. Each one embodies and emphasizes some special aspect of buddhahood, yet each is complete and perfect in itself. The deity chosen as the focus of one's practice represents total awakening, the essence of all deities; it is the meditated form of the practitioner's own awakened nature, his or her innate divinity. In the *Tibetan Book of the Dead*, we kept the Tibetan term *yidam*, but here I call it the "chosen deity," from the Sanskrit equivalent, *ishtadevata*.

During the stage of creation, the meditator transforms the ordinary world into a sacred world through creative meditation or imagination. This is often referred to as visualization, but the visual sense is only a part of the creative process. William Blake called imagination the "Divine Vision," which is exactly what is meant here. It involves all the senses and the totality of the meditator's body, speech, and mind. The actual feeling of the deity's presence and confidence in the reality of the deity's world are the basis of the meditation. The details of the imagery help to establish and stabilize that conviction. Every element of iconography has a symbolic meaning, so it provides a direct connection to the awakened state of mind. The success of this whole practice depends on our willingness to give up our ordinary view of ourselves and to recognize the illusory nature of our present perceptions. We realize that we are actually creating our everyday world all the time with our confused, limited, dreamlike imaginations, so it would be far better to create an enlightened world through the techniques of tantric imagination.

Throughout the stage of creation, the meditator must never forget that the deities are neither substantial nor separate from oneself: they are the spontaneous appearances of emptiness, the play of the awakened mind. All the forms are made of light, like rainbows, so gradually one's fixed concept of physical reality decreases and the meditator begins to experience even his or her own body as insubstantial. At a certain point, the deities and their environment dissolve away once more into emptiness, and the meditator rests in formless meditation. This is the essence of the stage of completion. The two stages go together right from the beginning, but eventually the stage of completion becomes much more profound and extensive.

Completion has two aspects: one that uses yoga practices working directly with the subtle vital energies (see chapter 9), and one that simply remains in the natural state of ultimate awareness. The techniques of yoga lead to a conscious experience of the inner dissolution process that occurs at death, culminating in the experience of luminosity. Then, within the meditative state, the yogin or yogini takes on the form of his or her chosen deity, which is known as the illusory body. Finally, one meditates that the illusory body manifests in a physical form as one returns to ordinary life. The completion stage takes one through a process similar to the sequence of death, the after-death state, and rebirth, a sequence that also occurs in sleeping, dreaming, and waking. By practicing first in meditation and then during sleep, one learns how to transform one's death into a means of liberation. It is only through this bardo of meditation that one can acquire the skills to implement the instructions for all the other bardos.

The six yogas of Naropa provide a systematic arrangement of the entire process. They are practiced mainly in the "new" traditions stemming from the second diffusion of dharma in Tibet, while the "old" Nyingma tradition has its own corresponding practices. There is a marked difference in style between these two in the way they are presented. Commentaries on the six yogas are often extremely complex and make it obvious that no one would be able to practice them without considerable training. Nyingma literature, such as *Natural Liberation* and Trungpa Rinpoche's own teaching on the bardos, sometimes appears to have a deceptive simplicity; its ideas are expressed in very inspiring language that continually reminds us of our innate buddha-nature here and now.

In a general sense, the stages of creation and completion are present in all aspects of life. In every learning process, there is a phase of effort and contrivance, which, if we persist long enough, bears fruit in a natural, unforced phase of accomplishment. If it is a physical skill, like riding a bicycle, it becomes instinctive and automatic; if it is a mental process, like learning a poem, it merges into the background of the mind and remains present as a store of knowledge and source of inspiration. In all the arts, it is essential to acquire technique and to practice constantly, yet at a certain point we have to abandon reliance on technique, let go of deliberate effort, and allow spontaneity to take over—exactly the same principle applies to meditation.

The peak of this bardo is the ego's attempt to solidify the open space of meditation. Even at an advanced stage, attachment to the most subtle levels of realization can arise, producing a feeling of conflict. We are caught between the two extremes of dwelling in the blissful experience of eternity and sudden doubt about its validity, which comes from the emptiness of space. Perhaps we are losing our balance or losing our mind, we might even lose everything and cease to exist. This is the opportunity to let go completely and simply rest in the boundless state of the openness and clarity of the true nature of mind, experiencing everything just as it is.

The Bardo of Dream

Now when the bardo of dream is dawning upon me,
I will abandon the careless, corpselike sleep of delusion
And enter the abiding state with undistracted mindfulness,
Holding dreams, transforming emanations, purifying in
   luminosity.
Do not sleep like an animal, but treasure
The practice that mingles sleep with direct perception!

The bardo of dream includes both dreaming and dreamless sleep. It lasts from the moment of falling asleep until the moment of waking up again. As we fall asleep, we go through a process analogous to death, as the perceptions of waking consciousness dissolve and fade away. We consider this to be falling into a state of unconsciousness, but really the mind is resting in its most profound, natural state, which we are unable to recognize as such because of our confusion.

According to the teachings of *Natural Liberation*, the instructions concerning this bardo are in three parts: illusory body, dreaming, and luminosity (or clear light). The practice of illusory body trains us to see waking life as a dream and to realize that our whole subjectively experienced world is the creation of the mind, just like a magician's illusion, insubstantial and impermanent. This realization is fundamental to all practices related to the bardos. It is a particularly necessary preparation for working with dreams, because dreams arise from karmic traces deeply imprinted in the mind, and so they are very hard to influence directly. Only after our intense attachment to our ordinary concept of reality is loosened does it become possible to perceive the world of dreams, too, as our own creation and to control it. The practice of luminosity is simply to recognize and rest in the basic nature of mind itself, in its emptiness, radiance, and clarity. A momentary glimpse of luminosity appears at the moment of falling asleep, just as it does at the moment of death, but ordinarily we are unable to recognize it or even to notice anything at all.

Traditionally, there are two methods of approaching the dream practice. One is through an intense wish and determination to remain aware during sleep, assisted by certain meditations. This is a difficult and unreliable method, although it can occur naturally under certain circumstances. The other is by training in the completion-stage yogas and applying them here. As we fall asleep, we recognize and retain awareness of the state of luminosity, and then transform the dream experience into the illusory body of the practice. This is particularly recommended in order to gain confidence that we will be able to apply the same techniques at death.

In the verse, holding dreams means first recognizing the dream as a dream the moment it arises. This leads to the ability to cultivate lucid dreams and remember them. Gradually one learns to hold the clear awareness of dreaming so that one can transform one's emotions and reactions and control the dream events in various ways. Practitioners who achieve control over their dreams can transform whatever appears, changing its shape, color, and size or multiplying it into countless numbers. Then they can create emanations and go anywhere they wish in any form. All this activity takes place within the awareness of luminosity, out of which all appearances arise and into which they dissolve again. Through this practice, one gains insight into the illusory nature of all phenomena, in waking life just as in dreams.

In commenting on the bardo of dream, Trungpa Rinpoche emphasized the dreamlike nature of ordinary life: how we continually create an imaginary world out of our concepts and desires, our hopes and fears. The key to finding the gap, the intense in-between quality of this particular state, is to feel vividly the confusion between waking and sleeping and to catch a glimpse of our own uncertainty about what we really are. Dreams seem absolutely real while we are dreaming, so how can we be sure that waking life is not the same as a dream? Perhaps dreams are more real than waking life! This kind of uncertainty can act as a sudden inspiration to let go of all fixed concepts, and it may enable us to break through for a moment into the open space of luminous emptiness, whether we are awake or dreaming.

The three remaining bardos are concerned with the process of dying, the period after death, and the approach to rebirth. They will be introduced only briefly here, as they are the subject matter of *Liberation through Hearing* and are described in detail in part 2.

THE BARDO OF DYING

Now when the bardo of dying is dawning upon me,
I will abandon grasping, attachment, and the all-desiring mind,
Enter undistracted the clear essence of the instructions
And transfer into the space of unborn self-awareness.
As I leave this conditioned body of flesh and blood
I will know it to be a transitory illusion.

Death is a process of dissolution, described in terms of the elements of body and mind being progressively absorbed from coarse to subtle, one by one. It seems to be a unique and final event, yet this transformation is actually taking place all the time. All the elements that make up our existence are continuously arising and dissolving again: birth and death occur at every moment. Whenever we have the feeling of something coming to an end or of trying to hang on to it, that is a taste of the bardo of dying.

Even when the ordinary coarse and subtle elements have dissolved, grasping continues, and so the continuity of the mindstream is kept going on a very subtle level, along with its associated karma. It is said that at the final moment of the dissolution process, the luminosity of death appears to all sentient beings. Just before that moment, we experience the peak point of this bardo, where we are caught between the desire for continued existence and the fear of annihilation. To the ego, there seems to be nothing besides these two alternatives; we are imprisoned by the logic of either existence or nonexistence, since we have no experience of a state that transcends them both. The confusion of most living beings is too great to face such an inconceivable dilemma, and they simply black out into unconsciousness.

The instruction given for this bardo is the practice of transference, the total transformation of one's consciousness, at the moment just before death. This practice can be done in several different ways, according to one's level of understanding and experience, so that the mind merges either directly into the awakened state itself or into some particular aspect of it, to which one feels connection and devotion. If the mind of the dead person has not been liberated in this way, it will awaken in the next bardo after a period of unconsciousness.

THE BARDO OF DHARMATA

Now when the bardo of dharmata dawns upon me,
I will abandon all projections of fear and terror,
Recognize whatever arises as the self-display of awareness,
And know it to be the visionary nature of the bardo.
When the time comes to reach the crucial point
Do not fear the self-display of peaceful and wrathful ones!

This bardo brings us to the heart of *Liberation through Hearing*, the visions of the peaceful and wrathful deities. *Dharmata* is the natural state of the true nature of all phenomena, the essential quality of reality. The bardo of dharmata is the gap that occurs when one thought has vanished but another has not yet begun to arise in its place. The mind is plunged into its own essential nature of luminous emptiness, which is identical with the nature of all phenomena, and the peaceful and wrathful deities appear as natural manifestations of that ultimate reality.

Because of the sense of individual self, which still continues, we do not recognize the deities as our own nature; instead we feel afraid of them, thinking they are separate and external. The basic instruction is simply to recognize them, and thus to be naturally and spontaneously self-liberated. However, we have a deep, instinctive longing to return to individual existence, and so, at the same time as the visions of enlightenment, we dimly perceive pathways leading back to the six realms of samsara. As we go further into the experience of the bardo, the awakened energy becomes more and more intense, but to the bewildered consciousness, it appears more and more terrifying.

The form in which these visions are described is similar to that of deity yoga. This imagery is never accidental or arbitrary. The deities, with their colors, attributes, and so on, reveal the different qualities of our awakened nature, and at the same time, they each relate to some aspect of samsara. The illusory nature of ordinary life is called impure perception because it arises from ignorance and is dominated by passion, aggression, and delusion, while the appearance of the deities is pure perception, or pure vision; Trungpa Rinpoche used to call it sacred vision or sacred outlook. Working with this imagery helps us to make connections between ordinary life and the awakened state and shows us that in reality the two are indivisible.

If the departed consciousness does not recognize its own intrinsic nature during the bardo of dharmata, it will be pulled onward toward rebirth by the irresistible force of karma and find itself in the next bardo.

The Bardo of Existence

Now when the bardo of existence dawns upon me,
I will hold my aspiration one-pointedly in mind
And strive to prolong the course of good karma.
I will close the womb door and remember resistance.
This is a time for strength of mind and pure vision,
Abandon jealousy and meditate on the guru as father and mother!

The bardo of existence is the decisive period that determines either liberation or rebirth in one of the six realms of samsara. Previously, we translated it as the bardo of becoming, but Trungpa Rinpoche used both in his teaching, and I feel that existence is a better translation. Here it means the process of coming into existence as an embodied sentient being.

As the bardo of dharmata fades away, our experiences become more and more confused and frightening, and we are impelled onward by the power of our past actions. Then we find ourselves being drawn back into our habitual manner of perception, the environment begins to look familiar and we feel we are coming home again. As soon as we see a man and woman in the act of making love, we grasp eagerly at any opportunity of entering a womb to be reborn. Even at this late stage, there are instructions for avoiding rebirth or, if that is not possible, for choosing the best possible conditions in which to be born. Since we are continually creating our own world through our perception, the cultivation of pure vision makes all the difference at this point. We should try to perceive everything we experience as the pure land of a buddha and resolve to retain that kind of perception in the next life. At the moment when our new existence is about to be conceived, we should look upon our future parents as our guru or chosen deity, manifesting in the form of male and female in union.

During this bardo, we vividly experience the power of karmic cause and effect. Just as everything is dissolving away at every moment, so it is also continually reemerging. Everything appears again in the same old way through the force of habit. Sometimes in the course of daily life, we can see quite clearly how an action or an emotion is going to bring about a predictable result, and there is a certain moment when it could be averted. Usually, we are so attached to our habitual ways that we just let them take their inevitable course. We believe that this is what we are, this is our personality, and we are afraid of letting go into the unknown.

All six bardos have distinctly different qualities or flavors, whether we think of them as specific states that last for defined periods of time or as the essence of those states occurring during our daily life. Trungpa Rinpoche related them to the six realms of samsara, a subject that is explored further in chapter 8. Like the bardos, the six realms represent modes of consciousness, although in a rather different way. As well as referring to the six possible conditions of rebirth, they can be seen as descriptions of the various states of mind we inhabit: animal-like, god-like, hell-like, and so on. At present, we have been born in human form, so in the ordinary sense we are experiencing the bardo of this life in the human realm, but within that basic framework we continually experience psychologically all the other realms and all the other bardos. When the characteristic energy of whichever realm we are in becomes especially intense, it builds up to a crescendo that has the nature of a bardo: "it is the embodiment of the whole experience of each different realm."[7]

The experiences of the six realms and the six bardos do not exist by themselves; they arise from the open space of the primordial nature of mind. Luminosity is the aspect of mind that gives rise to all these appearances: it is the environment that surrounds them, out of which they emerge and into which they dissolve. It is always present, like the sun in the sky, hidden behind clouds. At the moment, because of ignorance of our real nature, we experience everything as the confused manifestations of samsara. The sense of self creates a feeling of solidity, like the apparent solidity of the clouds veiling the face of the sun, but at certain moments a gap is opened through which we may receive a glimpse of the light of reality.

This gap is brought about by the intensity of emotional experience, which is always accompanied by an equal and opposite reaction, so that we are thrown into a situation of conflict and uncertainty. Two contrasting extremes are present simultaneously. Trungpa Rinpoche described it as being drenched with boiling hot and freezing cold water at the same time. At that very moment, there is nothing to do but let go: give up trying to hold on to one extreme or the other, abandon the battle between life and death, good and bad, hope and fear. Then, in that instant of relaxation, there comes a sudden flash of realization. There is always the possibility that, in the midst of an everyday situation or at the height of some emotion, we may suddenly catch a glimpse of its essential emptiness and luminosity—a moment of sacred vision.

Entering the awakened state of mind, even for a moment, is always preceded by an experience, however fleeting, of extreme contrast and conflict. Even on the highest and most subtle levels of attainment, negative and positive continue together side by side until we make the leap beyond them both. Deliberately inducing paradoxical situations or being confronted by paradoxical statements that the rational mind is unable to reconcile can sometimes shock a person who is ready for it into a breakthrough. Great teachers have been known to precipitate an awakening in their students by a sudden outburst of anger or some other totally unexpected action. There are many stories of this kind in tantric literature, such as when the great siddha Tilopa hit his disciple Naropa in the face with his shoe.[8]

Even in ordinary life, gaps of this kind can occur. It might happen when we are in a state of complete exhaustion, feeling that we cannot stand it any longer and are just about to tip over the edge into madness. Or it might come at the height of extreme emotion, when our emotional energy reaches its peak and we are suddenly no longer sure what we are doing or what caused it. Suddenly time seems to stop and we feel calm and detached, suspended in a state of absolute stillness. For a moment, we enter a different dimension of being, but without training it is impossible to stabilize these experiences and take advantage of the opportunity they represent. To be able to recognize and use such moments of heightened intensity requires the firm foundation of a calm and steady mind and confidence in the basic sanity and goodness of our own nature.

All the instructions concerning the six bardos basically deal with allowing that gap to open by undermining our belief in the ordinary world that we take for granted, and then letting go into the space beyond. The bardo experience is a doorway to awakening that is always present. In Trungpa Rinpoche's words, "Bardo is a very practical way of looking at our life."[9]

T̶h̶ ̶ ̶ ̶ ̶f Elements

THE ENTIRE MANIFESTE   1ether it appears as the
confused phenomena of sam: ions of the buddhas—is
composed of earth, water, fire   vhich are known as the
five great elements. They are the basic materials of existence. But they
are not just the ordinary earth, water, fire, air, and space that we experience in everyday life. The elements we see in nature are only the material or outer forms of subtle, elemental qualities. These are the inherent
qualities of awakened mind, and they manifest in all aspects of life,
whether physical, mental, emotional, or spiritual.

The elements and everything composed of them exist on three
levels, called the coarse, the subtle, and the secret. This universal threefold principle is discussed more fully in chapter 9.

The coarse, gross, or material level refers to the physical reality of
our bodies and our environment. It includes whatever can be perceived
by the senses, even with the aid of scientific instruments, whose use
allows us to penetrate far beyond the reach of normal perception but
still remain within the physical realm. This is the sphere of ordinary,
everyday life.

Behind this plane of existence lie the immaterial qualities of the
elements, which determine how they manifest and function in the outer

world. This is the subtle level of energy. It cannot be scientifically defined or measured. Within these two dimensions is a continuous spectrum from material to subtle: earth is the densest and heaviest of the elements, while space is the finest and most subtle. Moreover, each single element contains all five elements within itself, so there are worlds within worlds, all interconnecting and interdependent.

The innermost dimension, the subtlest of all, is called the secret essence. This is none other than awakened mind, the ultimate state of emptiness and wisdom. The secret essence of the five great elements is the feminine principle of enlightenment taking the form of the five female buddhas.

The external world of the environment and the internal world of individual living beings both have the same origin and display the same characteristics. On the physical level, we are literally made from earth, since everything we eat comes from the earth. In the same way, a large proportion of our food and our bodies is made of water. We possess fire in the warmth of the body and we take in air with the breath, while space surrounds us and pervades us right down to the core of our atomic structure.

All material substances possess a subtle nature that shapes their outward form. Traditional and complementary medical systems make use of the subtle elemental qualities of plants and minerals in healing. These qualities act through their similarities with the subtle elements in human beings. Our physiological, psychological, and spiritual states all play a part in the condition of our health, and all these different dimensions are linked together by the theory of the five elements.

The subtle qualities of the elements also give rise to our five senses: subjectively to the development of the sense organs, and objectively to their spheres of operation. That is to say, they produce the subtle properties in matter that make it perceptible to the various sense organs. The relationships between the elements and the senses given in this chapter are according to Indian tradition, which was adopted by the Tibetans. It is mainly applicable to medical theory, for instance, in describing the development of an embryo in the womb. However, there are many other ways of relating the senses to the elements in different contexts—in fact, almost every possible combination can be found—and we shall see a completely different set of relationships when we come to the description of the dissolution of the body at death. Those given here refer to the basic, inherent qualities of the elements, while the other systems could be regarded as expressing additional, transient relationships arising from the context of a particular view or practice.

We can find innumerable parallels to the five great elements everywhere we look. Each element has its own color, shape, temperature, texture, season, bodily organ, direction in space, and many other characteristics. We know instinctively what is meant by a fiery temperament or a hot color. In fact, we use descriptions relating to the elements all the time in ordinary language. Certain traditional associations occur frequently in Buddhism, especially in the tantras. Generally, with a few exceptions, the same associations are found in the Hindu tantras. Other systems, such as the Chinese, Native American, and Western alchemical traditions, differ considerably in their details. But they are all based on the same fundamental principle that links can be made between the various levels of existence. These links are not just theoretical, but can be used in our understanding of life, in healing, and especially in spiritual practice.

EARTH

The element of earth is the densest of the five great elements and has the characteristics of solidity, weight, immobility, and hardness. Degrees of weight and hardness are relative; even the soft feeling of water, for instance, comes from the quality of earth that is inherent in water. Earth has a resistant nature that prevents it from merging and coalescing. It is this resistance we feel when we experience relative hardness and softness.

The subtle quality of earth is the origin of the sense of smell and, corresponding to it in the external world, of all scents and odors. Smell is the most earthy, the most physical, of our senses. It is often said that smell brings back memories more strongly and vividly than any of the other senses; it binds us to our earthly natures in a very deep and instinctive way.

Earth gives both living beings and inanimate objects their shape

and form. Like all the elements, earth is subject to impermanence, but
it changes so slowly that it produces an illusion of permanence. Mountains and rocks seem everlasting, and even our bodies appear more or
less the same from day to day, so we become accustomed to thinking
they do not change. Earth is our home, our familiar environment, the
solid ground on which we can walk safely and feel secure. Earth is a
treasure-house, the source of all wealth, a mine of gold and precious
gems.

Within the human body, the earth element provides our flesh and
bones. It gives us form, structure, and strength. It supports and contains
the other elements within us. Earth provides the food that sustains our
bodies. Whatever we eat, whether it is mineral, vegetable, or animal, is
a transformation of earth. The earth can withstand all kinds of attacks
and upheavals, and bears without complaint whatever heavy weight is
laid upon it. In the classical dances of India, the dancer always begins
by touching the ground in salutation to thank the Goddess Earth for
acting as a dancing floor. But earth is not only the actual ground we
walk upon; tantra sees all life as a dance or a play, so the subtle element
of earth becomes the dancing ground of our whole existence. Within
the mind as well, earth is the origin of everything that arises; because
of this quality, mind has the inherent capacity to act as a basis and a
ground.

The qualities of earth are also found in the emotional and psychological realms. They make a person steady and reliable; they bestow
patience, endurance, and loyalty. Earth conveys a feeling of inexhaustible resources and richness. When people act in a supportive role or
exert a grounding influence, they are displaying the qualities of earth. If
an emotion is unwavering, an idea weighty, or an opinion well founded,
they all partake of the earth element. Earth is the basis of spiritual
practice; in meditation we come home to ourselves, grounded in reality.

The earth element is present in all the structures of our lives, in the
family, in society, in politics, and in organizations. Every plan, group,
or activity needs some kind of basic structure and foundation, or else
it will fall apart. Earth is the womb of life. Just as seeds grow in the
soil, so imagination grows in the fertile earth of the mind, and projects
come to fruition within a supportive and nourishing environment.

Every characteristic can have a positive or negative effect according to the circumstances. Earth supports and contains, yet it can also destroy. We can be wounded by its hardness or crushed beneath its weight. The five elements cooperate together throughout every aspect of existence, but if there is an imbalance between them, problems arise.

If there is too much earth quality in the body, we may feel dull, heavy, and unable to rouse ourselves; our flesh may seem gross, our limbs stiff and leaden. We have lost touch with the fluidity and suppleness of water, the warmth and radiance of fire, and the lightness and mobility of air. Psychologically, an imbalance of earth can result in a rigid, unbending personality, an inflexible attitude toward life, or an overreliance on formality and convention. It is one thing to be down-to-earth, but quite another to be earthbound or stuck in a rut.

If we are out of touch with our own natural earth element, it can become oppressive and constricting. We may feel as if we are weighed down and hemmed in on all sides, or even that we are being buried alive. Earth seems to be all around us, suffocating us, instead of remaining beneath our feet where it belongs. Then we need to return to the firm ground of our being and establish our own inner foundations to regain our strength and stability

Earth is the basis of all the elements. It forms a vessel to contain water. It provides fuel to produce fire. Its presence allows air to circulate around it. Trees can grow tall, reaching up into the sky and bending flexibly in the wind, only because their roots spread deeply into the earth. Without earth, we would be drowned in floods of water, swept away on currents of air, burnt up in the heat of fire, lost in the vastness of space. Without earth, we would have no home, no resting place. Without earth, we could make no journeys in either body or mind. Without the planet Earth, we could not take off into outer space. Without the mental quality of earth as a firm ground to start from, there could be no leaps of the imagination and no adventures into inner space.

Each of the elements has a symbol that embodies its essence in an abstract, geometrical form. The symbolic form of earth is a square, and its color is yellow. The square expresses completeness, solidity, and immobility. It forms the foundation stone of the world of the elements. Yellow is the color of clay and sand, our basic building materials. It is also the color of precious gold and of grains ready for harvest. It con-

veys a feeling of the richness and ripeness of the earth. All these qualities are explored in greater detail in chapter 7 in connection with the
five buddha families.

The first four elements—earth, water, fire and air—are associated
with tantric practices known as the four vajra karmas, or indestructible
activities: pacifying, enriching, magnetizing, and destroying. These are
enlightened activities performed with an attitude of compassion for the
good of all living beings. Because they are not involved with attachment
or ego, they do not create the chain of cause and effect. Here karma is
used in its true meaning, simply action, rather than action and its results. In fact, these activities cut through the karmic chain reaction and
break its pattern. They are called vajra because they are invincible and
irresistible, no power can oppose them or prevent them. They can be
performed ritually for external purposes, but essentially they are different styles of working on the path and of dealing with inner problems
and obstacles.

The symbols, or mandalas, of the elements are used as meditative
and ritual supports for the four activities. The square yellow mandala
of earth is associated with enriching or increasing. The quality of earth
naturally produces riches of all kinds. In the outer world, this ritual can
be performed to obtain wealth and success, long life, good fortune, and
fruitful harvests. Internally, it enriches body and mind and removes any
sense of poverty and worthlessness. Dharma, the Buddha's teaching, is
the greatest wealth. Enriching creates an environment where favorable
circumstances for its growth spontaneously appear. Wisdom and compassion increase and meditation experiences arise naturally. It enriches
the spiritual life of individuals, communities, and the whole world.

WATER

The element of water embodies the principle of fluidity, which makes
cohesion possible. In this, it is the opposite of earth. If we try to mix
different foods together, it is the moisture in them that allows them to
mix, while their inherent earth quality tends to keep them separate.
Glue must be moist and sticky to join two surfaces together, but when

it has hardened, they become one, as solid as earth. Water is seamless; it flows in a continuous, unbroken stream. Unlike solid matter, two drops of water will merge together indistinguishably. Whatever is liquid and fluid, literally or metaphorically, is a manifestation of this element.

We are surrounded on all sides by the water of oceans, lakes, and rivers; above us, water falls as rain from the sky; and below us, water wells up from the ground in springs. But the water element also appears as oil, milk, sap, and juice; as anything that oozes, drips, or flows; as wine and nectar. Everything we drink is a gift of the element of water. It is water that makes earth fertile, and in water, life begins.

Water pervades our bodies just as it pervades the external world. It dwells within us in the form of all our bodily fluids: lymph, pus, phlegm, sexual fluids, sweat, and most importantly blood, the potent symbol of life itself. The inherent quality of water is responsible for the sense of taste and its objects, the variety of flavors. It is the liquidity of saliva that enables us to taste, and the fluid in food that carries its flavor. In the realm of the mind, the subtle quality of water imparts fluidity and adaptability. Mind is a stream of experiences, continually changing yet never breaking its continuity. It is often compared to a river, endlessly flowing, or to the ocean, deep and vast.

Water has no shape of its own; it fills whatever will hold it, adapting itself to any form. As long as it is not contained, it always continues in motion, trickling through the smallest of cracks, flowing downward, searching for the lowest point where it can come to rest. It gives its fluid and pliant quality to everything it infiltrates. A branch that is dry and brittle can easily be broken, but one that is full of moisture is flexible and resilient.

Water softens and loosens whatever is hard and stuck. It cleanses and purifies, lifting off dirt and washing it away in its ceaseless flow. Sprinkling with sanctified water is a universal ritual of purification. Water cools and refreshes us when we are hot and tired. In the past in many Eastern countries, guests were welcomed with water to wash their feet as well as water to drink, and these two offerings are still an important part of Buddhist ritual. In the West, they may have been replaced by showing guests the way to the bathroom and suggesting a drink of tea, coffee, or alcohol, but nevertheless these gestures of hospitality still represent the sacred offerings of the element of water.

Water is connected with feelings, emotions, and desires. It is sympathetic and intuitive, responsive to people's moods and needs, just as a pond reflects the changing colors of the sky above it. It provides the cohesiveness of friendship and affection that holds people together in relationships. When water is perfectly in balance with the other elements in a person, it can bring a reflective power to the personality and a spiritual quality of depth and stillness. Being in the presence of such people can make us feel as if we are looking into a deep, clear pool that reflects our true nature, and listening to their words is like drinking pure, sweet, refreshing nectar. Water softens the rigidity of earth, but at the same time it needs the qualities of earth to support it and give it form. The element of water in people's psychology makes it possible for them to move forward and adapt easily to changing circumstances.

Negatively, the water element can easily be overpowered by the characteristics of the other elements. Wind can disturb it, earth can dam it up, and fire can make it evaporate. If, on the other hand, the other elements are too weak, water will flood, breaking down the restraining walls of earth, putting out fire, and saturating the air, making it heavy and oppressive. A mental state dominated by water becomes completely fluid; although it is sensitive, it is ineffectual; its power flows away uselessly, unharnessed and undirected. Enthusiasm is dampened and no activity is possible. In the mind, just as in the environment, an imbalance of water destroys instead of fertilizing.

When it is concentrated and channeled, water has tremendous strength. Its power is gentle but persistent, and in time it can wear away the hardest rock. Huge weights can be transported by water with much less effort than over dry land. This characteristic helps people to bear burdens lightly and to persist steadily and calmly, overcoming obstacles just as a river flows irresistibly onward to the sea.

All the various ways in which we may describe the material element of water can also be applied to mental states, which are expressions of the subtle qualities of the elements. Water, like the mind, can be clear and bright, sparkling and vibrant, or it can be muddy, dull, and stagnant. Its ripples can spread out in a peaceful, harmonious pattern, or its surface can be ruffled and opaque. It can flow swiftly or sluggishly, just as the mind can. The restless current of thoughts that too often occupies us is like a shallow, babbling stream, but when the mind is still, it becomes like a calm pool reflecting the clear sky.

The symbolic form of water is a circle, and its color is white. White expresses purity and peace. The white circle of water is used in the activity of pacifying. It creates a peaceful environment to allow the appeasement of aggression, the reconciliation of enemies, the healing of mind and body, or the pacification of one's own inner turbulence. The cleansing, cooling, and soothing nature of water is invoked to cool the fever of sickness as well as the fires of passion, lust, hatred, and anger. Pacifying is a path of peaceful liberation, allowing thoughts and emotions to dissolve in the openness of empty mind so that no karmic result follows from them to create suffering.

FIRE

The element of fire gives us heat and light; its nature is to radiate, to burn, and to transmute; and its characteristic is temperature. Seeds that have been protected in the earth and brought to life by water are stirred into growth by the warmth of fire. Among all the outer manifestations of the fire element, the most important to us is the sun. Our world owes its very existence to the sun, all life on Earth is dependent upon the sun, and in time the sun will eventually destroy it. The sun warms and lights us during the day, but even after it has set, the element of fire still remains with us at night in the light of the moon and stars.

As an elemental force in the universe, fire is equivalent to light, and we actually experience it more in the form of light than of heat. Seeing depends on light, so fire is the subtle origin of both the sense of sight and its objects of perception, the properties of form and color. We also speak of the mind seeing or perceiving its objects. The mind possesses an inherent power of illumination, from itself and within itself, which is called its clarity or luminosity; it is the very quality of awareness itself.

The symbol of fire is a red triangle, the abstract form of a flame leaping upward. When we think of the principle of fire, we immediately imagine flames, in spite of the fact that many people no longer come into daily contact with natural fire. We have almost forgotten the tremendous importance of fire to human life, so we no longer think of it as the powerful, divine presence it once was. We do not realize that sacred fire is still among us all the time, in all kinds of disguises. It is present in central heating just as much as in a fire of wood or coal, and in electric light just as much as in the flame of a candle. Whenever we switch on a light, a gas cooker, or an electric kettle, we are using the gift of fire.

In humans, the fire element provides body heat, which is so vital that it is almost synonymous with life itself. Without warmth we feel miserable, stiff, and lifeless, deathly cold, as cold as the grave. Any sensation of temperature, whether it is hot or cold, comes from the quality of fire. Fire is the alchemist among the great elements. With its function of transmutation, it rules digestion and metabolism. Outwardly, it consumes gross forms of matter, transforming them into vapor and gas, heat and light. It cooks our food and then, internally, transmutes the food into the living cells of our bodies. The subtle element of fire within us transmutes our mental and spiritual food: all the sensations, impressions, ideas, and emotions that we receive through the senses and the mind.

Fire burns away impurities, not just washing them off as water does, but completely consuming them. At the same time, it tempers, refines, and strengthens. Fire stands in the center between the densest and the lightest of the elements—between the tangible, substantial nature of earth and water and the insubstantiality of air and space. It arises out of solid matter and disappears into nothingness. It is the ancient messenger of the gods, the link between the human and the divine. In India, ritual offerings are made through Agni, the god of fire, who devours them and carries their essence to the subtle realms of the deities.

Emotionally, fire manifests as both love and anger. We have many expressions in our language that indicate fire's connection with love in all its aspects. Men and women in love radiate the intensity of their feelings. Sexual desire burns in the body and the mind. Friendship and affection are like a warm, glowing, domestic fire. Love can melt the hardest heart, while compassion burns away selfish concerns and fears. Genuine love is the true alchemical fire that can transmute the human personality from lead into gold. Generous and affectionate people are described as warm-hearted. A smile can light up a room, a person can glow with happiness.

The quality of fire may be expressed through passionate anger as well as through passionate desire. One can burn fiercely with anger, have a fiery temper, or become incandescent with rage. But fire is always associated with a positive feeling of relationship. Even in the case of hatred, it suggests a hot, blazing, engaged kind of hatred rather than a cold, icy rejection. Flames reach out to touch whatever comes within their grasp, and their warmth and light draw living beings toward them, yet they can easily destroy the very things they hunger for. They are insatiable, like the grasping nature of greed and lust. A fiery personality will bring an intense, all-consuming passion to every emotion.

Without sufficient heat from the sun, life would disappear from the earth. Without inner fire, living bodies could not stay alive. Without enough of the element of fire in the heart, our natures remain half-asleep, as though hibernating in the cold, heavy earth. Without fire, the flowing water of feeling and responsiveness becomes frozen. We lose enthusiasm, hope, and aspiration, and our thoughts can no longer leap upward like flames toward the sky.

The three basic evils of passion, aggression, and delusion are all symbolized by raging fires. In tantric art, both the wrathful deities and the passionate, seductive deities dance within a circle of flames, symbolizing the pure, essential energy of their natures. Because of its destructive potential, fire is also a protector, so meditators visualize themselves surrounded by a protective wall of the blazing fire of wisdom.

The red triangular mandala of fire is used in the activity of magnetizing. It literally means "bringing under control," and is sometimes translated as controlling or subjugating, but Trungpa Rinpoche used the word *magnetizing*, which is really very appropriate. It exerts its power by attraction rather than by force. It draws everything into the orbit of its energy. It can be used to attract living beings, especially to influence their minds; to draw to ourselves everything that we need in a spiritual sense; and to control the harmful forces in our lives that hinder spiritual progress. Through it, we attain power in all aspects of life. In some traditions, fire is also associated with the fourth karma, the activity of destruction, because of its fierce nature.

Fire is the most dramatic, the most vivid and fascinating of all the great elements. It is essential and it is beautiful, yet at the same time, it is highly dangerous; there is always something threatening about it, as though the very nature of fire is to be beyond control.

Fire could not exist without earth and air; it feeds on both, requiring both fuel and oxygen to exist. It must be contained by earth, confined within a hearth or an oven, so that its power can be concentrated and put to use. If it gets too low, it needs to be fanned by air, and if it gets too high, it must be doused down with cooling, pacifying water. As it burns, its flames vanish into empty space, its final home.

Air

The fourth great element can be called either air or wind. Its characteristic is movement. Wind is simply moving air, which is inhaled and exhaled by living beings as breath. Air is constantly in motion, although when it is relatively still, we barely perceive its presence. Perhaps we may feel the very slight stir of a breeze against our skin or the clammy weight of the atmosphere on a humid day. When it moves more violently, although it is invisible in itself, we can see its effects as it rushes through trees and grass or whips up the surface of water, and we can hear the sounds it causes as it howls around buildings, making things whistle, groan, creak, and bang. We can feel the tug of a kite on its string as it tosses in gusts of wind, and we can watch birds soaring through the sky on thermal currents. On a windy day, we feel the presence of air around our bodies as we either struggle against it or are pushed along by its force against our backs.

The subtle quality of air gives birth to the sense of touch or feeling, and to the sensations that are felt. Air is less material than earth, water, or even fire, so it is less perceptible to the physical senses. It has no taste; we cannot see or hear it, only the effects it causes; we can smell the scents carried on the wind, not the wind itself. But we can feel its movement against our skin; touch is the only direct sensory experience we have of air.

Air is the breath of life to living things. A seed in the earth or an embryo in the womb, after having been nourished by liquid and invigorated by warmth, must eventually emerge into the air and start to thrive independently. It is the mobile quality of air that makes growth and development possible from the very start of life, since growth itself is movement and expansion.

We can most fully appreciate the importance of air by becoming aware of our breathing. When we are out of breath, suffocating and gasping, we gulp in great mouthfuls of air as though it were a life-giving drink. When we are calm and peaceful, breathing very gently, we can feel the slight movement of breath in and out of the nostrils, alternately cool and warm, and become intuitively aware that it is indeed the breath of life. The close connection between breath and emotion has long been recognized: we are often advised to take a deep breath before acting impulsively and to breathe slowly and deeply when we feel frightened or aggressive.

Breath is a direct link to the external world. When we experience any kind of sensation, the mind acts as an intermediary between the environment and ourselves, instantaneously interpreting all the impressions received through the senses. But in the act of breathing, the environment actually enters our bodies without any intermediary. It is direct communication between ourselves and the universe.

Conscious awareness of breathing is the most basic and powerful method in meditation practice. The breath is also used as a vehicle or medium for various kinds of exchanges in meditation. We can draw in the essences of all five elements on the breath, because all five are inherent within each of them. We can renew our energy by breathing in tranquillity and peace and let go of all our tensions and worries as we exhale. In a very important mahayana practice, we breathe in the pain and suffering of all living beings and breathe out goodness, happiness, and healing.

Breath does not only refer to the air we inhale and exhale. The word for breath in Sanskrit is *prana*, which means not just ordinary breath, but life itself. It is life force, vital energy, and spirit. Prana is always in motion, like a restless horse; the horse is an ancient symbol both of prana and of the wind. The mobility of air makes movement possible within the mind and body; not just the movement of breath, but also movement of the limbs, circulation of the blood, messages from the senses, instructions from the brain, and transferal of awareness from one part of the body to another. As a fundamental quality of mind, air is its continual movement, mutability, and activity.

Psychologically, the air element provides a sense of freedom and dynamism. A personality dominated by air is tremendously active physically and mentally and hates to be tied down. Air effortlessly penetrates everywhere and simply floats away from all constraints. Free as air and light as air accurately describe its nature. But all movement needs a reference point. If air is in motion, then it must be moving away from somewhere, toward somewhere, or around something, and that fixed point is provided by the element of earth. Air is always related to earth as its center of motion. The subtle qualities of air give us the power to lift ourselves up from the ground, to raise our arms to the sky, and to dance. It allows our thoughts to fly upward and our hearts to feel light and joyful. Without air there would be no lightheartedness and no laughter.

If there is too much air with not enough earth to balance it, activity will lose its sense of purpose; it is no longer grounded and becomes pure restlessness. People suffering from this kind of imbalance can easily lose touch with reality; they become extremely volatile, their ideas are insubstantial, and their emotions are fickle, blowing here and there like the wind.

If there is an excess of air but no fire of passion to warm it, activity becomes cold, mechanical, devoid of life and meaning. But if there is too little air, then fire cannot burn at all, water will become stagnant, and earth will grow leaden, like dough that cannot rise. Without movement and a sense of freedom, people sink down into despondency, become closed in on themselves and cease to respond or feel emotion.

The symbol of air is a semicircle, which can also be pictured as a fully drawn bow or as a crescent moon. Its color is green or sometimes black. Green seems a peaceful and restful color because of its association with nature, but in reality, nature is always active and on the move. Green is the color of growth, youth, and freshness. It is the color of unfurling leaves and thrusting shoots. If we think of meadows of rippling grass or leafy trees swaying in the wind, then we can see that green is truly appropriate to be the visible sign of the restless, invisible element of air.

The mandala of air is usually associated with the enlightened activity of compassionate destruction. If pacifying, enriching, and magnetizing have not succeeded, it is sometimes necessary to destroy evil outright, whether it appears in the external world or is a manifestation of one's own negativity. Destruction is based on realizing the essential emptiness of all phenomena: evil forces are liberated into their true nature and all obstacles to enlightenment are overcome. By understanding that in reality there are no such things as hindrances, they are all transformed into opportunities and inspirations on the path.

SPACE

Space is simultaneously the first and the last of the great elements. It is the origin and precondition of the other four, and it is also their culmination. It is the most subtle, the least material, of the elements. Within it, they exist and function in harmony together. The Sanskrit word for space is the same as for the sky: *akasha*, which means "shining and clear." What is it that we call the sky? It marks the boundary of our vision, the limit our sight can reach. If we could see more clearly, the sky would extend infinitely into outer space. The sky is an imaginary boundary set by the limitations of our senses, and also by the limitations of our mind, since we find it almost impossible to imagine a totally limitless universe. Space is the dimension in which everything exists. It is all-encompassing, all-pervading, and boundless. It is synonymous with emptiness: that emptiness which is simultaneously fullness.

The inherent quality of space gives birth to sound and hearing. One of the definitions of akasha is the element in which vibration takes place. This vibration is the primordial pulsation of life; its first manifestation as sound is the seed syllables of mantra, which in tantric theory are the cause of all existence.

The element of space dwells within us as mind or consciousness. Like space, mind is infinite and boundless; it has no shape or size, it does not dwell anywhere, it has no color or characteristics. Space is mind's fundamental, intrinsic quality of openness. In Indian poetry and philosophy, the mind has often been compared to the sky. Mind is the mirror of the sky, space is the mirror of mind. In essence perfectly clear and empty, it remains untouched by the clouds that drift across it. Our mind is inner space, the space within the heart, where we can journey infinitely and timelessly. But consciousness is not limited to the mind alone. Every cell in our bodies and every particle throughout the universe possesses its own kind of intelligence, by means of which it continues to exist in its own particular form and carry out its own special function.

Space contains all the elements within itself, yet it is beyond all characteristics. It is pure, shining intelligence, complete openness, and all-seeing awareness. When it is obscured, we experience confusion, dullness, and ignorance; we become enclosed, limited beings.

Earth, water, fire, and air cannot exist without space, but they are also necessary for its manifestation. Space expresses itself through the dance of the elements. If they are not all functioning properly within a personality, if there is too much quality of space, a person will lose touch with reality, feel spaced out, lost in a realm of illusion. But when there is a lack of space, one feels crowded, oppressed, and claustrophobic.

Space in harmony with the other elements gives one a sense of relaxation and accommodation, a feeling that there is plenty of room for everything. Nothing need be excluded or suppressed, but just left to be as it is. The mind rests in its natural state, which is discovered to be none other than the state of wakefulness or enlightenment.

The symbolic color of space is blue, the blue of a clear, luminous sky. Space has no color of its own, but when we gaze into its infinite depth, we perceive it as blue. Blue is a color of mystery and spirituality; it is associated with heaven, and therefore it has always conveyed the ideas of peace, happiness, beauty, and perfection. But the unfathomable depth of blueness can also carry a threat and a sense of fear. Gazing out into space, people have sometimes felt that they might drop off the edge of the world and fall forever into that vast emptiness. It is the fundamental fear of death, the terror of losing the sense of self, that we confront when we look into the face of the element of space.

The symbolic form of space is a point or dot, sometimes drawn as a small circle elongated into a flame at the top. This point is simultaneously zero and infinite potential, the creative seed of the universe.

THE FIVE DEVIS

As long as we perceive the elements only in their material forms, they remain within the realm of samsara or worldly existence. In this sense, they are like a prison or a tomb. They appear and disappear, they change and decay, and eventually everything composed of them—our bodies and our world—will die. But the jailer of the prison is our own mind, unable to see beyond their surface appearances and understand them as they really are.

The five elements arise from awakened mind, therefore they themselves are aspects of that awareness: they are buddhas. This is their secret essence. This essence is empty, and yet it is also luminous; it shines forth with the pure qualities of the five elements. In *Liberation through Hearing*, the pure essence of the elements simply appears as light of the five colors. The essence of earth is a yellow light, the essence of water a white light, the essence of fire a red light, the essence of air a green light, and the essence of space a blue light. Essence is invisible, therefore these colors do not appear externally; if they did so, they would have entered the realm of the material elements. They are visionary colors, perfectly pure, clear, and luminous, like a rainbow seen within the heart.

Emptiness is the realization that nothing has a permanent, substantial, independent existence of its own. Since this is so, since nothing is fixed and static, there is infinite potentiality and dynamic transformation. It is this alone that makes it possible for the ever-changing display of life in all its multiplicity to arise. Therefore emptiness is regarded as the creative feminine principle. The five great elements, arising from emptiness, are the mothers who give birth to all phenomena. When they are perceived in this way they are known as the five female buddhas. In the tantras, they are called devis, dakinis, mothers, or queens, and I generally refer to them as devis in this book.[1]

The devi of earth is called Lochana or Buddha-Lochana, the Eye of the Buddhas. Her name does not refer to ordinary sight and has no connection with the relationship of the five senses to the five elements mentioned earlier, where earth is associated with the sense of smell. She represents the pure vision of the buddhas, the awakened experience of the world as it truly is, seen through the buddha eye. On this level of unified awareness, she is the perceiver, the perceived, and the act of perception, all at the same time. She embodies the aspect of wakefulness called equanimity and equality: the one, same, basic nature of everything that exists, the ground of being that manifests outwardly as the qualities of earth. In a meditation practice that he composed, Trungpa Rinpoche described this state of sacred vision: "you won't find ordinary earth and rocks here, even if you look for them. All the mountains are Buddha-Lochana, who is the all-pervading wisdom of equanimity and unchanging stillness."[2]

Mamaki is the devi of water. The same meditation practice says of her: "the water which flows here is the Buddha Mamaki, who is the lake of the mirrorlike wisdom, clear and pure, as though the sky had melted." The name *Mamaki* means Mine, not in the sense of possessiveness, but of affection and belonging. She looks on all beings as her own, and she belongs to each and every one of them. This relates to the emotional quality of water; she expresses the clarity and purity of the heart when the confused aspect of feeling has been cleared away and its innate sensitivity is revealed. When we catch a glimpse of Mamaki's state of awareness, we feel empathy with all beings; we can enter their minds and hearts just as a drop of water merges with other drops. Mamaki is the loving mother who treats all sentient beings, without exception, as her own children. She infiltrates everywhere, she surrounds us, she pervades us, she is the water of life.

The essence of fire is Pandaravasini, the White-Robed Devi. White is the color of purity, usually associated with water, but in this case it has slightly different implications. Fire does not just wash away dirt, it burns it up completely. The dazzling brightness of the devi's white garments radiates light all around her; it expresses the white heat of the compassion of the buddhas as well as the purifying and transmuting power of fire. Since she is the embodiment of fire, she is filled with the energy of passion, which, as an aspect of enlightenment, is identical with compassionate love. Our ordinary greed, lust, and desire must be transmuted and their essence freed in order to realize this state. Pandaravasini is that transmuting energy itself, inherent within our own being. Just as the element of fire exists everywhere in the physical world, so Pandaravasini is always present in every aspect of life. Once we awaken to her presence, every circumstance becomes an opportunity for transformation, a manifestation of the essence of fire.

The name of the devi of air is Samaya-Tara. *Tara* means Savior, she who carries all beings across the ocean of samsara, and *Samaya* refers to the promise she has made to accomplish this task. Tara is one of the most beloved of all Buddhist deities, and she has many different manifestations. But all her forms spring from the basic quality of air: unobstructed speed and activity. She is known as Swift Tara because she always responds with immediate, compassionate action. Tara embodies that state of being in which wisdom, compassion, and activity are inseparable. She acts without thought: as soon as she sees the need for action, the knowledge of what must be done is instantaneously present, along with the infallible power to accomplish it. Samaya-Tara, the essence of air, is our breath of life, inspiring us to live, to move, and to act in accordance with truth.

The devi of space is called Akashadhatvishvari. Her name means Lady of the Element (or Realm) of Space; we can call her the Queen of Space. She is the feminine principle of space and emptiness, the creative matrix of the whole of existence. Like her element, she is impossible to capture or define with words; she cannot be described in human language. Her nature is immensity, expansiveness, and openness, all-embracing and all-pervading. She reigns at the center of the mandala and gives birth to all the elements.

The five devis embody the ultimate, empty, yet luminous essence of the elements. They are aspects of pure enlightened energy shining forth from the state of nonself and nonduality. So they must not be confused with nature-spirits or element-deities in the usual sense. Buddhism in India and Tibet, as well as in the other countries to which it spread, has always recognized many kinds of spiritual beings belonging to the different realms of samsara on various levels. Since in the West we do not have much feeling for this kind of deity, this issue may seem irrelevant to most people. But for those who do believe in them or who can appreciate them as metaphors, the distinction is very important. The deities of samsara are forces that may have greater or lesser power for both good and evil, but are all subject to the laws of cause and effect. Even great deities like the goddess of earth, who witnessed the Buddha's enlightenment, or Agni, the god of fire, remain within the sphere of samsara, albeit on a very high level. This is accepted in Hinduism as well as in Buddhism. An impression is sometimes given that Buddhism disparages the Hindu deities by treating them as relative, but this is not so; they were always regarded in that way, part of a beginningless and endless cycle of existence, completely unlike the absolute God of monotheistic religions.

We are made of the five elements and we are utterly dependent on them, so when they begin to disintegrate at the time of death, it means our ordinary world is coming to an end. If we take them as real, it may seem that they have turned against us and are destroying our very existence. But if we understand the nature of the five devis, we shall see that there is really nothing to fear and nothing that can be destroyed. One of the sets of verses connected with *Liberation through Hearing*, called the *Aspiration-Prayer for Deliverance from the Dangerous Passage of the Bardo*,[3] says:

> May the elements of space not rise up as enemies,
> May I see the realm of the blue buddha.
> May the elements of water not rise up as enemies,
> May I see the realm of the white buddha.
> May the elements of earth not rise up as enemies,
> May I see the realm of the yellow buddha.
> May the elements of fire not rise up as enemies,
> May I see the realm of the red buddha.
> May the elements of air not rise up as enemies,
> May I see the realm of the green buddha.
> May the rainbow of the elements not rise up as enemies,
> May I see the realms of all the buddhas.

This verse is not just a prayer, but an aspiration or resolution; it is meant to be a way of inspiring ourselves and influencing our state of mind rather than a request. It arouses us to cut through our perception of the material elements as real and solid, whether in their creative or in their destructive manifestations, and to recognize their empty essence. If there is a very strong sense of self-preservation in the mindstream, then we will hold on fast to apparent reality and fear its dissolution. But since we are naturally composed of the five elements, it is beyond doubt that we also possess the inherent nature of the five devis and the potential to awaken into their state of being and awareness.

Chapter Six

The Five-Step Process
of Ego

ANOTHER WAY OF LOOKING at the nature of existence is from the point of view of our own perception, the way we experience the individual world each of us inhabits. All the phenomena that appear to exist outside us are also contained within this world, because our actual experience of them only exists within our own minds, mediated through the senses. Buddhism analyzes this realm of our experience in terms of basic units, or dharmas in Sanskrit. In a Buddhist context, dharma in the singular (often given a capital letter in English) usually means the teaching of the Buddha, but these two meanings of the word share an underlying principle and are not so different from each other as they at first appear. Sometimes in translating one cannot tell which of the two is intended, and sometimes both are implied at the same time.

The word *dharma* has the basic significance of holding and supporting. Its primary use is to convey the ideas of law, religion, and duty that uphold human society and are upheld by it in a reciprocal relationship. On a personal level, it means the special role in life that each living being is born to fulfill—one's inner truth, the law by which one lives. It can also mean the inherent nature or quality of anything, the law that determines exactly what that thing is and does. Just as the dharma of a king is to rule, so the dharma of fire is to burn. In this

sense, there are innumerable dharmas, the fundamental laws of everything that exists. Among them, certain particular physical and psychological elements were identified in Buddhism as lying at the root of our
way of perceiving the world.

The link between dharma and the dharmas is this very idea of
inner law and truth. The dharma taught by the Buddha reveals the
truth about existence, the ultimate law of life. Dharma, the truth itself,
spontaneously manifests as the many dharmas, the fragmented realities
of temporary, relative existence. They take many forms, they appear
and disappear, yet in essence they are never anything other than the
truth.

In Buddhism, the external world is never considered separate from
the observer. We can only know the world as we experience it. The
physical universe is certainly not ignored, but it is always treated as
indivisibly linked with the inner world of consciousness. So, in the
Buddhist analysis, it is represented by only five dharmas: the fields of
the five senses. All material phenomena are defined by the fact that they
can be seen, heard, smelled, tasted, or touched. If they were not perceptible by the senses, we would know nothing about them, and whatever
we do know comes to us only by means of our senses. All the other
dharmas are concerned with the processes of perception and consciousness and with psychological states. These states of mind condition the
way in which we experience the world, so that mind and body, inner
and outer, can never be separated. The system of dharmas describes
existence, not in a theoretical way, but as it is actually lived by sentient
beings from moment to moment.

The various early Buddhist schools developed different lists and
numbers of dharmas, but their purpose was always the same. They are
a tool for analysis, in order to observe how the sense of self arises out
of a combination of many different factors and how it evolves and
perpetuates itself, yet has no independent reality of its own. In the best-
known method of analysis, all the dharmas are grouped together into
five categories. These are the five skandhas: form, feeling, perception,
conditioning and consciousness, which are described in detail later in
this chapter.

The Sanskrit word *skandha* has a double meaning: it can mean a
group composed of smaller units, or a single unit that makes up part

of a bigger group, like an army division that contains many soldiers yet is part of a much larger force. Traditionally, in its Buddhist usage, the emphasis was on the first sense, the idea that each skandha is composed of a group of dharmas. The Tibetan, *phung po*, literally means "heap," while the first translations into English used "aggregate." To me, both these words sound rather strange and unnatural. The alternative meaning has often been preferred, especially by Western scholars, who have used expressions such as "constituents of personality" or "psychophysical components." On the whole, I feel that it is better kept in Sanskrit.

Buddhist philosophy is always practical and relates directly to experience, so it often seems to be more a spiritual psychology than a philosophy. The system of the skandhas demonstrates how they combine together to produce the illusion of a self, and yet that self has no basis in reality. Although we are so thoroughly attached to it, everything we are and everything we experience can be explained perfectly well without it. Trungpa Rinpoche described the five skandhas as the five-step process of the development of ego. This is why I am not entirely happy to translate skandha as "component," which gives an impression of separate entities rather than interactive and interdependent elements of a process. They are not so much what we are made of as how we function.

We each think of ourselves as a single, unified personality, but if we examine our experience carefully, we can see that our thoughts and feelings are changing all the time. One moment I am happy, the next moment I feel upset or angry, then something catches my attention and the anger is forgotten in a new interest. I begin to concentrate on some plan, only to find a few minutes later that I am thinking of something completely different, without even having noticed. If a part of my body is hurting, then I feel that I am nothing but that pain. In other words, the "I" is continually changing. There is no unifying conscious thread running through all these different thoughts and feelings. Even the body is changing, although we only notice it over a longer time scale. We are an endless stream of momentary, interconnected, psychophysical states. This is how a person is viewed in Buddhism. Instead of a fixed self, there is a continuous flow of moments of consciousness, which is called the mental continuum or mindstream. The dharmas are momentary particles of experience, like drops of water that make up the flowing stream, whereas the skandhas might be seen as patterns in the flow.

Buddhism presents different ways of viewing this situation and of working to overcome our misconceptions. Traditionally, the Buddha's teaching is divided into three phases, known as the three turnings of the wheel of dharma (not exactly the same as the three yanas described in chapter I). The first of these is especially focused on the realization of impermanence and absence of self. It is here that the analysis of experience into dharmas and skandhas is particularly helpful. The first step toward awakening is to overcome our ordinary, commonsense view of ourselves as real, solid, permanent beings. Investigating the basic units of existence undermines the solidity of our world. What we call our bodies—or a table, or a tree, or anything at all—are just names, just conventional terms; they are really only collections of dharmas, arising and falling away again, combining temporarily according to circumstances. From this point of view, the dharmas are real; they are the ultimate realities, because they are what we actually experience. It is self that is unreal, just a construct of the mind.

The second phase of the teaching is expressed in the collection of texts known as the *Perfection of Wisdom (Prajnaparamita) Sutras*. Here it is revealed that the dharmas themselves are empty of any independent existence or inherent nature of their own. At this stage, meditation expands beyond the area of one's own individual lack of substantiality to understand the dreamlike nature of the entire universe. This realization breaks down the barrier of the duality of self and other and arouses love and compassion for all living beings, who are suffering unnecessarily because of their confusion about existence. It is no longer necessary for the meditator to concentrate primarily on identifying the separate dharmas as an antidote to the sense of ego. Instead, with at least some basic experience of its absence, there is more emphasis on understanding the process by which our ego-based experience of life is continually built up and maintained by the five skandhas, and on seeing through their apparent reality.

Finally, the teaching of the third phase reveals that the realization of emptiness is really none other than the buddha-nature. The absence of a limited, individual self is not nothingness, but the experience of awakened presence. It is the great self, pure from the very beginning.

The potentiality for enlightenment exists within each one of us, as our genuine, true, original nature. These teachings are found in the sutras on the *tathagatagarbha* doctrine.[1] It should be pointed out that the interpretation of these sutras is controversial, and that the very positive view typical of the Nyingma tradition is not held by all Tibetan schools.

The second and third turnings of the wheel of dharma both correspond to mahayana teachings. Within that philosophical framework, vajrayana developed the dynamic, practical methods and vivid symbolism found in the tantras. Our fundamental awakened state has never been diminished or destroyed, only obscured by ignorance. But where did ignorance come from? It arose from that basic state itself, just like an illusion. The entire elaborate structure of ego and the samsaric world somehow developed without any reality of its own, as if in a dream. Therefore everything that we are, the components of our worldly existence, can be regarded potentially as components of enlightenment. In vajrayana, enlightenment is envisioned as having five aspects: the five modes of transcendent, primordial knowledge, embodied in the buddhas of the five families (see chapter 7). The higher tantras do not even speak in terms of potentiality or of transformation, but of complete identity. The *Guhyasamaja Tantra,* for instance, simply states that the five skandhas *are* the five buddhas.

In *Liberation through Hearing,* the buddhas of the five families appear during the bardo of dharmata, which literally means "dharmaness," the essential nature of all dharmas. Brilliant rays of light shine out from their hearts, which are identified as the lights of the five pure skandhas. The meaning of the five families is explained in the next chapter, where the correspondence between the buddhas and the skandhas is discussed fully, so this aspect, although very significant, is mentioned only briefly in the following description of the skandhas. Each of the five skandhas also has a particular association with one of the five great elements. This means that there is a connection between the five devis (who are the essence of the elements) and the five buddhas (who are the essence of the skandhas), but they do not always correspond in the way one might expect. This aspect, too, is left until later (see chapters 9 and 12), when these sometimes complex interrelationships will make more sense.

FORM

The first skandha is form. Normally form means appearance, the shape
and color of something; in other words, whatever is visible to the eye.
But here it is extended to mean everything that can be perceived by any
of the five senses. It includes one's own body as well as the environment.
Form is divided into eleven dharmas. The first ten represent the activity
of the five senses: these are the five sense faculties of sight, hearing,
smell, taste, and touch; and their five fields of operation, whatever can
be seen, heard, smelled, tasted, and touched (or felt, for instance, inside
the body). These ten dharmas are derived from combinations of the
elements of earth, water, fire, and air, all contained within the element
of space. As we saw in the previous chapter, our subjective senses and
the objective outer world are both composed of the same elemental
qualities, and it is because of this shared origin that they are able to
interact with one another. We experience the world in the way we do
because of what we are; we are made for this particular world, and it is
made for us.

The skandha of form refers to this interface, this sphere of relationship between subject and object, not to matter or material existence
itself. Form is very basic and straightforward: just simple, direct contact
between the senses and their objects, without any interpretations, reactions, or preconceptions. It is not yet perception, but without the foundation of form, complete perception could not develop. Form is our
fundamental sense of existing in this world, our experience of ourselves
as our bodies and of external phenomena as objects.

The eleventh dharma within this skandha is a subtle kind of form
called the unmanifest. It can appear to the mind in dreams, visions, and
visualizations, or it can be an invisible imprint created by meditation
or repeated thoughts and intentions. It also includes a special form
made by vows and solemn promises that create a pattern in the mind.
A vow modifies the personality, producing changes in behavior and
sometimes even physical changes, so it can be said to possess a form of
its own. Religious vows are regarded in Buddhism as sacred objects that
are given and received. If someone no longer wishes to remain commit-

ted to a vow, it should be given back by the recipient, not just neglected and forgotten. Curses are equally powerful, and if they are not carried out, they must be properly recalled and disposed of, like toxic waste, or they will continue to do harm.

Form corresponds to the element of earth; it provides the basic ground for the operation of the other skandhas. Like earth, form seems to be solid and lasting, but in reality, it is impermanent and destructible. The Buddha said that, when it is examined, it is seen to be full of holes and cracks or like an evanescent mass of bubbles. Even on the purely physical level, we know that things are not what they seem. A solid-looking table is nothing more than a collection of atomic particles. The apparently substantial universe is really a dance of energy in empty space.

Psychologically, form is the foundation for the development of ego. It is an expression of our conviction that we really do exist. We experience ourselves as separate because of the split between the senses and their objects. We think we are real and solid because we have bodies, and we think the world is real and solid because of the evidence of our senses. We base our whole lives on this conviction, which is ultimately an illusion. Form arises out of fundamental nonawareness; it is the first step in solidifying the openness and awareness of space. Form and ego mutually create and maintain each other.

This entire ego-based, self-centered experience of life is what we call samsara. Yet from the ultimate viewpoint, there is no distinction between samsara and enlightenment. It is possible, even in this life, to enter a state in which form becomes an experience of pure presence, free from identification with the body or attachment to it. Then the spontaneous dance of energy is revealed in all its natural splendor.

In the language of vajrayana, the skandhas are really the five bud-dhas, who express the different qualities of the awakened state. There-fore, to the awakened mind, form appears as the Buddha Akshobhya, the Unshakable. His family is called Vajra, the indestructible diamond-thunderbolt. In him, the false identification with the deceptive solidity of form is transmuted into genuine being, unshakable and indestructible because its essence is emptiness and selflessness. Nothing at all could possibly be disturbed or destroyed. Akshobhya embodies an aspect of enlightenment that is comparable to a mirror. In a mirror, all forms are reflected clearly and precisely; they appear to be real, yet they are not real, and the mirror itself is not affected by the images it holds. This is how we should view the skandha of form.

FEELING

The second skandha is feeling, our immediate response to the sense impressions provided by form. Feeling is both physical and emotional, but at this level, it is still very simple, direct, and uncomplicated—just an instinctive reaction that can be positive, negative, or neutral. As soon as we receive any kind of stimulus, we feel pleasure, pain, or neutrality, and along with that reaction goes an emotional feeling of happiness, sadness, or indifference. They do not necessarily correspond in that order. Sometimes it is possible to feel happy even when we are in physical pain or sad in the presence of pleasant sensations. The feeling that arises between these two, which is neither pleasure nor pain, may be confusion—not being quite sure what we feel—or it may be indifference as a result of apathy and dullness.

These feelings are not fully developed emotions; they are so basic that they are often almost unconscious, yet they are taking place all the time, forming the background to our thoughts and actions. If we look carefully, we can see how our automatic liking for or dislike of people, situations, and ideas continually influences us. After the first skandha, feeling is a step further in the development of duality, which strengthens the sense of ego in relation to its surroundings. The distinction between subject and object immediately seems more real and valid. Even at such a simple level, feelings are very important to us; they seem to prove our existence. Because we have a reaction to the outside world, we must be real and it must be real. Instinctively, we want to cling to pleasant sensations and avoid unpleasant ones, so attachment and aversion begin to grow. We find that the ego can use any kind of feeling, even pain, to reinforce its sense of its own importance. This is the most deep-seated form of attachment: it is not just a search for happiness, but attachment to our own identity.

Feelings may seem to be real and significant, but with insight, they are seen to be empty and transitory. They are compared to foam on the sea, which vanishes as suddenly and quickly as it arises, or to the flight of an arrow flashing into view and disappearing in an instant. Feeling is associated with the element of water. It has the liquid quality of water, flowing and changeable. It is affected by every new impression, just as water absorbs the colors and flavors of everything it encounters.

Through understanding the empty and transient nature of feeling, we develop stillness and equanimity. Beneath the constant push and pull of likes and dislikes, there is an underlying essence of the mind that remains the same in all experiences. This is the special quality of the Buddha Ratnasambhava, the Jewel-Born. His family is called Ratna, the precious jewel of our awakened nature. Ratnasambhava does not need to react with attachment or aversion in order to assert himself or to be assured of his own existence; he has complete confidence in the value and the richness of genuine feeling, so he can afford to be equal and unbiased toward all.

PERCEPTION

The third skandha is perception. At this stage, the act of knowing comes in, so it is sometimes and, strictly speaking, more accurately called "cognition" or "recognition." The mind is counted as our sixth sense faculty. It coordinates everything; it identifies impressions and the feelings they arouse and relates them back to the appropriate sense organ. It identifies objects and differentiates one from another; it recognizes and names them. The skandha of perception thus makes it possible to label experiences and express them in thoughts and words. In effect, it completes the process of perception set in motion by the first two skandhas of form and feeling.

When we look at something indistinct and we cannot quite make out what it is, there is a moment of uncertainty and confusion; although we can physically see the object, our perception of it is incomplete. We strain our eyes to try to see it more clearly, and once we realize what it is, our vision actually seems to improve; now we know what we are meant to be seeing, so we are able to perceive it properly. This is an example of how perception works as part of a complete experience.

Memory is linked to perception, but in this case the object is within the mind; perception takes note of the object and remembers it. We feel as if we are dwelling in the past when we remember, but the memory itself is actually in the present; it is always a new moment of perception, literally a "re-cognition."

That very quality of knowing, which is inherent in perception, intensifies the sense of separate individuality. It creates a centralized reference point, so that the duality of subject and object is strengthened. Perception is a two-way process of communication. From an ordinary point of view, it provides a link between subject and object, connecting the observer with the external world. But from an absolute viewpoint in which there has never been any division between self and other, perception separates them and emphasizes the gap between them. In this way, it contributes to the development of ego.

Perception is traditionally defined as the mind pursuing its objects. It is related to the element of fire, which reaches out with its flames like hungry tongues, grasping and consuming. Fire also illuminates, just as cognition does. And just as flames dissolve into thin air, perceptions seem real yet cannot be caught and held. Perception is comparable to a mirage, when a thirsty traveler sees a pool in the desert, but it is only an illusion created by the mind out of an intense desire for water.

Purified perception manifests as Buddha Amitabha, Infinite Light. In Indian thought, knowledge and perception have always been equated with light. Mind shines spontaneously with its own radiance, illuminating its objects. To be perceived is to shine in the light of consciousness. Amitabha's enlightened consciousness looks deeply into each object within the limitless field of his perception, recognizing and appreciating its particular qualities. This kind of knowing unites the subject and the object instead of setting them apart from each other. The pure energy of perception dissolves the boundaries in a transcendent unity of perceiver and perceived.

Conditioning

The Sanskrit word *samskara*, the fourth skandha, has been translated in many different ways; there does not seem to be any single word that is

entirely suitable or adequate. I have come across the following translations: thoughts, intellect, concept, mental events, mental occurrences,
mental factors, mental formations, mental constructions, volition, intention, motivation, impulses, forces, conditions, activities, predispositions, and habitual tendencies. Here I propose to use "conditioning,"
which seems to express its meaning overall, especially as the related
word *samskrita* is very often translated as "conditioned."

Conditioning is the largest group among the five skandhas, containing many different elements or factors. In a very general way, it can
be taken to represent the totality of everything that arises in the mind,
just as the dharmas can, roughly speaking, be taken to mean all phenomena. From this point of view, Trungpa Rinpoche used "intellect"
in his book *Glimpses of Abhidharma*, and in the *Tibetan Book of the Dead*, we
used "concept."[2] However, these conditioning factors do not really refer
to all the discursive thoughts and activities of the mind. They are specific types of causative mental states, giving rise to our characteristic
views, emotions, and ideas, which in turn are the causes of our actions.
They exist in the mindstream as latent predispositions, rather than as
fully developed thoughts or concepts. Although we possess all these
inherent tendencies, some of them become strengthened through repeated arising, while others seldom appear, thus creating the differences
between people. They are closely connected with character: with the
help of this skandha, the ego expands into a full-fledged personality.

The most significant thing about these particular mental states is
that they lead to action, which is the literal meaning of karma. They
can collectively be regarded as motivating impulses because they set in
motion the karmic chain of cause and effect. They are like the motors
driving the machinery of karma. All the activities of body, speech, and
mind—our manifested deeds, words, and thoughts—arise from this
skandha. They are karmic triggers. The word *samskara* conveys the ideas
of construction and completion: it completes the processes of reacting
and perceiving and constructs each person's version of reality. It also
carries a sense of artificiality; it is an alteration of the mind's natural
state.

There are different lists of conditioning factors among the various
Buddhist philosophical schools. In vajrayana, there are usually said to
be fifty-one or fifty-two of them, sometimes rounded down to fifty in

texts describing the iconography of certain deities. Many of the tantric deities wear garlands of skulls or severed heads that symbolize the conditioning factors in their purified nature. Each one is like a separate "I," sometimes taking over completely, sometimes subsiding into the background, but if we look closely at them, we find that there is no unifying self among them: none of them is "myself." So when they are thoroughly seen through and stripped of their apparent reality, these fragmented egos lose their vitality and become just like a garland of skulls that the awakened person wears as an adornment.

For our purpose here, it is enough to understand this general definition of conditioning, but some readers may be interested in looking at the traditional list of factors in more detail. Some are always found together, while others are mutually exclusive. They appear and disappear from moment to moment, continuously forming new combinations.

The first five are intention, attention, contact, feeling, and perception. They are always activated in the mindstream, whatever we are thinking, feeling, or doing. The most important of these is intention, defined as the first movement of the mind toward an object. It is not necessarily deliberate or fully conscious, but if we carefully examine our minds, we can often discover deeply hidden motivations of which we are unaware most of the time. Nevertheless, their presence indicates that the mind is constantly occupied with something or other, and therefore continually creating karmic causes. Karma depends upon intention; if there is no intention, there will be no karmic result, but intention itself lies much deeper than we normally suppose. The next two factors are attention and contact, in which the mind focuses on and then connects with its object. Contact is equivalent to the first skandha, form, which is the contact of the sense faculties with the sense fields. Then come feeling and perception, equivalent to the second and third skandhas, which have already been described. Although they are contained within this skandha, they are also treated as separate skandhas in their own right because they mark such significant stages in the development of total experience.

The next five factors also are always present, but in differing degrees, so their relative strength or weakness determines the quality of each mental activity. They are wish, decision, mindfulness, concentration, and understanding. Wish or desire is the element of attraction by which the mind is strongly drawn toward something; it may be for worldly concerns, or it may be for enlightenment and the benefit of others. Decision is the firm application of the mind. It can also mean devotion and trust; we could say that the mind is devoted to the object and entrusts itself to it. Mindfulness is repeatedly bringing the mind back to its object and is the basis of meditation. Concentration is more complete than mindfulness, it is the absorption of the mind in its object; understanding is the direct knowledge resulting from that absorption. The Sanskrit words for these last two mental formations are *samadhi* and *prajna,* which can also refer to the highest states of meditation and wisdom. Thus the potentiality for their realization is always present in our mindstream from the beginning, although in our ordinary condition they exist only as very weak versions of concentration and understanding. Nevertheless, without them no mental activity or bodily action would be possible.

Next come eleven conditioning factors classified as positive and helpful. It is often difficult to find a single English word to convey the meaning of these states of mind, so several words or a paraphrase may be necessary. They are (in no fixed order): faith, which is a combination of trust and confidence; vigilance over one's mental states; a sense of ease and harmony in body and mind as a result of thorough training; equanimity; shame inspired by conscience; fear of the consequences of wrongdoing; a combination of courage, enthusiasm, and energy; nonattachment; absence of hatred; absence of confusion; and nonviolence or harmlessness.

There are twenty-six negative and unhelpful factors: ignorance and delusion; desire and attachment; hatred; pride; doubt and uncertainty; false belief in the extremes of either the permanence or the annihilation of the self; anger; continual enmity and resentment; burning rage; violence or intent to harm; envy; deceitfulness; hypocrisy in pretending to possess good qualities; disparagement and concealment of the good qualities of others; lack of shame; lack of fear of consequence; avarice and selfishness; conceit and self-infatuation; lack of faith and confidence; heedlessness about accepting what is good and rejecting what is bad; laziness; lack of mindfulness; inability to apply one's understanding to life, resulting from lack of mindfulness; mental inertia; mental restlessness; and distraction.

Finally, there are four neutrals, which may be helpful or unhelpful, depending on how they combine with others. The first of these is sleep, which may be actual sleep or just drowsiness and which is appropriate or inappropriate depending on the time and place. Next is regret, which can manifest either as genuine remorse for evil or as useless guilt and worry. The final two provide an analysis of the thought process: first, conjecture, which is the initial movement or flash of thought, making a connection but still searching and uncertain; then reflection, sustained thought in which the mind settles on its object, examines it, and gains knowledge of it.

This list does not represent what we would ordinarily consider the entire range of human tendencies. The traditional conditioning factors are really just the basic materials for our more complex emotions and patterns of thought. Some of the early Buddhist schools had even longer lists, all along similar lines. They were compiled after the Buddha's death from his disciples' memory of topics that he had mentioned as being relevant to their training. Above all, the factors were specifically identified as being helps or hindrances on the path; they are related to the development or detriment of meditative awareness and virtuous conduct.

When we investigate this skandha and become aware of this level of functioning within ourselves, we begin to realize the extent to which we are programmed and how all these preconditioned, interdependent factors determine our behavior. The actual details of analysis are not regarded as particularly important in vajrayana, but it is extremely important to become aware of the principle of conditioning. Once we begin to notice these forces at work, we may feel that they are quite significant in our lives, that they make up our character and are essential to our identity; but looking into them to discover their reality is like peeling the skins from an onion: there is nothing solid inside. The traditional image for this skandha is the banana plant. The leaves of the banana plant grow straight from the stem in sheaths, rather like a giant leek, and however many layers you strip off, you never reach a central core.

Conditioning is associated with air, the element of movement and activity. It forms the springs of action, the causes of karma, so when it is purified, its essence is revealed as the effortless accomplishment of all actions. This is the special quality of Buddha Amoghasiddhi, Unfailing Success, who is lord of the family of Karma or Action. His enlightened activity does not originate from confusion; therefore it does not give rise to karmic cause and effect. It arises spontaneously from his insepa-rable wisdom and compassion. This is pure, dynamic energy no longer distorted by unawareness and no longer giving rise to any further delusion.

CONSCIOUSNESS

The fifth and last skandha is consciousness, *vijnana* in Sanskrit. Con-sciousness is that which knows or experiences. It does not imply a higher, or awakened, consciousness; that is expressed by the Sanskrit word *jnana*. The prefix *vi* in vijnana indicates division and separation: vijnana is divided, dualistic consciousness. It is no longer whole, but limited and fragmented; it is separated from its original, primordial state of nondual knowing and has become the ordinary consciousness of everyday life. In some cases, *vi* can even indicate negation of the word it prefixes. Metaphorically, we can truly say that ordinary con-sciousness is unconscious compared with the genuine wakefulness of jnana. Whenever we speak of consciousness in Buddhist psychology, it refers to all the functions of the unenlightened mind, including what Western psychology calls the subconscious or unconscious. We say that we are unconscious during sleep or in a coma; but the underlying sams-aric mind is still active in these states, so it is still categorized as vijnana.

Consciousness has eight aspects. The first six of these operate through the six senses. All the skandhas are interdependent, and con-sciousness pervades them all; none of them could function without the presence of consciousness, so it is already inherent even in the first, the skandha of form. Form is the bare existence of the senses and their objects; consciousness brings them to life, as it were. For its part, con-sciousness relies on all the other skandhas in order to operate. It is not a fixed entity, not some abstract state of pure consciousness, but an impermanent, changing, dynamic process. The first six aspects of this skandha are the consciousness of sight, the consciousness of hearing, the consciousness of smell, the consciousness of taste, the consciousness of touch, and the mental consciousness. The last of these, the mental consciousness, is equivalent to the thinking mind. It coordinates the input from the other senses and experiences thoughts and feelings. Everything that comes through the senses from outside and all the ideas and emotions that arise from within reach us as mental images and serve as objects of the mental consciousness. These first six types of consciousness are on the level of waking life.

The seventh aspect is called the defiled or afflicted mental consciousness and is responsible for our sense of self. Trungpa Rinpoche called it the "cloudy mind" because it is clouded over by ignorance, the fundamental emotional affliction. Affliction, or *klesha* in Sanskrit, literally means "a pain," something that hurts and torments us. It is the pain of not knowing our true, indestructible, awakened being. This ignorance pervades the consciousness of the six senses, so that all our perceptions are immediately influenced by confusion. This cloudy mind is the level of dreams, memories, subconscious images, and the confused undercurrent of thoughts. It also acts as a link between the first six consciousnesses and the eighth, which is the source consciousness, or "the storehouse of reference points" as Trungpa Rinpoche called it. The seventh consciousness looks in both directions. It sends messages from the senses and the mental faculty to be kept in the memory banks of the storehouse, and it draws them back to the surface again whenever they are required in waking life. It provides access to the vast, hidden library of information we each possess, which is continuously being processed and used as we go about our daily lives.

The eighth consciousness is the basis of the other seven. It holds the imprints left by past experiences that in turn become the seeds of future experiences. But it is diffuse and undifferentiated; it is not even dependent on this particular body and this lifetime. It is potentiality, a sense of being, but not quite a fully formed individual. It carries the continuity of karmic effects from one life to the next, and it creates a mental body during the bardo between death and rebirth. In some ways, it corresponds to our concept of the unconscious mind, but it is nevertheless called a consciousness because it is always present and potentially conscious, even in coma or deep sleep. Wherever there is mind, there is consciousness, the two terms are used interchangeably. Mind or consciousness is very closely linked with prana, the life force; it is equivalent to life itself, for we are still alive, as long as prana and mind have not left the body, even when we are apparently "unconscious." Through meditation, it eventually becomes possible to penetrate this level and to transform ordinary consciousness (vijnana) into pure, non-dual knowledge (jnana).

We can also look at the eight aspects of consciousness in reverse order to see how they give rise to the sense of self. The eighth is the source, containing the latent seed of ego's development; it is like the womb of ego. The seventh is the birth of ego through ignorance of one's true nature; here the seed stirs to life and becomes a shoot. Finally, the shoot grows into a fully developed plant with the mental conscious-ness as its stem, while the five sense consciousnesses are its leaves and flowers, springing out from the stem and communicating with the envi-ronment. The whole plant is pervaded with the flavor of "I, me, and mine." At the basic level of the eighth consciousness, ego is only a potential, but from the seventh onward, it is present in all experience. It is difficult even to imagine consciousness without an ego. We feel that to be conscious at all automatically implies being conscious of something other than ourselves. This is because we are so accustomed to thinking in terms of duality, with our divided consciousness.

But consciousness is just like a magic show: when we look care-fully, nothing is there and nothing has really happened. There is only a magical play of appearances, a dance between an imaginary observer and imagined phenomena. Another analogy is a crystal ball, clear and transparent in itself, but appearing to take on all the various colors that surround it.

Consciousness shares the qualities of the fifth element, space. Like space, it is the subtlest of the five and pervades them all. It is the first and the last, their source and their culmination. Consciousness is luminous. In essence, it is the Buddha Vairochana, the Illuminator. He embodies the knowledge of totality, the all-encompassing dimension of truth, the sphere of all phenomena as they really are. Awareness expands into infinity, no longer self-centered, because the distinction between subject and object is transcended. This is not some vague oceanic feeling, but a vivid, precise, direct knowing of things in their true nature. It is the genuine magic of selfless being, experiencing the characteristics of the eight aspects in a completely open and unlimited manner. This kind of awareness is symbolized by the circle of eight male and eight female bodhisattvas, who also appear during the visions of the bardo. The male bodhisattvas embody the eight types of consciousness, and the female bodhisattvas embody their respective objects of awareness. They dance together, enjoying the play of meeting and separation, yet always fully aware of their essential unity.

The *Heart Sutra*, the essence of the *Perfection of Wisdom Sutras*, describes how the bodhisattva Avalokiteshvara looked with his eye of wisdom at the five skandhas and saw their emptiness. He proclaimed that "form is empty, yet emptiness is also form." The same is true of the other skandhas: feeling is empty and emptiness is feeling; perception is empty and emptiness is perception; conditioning is empty and emptiness is conditioning; consciousness is empty and emptiness is consciousness.

The essential nature of the skandhas is emptiness; they have no reality of their own. This means that when we meditate on emptiness, we can free ourselves from the gross characteristics and activities of the skandhas and interrupt the relentless flow of cause and effect they constantly create. We stop holding on to our habitual idea of ourselves and relax into the openness and clarity of space. When the scriptures tell of buddhas and bodhisattvas entering states of samadhi and giving teachings, as in the *Heart Sutra*, they are describing states of meditation that are accessible to human beings. It is possible for us to look into our own true nature just as Avalokiteshvara did.

What he saw was emptiness not just as a negative condition, but as a positive one. The void naturally and spontaneously manifests as the universe, with all its marvelous and varied phenomena. Existence may not be real in the way we have always imagined, but it is real in a far more wonderful way, as the play of wakefulness. Everything in the universe is contained within the five skandhas, and every expression of enlightenment is contained within the nature of the five buddhas. Emptiness is inseparable from luminosity, the creative power of the awakened mind, and therefore the pure essence of the skandhas appears as radiant light shining out from the hearts of the buddhas.

The skandhas themselves are neutral; they are not something we should feel ashamed of or try to suppress. In any case, it is impossible to get rid of them. As long as we are alive we possess the five skandhas, but because we possess the five skandhas we also have the nature of the five buddhas. It is simply a natural process. As long as there is a body to receive sense impressions, there will be feeling, then perception, and then thought elaborating on what has been perceived. These elaborations give rise to an endless cycle of further thoughts and actions, so that we continually re-create ourselves from moment to moment. The practice of meditation enables us to become disentangled from the whole process and to stop being identified and involved with it. We can simply observe whatever arises in the mind without feeling proud of good mental states or depressed by bad ones. In meditation, we simply deal with the basic energy of the skandhas, which is freed to manifest as patterns of awareness instead of confusion. We need not fear losing our transient, illusory "selves." Even a fully awakened man or woman still has a sense of personal identity and generally radiates a very powerful personality.

Our physical existence, sensations, perceptions, conditioning, and all the contents of our consciousness build up our picture of who we are. We cling to this picture, fearing death and nonexistence. By identifying with the skandhas, we actually create a new life, a new "I," at every moment. We are constantly forming the conditions for our rebirth, whether it is in the next life or here and now. Even when the skandhas of this present life separate and dissolve at death, the chain of karma continues. It will never end as long as we still self-identify with the skandhas, as long as we continue to believe that we really are this body and mind.

Chapter Seven

The Display of the
Awakened State

AT THE HEART OF *Liberation through Hearing* lies the vision of the five buddhas, or, as they are often known, the five tathagatas: Vairochana, Akshobhya, Ratnasambhava, Amitabha, and Amoghasiddhi. They are the embodied manifestations of different aspects of enlightenment; through them, we can connect with our own intrinsic buddha-nature. The ultimate awakened state—what it really means to be a perfect buddha—is inconceivable and inexpressible. It is like pure light, which makes everything visible, but is itself invisible until it is refracted through a prism and split up into the colors of the rainbow. The vision of the five buddhas is the five-colored rainbow display of the awakened state.

In all the world's traditions, mystical experience, the experience of supreme reality, has always been described in terms of light. This is more than just a metaphor to express the inexpressible; spiritual insight is often experienced as an actual flooding of the mind with radiance, sometimes even with specific colors. Sound can also play a part in such experiences and is very significant in *Liberation through Hearing*; but above all, vajrayana is filled with the imagery of light. Rays of light, clouds of light, circles and spheres and points of light: shimmering, glowing, sparkling, dazzling; blazing masses of fire, rings of flame, and shooting sparks all appear spontaneously out of emptiness, displaying the nature of enlightenment. Although I prefer "awakening" or "wakefulness" to "enlightenment," there is a beautiful play on words in English between "light" and "enlightenment" that does not exist in Sanskrit or Tibetan.

That which makes a buddha enlightened or awakened is jnana, the true knowledge of reality. The five buddhas each represent and embody a particular aspect of this transcendent jnana. These five aspects are often known in English as the five wisdoms, but there is a problem here because wisdom is also commonly used to translate another Buddhist term, prajna, for instance in phrases such as "wisdom and compassion" or "the perfection of wisdom." Both jnana and prajna include everything that we imply by wisdom and knowledge, understanding and intuition; ultimately, they merge together, yet they are quite distinct from one another. So, although in a general sense it would be possible to translate them both as wisdom, it is important to be able to distinguish between them. Various other words and phrases have been put forward by translators recently, but I do not find any of them satisfactory. In both Sanskrit and Tibetan these are quite simple, ordinary words, and they are often used in poetry, so I feel it is inappropriate to translate them with more obscure English terms that introduce a very different tone.

When I first began working with Trungpa Rinpoche, we decided to translate prajna as "knowledge" and jnana as "wisdom," on the grounds that knowledge (prajna) leads to wisdom (jnana), the supreme state. However, I now feel that "wisdom" is more appropriate for prajna and "knowledge" is the most natural and straight translation of jnana. If we look at how these two words are used in English, the main difference between them is that knowledge has an object or a content, while wisdom is a faculty or quality of mind. In any case, they are interdependent: knowledge may lead to wisdom, but at the same time, wisdom is a precondition for the attainment of real knowledge. Although they may exist apart from each other on a mundane level, they are inseparable in the context of spiritual knowledge, a knowledge that transforms the mind and heart.

Prajna is defined as the state of mind that knows emptiness. It is an attitude and a way of being that results from the direct experience of emptiness and selflessness, so the emphasis here is more on the aspect of wisdom than of knowledge. It has elements of discernment and insight and is symbolized by a sharp sword that cuts through doubt and delusion. It is one of the six perfections or transcendent virtues. Prajnaparamita, the Perfection of Wisdom, is the feminine principle of enlightenment, the mother of the buddhas; she gives birth to wakefulness, whose very nature is jnana.

Jnana is the supreme knowledge of truth, of how things really are. A buddha is one who knows, one who has awakened to the truth. Supreme knowledge does have an object, even though the distinction between subject and object is transcended. It is nonconceptual and nondual: nonconceptual because it is not the result of a reasoning process but of immediate, direct experience, and nondual because it is complete oneness with that experience, so there is no longer any sense of a knower or experiencer. It is a state of knowing, a "being knowledge," in which the knower becomes one with what is known. This knowledge is innate; it has always been present within us from the very beginning, but it is obscured by ignorance and confusion. Awakening is really the recognition of what we already know, what we have always known. This is brought out by the Tibetan translation of jnana, *ye shes*, which literally means "primordial knowledge." It is timeless, without beginning or end, so it is always fresh and new; it is always direct, immediate knowing in the present moment.

The five jnanas are five ways of knowing reality, each revealing a different enlightened viewpoint. They complement each other and together form a perfect whole. They cannot be isolated from each other and, true to the principle of interpenetration, which we have already seen with the five elements, each contains all five within itself. They are not just attributes the buddhas possess; they are the fundamental nature of the buddhas. They shine forth as light of the five colors: white, yellow, red, green, and blue. We have already seen that the five skandhas and the five elements are, in their pure essence, the five male and five female buddhas. Now we shall find many other fivefold categories corresponding to them, and we shall see how their characteristic styles appear, in both the confused world of samsara as well as the enlightened realm.

Since the whole of existence, everything without exception, arises out of the awakened state, everything is ultimately an expression of the five buddhas and shares their characteristics. Thus everything belongs to the "family" of one of the buddhas. Human beings, all other living creatures, inanimate objects, places, events, activities, abstract ideas, emotions, whatever can be imagined, all have a particular affinity with one or more of the families. It is said that in reality there is only one family: the ultimate state of wakefulness to which all sentient beings belong. But then, because of the different characteristics of beings, there can be said to be three families, or five, or a hundred; if one analyzes it even further, there are countless families, as many as the number of all the sentient beings who exist. All the higher tantras of vajrayana use the system of five families, which creates the typical mandala pattern of a center and the four cardinal directions.

Fundamentally, the manifestation of the five aspects of knowledge is simply energy, and energy itself is neutral, but in the world of samsara, it appears as five kinds of confusion and negativity: delusion, passion, aggression, pride, and envy. These are the five afflictions, also called defilements, but I prefer another synonym widely used in Tibetan—the five poisons. They are really nothing but distortions of enlightened energy, therefore they too are included within the five families. Each of them is the antithesis of one of the five knowledges, yet at the same time, we shall be able to see how intimately they are related and how the characteristic energy of the poisons is also the basic ground from which knowledge is born. Knowledge is likened to *amrita*, the elixir of immortality, and it is said that the practice of vajrayana has the power to transform poison into elixir.

The whole meaning and purpose of the five families is to wake us up to our inherent buddha-nature by means of our own human nature. Not only do we already possess all the good qualities of the awakened heart, but we can even transform our faults and negative tendencies into aspects of enlightenment. In fact, according to tantra, the only way we can reach the knowledge of the buddhas is through using the energy of the five poisons. Becoming familiar with the system of the families can help us to make connections between the realms of confusion and awareness, as we realize that every aspect of body, mind, and environment is in essence an expression of the five principles of buddhahood.

The arena in which transformation takes place is the *mandala*.[1] A mandala is the dwelling of the buddhas; it is their world and their environment. Within this world, everything is an expression of wakefulness and a reminder to awaken. All the colors that are seen are the light rays of knowledge; all the sounds that are heard are the natural proclamation of dharma; if we were to eat the fruit of the trees that grow there, they would have the taste of supreme bliss. The bodies of the deities, the walls of the palaces, the trees, rocks, water, and whatever else may be found there are not solid and substantial, but appear as though they are made from rainbow light.

The word *mandala* literally means "round," and it has many applications, literal and metaphoric, similar to our use of words such as *circle, cycle, orbit, ring,* and *sphere.* The circle is a universal image suggesting wholeness and completion; this vision of an all-embracing totality lies at the heart of its function in Buddhism. Pictorially, it need not necessarily be a circle. Sometimes it may simply refer to the arrangement of deities or their symbols around a central figure. Often the deities are placed within a square, four-gated palace, which also is known as a mandala. The geometric forms symbolizing the five elements are called *mandalas;* they are the dwellings of the five devis, who are their essence.

The mandala is much more than a visualized or painted image to be used in meditation; it is a principle that applies to every area of life. The concept of the mandala is very simple, and something we are quite familiar with when we use words like circle or sphere metaphorically. We speak of the family circle and circles of friends or followers; spheres of interest, activity, and influence; the mental and physical spheres; and so on. In Buddhist terms, our environment, our bodies, and our minds are all mandalas. We can think of a mandala on any scale, for instance, the mandalas of home, neighborhood, country, or the whole human race. Any area of relationship constitutes a mandala. When we think of any group of people, things, or even concepts in relation to a central focus, it can be expressed in terms of a mandala. Each of us occupies the center of our own personal mandalas of friends, family, colleagues, and indeed everyone with whom we have ever come in contact. At the same time, we are each part of innumerable other mandalas: patterns of relationship in which there is a ceaseless flow of energy and communication, back and forth, between the center and the periphery. The mandala of guru and disciples is particularly important in vajrayana. These patterns of relationship, as they occur in everyday life, are unpredictable and disordered. Sometimes they work and sometimes they do not, but in general we do not have much control over them or much awareness of what is really happening within them. The mandala of the deities, on the other hand, arises from a state of natural perfection and harmony, reflected in the formal arrangement of mandala paintings and structures.

The mandala principle points the way toward transmuting the confused patterns of samsara into the harmonious patterns of enlightenment. We have seen that the five skandhas are in essence the five buddhas, and the five elements are in essence the five devis. Although from the ultimate point of view they are inseparably one, from our point of view, there appears to be a process of change, a transformation of the samsaric mandala of the skandhas, the poisons, and the gross elements into the mandala of the awakened state. This is not in any way a forcible imposition of order or a suppression of the free flow of energy, but rather an uncovering of the hidden order that dwells at the heart of chaos and confusion. Chaos contains enormous energy—it is the raw material of creativity—but the very confusion itself obstructs the expression of its creative power. The secret of the mandala is to tap into that raw, chaotic energy and transform it through awareness to reveal its inherent nature.

There are many different types of mandala in Buddhism. During the bardo of dharmata, the five buddhas each appear at the center of their own mandala, together with their devi consorts and their sons and daughters, the eight bodhisattvas. They also appear together in a great mandala containing all the peaceful deities, followed by mandalas of the wrathful deities, who are the most extreme expression of their irresistible energy. Here I will describe the simple, basic arrangement of the mandala of the five buddhas, together with the most important fivefold categories that correspond to them. (The five devis will not be brought in at this point because of certain inconsistencies, which can be explained better later on. They and the eight bodhisattvas appear in chapter 12.)

One of the categories consists of the fivefold division into body, speech, mind, quality, and activity. This applies to every aspect of existence: buddhas, ordinary living beings, and the whole of nature. The first three—body, speech, and mind—are explained at greater length in chapter 9. Briefly, body corresponds to the material form or visible appearance of anything; speech is the expression of energy and communication; and mind is the formless, empty essence. Quality is the totality of characteristics; in the case of the buddhas, it refers to all the enlightened virtues, such as wisdom and compassion. Activity is the way anything actually functions; the buddhas perform enlightened actions by means of the four indestructible activities.

The basic fivefold mandala is fundamental to all tantric practices. In these practices, the meditator identifies with the central deity and emanates the surrounding deities in the cardinal directions, starting with the east. Symbolically, the meditator always sits facing the direction of the rising sun, so that east is in front, south is to the right, west is behind, and north is to the left. When a mandala is drawn or painted, east is normally shown below the central figure, south on the left side of the picture as one faces it, west at the top, and north at the right (see plate 2). During the visions of the bardo, Vairochana, the central buddha, appears first, but in describing the five buddhas, I will come to him last, following the same sequence as the elements and the skandhas in the previous chapters.

AKSHOBHYA

The first of the five buddhas is Akshobhya, the Unshakable, who appears in the eastern direction of the mandala. His family is called Vajra, because it combines the strength, power, and energy of the thunderbolt with the brilliance, purity, and indestructibility of the diamond.

Akshobhya is visualized sitting cross-legged, touching the ground before him with his right hand. When Shakyamuni made his great vow to attain enlightenment, seated in meditation beneath the bodhi tree, Mara, the Evil One (whose name literally means "death"), came to try to prevent him from reaching his goal. First, Mara sent an army of terrifying demons to attack him, then his beautiful, seductive daughters to tempt him, but the future Buddha was unmoved. He touched the ground with his hand and called upon the Goddess Earth to witness his resolution. In response, Earth trembled and quaked in every direction, as though to emphasize his immovable steadfastness, as well as to demonstrate her awe at his great vow. Akshobhya makes the same gesture of touching the earth to show that he embodies this particular aspect of buddhahood.

Akshobhya is the embodiment of the mirror knowledge. This mirror is mind itself, clear as the sky, empty yet luminous. It is sometimes known as the great mirror, the cosmic mirror that contains the whole of existence. It is the purified nature of the skandha of form: all forms are like reflections appearing within it; it holds the images of all space and all time, yet it remains empty and untouched by them; nothing in the mirror has any intrinsic reality or independent existence of its own. It is a magic mirror, because it is the source of all the appearances that arise within it; they do not exist anywhere else, for there is no place outside the mirror. This kind of knowing perceives everything with precision and clarity; it does not judge or compare, it does not feel attachment or aversion. It is like watching a play. In the great mirror, the play of existence is performed without beginning and without end; it is colorful, intense, and real; perceptions and experiences are vividly real and alive, yet they have never arisen. The mirror knowledge is the understanding of simultaneous emptiness and appearance. It shines forth as a ray of pure white or blue light from Akshobhya's heart.

The kind of realization expressed by the mirror knowledge is a particularly Indian form of the mystical vision. It is found very strongly in the Hindu doctrine of *maya*, which is the creative, magical power of illusion. Sometimes people consider the concept of maya to be nihilistic, because they assume it means that everything is totally unreal and therefore valueless. But the essential nature of an illusion is that it does, in fact, appear thoroughly real; it has to be convincing or it cannot be called an illusion. In Buddhism, this is known as relative or conventional truth. As long as we remain under its power, we must respect its level of reality and obey its laws, or we shall cause harm to ourselves and others. It is only in the light of a higher and more comprehensive understanding that we finally recognize it for what it is. Then, knowing that it is not ultimately real, we can take part in it without being taken in by it. It can be fully enjoyed as the spontaneous expression of a greater reality. That vivid appearance of illusion's play is what we perceive with the mirror knowledge.

Yet the surface of our clear mind mirror is covered with dust and dirt, obscured by ignorance. Basic ignorance develops into the five poisons. In the case of the Vajra family, the characteristic poison is aggression, which grows from the instinctive negative reaction of rejection and swells into a huge complex of hostile feelings such as hatred, anger, rage, malice, enmity, and violence. Fundamentally, it is a force of separation, the instinct to assert one's identity by defending the boundaries between self and other. Aggression can only exist because we take as real the ever-changing appearances in the mirror, not realizing that our intrinsic nature is untouched by them. The mirror knowledge shows us that there is really nothing to fight against and nothing from which we need defend ourselves.

At this point, it may be helpful to remind ourselves that powerful emotions are only poisons if they are used in the service of ego. That is when they are selfish and harmful, when they protect the small, limited, divided self and cut it off from others. Emotions are simply expressions of energy: they can be poison or they can be food and medicine. The energy of anger can be extremely positive, as we shall find in a later chapter when we meet the wrathful deities. Their wrath is sometimes called anger without hatred; it is directed toward evil and ignorance and the suffering they cause, but it is entirely free from personal hatred toward living beings.

Akshobhya represents the eternal, changeless mind of all the buddhas, therefore, we find that the characteristics of this family are connected with intellect and intelligence. Intellect combines all the qualities of the vajra. It is bright, sharp, and penetrating like a diamond, and it is energetic and powerful like a thunderbolt. Its brilliance illuminates the darkness of ignorance, its sharpness cuts through confusion, and its shining clarity sees everything without obstruction. It has the tranquil, reflective quality of the mirror knowledge, together with the unshakable confidence and certainty of Akshobhya. All these attributes belong to the Vajra family, which is part of our own intrinsic nature. Everyone has the potentiality to release their awakened intelligence, however stupid they imagine themselves to be. It does not mean worldly cleverness or academic ability, but clarity and steadiness, which come about naturally if we can only allow our minds to relax and become calm and clear like the surface of a mirror.

When intellect is misused or allowed to run wild, it becomes destructive, and the cutting quality of the mind is transformed into a hostile weapon. We even have the saying, "You're so sharp, you'll cut yourself." This negative mind tends to notice every mistake and every fault. It develops an overcritical approach and easily gets irritated by anything it cannot control or understand. When its high ideals are not realized, it grows disappointed and hostile toward others or toward itself. Too much self-criticism, instead of helping one to improve, can quickly turn into self-hatred. Eventually, people who rely overmuch on their critical faculties may become completely intolerant and unable to see any good points in anything; they perceive those who are less intellectual as weak, muddled, and emotional, and they end up wanting to isolate themselves completely from the unreliable messiness of ordinary life.

The Vajra family is associated with the element of water. When water is frozen into ice, it becomes as hard and sharp, as clear and sparkling, as a cut diamond; but diamondlike intelligence, to achieve its full potential, must also be as fluid and adaptable as flowing water is in its natural state. When the mind becomes hard and hostile, the cool, refreshing quality of water has turned into icy coldness. It is very difficult to get through to people who are in an aggressive mood. They automatically reject every approach and surround themselves with hard, spiky edges so that nothing can touch them. Sometimes, however, the intellect may become excessively heated and boil over into furious rage. In their most extreme forms, these two tendencies develop into the states of mind of the cold and hot hells. Although water looks ethereal and weightless, it is really extremely heavy; anything that is wetted immediately becomes heavier: this is the immovable nature of Akshobhya. Even if the surface of the ocean is whipped up into violent waves, the depths below cannot be disturbed: this is Akshobhya's imperturbable being. Water always flows down to the lowest place it can find and settles there, creating a basis of unshakable stability. When a large mass of water begins to move, it overcomes everything in its path; it is unstoppable and invincible.

The color of the Vajra family can be either white or blue. White is the color of water: it can appear bright, pure, and translucent like a peaceful lake and a clear intellect, or else opaque and cloudy like turbulent water and an angry, disturbed mind. Akshobhya himself, however, is blue in color, and many of the wrathful tantric deities also are blue, because they embody the transmuted energy of hatred and aggression.

Vajra is connected with winter and with the dawn. First light is pale and clear with a sense of austerity; the wind blows from the east, bitterly cold and biting; the landscape is desolate, its features sharply defined, glittering and crystalline, or white and crisp with snow.

The symbol of the Vajra family is the vajra itself. It has five prongs at each end, which represent the male and female buddhas of the five families. This reminds us once again of the principle of universal interpenetration: all the buddhas and all the aspects of knowledge are complete in themselves, and each contains all five.

RATNASAMBHAVA

Moving in a clockwise direction around the mandala, the next buddha is Ratnasambhava, the Jewel-Born, seated in the south. The jewel (ratna) in his name is explained in the tantras to mean bodhichitta, the awakened heart and enlightened mind, "the jewel of all the buddhas." His family is called the Ratna family, and its symbol is the *chintamani*, a miraculous wish-fulfilling jewel of Indian mythology, which is also sometimes used as the name of the family.

The way of knowing expressed by Ratnasambhava is the equalizing knowledge. It could also be translated as the knowledge of sameness, evenness, equality, or equanimity. The inner state of mind and the outer realm of the environment always reflect each other. The mind resting in a state of equanimity intuitively perceives that all phenomena share the same essential nature, so it regards everything as equal; looking within, we could call it equanimity, and looking outward, equality. Sameness does not imply a blending of opposites into bland neutrality or the smoothing over of different characteristics in any way. It is a vision of the universal "same-taste," or "one-taste," of the awakened essence of all existence, so that in ultimate truth, there is no difference between samsara and nirvana. The buddha-nature is never obstructed or defiled; it is equal in all beings.

Ratnasambhava is the pure essence of the skandha of feeling. The polar opposites of attachment and aversion, pleasure and pain, which originate in this skandha, are balanced by equanimity. With this attitude of mind, they can be accepted and appreciated as part of our whole experience without causing any emotional disturbance. The quality of feeling is precious in itself—simply to savor the aliveness and intelligence inherent in the very possibility of feeling. Through it, we can discover a hidden essence in all sensation, the quality of everything being simply and nakedly as it is. This is what is known in the tantras as the same-taste, which in its highest form becomes the experience of great bliss.

The color of the Ratna family is yellow or gold. Everywhere in the world gold has the same significance: richness, both material and spiritual. The gold of money provides material security; alchemical gold represents spiritual perfection; a gold wedding ring symbolizes love and fidelity; gold jewelry lends its beauty and value to the wearer; angels, saints, and deities have golden halos to show their holiness; and a king's golden crown is the sign of sovereignty. In nature, golden yellow is the color of ripeness and harvest, of precious amber and saffron, of rich butter, sweet honey, and warm sunshine.

The season of Ratna is autumn, and the time of day is midmorning and noon. The warmth of the southern sun has ripened all the fruits of the earth; now it is time to enjoy them and to share them with others. Trungpa Rinpoche vividly describes Ratna as a huge, fallen tree that has begun to rot: mushrooms and fungi thrive on it, moss and lichen cover it, seedlings have sprouted all over it, worms and insects feed on it, and small animals take shelter inside it; it oozes sticky gum like amber, and its bark peels off, revealing fascinating colors and textures.[2]

The element connected with Ratna is earth. Earth has many different names in India, including Possessor of Wealth, Giver of Wealth, Womb of Jewels, Dwelling Place, She Who Supports, All-Enduring, and Patient One. Our planet Earth is literally a mine of gold and jewels, but beyond that she is ultimately the source of everything we possess. Mother Earth provides all our food, clothing, shelter, and material wealth; she shows complete equanimity and impartial generosity toward all her children.

With these associations, the general picture of the positive Ratna characteristics conveys an overall impression of inexhaustible richness, generosity, and goodness. Ratnasambhava himself represents the principle of the quality of all the buddhas. Quality means the spontaneous existence of the attributes and powers of enlightenment, the total conviction and perfect confidence in the awakened nature, by which the buddhas can awaken others and lead them to the same state.

The Ratna personality attracts good fortune and is able to appreciate and enjoy it to the full. Ratna is the ideal type to be the ruler of a country; in the ancient world, the most important duty of a king was to provide for all his people. Buddha Shakyamuni is said to have belonged to this spiritual family. He was born a prince and surrounded with everything he could wish for. At his birth, it was foretold that he would become either a great king or else a fully awakened buddha. In choosing to renounce his worldly power and wealth, he expressed the generosity of his nature not by benefiting people materially, but by giving the precious dharma, which removes all suffering, to the whole world. Ratnasambhava embodies this supreme generosity of the Buddha and reveals it in his special gesture of giving: the right hand held out with the palm facing forward.

Ratna generosity springs from unshakable confidence in the possession of goodness. In order to connect with this confidence, we need to let go of our limited self-concept and open up to the limitless power of the buddha qualities, allowing them to enter our own lives—or rather, to rediscover them there—and to radiate out to all beings. By definition, goodness cannot be kept for oneself; the virtue, goodness, and richness of the Ratna family are inseparable from its generosity. Bodhisattva Samantabhadra, whose name means Universal Goodness, belongs to this family. He is famous in the mahayana sutras for making inconceivably vast offerings to all the buddhas to fulfill his equally vast vision of liberating all the sentient beings of all time throughout the whole of space. The purpose of making offerings is not simply to please the recipient or to express one's own generosity, but to establish a connection and to initiate an exchange of energy between giver and receiver. When a material or mental offering is made to the buddhas, who are the power of goodness itself, it calls forth the immeasurably greater response of their adhishthana, their living presence flowing into the world. Therefore, in many ritual practices, offerings are made with the intention that they may be as limitless and as perfect as those of Samantabhadra.

The poison connected with this family is pride or arrogance, the inversion of equality. The expansive sense of existence shared with all beings contracts to the enclosed world of the limited individual self, and the joy of participating in the boundless wealth of the whole universe is reduced to pride in one's own particular virtues and possessions. Arrogance arises from being overly impressed with one's own good qualities and disparaging those of others. Because of the Ratna family's inherent quality of generosity, such a person may genuinely wish to benefit others, but somehow it comes across in an arrogant and patronizing manner. The basic awareness of equality has been lost, distorted into an unequal relationship between giver and receiver. Arrogant generosity can be humiliating when the dignity and self-respect of others are forgotten. Wealthy people who ostentatiously flash their money around, or hosts who insist on pressing too much food and drink on their reluctant guests, are examples of negative Ratna behavior. In the sphere of emotions, too, the basic generosity of Ratna may become a burden instead of a gift; for instance, in possessive love that smothers and inhibits growth instead of nurturing.

The distorted Ratna personality would like to expand its own territory into that of others, as though the earth were trying to fill up the whole of space. Pride wants to build great monuments to its own existence, impressive and overbearing, richly decorated with ostentatious signs of wealth. The sense of sameness or equality, on the other hand, is confident of its innate dignity and presence, and so has no need to impress others. Pride is prickly and defensive, whereas equality does not feel threatened by anything and bears no grudges.

Often a fear of poverty is hidden deep within the heart of pride. While one person may bestow gifts out of a genuine wish to help and give pleasure, another may do so out of an inner feeling of worthlessness. Accumulating many possessions or building up a collection of valuable objects is a way of gaining a sense of one's own value, but it may lead to a feeling of pride and superiority as well. In many of the world's mythologies, the creatures who dwell under the earth are the hoarders and guardians of treasure. Among people of the Ratna family, with its connection to the earth element, a love of hoarding can often be found alongside their generosity. In spiritual life, it is also quite easy to fall into an attitude of what Trungpa Rinpoche called spiritual materialism. This might involve visiting a lot of famous teachers, receiving many empowerments, or collecting instructions for different practices without taking any of them to heart.

Contemplation of the equalizing knowledge is the remedy for all the extremes of the Ratna psychology, creating balance and harmony. Through its wisdom, we recognize the inherent potential for enlightenment in all beings, making it impossible to disrespect them simply because they are different. Feeling our essential sameness deeply, however strange others may sometimes seem to us, gives us the power of sympathy and empathy. Emotional reactions of liking or disliking begin to lose their importance, so that impartial, all-embracing love can blossom in their place. Inner equanimity develops from seeing that the same opportunity for awakening exists in all circumstances, whether happy or sad, pleasant or unpleasant, privileged or deprived. These realizations make it possible for all the spiritual qualities of the earth element to manifest. From a firm, balanced foundation with unshakable security and confidence, the awakened Ratna personality can act as an inexhaustible mine of spiritual treasure for others, without pride, arrogance, or possessiveness.

Amitabha

In the western direction of the mandala sits Amitabha, the Buddha of Infinite Light, who is lord of the Padma, or Lotus, family. Everything about this family is red: the glow of Amitabha's radiant light is like the sunset in the western sky, expressing the total love and compassion of the awakened state; the lotus symbolizing the family is red; its element is fire; and the poison that is to be transmuted into love is the consuming heat of passion.

The Sanskrit word for this particular poison is *raga*, which inter-

estingly has the basic significance of color, especially red. It also means
a musical mode, because music, above all the arts, expresses the various
colors of emotion. Finally, it means love, lust, desire, and passion. All
its related meanings convey the passionate, emotional quality characteristic of this family. The positive aspect of the Padma personality is
warm and enthusiastic, loving and affectionate; it is sexually attractive,
sensual, and magnetic; it appreciates beauty and delights in all the pleasures of the senses; it is naturally compassionate, feeling the pain of
others and reaching out to embrace the world. Padma energy brings out
all the joy of life; it is romantic, poetic, musical, and artistic; it impels
people to make their surroundings as beautiful as possible, to decorate
their homes and create gardens for enjoyment and relaxation. Lovers
radiate Padma light all around them. Padma energy can be erotic, but
it is equally present in all the varieties of love; a mother with her baby
and someone caring tenderly for a sick friend also emanate Padma
radiance. In religious people, this quality manifests as intense devotion.

Negatively, the Padma style can appear as greedy and grasping,
consuming indiscriminately like hungry flames. It can develop into an
addictive personality, wanting more and more, never knowing when to
stop. Its intense grasping quality can slide over into possessiveness
toward both people and things. In relationships, Padma-dominated
people may become overemotional, sentimental, and clinging. Alternatively, they may become intoxicated with their own brilliant seductive
power, attracting lovers or followers only to abuse and discard them,
or they may become deceitful and manipulative in their attempts to
control others. While the Ratna tendency is to expand and cover everything, Padma energy magnetizes and sucks everything in.

Fascination with the pleasures of the senses and with beauty in all
its forms can easily turn into self-indulgence. Another danger is that
the Padma personality may not be able to see beneath the surface or
behind the mask of an attractive façade. Amitabha's particular qualities
give those who belong to his family a great sense of curiosity and
interest in all the details of life, but once the initial curiosity has been
satisfied, they may not feel any need to look deeper into an object's real
meaning. Or they might feel intensely moved and inspired by the beauty
of religious art and the language of liturgy and think that is enough,
without attaining any genuine spiritual realization. There is a tendency

to focus on the surface, captivated by glamor, and at the same time a capacity to ignore anything unpleasant.

Padma's time of day is evening, when the world is suffused with the glow of sunset and thoughts turn to romance. This is the time when families are reunited after the day's work, when friends get together for relaxation and pleasure, and when lovers meet. The season is spring, with its seductive youthfulness and promise. After the hard winter, nature becomes soft and gentle once more. In Indian mythology, the god of spring is the constant companion of the god of love, always at hand to create a perfect scene for romantic encounters, with flowers blossoming, birds singing, and scented breezes wafting through the air.

Craving and attachment are regarded in Buddhism as the most powerful forces that keep us bound to samsara through life after life, yet the energy that fuels them is also the driving force of love, compassion, and the striving for enlightenment. The energy of passion is the source of life, the fire of life. The fire that burns us is also the warmth that gives us life and the light that illuminates our path. Nothing would be possible without desire and passion. It is only the root problem of grasping at a permanent self that turns them into poison. Consideration of the qualities of the Padma family reveals exceptionally clearly that the five poisons cannot simply be denied, but must be transmuted through the understanding of their true nature into knowledge and wisdom.

The knowledge embodied by Amitabha is generally called "discrimination" in English. I have never felt happy with this translation; here I prefer to call it the knowledge of investigation or investigative knowledge, although, as we shall see, this too does not do justice to the original Sanskrit *pratyavekshana-jnana* (Tibetan *so sor rtogs pa'i ye shes*). *Pratyavekshana* is a very interesting word, and it contains several implications that may help to illuminate its meaning here. Let us look at its practical application first and then return to the actual name.

Amitabha's mode of knowledge complements those of Akshobhya and Ratnasambhava. First, the awakened mind perceives the whole of existence within the great mirror as simultaneous emptiness and appearance; then, it experiences the essential same-taste of all existence; now it looks in detail at the different, distinct natures of each individual object and living being. On the level of ordinary life, this knowledge makes it possible both to distinguish one thing from another and to consider each in its own right. It is connected with the skandha of perception, which allows us to recognize, name, and remember all the objects of the senses. It is the acknowledgment of multiplicity within unity. For buddhas and bodhisattvas, this is the wisdom through which they understand the minds of living beings in order to help every single one using the method best suited to their characters and needs.

To return to its Sanskrit name, the word *pratyavekshana* is composed of three elements: *prati* + *ava* + *ikshana*. *Ikshana* gives the word its basic meaning of looking and seeing. The prefix *ava* means "downward," and here it is intended to emphasize a higher order of vision rather than the literal action of looking down. The prefix *prati* is complex and ambiguous in its functions. It indicates motion toward, coming close to and being in the presence of something, but also motion in reverse, in return, and against. In certain circumstances, it can also mean each one or every one, but for grammatical reasons, this particular usage is unlikely here, although it is quite possible that the association remained in people's minds. Tibetan translators, however, almost always adopted the latter meaning of *prati*, as they did in this case, thus emphasizing the perception of individual objects.

Combining these three elements, the complete word can be used in several different but related ways. First, it has the significance of watchfulness and attention. The back-and-forth movement of *prati* often indicates reciprocity, like gazing at a reflection that gazes back in return, or repetition, as in contemplating the object again and again. This is carried over into its Pali equivalent, *pacchavekkhana*, where it means "reflection and contemplation." The image of Amitabha seems to suggest this idea: he sits in meditation, with his hands resting together on his lap and his eyes half-closed as he looks deeply into his object of contemplation and attains profound insight with his inner vision. This replicates the posture of Shakyamuni beneath the bodhi tree in samadhi before his supreme awakening.

Second, the sense of watchfulness and taking care expands into watching over, taking care of, caring for, and looking after. There is an emotional content of both concern and appreciation. Pratyavekshana can also mean consideration, respect, and regard. Of course, we cannot be sure whether or not the Indian Buddhists who originally used the word had that particular implication in mind, especially as it is not carried over into the Tibetan translation, but it does fit perfectly with

the compassionate and caring qu   ily. The sense
inherent in *prati* of going toward s   ʲevant here. It
is a characteristic of the Padma fam   every aspect
of life, face to face, never rejecting th

Third, there is an inquisitive ele   curiosity
that predominates in the way *pratyaveks*   Indian
languages. There it means investigation,   ᵈ research, all stemming from the basic signi   ˙ at
something. This is obviously present in t   ˌ,
which examines the distinctions between vari   ˙
discrimination seems to imply something more th
act of distinguishing; it includes a sense of con
Here there is no question of judging or of ch
rejecting another, but only the awareness and appr
We could even say that this mode of knowledge do
since it is springs from unconditional, impartial love.
remember that we are talking about an aspect of jnana,
supreme knowledge, intuitive and nonconceptual. So, t   ˌanslate *pratyavekshana* as "discrimination" seems to me inadequate as well as possibly misleading.

Clearly, from traditional explanations, the primary intention is to
convey the enlightened awareness of individuality. Translations such as
"discernment" and "distinguishing" also have been used, but I feel there
is more to it than that. It is possible that all the different implications
inherent in the original Sanskrit word may be present simultaneously:
not just the ability to distinguish between different objects of perception, but even more importantly, the capacity to look deeply into each
one, appreciating its unique qualities and entering into its very being
with love and understanding. Unfortunately, it does not seem possible
to convey all this concisely in English any more than it proved to be in
Tibetan. My suggestion here of "investigation" or "investigative knowledge" is also inadequate, but I hope a little better than "discrimination."
At least it carries the implication of looking carefully at things and
paying attention to individual details.

The grasping nature of the poison of passion is transformed by
the investigative knowledge. Passion in its crudest form simply wants
to possess. It sees all kinds of different objects of pleasure, without
distinguishing between them, and immediately grasps blindly at them

all. But the awakened mind, instead of being overcome by desire when it sees these objects, examines them attentively, respecting their individual natures and enjoying them without attachment. When one allows people and things just to be as they are, without any thought of possessing or controlling them, they immediately appear in a different light—more wonderful, more interesting, and more enjoyable. Desire and attachment are rooted in duality, yet they are driven by an impulse toward oneness and a longing to overcome the loneliness of separation. The investigative knowledge arises from nonduality, so it can afford to relax and rejoice in the appearance of separateness and to take part in the dance of multiplicity with all its various forms and attributes. Purified by insight, the impulsiveness of passion turns into genuine care and interest; instead of grasping, it sees with sensitivity and empathy. Desire is transmuted into love, and passion into compassion.

Without desire and passion, we could not long for enlightenment or practice dharma, and without them dharma could not be transmitted. Amitabha represents the sacred speech of the buddhas: speech that is always truthful. He himself *is* the expression of dharma; indeed, Dharma is sometimes used as an alternative name for this family. Communication springs from passion, from reaching out, from relationship. The Padma personality has a tremendous ability to communicate. Just as we are drawn to the warmth of fire, the whole atmosphere of this family is extremely attractive to human beings. Amitabha is probably the best known and loved of the five buddhas throughout Tibet and the Far East. Avalokiteshvara, the Bodhisattva of Compassion, belongs to this family and is supplicated with intense devotion, under different names, wherever Buddhism has spread. And Padmakara, the Lotus-Born Guru, is the direct embodiment of Amitabha. His nature fully manifests both the compassion and the communication of the Padma family, boundlessly radiating the light of dharma, which is the significance of Amitabha's name.

AMOGHASIDDHI

In the fourth quarter of the mandala, the northern direction, is Amoghasiddhi, the Buddha of Unfailing Success. His family can be known as either Karma or Samaya. *Karma* means "action" and *samaya* means "a promise" or "commitment." The supreme commitment is to attain enlightenment and lead all beings out of the suffering of samsara. Combining these two ideas, Amoghasiddhi represents the enlightened activity of all the buddhas, fulfilling their commitment to universal awakening. As well as two names, this family also has two symbols: one is a sword, which symbolizes dynamic energy and penetrating force; the other is a double vajra, two vajras in the form of a cross, which expresses the universality of enlightened action spreading out in the four directions. Amoghasiddhi raises his right hand with the palm facing outward, as though pushing away danger, in the gesture of fearlessness, just as Shakyamuni fearlessly opposed the onslaughts of Mara, completely confident of his success.

Amoghasiddhi embodies the action-accomplishing knowledge. This is the actual functioning of the awakened state, putting it into action. It combines the intuition of knowing exactly what needs to be done in every situation with the infallible power to bring it about. It is the natural fulfillment of the previous three aspects of knowledge. The awakened person, having fully realized the essential nature of reality, its unity as well as its diversity, must then act on that insight. Enlightenment does not consist only in knowing the truth, but in expressing it. As long as there are living beings still suffering in samsara, the buddhas and bodhisattvas cannot remain inactive; their compassionate activity flows forth spontaneously from their very nature—this is the essence of the action-accomplishing knowledge.

In everyday life, we all possess this kind of knowledge in our basic ability to act, which is necessary in order to manifest any of our other qualities. Those in whom it predominates show unusual dynamism and energy; they often have great ambition and reach positions of power and influence. They are confident and decisive, and they have no doubts that they will succeed. Karma personalities are speedy, always busy and on the move; they are restless and generally find it hard to relax. Such people may become notorious busybodies, interfering in other people's lives, but at the same time they are the ones who really get things done. They are the ones who organize, complain, protest against injustice, and badger the authorities to shame them into reform.

Bravery and heroism are also attributes of this family. Great military leaders and warriors of history have demonstrated the confidence and courage of Amoghasiddhi's symbolic gesture of fearlessness. Others, such as diplomats and advisers, prefer to act behind the scenes, using mental skills instead of physical action. Nowadays, we are led by politicians instead of kings and warriors; politics and big business have become the most important arenas for the exercise of Karma characteristics. But whatever their chosen field, the Karma family's outlook is to see life as a call to action: if one does not achieve, then one is nothing.

The Karma family is associated with the element of air, which possesses the quality of constant movement. The cold, sharp wind blowing from the north cuts like a sword, just as decisive action slices through the knots and tangles of confusion and doubt. Amoghasiddhi is the perfected nature of the skandha of conditioning: the skandha that leads to the karmic chain reaction. Karma is associated with the night, when all one's work has been done and there is a sense of accomplishment. Its season is summer, because in summer nature is at its most active. Fruits are ripening, young animals are growing strong; everything is trying to fulfill its potential at this time of year. Trees are dense and green; flowers explode in a riot of colors; and dense, black thunderclouds bring tropical storms.

The color of Karma is primarily green. As we have seen in connection with the elements, green conveys a feeling of youthful energy and the restless activity of nature. It suggests freedom and the space to expand and express ourselves. We even have the green light as a sign that we can move ahead and put our plans into action. In Indian culture, green often symbolizes strength and bravery; in Kathakali dance-drama, heroes and warriors wear green makeup. But Karma's color is also sometimes given as black or multicolored. All colors are contained in black, so both of these suggest the sense of universality, covering all areas and fulfilling every aspect of life.

The poison of the Karma family is jealousy and envy, which incidentally provides another link with the color green, which in Western culture (although not in Asia) is the color of envy. Generally, envy develops from a hidden fear of failure and of not being able to live up to one's own highest expectations. Fear can make one feel that everyone else is doing better than oneself, or that they are being given unfair advantages. These fears arouse not only straightforward envy of others' success, but a kind of additional paranoia, the feeling that everyone is against one. The Karma personality has such an urge to forge ahead that it cannot bear any restriction on its speed and dynamism. There is resentment both when colleagues are not as efficient as oneself and when they are more so. The spirit of competition turns into suspicion of everyone else's motives, and one ends up being constantly on the defensive and afraid of attack. Touchiness and oversensitivity to criticism are manifestations of this tendency. The Karma family's natural ability to lead and inspire others can turn into manipulation and deviousness. Karma people can become obsessed with measuring their progress, worrying about their position, and comparing themselves with others. In spiritual life, they may be inclined to treat the path as a racecourse, with enlightenment as a prize to be won at the end. They can be impatient and impetuous. At first, life appears to be a motivating challenge, but eventually it may develop into an overwhelming struggle: the original inspiration of whatever they are striving *for* becomes lost in the urgency of overcoming obstacles, and they end up only seeing enemies to fight *against*.

All these problems in relation to action arise from our original mistaken identification with the limited, individual self. We have to go back to the beginning to see the unreality of ego and understand that it is, by its very nature, conditioned and impermanent, therefore incapable of achieving anything. Once our confused, distorted view of things is cleared away and traced back into emptiness, whatever appears can be recognized as the spontaneous play of the awakened state. The awakened state is not a passive condition; it is the primordial ground of being, whose inherent nature is to express itself, and all expression is a form of activity. The action-accomplishing knowledge is real and effective because it flows straight from the power of universal goodness, completely free from self-interest. It has no limitations and nothing can obstruct it, and it always achieves its aim for the benefit of all beings. In the ultimate sense, everything is already accomplished and all sentient beings have always been awakened. In the realm of enlightenment, cause and effect are reversed: the result is already certain and already exists, so the actions that appear to be its cause are automatic, spontaneous, and effortless.

VAIROCHANA

Finally, in the center of the mandala, we come to Vairochana. He is the Illuminator, the Radiant One who shines in all directions. He is the universal sun, whose light penetrates every corner of the universe. His family is simply known as the Buddha or Tathagata family. This family represents the natural, primordial condition of awareness, all-knowing and all-pervading. It can be considered the first or the last of the five families, just like the element of space and the skandha of consciousness to which it corresponds. It is the basis of the whole mandala, from which the other four families arise.

Vairochana is pictured with his hands held at the level of his heart in the gesture of teaching; his fingers form a circle representing the *dharmachakra*, the "wheel of dharma." With this gesture, he reveals the knowledge of the heart that we already possess deep within us; it stands for the whole teaching activity of Buddha Shakyamuni and of all buddhas in all times and places. The dharmachakra, a wheel with eight spokes, is the symbol of the Buddha family, and it is also a symbol of Buddhism itself, the noble eightfold path.

Vairochana embodies the knowledge of the dharmadhatu. *Dharmadhatu* is a term that needs to be explained rather than translated. We have already looked at the significance of the word *dharma* in connection with the skandhas. Here it carries both its meanings: the dharma as "truth and reality" and dharmas in the general sense of all phenomena. *Dhatu*, in this context, can be translated as "realm," "dimension," or "space." The dharmadhatu is the dimension that contains the whole of existence, past, present, and future. Since Buddhist terms always relate to the mind, it is not an external dimension but a level of consciousness, an actual direct experience of the true nature of existence. Trungpa Rinpoche frequently called it all-encompassing space, so I shall call the knowledge of the dharmadhatu the all-encompassing knowledge. It is an awareness that clearly sees the ultimate nature of everything, everywhere and at all times, as it truly is. Its flavor is of a vast, boundless expanse.

The dominant characteristic of this family is a wide-awake openness, an all-embracing awareness that shines out like the sun in every direction. It has a quality of purity and clarity, and a calm, peaceful serenity flowing naturally from its centered yet limitless nature. People with Buddha family personalities are open-minded, responsive, and welcoming. They are able to retain a childlike sense of wonder at the beauty and vastness of the universe and the magic of life. They are relaxed and unhurried, magnanimous and serene.

When our natural, innate knowledge and wisdom become distorted, we find ourselves in the confused condition of ordinary life. Ignorance of the true nature of existence is the fundamental distortion, which gives rise to the five poisons and thence to all the problems of samsara; it is the original problem underlying and pervading all others. Passion, aggression, pride, and envy are just different styles of expressing and indulging in the fundamental decision to ignore reality. The poison particularly connected with the Buddha family, the antithesis of its knowledge, is a more developed version of this basic ignorance: in Sanskrit it is called *moha*, which can be translated with increasing degrees of intensity as "confusion," "illusion," or "delusion." It is not merely ignorance as an absence of knowledge, but a deliberate, sustained ignoring of our inner truth, resulting in a state of self-deludedness. The ego, our limited and separated being, is continuously spinning its own web of delusion, creating samsara and becoming more and more trapped in the net it has brought forth out of itself. To the ego, this web no longer seems like a trap, but like a soft, warm cocoon, inviting and protective. Securely wrapped up inside its habitual way of perceiving life, the last thing it wants is to be woken up and stripped naked.

The negative aspect of the Buddha family's psychology is the capacity to create and inhabit a world of one's own dreams. This can even happen on a spiritual level. The Buddha qualities give one a natural ability to meditate, but if this talent is not properly directed, one can happily live in a beautiful state of delusion; perhaps one may even start going into trances and seeing visions, which can subtly enhance the sense of a superior self. On a more ordinary plane, gentleness and calmness can become too passive and develop into complacency and laziness. The Buddha personality will put up with all kinds of trouble for the sake of a quiet life. There is a tendency to withdraw, like a tortoise into its shell, and to cut oneself off from all contact; it is the view that "I don't want to know" and "ignorance is bliss." Even a tiny glimpse of the vastness of the all-encompassing knowledge can seem overwhelming and threatening, so that one tries to run away from it and hide by acting deaf, dumb, and blind. Luminous awareness turns into dull, stubborn stupidity.

The self-absorption of living in one's own little world does not only apply to individuals: it can be seen in groups of people, too, in exclusive societies and inward-looking communities that are intolerant of differences and suspicious of outsiders. All these negative characteristics are inversions of the Buddha family's inherent positive attributes. If the open-minded, all-embracing intelligence of the personality is suppressed or denied, it can turn in on itself and lead to apathy, depression, and even deep despair. This is the ultimate rejection of the all-encompassing knowledge, the very opposite of its vast, open quality. The all-encompassing knowledge arises from the experience of letting go and opening out into the radiant infinity of wakefulness, where all potentialities can be realized. Dissolving the tightness of ego-centered existence into the vastness of space releases the fears and tensions that make us want to go on taking refuge in ignorance.

Vairochana represents the indestructible body of all the buddhas, just as the dharmadhatu could be considered the body of the whole of existence, or space as the body of the universe. It is an insubstantial body, a body of nonself, which, because it is not limited by any self-defining notion, can manifest out of emptiness in any form whatsoever. On the relative plane, our physical bodies are the outer expression of inner presence and our means of relating to the world. We can turn our faces and bodies toward the world, radiating outward like Vairochana, or else we can turn our backs on the world and hide, using the body as a means of self-protection to conceal our innermost being.

The Buddha family has no special affiliation with a season or a time of day. In terms of visual qualities and so on, it seems neutral because it is so inclusive; as Trungpa Rinpoche observed, it is rather dull and uninteresting! It embodies the totality of time and space and forms the background for the more distinctive manifestations of the other families.

The all-encompassing knowledge of the dharmadhatu is the pure essence of the skandha of consciousness and the element of space; therefore, its color is the blue of space. Infinite space and boundless sky are symbols of the mind in its natural state: open, clear, and luminous. The blue of the sky suggests the spirituality and joy of the positive side of the Buddha personality, while at the other extreme, "the blues" indicates the sadness and despair of its negative aspect.

The Buddha family is also connected with the color white, since Vairochana is generally depicted as white. This color conveys the peace and purity of the Awakened One, who is the very source of light. White is particularly associated with the peaceful deities, and blue with the wrathful deities, while red represents their passionate aspect. As we shall see, mandalas of all three appear during the visions of the bardo. The peaceful deities represent the fundamental, ever-present nature of enlightenment, so in depicting the basic principles of the five buddhas, it is Vairochana with his white body who dwells at the center of the mandala and pervades it with his peaceful presence.

The five ways of knowing are essentially one, but we can look at them from different angles, like the facets of a crystal shining with different colors, balancing and complementing each other. In a certain way, they can be viewed as a progression, yet each depends on the simultaneous realization of the others. In a tantric version of the Buddha's enlightenment, he attained all five in sequence, beginning with the mirror knowledge and culminating with the all-encompassing knowledge.

All-encompassing knowledge pervades the mandala. It is the direct experience of the whole of reality, complete and perfect, embracing all phenomena, past, present, and future. It is the state of being fully awake, on which all the others are based and into which they all flow.

The great mirror reflects the dharmadhatu. Within it, the awakened mind perceives the whole of existence—illusory yet real, apparent yet empty. Because the essential nature of all things is emptiness, equalizing knowledge is inherent in the mirror knowledge; and because all things appear out of that emptiness, investigative knowledge also arises simultaneously. Emptiness and appearance cannot be separated; oneness and multiplicity cannot be separated; sameness and difference cannot be separated.

Equalizing knowledge springs from the realization of emptiness and nonself, for when there is no grasping at a self, one is able to experience the basic ground of being, which is none other than universal goodness. Where there are no longer any barriers between self and others, love, which is the essence of investigative knowledge, cannot help arising.

This love is the understanding of all living beings, the aspiration for their happiness, and the compassion for their suffering that automatically arise as a result of feeling one's connection with them; it spontaneously expresses itself in activity. This is the infallible, unobstructed action-accomplishing knowledge, whose purpose is to bring about the enlightenment of every particle of existence.

Enlightenment cannot be for oneself alone. As long as one feels the separation of self and others, one is not fully awakened. So it is taught that the bodhisattvas can only save all beings by realizing the paradox that there are really no beings to be saved and no one to save them. At the same time, they can only help them by understanding their individual natures, as well as by seeing clearly into their essential buddha-nature. The irresistible power and effectiveness of enlightened action can only result from completely selfless motivation, that is, from the insights of emptiness, equality, and love within the all-embracing experience of absolute reality. Thus, all five aspects of knowledge flow naturally into each other and are mutually fulfilled.

In the same way, all the other sets of five are interdependent and inseparable. The mandala is a vision of wholeness, a way of looking at the totality of our being. The five emotions, which can be experienced either as poisons or as the basic ground of the five ways of knowing, continually intermingle; our energy is never exclusively confined to one compartment. Our whole existence is a dynamic interplay of forces; the mandala is only presented in a static form so that we can begin to comprehend it in some way, however incompletely. It is a dance captured in a freeze-frame, in order that we may identify the dancers and catch a glimpse of the pattern of their movements.

The five families have all sorts of associations and correspondences, many more than can be listed here. More details are given when we examine the bardo visions in part 2. It is not only living beings that belong to the families, but every possible aspect of existence. We can recognize Vajra, Ratna, Padma, Karma, and Buddha qualities in everything around us: in seasons, landscapes, countries, cultures, ideas, works of art, films, literature, fashion, and so on, endlessly. There is no need to restrict ourselves to the traditional connections; associations from other cultures and other times can bring unexpected insights into the nature of the families. The point is not to divide everyone and everything into categories. Classifying people and things in this way can easily become just a fascinating and rather superficial game. The essential thing is to use these images and analogies to bypass the discursive mind and reach an intuitive perception of the all-pervading presence of wakefulness in its infinite manifestations.

At first, all these connections may seem arbitrary and artificial, but if the mandala principle is approached and practiced correctly, it opens up a magical view of life. Everything becomes significant and a source of inspiration. All experience is imbued with symbolism relating to the five families. This is what Trungpa Rinpoche called natural symbolism: the symbol points not to something other than itself, but to its own inherent, empty-luminous nature. Everything becomes a spontaneous reminder of some aspect of the five families and automatically links back into the wisdom and knowledge at their heart. We begin to see the whole of life in the light of the mandala. The aim of vajrayana practice is to live in such a way that all sights are seen as the appearances of the buddhas; all sounds are heard as mantras, the sacred speech of the buddhas; and all thoughts and feelings arise as the natural expressions of the awakened mind of the buddhas.

The mandala principle means that absolutely everything is included: the whole confused world of samsara, as well as the whole realm of enlightenment. Nothing is rejected or left outside the circle. All our problems and emotional conflicts, all our good and bad characteristics, can be used on the path. In many of the actual practices derived from the various tantras, the five buddhas are not imagined in their peaceful forms as they have been described here; instead five devis or five wrathful herukas may manifest the qualities of the five families. The important thing is to experience the flavor and feeling of the different families and to develop confidence in the particular kind of transmutation they each bring about. The mandala is the sacred space in which transmutation is accomplished.

It should be mentioned that the system of correspondences given

here is that found in *Liberation through Hearing*. In other vajrayana traditions, and even in other practices within the Nyingma tradition, there
may be some deviations from it. In particular, the *Kalachakra Tantra* has
an entirely different system. The other main tantras largely follow the
outline presented here, although one or more of the buddhas may be
placed in a different position in the mandala. Theoretically, any of the
five may be at the center, which will then involve a series of displace-
ments.

   The most significant difference that occurs is the alternation of
Akshobhya and Vairochana, since these are the two most likely to be
found at the center. We have already seen that they share the colors
blue and white. Akshobhya is almost always blue, while Vairochana is
white, but the color of light surrounding them and emanating from
them can be either one, as we shall find in *Liberation through Hearing*.
Speaking in terms of the families rather than the buddhas, Trungpa
Rinpoche sometimes describes the Vajra family as blue and the Buddha
family as white, and sometimes the other way around.

   In vajrayana, one comes across many discrepancies of this sort,
and we shall find several later in this book, but they should not cause
confusion or concern. Each system of correspondences possesses its
own truth and its own power, revealing marvelous insights through the
web of relationships it embodies. Each is designed for a particular purpose and has been shown over many centuries of practice to be effective.
It is true because it works, so it should be observed exactly as it is
within its own context and not compared with others or altered to fit
into some scheme that may appear more logical. The mandala is not a
static diagram, but an ever-changing dynamic display, a magical dance
of life.

Chapter Eight

Six Styles of Imprisonment

ALL LIVING BEINGS ARE FORMED by the five great elements and function by means of the five skandhas. Their true nature is the awakened state, expressed as the five families of buddhas, but their enlightened energy has become confused and distorted into the five poisons or afflictions. Under the influence of the poisons, living beings manifest in various characteristic ways, which form the six realms of samsaric existence.

The six realms are illustrated in the wheel of life: they consist of three higher realms of gods, jealous gods, and humans and three lower realms of animals, hungry ghosts, and hell-beings. Alternatively, they can be classified as two higher realms of gods and jealous gods, two lower realms of hungry ghosts and hell-beings, and two intermediate realms of animals and humans. In the lower realms, the effect of negative karma is very strong, so that there is great suffering and it is very hard to change the tendencies that keep one imprisoned in that condition. In the higher realms, there is less suffering and greater freedom, because the results of positive actions outweigh the negative.

Where do the six realms exist? In the outer sense, they refer to all possible forms of sentient life, divided into these six main types. Among them, we only have direct knowledge of human and animal life. Some people believe in ghosts, but the actual existence of living beings in the realms of heaven and hell is probably a very strange idea nowadays to many people in the West, although it would not have been in the past and it is taken for granted in Buddhism.

All these supernatural beings belong to the rich and fascinating treasury of Indian legend, which provides the common background to the religions of India, and the descriptions of their realms are based, with some adaptations, on this mythology.[1] Sadly for lovers of stories, most of these legends have not become part of Buddhist tradition, because they belong to the drama of samsara and were not seen as relevant to the Buddha's teaching of liberation from samsara. The system of the six realms is based on the psychology of the various classes of beings rather than on their mythological origins. But some of the stories I shall refer to in this chapter shed light on the nature of the realms. After all, the Buddha never rejected his own cultural heritage; he only disputed certain ways of interpreting it, and its basic assumptions remain very much part of the Buddhist worldview.

This vision of the universe is unimaginably vast, both in space and in time. It contains many levels or dimensions interpenetrating and interacting with each other. Forms of life that are imperceptible to our senses coexist alongside us, simultaneously occupying the same space. Our own senses, perceptions, and consciousness determine the kind of world we live in; we, as human beings, can only experience the universe in our specifically human way. Animals have much in common with us physically, but even they perceive the environment quite differently, while beings of the other realms differ from us so greatly that we generally remain completely unaware of them. We can only conceive of them in terms of what we already know, so we imagine them as having somewhat humanlike or animal-like forms; in legends throughout the world supernatural beings are able to change their forms and appear in different ways.

Samsara is the state of wandering round and round. The wheel of life presents us with a picture not just of human life, but of life as a whole—manifesting in all the multitudes of possibilities within the six realms, endlessly moving from one to another, transforming from one kind of consciousness to another. In ordinary language, the six realms are generally understood to mean the various kinds of existence in which sentient beings can be born. We have been born as human beings in this life, but it is theoretically possible that we could be reborn into any of the other realms as a result of our actions. These actions determine our physical embodiment, our underlying states of mind, and the way we experience the world and other beings. Body, mind, and environment are inseparable. For instance, we could not suddenly find ourselves in an animal body with a human consciousness; we would first have had to develop an animal consciousness and perceive our whole environment with the mind of an animal.

Traditionally, this outer interpretation of the six realms has been emphasized strongly as an incentive to practice dharma.[2] In a culture where belief in rebirth is accepted, contemplation on the endless cycle of life after life is very powerful and effective. But for those of us who have not been brought up with these ideas as part of our cultural background, it would be artificial just to accept them as an article of faith. We need to come to a deeper understanding of their inner meaning before we can usefully integrate them into our view of life. Many Western Buddhists have difficulties with the concept of rebirth in the six realms, or even with rebirth at all. No one can prove to us what lies beyond death. However, we *can* investigate our minds here and now and discover all the worlds contained within. We can find out what life as a human being really means at this very moment, and this may lead us to a reasonable belief, based on our present experience, about what happens after death.

When we watch the mind in meditation, we can see clearly how each thought arises and ceases, how cause and effect operate, how states of mind succeed each other just like one life after another, and how our imagined permanence is really a process of continual change. If we learn to observe all these things taking place in this life, it is not so hard to accept the idea of them all continuing after death. Our own mind is the only thing we can really know. We can learn to see, beyond any doubt, how we continually create our own world by the power of mind, and how the six realms have a very real significance in the psychology of everyday existence. As Milton wrote:

> The mind is its own place, and in itself
> Can make a Heaven of Hell, a Hell of Heaven.[3]

Trungpa Rinpoche always spoke of the six realms as states of mind, and he emphasized the importance of understanding them in this way while we have the opportunity in this life. He referred to them as styles of imprisonment, styles of confusion, styles of insanity, and fantasy worlds.[4] They are all strategies for maintaining what he called ego's games in the face of the possibility of awakening. They arise from the poisons, and when we allow one of these powerful emotions to build up and take over our lives, we find ourselves in the particular realm associated with it. The poison eating away at the heart of the beings who inhabit each realm comes from the basic fear of losing ego, expressed in these six characteristic ways. All the realms are based on grasping and holding on, not allowing ourselves to let go into spaciousness.

When we are completely immersed in an overwhelming emotional state, our whole world becomes colored by it; we tend to see the environment and other people in the same light, so that it becomes impossible to distinguish inner from outer reality. When we are happy, we find that our happiness affects everyone around us, people respond to us and feel happier themselves; we are able to enjoy the weather even if it is dull or unpleasant, and we see beauty even in the ugliest environment. In the same way, when we are consumed by anger or hatred, everything becomes hateful; we cannot take any pleasure in our surroundings, and we feel that everyone is directing their aggression toward us. We bring out the worst in other people, and even inanimate objects seem to reflect our bad mood, breaking down, getting in the way, and causing accidents. These are everyday examples of dwelling in the realms of heaven and hell. The descriptions of the six realms that follow may appear extreme; they show each realm at its most intense, undiluted by any other characteristics. For us as human beings, the experiences of the other realms always take place within our basic human nature; it is as though we see only their shadows or their reflections.

The characteristics of the six realms share many features with those of the five families. In *Liberation through Hearing*, the five peaceful buddhas appear successively over five days, and simultaneously, on each day, a path of colored light leads to one of the realms. Brilliant, dazzling rays shine out from the hearts of the buddhas, and the dead person is presented with a choice between the penetrating light of awakening and the softer and more comfortable light of the pathways back into samsaric existence, created by the poisons. Here there is an obvious difficulty in relating a sixfold system to a fivefold one. The traditional method is to identify a sixth poison, greed, as distinct from passion. Hell-beings are associated with aggression, hungry ghosts with greed, animals with delusion, humans with passion, jealous gods with envy, and gods with pride. However, this is not entirely compatible with the mandala of five buddhas, and as a result, the text comes up with some unusual connections, which are discussed in dealing with the individual realms.

Trungpa Rinpoche also related the six realms to the six bardos. Living beings in all the realms go through all the bardos, but there is also a special one-to-one correspondence. Here the bardos are seen as highlights of the nature of each realm. The experience of in-betweenness has an extreme quality: it is as if we are standing on the edge of a cliff, just about to leap over the edge into space, but we are not certain whether that leap will kill us or set us free. This happens whenever the heightened, intensified quality of emotion reaches a peak; it suddenly presents a gap, which is a gateway to awakening. We can either go through it and awaken from the dream of the realm we were in, or remain imprisoned in our habitual patterns of thought.

THE REALM OF HELL-BEINGS

The realm of hell-beings is the lowest of the six realms and is caused by extreme aggression. It is the most intense, the most confined and claustrophobic. All the emotional poisons are addictive; when we are in their grip, they appear absolutely necessary to keep us going, and they provide a reason for our very existence. In some ways, aggression is the most difficult to let go of, because it makes us feel so strongly that we are in the right. The problem is always someone else's fault, and there seems to be nothing we can do except react with hatred or anger. Acting out our aggression may provide a little short-term relief, but it does not really produce the desired result. We want to destroy the world around us, which is causing us so much pain, but instead we find that the world is a mirror filled with our own reflections. Our own aggression bounces back at us from every angle, magnified and transformed into terrifying hallucinations. It develops into a situation of extreme claustrophobia, with no space to open out into and no time for relaxation. That is why, in all traditions, hell is the underworld: it lies deep beneath the earth, crushed down and enclosed on all sides, offering no hope of escape.

In other religions, too, hell is fiery; but in Buddhism, there are two kinds of hell: one burning hot and the other freezing cold. Both contain eight regions of varying intensity, where different kinds of torment are inflicted. The descriptions of the hells are so horrible that we may find it difficult to relate them to our own lives. Since we are in the human realm, at present we only experience shadows of the other realms filtered through our human nature. Yet terrible as it may sound, hell is a condition that human beings know only too well. We often describe its outer manifestations, such as war, terrorism, torture, and degradation, as hell on earth, yet these are only projections of the hell that is experienced first within the human heart.

Blazing fury and incandescent rage conjure up the atmosphere of the hot hells. We would like to burn up the whole world with the force of our anger, but instead we find that we ourselves are being consumed. Full of the need for revenge, we would like to terrorize our enemy, but instead terror haunts us in our dreams and even in our waking hours. People in this state of mind often cannot see their own aggressiveness and are unaware of the effect they have on others; they feel it is only they who are suffering, they who are the victims of the hostility of others. Everything they do turns back on them with the same hatred that is burning in their own hearts. Even the elements join in the conspiracy against them. The earth becomes red-hot iron; water turns into molten metal; fire breaks out from every fissure in the ground; and the air is a suffocating, scorching wind. There is no escape in any direction.

In the first level of the eight hot hells, the inhabitants attack and kill each other over and over again. This image is something we can recognize in human life, when blind aggression makes people lash out in all directions, seeing everyone else as the enemy. In the remaining hot hells, the hallucinations escalate into fantastic extremes. The beings there are ceaselessly tormented by the servants of Yama, the Lord of Death, in increasingly horrible ways. But these torturers are not external creatures like devils; they are the projections of the mind consumed by hatred. The only sentient beings in the regions of hell are those who suffer there. The stronger the grasping, the stronger the sense of projection, so that our inner situation seems to be completely dependent on outer circumstances.

In the traditional descriptions, a series of additional neighboring hells surrounds the lowest and most terrible of the hot hells. There are ditches of burning coals, swamps filled with rotting corpses, broad highways paved with razor blades, forests whose trees have leaves of blades and metal spikes, and rivers of boiling water. From a distance, they seem to provide an escape route from the fires of hell, so the very sight of them arouses joy and hope in those sufferers who have at last been released. But it is not so easy to give up the intensity of grasping that has plunged someone into such an extreme experience as the hell realms. Obliged to journey through the neighboring hells, it is as though one is haunted by recurrent nightmares and hurled back again and again into a state of suffering, unable to let go.

Then there is that kind of icy hatred, repressed or tightly controlled, filled with pride, resentment, and bitterness, that leads to the cold hells. Rather than going on the attack, we try to freeze other people out with our contempt. Instead, our own hearts freeze as we look out on the world with the cold eyes of hate. This frozen world is also the hell of depression and despair, anger directed toward ourselves rooted in self-hatred. We feel utter self-loathing, and we cannot imagine how we could ever change because we are so despicable and always have been. As though locked in a pillar of ice, we are unable to communicate or respond to others. Since there is no sense of relationship, there are no external tormentors here; it is a world of self-enclosed isolation. The naked bodies of sufferers crack and blister in the intense cold, producing the appearance of red and blue lotus flowers, which give their names to some of these hells. Here, just as in the hot hells, there is no sense of space or openness. Earth is like frozen iron; water has solidified into ice; air cuts like a sword. Everything has become solid, hard, and sharp. We are surrounded by walls of ice, and our own reflections haunt us and our own voices echo back at us.

Finally, there are ephemeral hells, which last for a much shorter time. This type of hell can be found in different locations all over the earth. Beings there may be trapped inside rocks, trees, lakes, ice, fire, or any kind of inanimate object. Their sufferings are said to be the result of single actions or actions done within a single lifetime, rather than the effect of negative karma accumulated over extremely long periods. This idea, like that of hellfire, seems to be universal; it corresponds to legends found in the mythologies of both East and West, where spirits are imprisoned, like Ariel in *The Tempest* before Prospero freed him.

There is a distorted logic associated with aggression, by which it always justifies itself and puts the blame on others. We become so convinced that our suffering depends on the external situation that we feel we cannot possibly change our own attitude. Others have done wrong, therefore we must not give in to them and give up our anger; or others have hurt us so badly that we can never stop hating them and be happy again. What has been done cannot be undone; we owe it to ourselves never to forgive or forget. We radiate the flames of our burning hatred, and they shoot back at us from earth and sky. We emanate the waves of our icy hatred and turn the whole world into a freezer.

Life in the various hells is said to last for thousands of millions of years by human measurements. Aggression creates an environment of total constriction in which we feel trapped forever; we lose all hope and cannot even begin to see a way out. For a person in utter misery, time hardly seems to move, or it might be truer to say that time loses its meaning altogether. There is no longer any sense of past or future, only the unbearable present, which feels eternal. Yet the attachment of living beings to their own identity is so strong that it seems indestructible. They long to die and put an end to their torment, but they cannot; they are cut to pieces over and over again, but they always revive.

Yet even the results of the most negative actions come to an end at last. The seeds of goodness in the mindstream gradually emerge, and a hell-being might begin to feel remorse or pity for a fellow sufferer. That little glimmer of compassion is enough to start the process that eventually leads to rebirth in a higher realm.

In all six realms, the Buddha manifests in the form most suitable to communicate with the beings who dwell there. In hell, he appears as Dharmaraja, the Dharma King, another name for Yama, the Lord of Death. According to Indian legend, Yama was the first mortal to die, so he became the guide and judge of all the dead. As Dharmaraja, he is black or dark-skinned, and he holds vessels of water and fire in his two hands to relieve the sufferings of burning and freezing. Here there is no room for subtlety: the pain of those who suffer in hell is so intense that only a direct antidote will help them, before they can open their hearts to the message of the Buddha. On a deeper level, by showing them both fire and water simultaneously, he is letting them experience the sense of contrast that is completely absent from their lives. Hell-beings are imprisoned in their pain because they are convinced that it is real: the burning or the freezing has become their whole existence. Seeing the simultaneous presence of fire and water in the Buddha's hands opens the way for a sudden moment of doubt about their condition—perhaps there is an alternative after all.

In *Liberation through Hearing*, the path leading to this realm appears at the same time as Akshobhya, the buddha of the Vajra family, who transmutes the poison of aggression. The overwhelming weight of negative karma in this lowest realm seems to place it at a vast distance from the awakened Vajra qualities. Yet there is still the possibility of intelligence and clarity breaking through. Any glimpse of awakening is always connected with a bardo, in the sense of a gap where solidity and certainty dissolve. Since hell is the realm of the most intense grasping and the greatest solidification, it is particularly associated with the bardo of dying, where all the elements and components of self dissolve. To hell-beings, abandoning their aggression seems like death because they are identified so completely with it. The bardo is the highest point, the most extreme experience of the realm. At that moment of greatest intensity, poised between two alternatives, there is a sudden opportunity to see beyond the two extremes of the existence and the annihilation of ego.

THE REALM OF HUNGRY GHOSTS

The hungry ghost realm is a condition of extreme frustration and unsatisfied desire. Its suffering is less intense than that of hell, in that the beings here do not feel so totally oppressed and confined, but it is still very great because of the weight of negative actions that have caused them to be born in such a state.

The original "ghosts" are only one group among the many who inhabit this realm; their Sanskrit name is *preta*, which simply means "the departed." Originally, preta referred to a spirit of the dead whose funeral rites had not been performed, so it could not continue to its destination of rebirth or liberation. It would remain haunting the burial or cremation ground, waiting to receive the ritual offerings to the dead that would set it free. An interesting sidelight is thrown on the nature of pretas by a later Hindu legend concerning the god Brahma, who embodies the creative energy of desire. By his mental power, he created the first female, his mind-born daughter, but immediately his inherent nature impelled him to feel lust for her. Since he also embodies goodness, truth, and purity, he struggled to control his feelings, and the pretas were born from the sweat that poured from his body during this intense inner conflict. In several legends, other strange creatures arise in a similar way from the residue of desire or anger which, although they have been overcome, cannot be destroyed entirely; in other words, they always give birth to karmic consequences, ghosts that remain to haunt us.

The term *hungry ghost* comes from a Tibetan interpretation of the name (Tibetan *yi dvags*)[5] and seems a good choice because it describes this type of being's chief characteristic. In English, ghost has popularly come to mean a spirit suspended between this life and the next, just like the original meaning of preta, so we must be aware that in Buddhism it actually refers to a new existence, a state of rebirth. All the same, our idea of ghosts seems to correspond very well to the psychology of this realm. All ghosts are hungry and unsatisfied in one way or another, wandering restlessly, obsessed with what they lack and haunting others with their insatiable demands.

Another class of beings in this realm is the *gandharvas*, mysterious supernatural beings of Indian mythology who are identified with the moon and have a strange power over women. They eat only fragrances and are great physicians, musicians, and lovers. Probably because of their connection with women, they became identified with the spirits of the dead searching for a womb in which to be reborn. The consciousness of the dead person during the bardo of existence is known as a gandharva, and this realm of the hungry ghosts is linked with the bardo of existence. The gandharvas in the bardo are outside the context of the six realms since they have not yet been reborn, but if they stay too long in the bardo without entering a womb, they may eventually become permanent hungry ghosts in the full sense.

Various spirits inhabit the hungry ghost realm, including most of the vast array of beings in Indian mythology who are neither fully human, fully animal, nor fully divine. There are a large number of wraithlike, tormented spirits haunting cremation grounds and other desolate places, including some who enter corpses and reanimate them.[6] Many of them are malevolent and twisted in some way, constantly making trouble for other living creatures by causing misfortune, disease, or insanity. Some have died violent deaths and are still bewildered by pain and fear, and some wish to hurt others because of injuries that have been done to them in previous lives, such as the female spirits who try to harm children and pregnant women.

Then there is a whole host of negative forces that cause physical and mental illnesses. In books on Tibetan medicine, they are often referred to as demons and are taken very seriously in diagnosis and treatment.[7] There is always some sort of karmic connection from the past between these negative forces and their victims. Such connections could result from a very strong emotional energy or some kind of fixation that takes on a life of its own, or they might arise from injuries done to others.

Another kind of demon is the flesh-eating, blood-drinking nocturnal spirit called *rakshasa*. Rakshasas are described as huge, ugly, and violent, full of greed and lust; they typify the forces of evil, just as demons do in the West. When translations of Buddhist works refer to gods and demons, rakshasas are often meant. Trungpa Rinpoche explained that demons represent everything we would like to be rid of, while gods and goddesses embody everything we want to attract into our lives. Certain rakshasas belong to a higher level, more like minor gods or jealous gods, and there are many other beings in this realm that are less malignant and less tormented than the lower class of hungry ghost. They sometimes possess great power, which they can use for good if they so wish, but they are still obsessed with their own needs and this makes them deceitful and unpredictable.

Tibet had its own traditions of supernatural beings, which were incorporated with the Indian ones, and the same thing has happened wherever Buddhism has spread. We can do the same; we could imagine all the gnomes, goblins, giants, genii, and vampires, the fair folk and the little people of Western folklore in this realm—all the "ghoulies and ghosties and long-leggety beasties, and things that go bump in the night."

These various spirits may live on the earth, beneath its surface, in the ocean, or in the air. Although there are many different kinds, traditionally they are all pictured as one type, a kind of caricature expressing their hungry nature. They have tiny mouths, long thin necks, and huge, swollen bellies, which of course can be a sign of starvation as well as greed. Their inability to satisfy their hunger manifests in different ways, according to whether they have distorted perceptions of the external world, of their own inner condition, or both.

In the first case, some search desperately for food and drink but can never find any. Some imagine that they can see it in the distance, like a mirage, but when they get nearer, it turns out to be an illusion. Others can see a feast laid out for them and are just about to eat it when fearsome guards appear and chase them away.

The second category of hungry ghosts have food and drink available to them, but their mouths and throats are so small and their stomachs so large, that they would never be able to consume even a fraction of the amount they need. They have long, grasping fingers, with which they frantically grab and try to swallow whatever they can, but it only makes them feel more and more empty.

Hungry ghosts in the third category are subject to various inner and outer hallucinations, so they cannot benefit from their food. For some of them, food and drink burst into flames inside them and burn them from within. For others, it turns into revolting substances like blood, pus, and urine, which they eat; still others find that they are biting into their own flesh; and for some, food becomes inedible material, like iron or straw.

The basic subjective feeling of this realm is overwhelming deprivation, a sense of poverty combined with greed. Paradoxically, the hungry ghosts are surrounded by an environment of richness and abundance; everything they want is already there, but their hunger prevents them from enjoying it. Self-preservation is very strong, so there is little sense of openness or relaxation. They are totally obsessed with trying to satisfy their own needs, so they cannot afford to feel the pain of others or arouse the slightest generous impulse. Birth in this condition of existence is the result of extreme avarice, meanness, and stinginess.

It is easy to find hungry ghost characteristics in all areas of human life: material, emotional, intellectual, and spiritual. It has nothing to do with external conditions; even a billionaire can have the mentality of a hungry ghost. People who have made fortunes through scrimping and saving are often unable to enjoy their wealth properly; they are always trying to increase it and are afraid of losing it. Conspicuous consumption and addictive collecting are other manifestations of this tendency in the material world. At first, buying a desirable object gives pleasure, but after a while, the activity of shopping or collecting becomes an end in itself. It no longer brings real satisfaction, but actually arouses even greater hunger. Clothes are kept in the wardrobe and never worn; collections of beautiful objects are locked away and never enjoyed or shared with others.

Often, we devour sensations in a hungry ghost manner, although this is harder to catch and identify as it is so ephemeral and almost abstract. Our avidity for beauty can be like this; for instance, when we drink in the richness of color and texture or the scent of flowers, often with a literal intake of breath, as though trying to solidify the sensation, draw it into ourselves, and possess it.

Emotionally, the hungry ghost is insatiable. It might be someone who tries desperately to make friends, is extremely demanding for a while, but then loses interest. Or someone who falls in love over and over again, but never meets the right partner to settle down with. The eternal student, forever wanting to accumulate more information, but not putting it to use, is an example of the hungry ghost tendency in the realm of ideas. In the same way, searching for a spiritual path can become a way of life, sampling them all without ever making a commitment. In all these cases, the search, the hope, and the expectation have become more important than the attainment. In fact, Trungpa Rinpoche said that any kind of hunger—whether for knowledge, skills, or even enlightenment—and any process of learning belongs to the hungry ghost realm.

We can connect various examples of hungry ghost psychology to the three categories of distorted perception in the traditional descriptions. Sometimes people feel that if only they could find the ideal place to live or the ideal job, they would be perfectly happy: this is like the hungry ghost who cannot find food or for whom it is only a mirage. The endless search for love or perfection is the same. The hungry ghost who is chased away from food and drink is an example of those people who, deep down, do not believe they deserve to get what they want. No one really prevents them, but they perceive all kinds of obstacles in order to deny themselves the opportunity of fulfillment.

Those who are not obstructed from outside, but who nevertheless are unable to consume and make use of nourishment, are like the ghosts with huge stomachs and tiny mouths. They acquire and collect all kinds of things, without obtaining any real benefit or satisfaction. To use a food-related metaphor, they might consume vast amounts of knowledge and information without digesting it. Sometimes we do not savor the experience of the present moment because we are so anxious to capture it for the future: a student intent on taking notes misses the essence of what is being said; a tourist busy taking photographs does not really enjoy the living quality of the scene. Whatever we receive through any of our senses is food for our whole being, yet it cannot nourish us unless we take it in properly and completely.

When food does not fulfill its proper function of nourishment, it causes harm instead; this is the situation illustrated by the third category of hungry ghost. If the wanting itself becomes all-important, when we obtain what we want, we lose interest in it or find that it is useless to us or not what we really wanted at all: it has turned to straw. Sometimes we get what we want and find it is a heavy burden, like a lump of iron; or it may even sicken and revolt us like pus. If we misuse the gifts and opportunities of this life through greed and meanness, we may end up feeling disappointed, cheated, and bitter, even to the point of burning up inside with despair. This is particularly true in the spiritual sphere. If we follow a path with an attitude of grasping—what Trungpa Rinpoche called spiritual materialism—whatever we learn may become an obstacle to genuine realization.

The hungry ghost mentality is "all take and no give." It uses people and situations; it treats everything and everybody as objects of consumption. In folklore, ghosts draw all the warmth out of the atmosphere around them. People in a hungry ghost state of mind suck energy from others, making everyone in the vicinity feel drained and exhausted. However much you give them, they still ask for more.

This realm has affinities with both the Padma and Ratna families. In *Liberation through Hearing*, it is linked with Amitabha, the buddha of the Padma family. The path that leads to it is described as "produced from passion and meanness" and "accumulated by intense passion." Emotions such as passion, desire, greed, and wanting are usually considered Padma characteristics. However, Trungpa Rinpoche relates the hungry ghost realm to the Ratna family. Two other texts in the same cycle as *Liberation through Hearing*, called *The Hundred Homages* and *The Dharma Practice*,[8] only mention meanness or avarice as the cause of birth as a hungry ghost. This would fit in with Ratna psychology, since it is the other side of that family's generosity and expansiveness. Pride is the poison normally associated with Ratna, but here, instead of pride in riches, it is a twisted pride in the sense of deprivation, inseparable from the fear of poverty. It is a hollow void crying out to be filled.

The buddha appearing in the realm of the hungry ghosts is called Jvalamukha, Mouth of Flame. He is red in color, which relates him to the Padma family. He glows with Amitabha's limitless light and warmth, which can never be drained away, and with boundless compassion that can never be exhausted. He holds a vessel of divine ambrosia to satisfy every need. But this gift of perfect food, which would end the hungry ghosts' hunger forever, presents them with the ultimate dilemma: to accept it would mean giving up their existence as hungry ghosts. This is the suspension between hope and fear, grasping and letting go, typical of the bardo of existence. Existence is based on grasping, as we saw in the wheel of life; the hungry ghost is always searching for something else, hungry for a new life, yet fearing the loss of the old one. The gap of the bardo is a moment of opportunity in which to give up the extremes of hope and fear.

THE REALM OF ANIMALS

The animal realm is the only one in which we are able to observe the living beings who inhabit it. Here it becomes particularly obvious that the descriptions of the six realms are not intended to give a complete, literal picture of life within them, but to bring out the essential, underlying, emotional quality of each type of existence. Animal life covers a huge spectrum of species, and the countless creatures within this realm display a vast range of different behaviors. If we watch animals closely, especially those that are domesticated, we can see that they show characteristics of all the six realms at various times, within the limitations of their own consciousness. But coloring their experience of all the others is the poison made up of ignorance, confusion, and delusion. *Liberation through Hearing* warns that one may "fall into the animal realm of delusion and experience the suffering of stupidity, dumbness, and slavery."

From the Christian and even a secular Western point of view, animals are regarded as innocent and not responsible for their actions, because they do not understand good and evil. For the same reason, they are considered inferior to human beings and, in Christian terms, as having no soul. The Buddhist view is entirely different. All sentient beings in all six realms possess buddha-nature. But because their essential nature is obscured by ignorance, they are all equally subject to the law of karma, and the law of karma is simply a matter of cause and effect. Since everything is continually changing and no condition is permanent, they will eventually be reborn in more favorable states. Every living being has experienced birth in all six realms over and over again. The realms of animals, hungry ghosts, and hell-beings are called the lower realms because they are caused by a predominance of negative karma, and they are also extremely difficult to escape because such strong negative karma tends to be self-perpetuating. The torment of the hell-beings produces even greater anger and hatred, and the hungry ghosts' feeling of deprivation makes them even more avaricious. Similarly, the suffering felt by animals continually leads them into further bewilderment and confusion.

Animals have their own kind of intelligence, which is appropriate to their state of existence. They act directly and instinctively, without doubts or hesitation; they have extremely acute senses, ranges of perception that we have lost, and sometimes even what appear to be powers of extrasensory perception; they also have wonderful physical abilities and coordination. But their intellect and power of reason are undeveloped. They cannot ask questions about their existence or look into their own minds. They simply live their lives with total involvement and absolute self-absorption.

A psychologist would say that animals have no self-awareness or self-consciousness, but from a Buddhist point of view, one could say that they are conscious only of self. They perceive the world entirely in relation to themselves: it only has meaning insofar as it affects them and their reactions. They obviously experience the duality of self and other in a practical sense, but the other exists only in terms of self. This is exactly what Buddhism means by delusion. It is the creation of a world of one's own, a cocoon for one's separate, individual existence. It is like a dream world where everything is a manifestation of the dreamer, so the animal realm is related to the bardo of dream.

Almost all the activity of animals is directed toward the immediate satisfaction of their needs. They are extraordinarily patient, persistent, and stubborn in this pursuit; they instinctively take advantage of every opportunity that comes their way, and they do not worry about the consequences to themselves or others. This is only possible because they lack the vision of a wider horizon; their world is narrowed down to their own survival and the propagation of their species.

Much of the suffering of the animal realm derives from the fight for survival. In the wild, many animals are continually either killing or being killed. Prey animals are constantly in fear of losing their lives; they cannot relax for a single moment. Predators exhaust themselves in hunting, while those that are not carnivorous spend all their waking hours searching for food; they are entirely at the mercy of the environment and climate. Thus they are continually reinforcing their state of self-concerned delusion, which binds them to rebirth in the same realm, or else creating karma of greed or aggression, which may eventually lead them down into the hungry ghost or hell realms. But above all, animals suffer at the hands of human beings. In spite of their often superior physical strength, we hunt them, kill them, destroy their habitats, enslave them, exploit them, and abuse them, and we are able to do this because of our greater mental power. Through their lack of the right kind of intelligence, they allow themselves to be trapped, manipulated, and controlled.

The animal realm is very close to the human realm. Much of everyday human existence seems to be spent in an animal state of mind, accepting life as it comes, half-asleep, intellectually unchallenged, and spiritually unaware. It is quite possible to live a very contented and materially productive life in this manner. People with characteristics of the animal realm are usually conventional, dependable, serious, and efficient. They have a firm sense of priorities and hierarchy. They are probably excellent parents and pillars of the community. They are extremely loyal to their families and whatever groups they feel they belong to, but intensely distrustful of outsiders, which may easily lead them into attitudes of chauvinism, racism, or religious intolerance. They are the sort of people who might say "my country right or wrong," and "if it was good enough for my parents, it's good enough for me." They are fond of clichés and secondhand opinions because they do not really want to think things out for themselves. They believe in honest hard work, but they are not particularly ambitious; they would rather be employees than take on the challenges of leadership. Even intellectual work can be done with an animal-like attitude: one may be highly educated and have absorbed a lot of knowledge, but lack the imagination to make use of it in an inspiring or innovative way.

Any behavior that we think of as instinctive, automatic, or habitual partakes of the animal mentality. Animals like routine, and they become anxious when it is disturbed. On the most basic level, life revolves around food, sleep, sex, and self-preservation. There is always a sense of restriction and limitation, an absence of vision. Anything new or unknown is upsetting and threatening and is viewed with suspicion. The animal mentality is down-to-earth and practical, but it is indifferent to beauty. It cannot step back and look at itself objectively, so it has no sense of irony, and it is not in the least interested in self-knowledge. It is utterly serious and sincere, and it hates being laughed at or criticized. Human beings are animal-like in being easily controlled and manipulated by society, religion, education, advertising, and all kinds of other influences. It is the ignorant and credulous part of our nature that allows us to be used in this way.

When people accuse other human beings of behaving like animals, they are generally referring to extreme violence, cruelty, or destructiveness, or gluttony and overindulgence, which in fact are not typical of animals at all, but are more likely to be manifestations of the hungry ghost and hell realms. The flavor of the animal realm is confusion and unawareness. Actions are carried out instinctively, through habit, with a quality of mindless ignorance.

The animal realm has a lot in common with the characteristics of the Buddha family and is normally connected with it. However, in *Liberation through Hearing*, it is not specifically linked to any of the five families. During the appearances of the five buddhas, one of the six realms must necessarily be omitted, so the pathway leading to the animal realm appears later, when a different aspect of the awakened state manifests. This is the vision of the five vidyadharas, embodying the principles of awareness, communication, intelligence, and profound insight: the ultimate transmutation of our animal nature.

The buddha who appears in the animal realm is called Dhruvasimha, Steadfast Lion, since the lion is the king of animals. His color is blue, one of the two alternative colors associated with the Buddha family. He holds a sacred text in his hands. As a Buddhist symbol, a text represents the entire dharma, whether spoken or written. There are many different ways of teaching dharma, and the buddha could, of course, communicate with animals intuitively; but there is significance in the fact that he actually presents it to them in the form of a book. Language marks a crucial stage in the evolution of consciousness: the development of reason and the ability to express thoughts go hand in hand. The gift of language symbolizes the higher intelligence that must be awakened in order to free animal nature from the bondage of its self-satisfied existence, which is similar to the bardo of dream. How can those in the animal state of mind be shown that they are asleep and that whatever they are experiencing is a dream? By seeing the book of dharma in the buddha's hand, they receive a glimpse of a different world, and a sudden gap of uncertainty opens up. Am I awake or asleep? Is this real life, or is it just a state of delusion?

THE REALM OF HUMAN BEINGS

According to ancient Indian cosmology, races of humans dwell on four different continents or worlds (literally "islands"), situated in the cardinal directions around Mount Meru, the axis of our world system. Our home is the southern continent, Jambudvipa, the Rose-Apple Island. Originally, Jambudvipa referred only to India or South Asia, but nowadays it is often taken to mean the whole planet Earth.

When we consider the human realm, we must remember once again that we are looking into what particularly distinguishes it from the other realms rather than describing the whole spectrum of human existence. As human beings, on a psychological level, we continually pass through all six realms during the course of our daily lives, yet there is a quintessentially human quality that pervades all our experiences. The traditional correlation is with the Padma family, although in *Liberation through Hearing* it is with the Ratna family. The human realm has great affinities with both, as does the hungry ghost realm, but here there is a completely different flavor from that of the hungry ghosts.

The Padma family expresses the transmutation of passion and desire. It is the family of Buddha Amitabha and Bodhisattva Avalokiteshvara, the two most beloved manifestations of enlightenment wherever Buddhism has spread in this world, so there is obviously a deep attraction inherent within the human mind to all that Padma represents.

Trungpa Rinpoche described the human realm as the epitome of communication and relationship, which in turn is the essence of passion. We can see that this is true by comparing it with the other realms. The intelligence of animals has not developed far enough for them to communicate fully, while hungry ghosts and hell-beings are too immersed in their suffering to relate with others; gods and jealous gods possess higher intelligence, but their minds are entirely occupied with their own concerns. Only human beings are so curious about everything around them, so emotional, so affected by others, and so anxious to make contact. Along with communication, there is a creative urge and an idealistic striving for perfection. Human beings are desperate to know all there is to know; they want to attract everything into their own sphere and bring it under their control. Scientific research is essentially a passion for knowledge and art a passion for expression. This passionate quality of magnetizing, curiosity, and creativity has fueled human development from the very beginning of history.

It is this quality that gives human life its unique value in the Buddhist view. It is called precious human life, because among the six realms, it offers the best opportunity to practice dharma and attain enlightenment. Here we are talking about embodiment as a human being, rather than experiencing the human realm as a temporary state of mind. We are born with a longing to find out the meaning of our existence, a desire to attain perfection, and an instinct for relationship; all these qualities allow us to receive the communication of the dharma and open our minds into the space of awakening.

When passion becomes obsessive, it degenerates into grasping, greed, and lust, which result in the great suffering that afflicts the human realm: the suffering of loss and not being able to keep what we love; the suffering of not getting what we desire and having to endure what we dislike; and the suffering of pain and death, which is the result of attachment to the body and grasping at the idea of self.

In *Liberation through Hearing*, however, the pathway leading to the human realm appears at the same time as the vision of Ratnasambhava, the buddha of the Ratna family, and is said to be "accumulated by intense pride." *The Hundred Homages* and *The Dharma Practice*, on the other hand, connect the human realm with passion. It is interesting that both these connections are made. As we saw in the realm of the hungry ghosts, Padma and Ratna characteristics are closely related, but in the case of the hungry ghost mentality, their passion is extremely grasping and avaricious, and their pride is combined with meanness and selfishness. In the human realm, we find a more positive, expansive feeling of pride, a pride that feeds on relationships rather than turning away from them. The wish-fulfilling jewel, which grants all desires, is the symbol of the Ratna family, so it could be seen as the natural complement to the desire of the Padma family.

By contrast, Trungpa Rinpoche said at one point that "the human realm seems to have less pride than any of the other realms."[9] He explained that he meant the pride of self-satisfaction and complacency. On the whole, it is a human characteristic not to dwell on one's achievements, not to remain satisfied, but always to move on to something new. There is a restless, searching energy in human nature that prevents one from becoming stuck, and this makes it possible to be open to new possibilities and receptive to spiritual teachings.

However, there are many different aspects of pride; it can easily turn into arrogance and superiority, which all too often dominate human relationships with other living beings, especially animals. This

aspect of pride appears to be a particularly human characteristic compared with the inhabitants of the other realms. It has actually been a
basic factor in human evolution, since only an inherent attitude of
arrogance, combined with passionate curiosity and creativity, could have
enabled humankind to dominate nature to such an extent. The Sanskrit
for pride is *mana,* which is related to the words for mind and man.
Homo sapiens evolved through the development of mental power, and
this mind, inquiring into everything with its insatiable inquisitiveness
and boundless inventiveness, has built up the civilization in which it
takes such pride. The history of the human race really does seem to be
a drama of both passion and pride intermingled.

Trungpa Rinpoche relates the human realm to the bardo of illusory body, replacing the bardo of dharmata in the usual list of the six
bardos. The practice of illusory body is one of the completion-stage
yogas, but is not generally classed as a bardo. In *Natural Liberation,* this
practice is included as part of the instructions concerning the bardo of
dream; in commenting on it, Gyatrul Rinpoche remarks that it can be
regarded as a preliminary practice for all the bardos.[10] Trungpa
Rinpoche presents it as the epitome of the bardo experience, a state of
suspension in which we begin to see the ambiguity of our situation in
any of the realms: "You are between extremes, and you realize that that
in itself is an extreme situation."[11]

The essence of the yoga of illusory body is the realization that
one's own body and mind, as well as all external phenomena, are unreal,
just like an image in a mirror or a reflection of the moon on water.
This practice cuts through the belief in our substantiality and our attachment to it and places us in a position of total uncertainty about
our own existence. Trungpa Rinpoche relates it to the intensely personal
and sensitive nature of passion in the human realm, which makes us
uniquely vulnerable and frequently produces a feeling of conflict and
ambiguity. We never know quite where we are, whether things are real
or unreal, solid or transparent, friendly or threatening. Once we realize
that things are not what they seem, we can begin to see them as they
really are. Understanding this principle is the first step toward attaining
the pure illusory body of the deity, which links to the appearance of
the peaceful and wrathful deities in the bardo of dharmata.

The buddha of the human realm is Shakyamuni himself, who

belongs to the Ratna family, portrayed with his glowing golden body and saffron robes. Shakyamuni is the Sage of the Shakya Clan and is also sometimes called the Lion of the Shakyas. He holds a begging bowl and a mendicant's staff, which symbolize the antidotes to both pride and desire. He gave up the life of a prince, the pinnacle of worldly existence, and became a homeless beggar with no status, no possessions, and no sensual pleasures. In the eyes of worldly people, he was a complete failure, yet his appearance radiates absolute joy, fulfillment, dignity, and peace. This is a supreme challenge to the basic assumptions of the human mentality. His empty begging bowl presents the ultimate paradox, and seeing it can suddenly plunge the mind into the open space of wakefulness.

THE REALM OF JEALOUS GODS

The jealous gods are the opponents of the gods, continually at war with them through jealousy and envy. In Sanskrit they are called *asura*, which is often literally translated as "antigod." In translations of Hindu legends, they are sometimes called demons; this is probably because many of them are also rakshasas, those fierce and bloodthirsty creatures that are classed among the hungry ghosts in the Buddhist system. In most legends, they certainly appear as evil and demonic, intent on the destruction of the world, while the gods fight on the side of good. It is said in the Vedas that the gods chose truth and rejected falsehood, while the jealous gods chose falsehood and rejected truth. Yet this realm is still one of the three higher realms in which positive karma predominates over negative. The jealous gods were the elder brothers of the gods, and fundamentally they have the same divine nature, with all its intelligence, powers, and advantages. Their character is not so completely dominated by negativity as those of the beings in the lower realms. They are not so overwhelmed by the suffering of the emotional afflictions, and they have much more freedom of action. However, in spite of their great intelligence and potential, they can easily fall into the three lower realms. Their tendency toward aggression and violence often makes them appear demonic, which suggests the hell realms, and their rakshasa characteristics connect them to the hungry ghost realm. In the Hindu legends, they often assume the form of animals; a god or goddess fights with them and kills them, liberating them from their bestial nature, which represents their extreme delusion.

In these legends, we generally find that some impulse of jealousy sparks their aggression, so the name jealous god is quite appropriate. It may be jealousy of someone else's wife or status or possessions, aggravated by the conviction that all these things belong to them by right and are being denied them. Sometimes they seem like revolutionaries: good or bad depending on which side one supports. They are portrayed in the wheel of life as warriors dressed in armor and bearing weapons. They possess all the qualities associated with warriors and heroes throughout history: courage, leadership, dynamism, and, above all, tremendous energy. They are capable of doing great good as well as great evil, and their character ranges from noble and highly civilized to coarse, ruthless, and tyrannical, not unlike dictators in our own world. They are renowned for their magical powers, and if they are attracted to religion, it is generally in order to gain power. They often attain highly advanced spiritual states through ascetic practices, which they pursue with single-minded ambition like everything else they undertake.

Trungpa Rinpoche describes the process of developing a jealous god mentality through discontent and disillusionment with the realm of the gods, which grows into a reaction against it. When the positive karma that caused rebirth as a god is exhausted, the only way to go is down. The god realm is a place of pleasure, perfection, order, and civilization containing within itself the seed of this reaction. It gives birth to an element of rebelliousness, a desire to experience something more crude and down-to-earth, and an impulsive need to express one's energy without any constraints. Once we have developed this attitude of discontent, it is no longer possible to relax and enjoy the blissful existence of the gods. Yet there remains an underlying envy of those who can still enjoy it, a feeling of being cheated and a fear of losing what was ours by right. Then we begin to feel shut out and excluded, and suspicion grows rampant. Nobody can be trusted; we imagine that everyone is spying on us and gossiping about us. Soon every attempt to communicate appears as a threat and conspiracies are seen in all directions. This is paranoia, the extreme of the jealous god state of mind.

The jealous gods dwell on the slopes of Mount Meru, just below the realm of the gods. In many paintings of the wheel of life, these two realms are depicted as one, divided only by a great tree. This is the wish-fulfilling tree, the *kalpataru*, which grants all desires. The jealous gods are continually taunted by the sight of it, for although its roots grow in their territory, its magical fruit is accessible only to the gods.

Another great treasure that the gods possess and the jealous gods lack is the elixir of life. In this case, jealousy seems fully justified, because the gods won it by cunning and deceit. In spite of their love of truth, many stories show the gods following truth only in the letter and not in spirit. In this particular legend, the gods planned to raise a hoard of treasures lying in the depths of the cosmic ocean, which included the wish-fulfilling tree and the elixir of life (*amrita* or *soma*). They made a truce with the jealous gods and persuaded them to help in churning the ocean, a task that required all their combined strength. Many marvelous treasures appeared: divine courtesans, miraculous animals, the five trees of heaven, invincible weapons, and magical jewels emerged from the churning water like butter out of milk. Finally the elixir itself arose, borne aloft by the divine physician, whereupon the jealous gods, quick off the mark as always, seized it and almost succeeded in carrying it away. But the god Vishnu transformed himself into an enchantingly beautiful woman, the personification of delusion, and tricked them into giving it up. As a result of this deception, the jealous gods are condemned to suffer terrible wounds and to die in large numbers during their battles, while the gods are miraculously healed and live immensely long lives through the power of the elixir.

This story throws an interesting light on the jealous god mentality: as the saying goes, "just because you're paranoid, it doesn't mean someone isn't out to get you." Their resentment may well be caused by some sort of injustice, but it is the grasping nature of ego that produces the distorted response of jealousy and envy. Then, just as with the other poisons, a vicious circle is created: they continually feed their suspicions and find more causes for resentment, provoking ever-greater paranoia.

The path leading to the realm of the jealous gods appears on the fifth day, along with the mandala of Amoghasiddhi, lord of the Karma family. Their characteristics are very close to the description of the Karma personality. They always feel that their neighbors have got something better, that the grass is greener on the other side of the fence. Whatever they possess, they are afraid that someone is plotting to steal it, just as they would themselves, so they have to remain constantly on guard. They are always prepared for war; warfare is both their work and their play. Diplomacy has been defined as war continued by other means, and jealous gods have the qualities of diplomats or spies, for whom every relationship is an opportunity for intrigue. With their sharp intellect, they imagine that everyone is playing some complicated game or engaged in some conspiracy. In spiritual life, they are ambitious; their energy leads them to extremes and they can easily become fanatics. They are intensely competitive, seeing rivals everywhere. They are manipulative and use people for their own ends. They are constantly comparing their situation with that of others and are quick to sense any insult, real or imagined.

The Karma family is connected with speed, and the increasing speed of our culture and way of life could be said to encourage the jealous god state of mind. We live in a speedy world where it seems more and more important to get whatever we want right now. Karma family activity often arises from a concern with justice and human rights, but its distortion into the politics of envy is typical of this realm. It demonstrates clearly how the energy of action can become demonic if competitiveness and suspicion are allowed to get out of control.

This realm is related to the bardo of this life, lasting from birth to death, which is also based on speed. Once a state of mind has come into existence, it must be kept going; the emotional impetus must be maintained. Simply staying alive entails a constant battle against the forces of decay, and the furious energy of the jealous gods is the survival instinct carried to its extreme. So the gap, the pause in their activity that could open up a glimpse of liberation for them, is the peak experience of being poised between intense speed and total stillness, or between winning and losing, and the uncertainty about which is which.

In this realm, the buddha appears as a warrior, green in color, holding a sword and shield and dressed in shining armor. His name is Vemachitra, He Who Wears a Brilliant Garment. The jealous gods would not be able to hear the buddha's message of compassion; they would distrust his motives and despise his gentleness. Since they perceive everyone as an enemy, the only way he can communicate with them is on their own ground, face-to-face as warriors. He does not manifest as a wrathful deity with a terrifying form, but is invincibly peaceful and absolutely powerful. He simply blocks all the attacks of the jealous gods and brings their headlong rush to a stop, so that by confronting the buddha they are forced at last to confront themselves.

THE REALM OF THE GODS

The realm of the gods is a realm of indulgence: material indulgence on its lower levels and spiritual indulgence on its higher levels. It is the highest realm within samsara, so it is placed at the top of the wheel of life. Just like the popular ideas of heaven in all cultures, it is a place of pleasure and perfection, the ideal toward which human beings strive. The gods enjoy everything they could possibly desire, they are highly intelligent and creative, they possess magical powers, and they are able to attain the most advanced states of meditation. Yet they are still bound within samsara and are part of the endless cycle of the wheel of life.

The realm of the gods is divided into three parts: the world of desire, the world of form, and the formless world. This threefold classification actually includes all six realms; the whole of samsaric existence is known as the three worlds. But the worlds of form and formlessness comprise only the higher levels of the realm of the gods, while the world of desire includes the other five realms as well as the lower levels of the god realm.

The world of desire is the world of the senses. It means desire for the pleasures of all the senses, including the pleasures of the mind. The five other realms and the lower levels of the realm of the gods are completely dominated and determined by sensory experience, ranging from almost entirely painful in the hells to almost entirely pleasurable in the heavens. There are six heavens in the desire world of the gods, inhabited by various classes of deities and all containing magical palaces, magnificent pleasure gardens, and every kind of perfection and satisfaction that could possibly be imagined.

According to mythology, the lowest of these heavens is situated on the slopes of Mount Meru and is ruled by the four great kings of the cardinal directions. It appears to be a very worldly and materialistic kind of paradise whose inhabitants enjoy power, grandeur, wealth, and status. In pictures of the wheel of life where the jealous gods are not given a realm separate from that of the gods, they also inhabit this region.

Above it, on the summit of Mount Meru, is the heaven of the thirty-three gods—a traditional formula for the ancient Vedic pantheon, although it does not include all of the later, better known Hindu deities. This is the heaven depicted in the wheel of life, the prototype heaven of Indian mythology. Its ruler is Indra, a powerful deity who was greatly revered at the time of the Buddha. He was the god of sky and storm and a great hero in battles against the jealous gods. His weapon is the thunderbolt, the original form of the vajra. The wish-fulfilling tree grows in his paradise, and here are found many other magical treasures that emerged from the churning of the ocean. Above all, the gods possess the elixir of life, which is an all-healing medicine and bestows longevity. But this, their greatest blessing, is at the same time their greatest curse. For the gods are not really immortal; they live unimaginably long lives in human terms and show no signs of aging, but eventually their lives must come to an end. They cannot imagine their own death, they never contemplate it or prepare for it, so when it actually arrives, it causes them extreme suffering.

Above these two terrestrial heavens are four more heavens in the sky around the summit of Mount Meru. The first of these is characterized as free from all strife, since the deities there are beyond the reach of the jealous gods' attacks. The second, Tushita, is a realm of complete satisfaction; this is where the Buddha Shakyamuni dwelt before his birth as a human being, and where Maitreya, the buddha of the future, now waits for his time to descend to Earth. In the third heaven, the deities can magically emanate everything they desire; in the fourth, they have only to wish and whatever they desire is spontaneously produced for them by others.

Human beings can be reborn in these lower heavens by following conventional religious practices and doing good deeds. Although they are still within the world of desire, they are considered to be very fortunate places of rebirth, the reward for many successive lives of virtue. The disadvantage is that, with so much pleasure and fulfillment, it is difficult to find enough motivation to practice dharma; so from that point of view, birth as a human being is considered the best. Mara, the Evil One, who tempted the Buddha on the eve of his enlightenment, is also known as the sovereign of the world of desire and dwells in its highest heaven. He represents the seductive aspect of spirituality, which is appropriated by ego to convince us that we are making great progress and becoming highly evolved beings.

The worlds of form and formlessness are levels of existence of a quite different order. Here form does not mean materiality but simply appearance: the qualities of color and shape. The deities in the world of form are no longer dominated by desire for sensual pleasures and have lost their attachment to coarse sense perceptions; they experience themselves as immaterial, so they are said to have subtle bodies of light. In the formless world, they have transcended attachment to all the senses except the mind; they are pure spiritual beings with mental bodies that have no visible form. Since these deities have no physical bodies, they cannot undergo death in the ordinary way, so when their immensely long lives eventually come to an end, they simply awaken in a different realm or on another level of the god realm.

Together, these worlds contain twenty-one levels of profound meditative states. In the world of form, the first four levels (the four meditative absorptions) are each divided into grades of weak, medium, and strong, making twelve in all. They represent increasing purification of the meditation process. Above them are five further levels known as pure abodes; the highest of these, Akanishtha, is the heaven in which the Buddha became enlightened.

The formless world consists of four extremely subtle and profound levels of meditation, which the Buddha mastered under the guidance of his teachers before he set off on his own to attain enlightenment. He realized that these states, high as they are, do not result in liberation from the cycle of rebirth. For the deities in these heavens, the skandha of form no longer functions as a means of ego grasping, because they do not identify with the body; but they still retain a sense of self through the activity of the other four skandhas— feeling, perception, conditioning, and consciousness. In the first stage of absorption, everything is perceived as being like infinite space: open, empty, insubstantial, and unobstructed. The second is the experience of the infinity of consciousness. The third is the experience of there being absolutely nothing. In the fourth, one transcends even the concept of nothingness and enters a state in which there is neither perception nor nonperception, the highest point of existence.

All these heavens in the worlds of form and formlessness are ruled by the god Brahma. In Hinduism, Brahma is the masculine personification of the formless, absolute principle, the neuter *brahman*, which simply means "expansion" or "immensity." Brahma and Indra (the ruler of the lower god realms) were the two foremost deities at the time of the Buddha, although later their importance declined. They both played a significant part in the Buddha's story as supreme representatives of all living beings in the universe: first encouraging him in his efforts to attain enlightenment, then praising his success and worshiping him with offerings, and finally requesting him not to remain silent but to teach the dharma. As we have already seen in connection with the hungry ghost realm, Brahma represents both the supreme good and the creative principle. He is subject to the law of karma and is only one of an infinite series of brahmas. His name in Tibetan means "the Pure One," and in Buddhism he is regarded not as the creative principle, but as the embodiment of truth, holiness, and purity. Brahma, with his qualities of excellence, was incorporated into Buddhism to represent the supreme levels of attainment within samsara.

Traditionally, the poison that most affects the gods is said to be pride, connected with the Ratna family. This tradition is followed in *The Hundred Homages* and *The Dharma Practice*, but in *Liberation through Hearing*, the path leading to their realm appears along with Vairochana, lord of the Buddha family, associated with delusion. In his commentary, Trungpa Rinpoche relates the gods with pride, which he defines as "intoxication with the existence of ego,"[12] although elsewhere he also associates them with the Buddha family. He describes their dominant state of mind as one of complete self-absorption, suggesting a combination of pride and delusion.

Self-absorption is the key to the human experience of the realm of the gods. On the lower levels, the world of desire, it appears as indulgence or dwelling on the enjoyment of such things as health, wealth, beauty, education, and all kinds of pleasures. Many of the normal aspirations of human beings could be considered expressions of the god realm or "heaven on earth." But to be in that realm psychologically means that one is not simply enjoying them, but using them as a means of maintaining one's sense of self. Life is seen as a search for happiness and fulfillment; when that search becomes the whole purpose of life, it can easily develop into an obsessive concern with youth and beauty, healthy living, self-improvement, emotional growth, and so on. There is always a certain amount of self-consciousness and self-congratulation in these endeavors. The notion of spirituality may be mentioned frequently, but this spirituality is really based on ego. It is a way of trying to manufacture love, light, and peace by shutting out all darkness and unpleasantness. All this is very similar to the picture of the distorted qualities of the Buddha family, which is connected with the animal realm. But the ignorance and delusion of the gods is extremely intelligent, sophisticated, and creative, unlike the confused and undeveloped mentality of animals. The gods are the supreme exponents of illusion, of building castles in the air, but they have become entranced by their own magical creation and are convinced that it is all real and permanent.

The feeling of being immortal is a very powerful godlike characteristic that we, as human beings, secretly have within us most of the time. Again and again, great teachers have reminded us that only an awareness of the inevitability of death can wake us from our complacency. And corresponding to our feeling of immortality during life, there is a longing for eternity after death: eternal heaven, eternal peace, or even eternal nonexistence. As Trungpa Rinpoche said in discussing this realm, "ego's ultimate dream is eternity, particularly when eternity presents itself as meditation experience."[13]

In the higher god realms, the worlds of form and formlessness, we become entirely absorbed in states of meditation, so the sense of self becomes much more subtle, beguiling, and dangerous. It is only natural, from the point of view of ego, that once we have reached such a wonderful place we would like to stay in it forever. But if we have no vision of vast emptiness and cannot dissolve into the open space of meditation, there will always be the little voice of ego thinking, "*I* am experiencing this awareness, this peace, this bliss."

In the tantric account of Shakyamuni Buddha's enlightenment, all the buddhas of the universe came to him and told him that it was impossible to attain liberation through the samadhis of the formless world. They took him down to the Akanishtha heaven, the summit of the world of form, and there he became fully enlightened. This story is very significant, for the formless absorptions into infinite space, infinite consciousness, nothingness, and nonduality are the most seductive of spiritual experiences. At this stage, it is extremely difficult to distinguish subtle grasping from genuine realization, or the dissolution of ego from its crystallization. If any attachment remains, the meditator would probably experience these states as union with God or with a formless Absolute; for as long as there is a self to attain union, there must also be a transcendent other with which to be united.

Not surprisingly, the realm of the gods is linked with the bardo of meditation. All meditation practices on any level can be done with an attitude either of letting go or of grasping. In genuine samadhi, the most profound state of meditation, there is complete nondual absorption, so that self dissolves; but with the gods, the very experience of absorption becomes an object of grasping and a means of self-preservation. The gap that occurs here is the contrast between this dwelling on our experience, this solidification, and a sudden simultaneous doubt, a flash of openness. We are not sure whether we are about to become enlightened or actually going mad. At the peak of that intense ambiguity, we could either leap through into the awakened state or fall back into the godlike trance, "the absolute, ultimate achievement of bewilderment, the depths of ignorance,"[14] as Trungpa Rinpoche called it.

The buddha appearing in the realm of the gods is called Shata-kratu, one of the names of Indra; it means Performer of a Hundred Sacrifices, a most respected and holy person. He is white in color, like Buddha Vairochana, and he plays a stringed instrument. As the gods are so immersed in pleasure, this buddha speaks to them in a language they will listen to, the language of music. Music is the most ephemeral of the arts; sound flows out of silence and returns again to silence almost as soon as it has arisen; the moments of silence are just as essential as the moments of sound. Music is constantly changing, movement is its very existence: it is the perfect teaching on impermanence for the gods, who are so attached to immortality and eternity.

Chapter Nine

The Threefold Pattern
of the Path

WHETHER WE CONSIDER the world around us, our own nature, or the nature of enlightened beings, we find that nothing exists in a static condition. Life is a continual dynamic process of appearance and disappearance. Reality is not just the phenomenal world, not just whatever appears; it is also nonappearance, potentiality. This is emptiness, the open dimension of reality. Between these two poles there is a third state, the flow of energy that links them together.

The highest or innermost level is emptiness, the essence of all phenomena. The intermediate level is the energy by which emptiness communicates and reveals itself. The lowest or outermost level is matter, the actual manifestation of physical form. Essence is invisible, completely beyond the sphere of the senses, a state of unity and simplicity. Matter is multiplicity and diversity, perceptible to the physical senses. Energy flowing between them partakes of both; it can be described in terms of the sensory realm, although it is not contained within it.

We shall look at the functioning of this threefold pattern in three different areas: first, the trikaya, the three dimensions of the awakened state; second, the body, speech, and mind of ordinary living beings; and last, the triad of coarse, subtle, and very subtle levels of existence. In addition, there are also categories of outer, inner, and secret, as applied to, for instance, the five elements or the mandala. These groups are all expressions of the same principle, so there are many similarities between them. As we have found so many times, they interpenetrate each other and each individual aspect contains all three within itself. We can discover all kinds of correspondences and relationships between them.

THE TRIKAYA

The threefold pattern of the awakened state is called the *trikaya*, which literally means the "three bodies." They are the *dharmakaya*, which is often translated as "body of truth"; the *sambhogakaya*, or "body of enjoyment"; and the *nirmanakaya*, or "body of emanation." *Kaya* means "body" in Sanskrit, both literally and metaphorically, as it does in English. Since they are such significant terms whose English equivalents do not really seem adequate, I will follow Trungpa Rinpoche's practice in keeping the Sanskrit words and refer to them as the three kayas, or collectively as the trikaya.

Trikaya is singular because the three kayas are an indivisible unity, three dimensions of totality. The sambhogakaya and nirmanakaya together are known as the *rupakaya*, the "body of form," distinct from the dharmakaya, which is formless emptiness. As the *Heart Sutra* says: "form is emptiness and emptiness is form"; form and emptiness are inseparable and they cannot be understood in isolation from each other. The two aspects of the rupakaya are the levels on which the mind of an awakened being manifests in order to benefit others. Dharmakaya represents the accomplishment of one's own aim to attain enlightenment, while sambhogakaya and nirmanakaya exist in order to accomplish the aim of others.

In a companion text to *Liberation through Hearing*, called *Self-Liberation through Naked Sight Pointing Out Awareness*, which we shall see more of in the next chapter, the trikaya is described as the very nature of mind itself. Speaking of this mind, or awareness, the text says:

> Within it the trikaya is indivisible and complete in one:
> Emptiness where nothing whatever exists is the dharmakaya,

Clarity, the inner radiance of emptiness, is the sambhogakaya,
Dawning everywhere without obstruction is the nirmanakaya,
These three complete in one are its intrinsic nature.

The last line refers to the indivisible unity of the three kayas, which is called the *svabhavikakaya*, the "body of intrinsic nature." This totality of "three complete in one" is the nature of our own mind; it forms the structure of our being and the pattern in which we function. The trikaya is an expression of how things really are, inherently pure and perfect, but under the influence of ignorance, we experience it as the three aspects of ordinary existence. It corresponds both to our ordinary body, speech, and mind and to our coarse, subtle, and very subtle levels. We also experience the three kayas in a confused way during the three states of consciousness that we go through every night and day: in deep sleep, we enter the dharmakaya; dreaming corresponds to the sambhogakaya; and the waking state is the nirmanakaya.

The three kayas naturally appear during the three bardos described in *Liberation through Hearing*. The luminosity of death, which the dying person enters at the culmination of the bardo of dying, is the dharmakaya. The radiant display of the peaceful and wrathful deities, appearing during the bardo of dharmata, is the sambhogakaya. Taking the form of a living being in the bardo of existence is the nirmanakaya. At those times, the person in the bardos has the opportunity to realize them by recognizing them for what they really are.

Trungpa Rinpoche explained the trikaya in terms of the way we relate to the spiritual path and to life in general, which always operates in accordance with this threefold pattern.[1] As it says in the root verse for the bardo of this life: "Making mind and appearances the path, I will manifest the trikaya." The bardo of this life is here and now, so manifesting the trikaya should not be regarded only as a transformation that miraculously takes place when we attain enlightenment or after death. The experience of the trikaya can be found everywhere; it is a continual presence in our lives. The dharmakaya is present in the sense of openness, the source and background of all phenomena. The sambhogakaya is present in the sense of energy bursting forth, the sacred, magical quality of life. And the nirmanakaya is present in the sense of phenomena continually arising, impermanent yet vividly apparent.

From a practitioner's point of view, we begin from where we are, as embodied human beings. The successive stages of practice lead us from the realization of nirmanakaya, through sambhogakaya, to the eventual accomplishment of dharmakaya. When this realization becomes stabilized, the journey is reversed, and we return through the kayas, manifesting sambhogakaya and nirmanakaya as the expression of the awakened state, from a completely realized point of view. This will become clearer in the following explanation of the individual kayas.

Dharmakaya

The different but related meanings of the word *dharma* were discussed in chapter 6, and we have seen how it forms a part of several other very significant terms. There is dharmata: the quality of reality itself, the true nature of all phenomena, free from the interpretations of the confused mind. Then there is dharmadhatu: all-encompassing space, the space that is nothing yet contains everything. Dharmakaya, the "body" of dharma, suggests the positive, living aspect of absolute reality. It is the totality of all possibilities, infinite potentiality. It is described as the empty essence, because all phenomena arise out of emptiness; emptiness is the essence of all existence. It is always present as the basis of existence, its secret, invisible dimension.

As Trungpa Rinpoche put it, the dharmakaya arises "unnecessarily" out of infinite space. It is the actual experience of space, and in a sense is its first embodiment; that is why it is known as a body. It is self-existing awareness; the pure, undifferentiated light of knowledge; the unborn, unchanging, undying state of absolute wakefulness. It is the universal, all-pervading buddha mind, the self-knowledge of the awakened state. Therefore it is called the original or primordial buddha (*adibuddha*), the buddha who has never needed to awaken. In the Nyingma tradition, the primordial buddha is called Samantabhadra, Universal Goodness. His iconography clearly expresses the nature of the dharmakaya. He is seated cross-legged, smiling slightly, in profound meditation, and his body is the deep blue color of infinite space. He is naked to express the state of complete simplicity and uncontrived naturalness. In that primordial sphere, the complexities of ego and the duality of samsara and nirvana have never arisen. His nakedness is also a reminder that, although we personify him as a buddha, the principle of buddhahood transcends all attributes, qualifications, and descriptions.

The verse states that "nothing whatever exists" in the dharmakaya, yet this is not a nihilistic statement; it goes beyond the ordinary concepts of both existence and nonexistence. Trungpa Rinpoche described it as "a sense of fertility" and "pregnant emptiness." In order for something to exist, there must also be a sense of its nonexistence, a sense of absence before it becomes present. Before words are spoken or thoughts arise in the mind, there must be a space in which they are unspoken and unthought; yet, because they do actually manifest, in a sense they are already there. Everything is already accomplished; cause and effect are simultaneous. The experience of dharmakaya as part of life is the recognition of this totality, an attitude of openness without expectation, seeing everything as it really is instead of how we would like it to be. It is total positive thinking, which is precisely the meaning of the dharmakaya buddha Samantabhadra: good in all ways, at all times, and in all places.

In the completion stage of vajrayana practices, the instructions will often say something like "rest beyond thought in the unborn dharmakaya" or "look into the face of the primordial dharmakaya." Even though we may only be able to manage a shallow and distracted kind of formless meditation, language of this sort is a very skillful part of the tantric method, reminding us that we really are the trikaya whether we know it or not. If we can simply relax into openness, neither following after thoughts nor suppressing them, without either acceptance or rejection, then the mind in its natural state is revealed as the dharmakaya.

Sambhogakaya

Sambhogakaya literally means the "body of enjoyment." It is the visionary form of the deities, the natural, spontaneous expression of the dharmakaya, ceaselessly radiating forth out of emptiness. It is the play of awakened energy, experienced as the fullness of joy and bliss. One of William Blake's proverbs describes it perfectly: "Energy Is Eternal Delight."[2]

The sambhogakaya is the dimension of communication, the medium through which the nakedness and simplicity of the dharmakaya communicates with the material level of existence. The dance of energy manifests as subtle vibrations of sound and light. In Indian tradition, the universe evolves from primordial, uncreated sound, a spontaneous, self-existent pulsation in empty space. Everything in existence resonates with its own particular vibration. In the sambhogakaya, all the sounds of the whole universe reverberate with their true meaning, as spontaneous expressions of dharma. Whether they are loud or soft, sweet or harsh, short or long, they are the natural sound of dharma, filling the whole of space. In terms of human speech, the primordial vibration evolved into the syllables of the sacred language, Sanskrit. These syllables, corresponding to the letters of the Sanskrit alphabet, are known as *akshara*, "imperishable"; they are the seeds that give birth to all phenomena. So it is said that the world is made out of the garland of letters. This is what lies behind the principle of mantra, sacred sound. The mantras of the deities are the nature of those deities expressed in the form of sound.

Light radiates from the emptiness of dharmakaya as the five colors of the five kinds of knowledge. It appears in shining rainbow clouds, in glowing circles, in scintillating pinpoints, and dazzling rays of light. Then the five colors crystallize into the forms of the five buddhas and all the other deities of the mandala. These divine forms are not solid like bodies of flesh and blood, but made entirely of light; they arise out of light and dissolve back into light. This is the realm of sacred vision portrayed in tantric art and brought vividly to life in meditation. The sambhogakaya is the bridge between emptiness and form: emptiness displaying itself as form, form revealing itself to be emptiness.

The experience of the sambhogakaya is to perceive the world directly and nakedly, welcoming whatever appears without preconceptions. Sense perceptions become clearer, sharper, and more colorful. The nature of the five buddhas spontaneously reveals itself in flashes of insight, and one sees intuitively how the whole of existence is pervaded by the qualities of the five families. The world is recognized as sacred, magical, and full of wonder; it becomes a boundless source of life and goodness. It contains all the vitality and passion of the emotions, free from the confusion that brings misery and pain. There is a sense of fearlessness and play and continual discovery: an invitation to take part in the dance of life. This is the meaning of symbolism in vajrayana— not contrived or imposed, but natural symbolism that is inherent in everything. Its sole purpose is to wake us up. The deities are nothing other than wakefulness, our own awake state. The natural, self-existent symbolism of the world points always toward awakening.

Nirmanakaya

The nirmanakaya is actual physical manifestation, energy solidified into matter. Literally it means the "body of emanation," because it emanates from the sambhogakaya as countless forms of awakened beings in all six realms. It is the practical application of enlightenment, the embodiment of the energy of compassion, totally responsive and sensitive to the needs of all beings. It is the activity of the buddhas in living form, the buddha that we can see and hear. It is unceasing in its manifestation, unhindered by any obstacles, infinite and all-pervading. It responds to the needs of living beings in whatever way is most appropriate for them. Buddha Shakyamuni is described as a perfect man in every respect, but awakened beings do not necessarily always manifest in ideal appearances like his. They can take any shape, pleasant or unpleasant, beautiful or ugly, and play any role in any situation, whatever is required for the benefit of others.

The principle of buddhahood can only fully reveal itself and carry out enlightened activities by means of embodiment. The title of *tulku*, given to those who are recognized as the reincarnations of great teachers, is simply the Tibetan for nirmanakaya (*sprul sku*) in its modern pronunciation. Men and women who have fully realized their buddhanature are able to take birth with the awareness of who they really are and with the conscious intention of helping others to reach that state. In their case, rebirth or reincarnation is quite different from that of ordinary people, because they do not cling to an imagined self that continues from one incarnation to the next. The nirmanakaya manifests directly from wisdom and compassion, not as the result of karmic traces in a confused mindstream. For us, the results of karma compel rebirth in one of the six realms whether we like it or not. An enlightened person, on the other hand, may have made a vow to take birth in a particular form, and the power of that intention will bring about its manifestation. There may even be several different emanations embodying different aspects of one powerful stream of enlightened energy.

In vajrayana, the guru is always regarded as nirmanakaya. It does not matter whether he or she has been recognized as a tulku, in other words, as having a particular link with some figure from the past. Learning to see the buddha in the guru is the first step toward seeing all beings as buddha. We are all really nirmanakaya, but we do not realize it. The sense of living the nirmanakaya principle comes about through applying the techniques of meditation in daily life: meditation in action. With this attitude, any situation is workable, whatever we do is appropriate, and all our activities bear fruit. The whole environment becomes our friend instead of our enemy, so that we feel completely at home in the world.

BODY, SPEECH, AND MIND

Every living being also consists of a threefold structure that mirrors the trikaya. These three aspects are body, speech, and mind, known as the three doors. All karma is created through the instigation of the three doors: our deeds, words, and thoughts. When they are transformed into instruments of awareness instead of confusion, they become vajra body, vajra speech, and vajra mind, three doors to awakening. An awakened person still has individual body, speech, and mind, but they are no longer identified with ego. Vajra mind is inseparably one with the buddha mind, the dharmakaya. Vajra speech is always the communication of dharma, the sambhogakaya. Vajra body is the authentic form of the buddha, the nirmanakaya.

Body

Body refers to our physical manifestation, the visible, tangible aspect of our being, corresponding to the nirmanakaya. It is the outward expression in material form of our mind and energy. It is the level on which other people see us and on which we perceive them. The body contains all our sense organs, through which we connect with the external world. We interact with the environment through them; sensation extends outward into the world, so in a certain way the environment is also part of our body. We are not enclosed within a solid wall, and there is no real barrier between inside and outside. Body is our total experience of ourselves as physical beings in a material universe.

The body is the basis of the spiritual path. Mindfulness, which is the foundation of all Buddhist practice, begins with the body. Because we are so attached to the body and so identified with it, we suffer endlessly during life and cling to existence even after death. Through the practice of mindfulness, we come to realize that it is impermanent and that it is not the self. Yet this realization does not diminish the body at all; on the contrary, it gives us a new appreciation of its true function. With awareness, sense impressions become more intense, movements more graceful and dignified, and actions more skillful and effective. We naturally become more sensitive and responsive to the environment on a physical level, which links in with the levels of speech and mind, how we communicate and how we think about the world. From the egoistic point of view, the body seems to isolate us and cut us off from others; the wall of our skin divides us from the atmosphere around us and encloses us in our separate shells. But from an awakened viewpoint, the body is our means of reaching out and touching others; it is the instrument by which we perform the activities of the nirmanakaya.

Vajra body means a body that is perfect and indestructible. This is not some egoistic dream of personal immortality, but, paradoxically, it springs from the realization of the body's unreality. The whole material universe, both the body and its environment, spontaneously appears out of emptiness at every instant; it has no solidity or substantiality; it is indestructible because there is nothing that can be destroyed. As Trungpa Rinpoche expressed it: "Things are there because they are not there—otherwise they could not exist."[3]

In vajrayana, the method of transforming ordinary body, speech, and mind into vajra body, speech, and mind is the practice of deity yoga. Deity yoga works with all three aspects simultaneously. It does not necessarily bring about any outwardly perceptible change, but is based on a new perception of oneself. The transformation of body comes about through meditating on the deity's form. The meditator is the central deity of the mandala and all other living beings are deities within it; the dwelling is a miraculous palace, and the whole world a paradise, the pure land of the deity. All these forms are made of light, as insubstantial as a rainbow, yet more vivid and beautiful than any light seen by the eyes.

This use of imagery in meditation is very important during the creation stage, but the most vital thing is to have complete confidence in the deity's reality. The deity is the actual living presence of the awakened state, possessing all the qualities of the five buddhas, and the whole mandala is also pervaded by these qualities. In the completion stage, all the forms dissolve back into emptiness. This cuts through any attachment we might have to them and prevents us from falling into the trap of belief in their substantial existence. The sense of presence continues into everyday life, gradually transforming our perceptions and our relationship with the world.

Speech

Like the sambhogakaya, speech is the dimension of energy, communication, and emotion; it unites body and mind. We are used to thinking of ourselves as body and mind, but we generally ignore or do not bother to identify this third aspect of our nature. Speech does not mean only words or sounds produced by the voice; these are only the outermost manifestation of speech. It also refers to emotional energy, which fuels all forms of expression, and to the breath, which is another aspect of vital energy.

The voice depends entirely on breath in its usual sense, but any form of creative expression, whatever medium it uses, depends on the flow of our inner breath or energy. We say we have found our voice when we discover how to express what we really want to communicate through words, music, art, dance, or any other means. Communication is the essence of speech, both between mind and body and between each individual and the world outside. Just as the sense of body includes the environment, so speech includes all the sounds in the world. Communication is a two-way process; we are continually receiving messages from everything around us and responding to them by sending out our own messages in all kinds of ways.

Although speech is a more abstract concept than body, we are just as attached to its apparent reality, and we believe in it just as much. In spite of evidence of their unreliability, we rely on words to convey our thoughts and trust them to express what we really mean. We feel that what we say wells up from our true nature and confirms our existence. The sense of vajra speech develops from becoming aware of the inherent emptiness of speech: the space around words, the silence that envelops sound, the openness from which communication arises, the absence of ego at its very root.

Speech is creative power, the power of mantra. All languages are sacred, not just Sanskrit, and any word or sound can be perceived as mantra. If we simply listen without expectations, hearing the emptiness behind the sound, we can become sensitive to its inner quality and the message it carries. It is the music of nonself and wakefulness. The poet Milarepa is often portrayed with one hand cupped to his ear, listening intently to his own songs as they arise out of his emptiness and silence. All speech can become the poetry of the dharma when it flows from that sense of spaciousness.

The transformation of ordinary speech into vajra speech is brought about by reciting mantras. Mantra is not just a prayer or an invocation; it is the deity itself. It is the living presence of the deity in sound, just as the visual image is its living presence in form. Mantra is also the deity's own speech, the word of power that accomplishes the deity's enlightened actions. Like the visualized forms, the sound of mantra dissolves back into emptiness at the end of meditation. Through this practice, we learn to experience everything we say and everything we hear as mantra, resounding yet empty like an echo.

Mind

Mind is the invisible aspect of our nature, the source of speech and body. Mind is not just intellect; it is heart and mind in one—our consciousness, perceptions, feelings, and reactions, as well as the vague undercurrent of thoughts that continually ebbs and flows. Sensations originate in the body, but it is mind that experiences them. We say emotions come from the heart, but it is mind that is aware of them. Thoughts, ideas, and concepts of all kinds are like waves rising and falling on the surface of the ocean of mind. All of them, however powerful they may be, however strongly they demand our attention, are just different kinds of mental activity. They all dissolve back into the emptiness of dharmakaya. In our ordinary, confused condition, what we call our mind should really be called mindlessness. But when confusion is cleared away, mind is revealed as direct, intuitive awareness, the intelligence of the heart. That is why the meaning of the Sanskrit word *chitta* encompasses both heart and mind, and why the place of the mind is in the heart, as we shall see.

The first step in meditation is to calm the mind; then we can begin to gain insight into its nature. Mind is like space; in the openness and clarity of the true nature of mind, all thoughts arise and fall, leaving no trace, like birds flying through the sky. Resting in this state, we just let them come and go, not fixating on any concept or grasping any thought or feeling. Only the clear sky remains; this is indestructible vajra mind. The practice of deity yoga provides the conditions for this experience to deepen and expand to its ultimate extent. The mind of the meditator becomes one with the mind of the deity, the state of wakefulness. From that state, the sense of relationship and communication in the realm of vajra speech and the sense of presence and accomplishment of actions in the realm of vajra body flow forth spontaneously and effortlessly.

In Trungpa Rinpoche's words:

> At the tantric level, the positive experience of nonexistence comes about when the mind is completely tuned in to the magical possibilities of life. At the level of the vajra mandala of mind, subconscious gossip, or the continual background of chatter and ongoing commentary of our thoughts, is completely cut through. Mind is completely open. This vajra experience of mind creates a continuous celebration in dealing with life directly and simply. At the vajra level of mind, every situation takes place very simply, on its own, and mind relates with whatever arises quite simply.[4]

THE THREE LEVELS

Another way in which the threefold pattern operates is as three levels or degrees of density, which we have already met in relation to the five great elements. They pervade the whole of the environment, and apply to living beings. In the context of human life, they are known as the coarse, subtle, and very subtle body and mind. Body simply means the aspect of form, while mind is the corresponding consciousness. Speech, their communicative potential, is implied, although it is not mentioned in this context. We should remember that the three aspects are indivisible; it is only on the coarse level of our ordinary existence that they appear to be distinct and separate.

These three levels correspond to the waking state, the state of dreaming, and the state of deep sleep. The outer realm emerges from the inner, subtle realm, the dimension of energy, and ultimately derives from the innermost, very subtle essence of our being. Once again, this threefold pattern mirrors the principle of the trikaya, the dynamic interplay of essence, energy, and material form. We should not picture them like a set of Russian dolls, one inside the other. Rather, they form a continuous spectrum of energy flowing back and forth from the most subtle to the most material.

Ordinary waking life corresponds to the coarse dimension. When we go to sleep, we think we are becoming unconscious, but in fact we are sinking into the level of subtle consciousness. We enter the world of dreams and experience it as a strange, hallucinatory version of the waking state; then we enter deep, dreamless sleep, which we cannot observe or remember at all, yet we are still living and breathing. Even while we are awake, our thoughts, feelings, and perceptions are continually appearing and disappearing, rising and falling through the levels of consciousness. All phenomena arise out of the infinite potentiality of emptiness, through the subtle levels, until they appear in the coarse realm, and everything dissolves back into emptiness in a never-ending process of transformation.

The Coarse Level

The coarse or gross body is our body as we usually think of it, the body of flesh and blood. It is the samsaric equivalent of the nirmanakaya. Most of the time, we are only aware of this superficial level of existence, and we identify with it completely. On this plane, we experience the apparent duality of subject and object to its greatest extent, so we think of the external world as totally separate from ourselves. The body is formed from the inner coarse elements, while the environment is formed from the outer coarse elements. Inner and outer are linked together by the senses. The coarse mind is the consciousness that operates through the senses; it makes up the whole experience of our everyday waking life. Although their ultimate cause is the very subtle mind, which continues from life to life, the coarse levels of consciousness are dependent upon the brain and the senses in order to function. That is why people who do not accept the reality of other levels conclude that there can be no consciousness of any kind after death.

The Subtle Level

Like the sambhogakaya, the subtle body-mind complex is the intermediary between essence and manifestation, also corresponding to speech, the link between body and mind. This is the level at which transmutation takes place. As it is the matrix from which the coarse body and mind arise, they are affected by any change that occurs within it, so these changes must be brought about carefully and gradually under the guidance of an experienced teacher. A sudden, complete transformation would be too great for an unprepared person to bear and could lead to serious physical and mental illness.

The subtle mind corresponds to the state of consciousness we have in dreams, when all kinds of strange illusory forms are created out of memories and other imprints in the mindstream. We also enter this state during the bardo of dharmata after death and can learn to enter it intentionally during the completion stage of vajrayana practice.

The subtle body itself is threefold, consisting of nadi, prana, and bindu.[5] These important terms each have several meanings depending on the context, so I prefer to keep the Sanskrit words for them. *Nadi* is analogous to the form or body aspect of the threefold principle, *prana* to the energy or speech, and *bindu* to the essence or mind. Nadi literally means a "tube" or "channel"; the same word is used in medical works for the veins and arteries, but in this context, they are not physical and cannot be perceived with the ordinary senses. They form a network creating the basic structure of the subtle body. They are imagined as luminous, hollow tubes through which vital energy flows just as blood flows through the veins. This movement or current is prana, which can mean "breath," "spirit," "energy," or "life," and is inseparable from mind. Bindu, literally a "dot" or "drop," is the creative essence of mind, and is carried by prana like a rider on a horse along the pathways of the nadis.

The details of the subtle body vary according to the tradition one follows and the specific practice one is engaged in. Theoretically, it is described and pictured as a defined structure like that of the coarse body, but in practice, it is much more elusive. This does not mean that it is purely imaginary. It is, as the name implies, subtle: only to be understood by intuition and direct experience. In a sense, the nadis do not exist as a ready-made framework, but are created as prana flows along them; they are the pattern of the flow of prana, like the flight path of a bird in the sky or the channel cut by a fish as it glides through water. The various tantric systems contain many different names and descriptions of the nadis, the different kinds of prana, and the bindus, which are often at variance with each other. In relation to *Liberation through Hearing*, we only need to have a broad picture of the subtle body, which will be helpful in understanding the process of death. More precise details are best learned from a guru in the context of a particular practice.

Forming the axis of the subtle body is the central nadi. At its fullest extent, it reaches from a point in the forehead between the eyebrows, up to the crown of the head, and then straight down to the genitals. It is called *madhyama*, the "middle one," or *avadhuti*, the "shaker," because it shakes off the duality of subject and object. When prana and mind are brought into the central nadi through the practice of yoga, one attains increasing realizations of emptiness and bliss. Ordinary dualistic consciousness (vijnana) becomes transformed into awakened knowledge (jnana), so it is also known as the nadi of knowledge (*jnananadi*).

Two other main nadis, called *lalana* and *rasana*,[6] run to the left and right of the central one. They terminate at the nostrils, where prana, in its outermost aspect as breath, enters and leaves the body. *Lalana* means "playful" or "seductive," symbolizing the objective pole of experience, the attraction of the objects of the senses. *Rasana* means "taste" or "tongue," symbolizing the subjective pole, the enjoyer of experience. Generally speaking, lalana is on the left of the central nadi and rasana is on the right, while some sources describe them as being the other way around. In certain practices, they may be reversed in women, although it is unusual to find this distinction. They are associated with several other pairs of complementary polarities, such as sun and moon, wisdom and method, red and white, female and male, inhalation and exhalation, attraction and aversion. Again, any of these pairs may be reversed, so completely different sets of correspondences can be found among the teachings of various traditions. The underlying significance of the right and left nadis is that they point to our fundamental duality, and this basic meaning is unaffected by which side is seen as white or red, male or female.

There are said to be seventy-two thousand minor nadis branching out from the central one. The image of thousands of nadis spreading throughout the body, bearing confused energy that flows in all directions, gives a vivid picture of the distracted, dispersed awareness of the human condition. Underlying all this confusion is the basic dualistic split into subject and object, self and other, symbolized by the two side nadis.

The function of the nadis is to convey prana. The word *prana* derives from a root meaning to live, breathe, and move, and is defined as the power of vibration or motion. Perhaps "energy" would be the best equivalent in English. Prana is universal. It is the essence of nuclear energy and cosmic energy. Every manifestation of energy in the natural world is the vibration of prana, and nadi is the pattern it forms—"the tracks of the world," as Trungpa Rinpoche called it. On the personal level, it includes everything that we might consider mental, emotional, physical, or nervous energy. It regulates the body along with all its automatic functions and carries every aspect of our experience, consciousness, sense perceptions, feelings, and so on. Prana is threefold: its outer aspect sustains the body, its inner aspect corresponds to the five elements and the five poisons, and its secret aspect is the five kinds of knowledge.

Besides denoting this subtle energy in general, prana is given different names to indicate its five main modes of operation in the body. They all contain the same root, meaning "breath," with prefixes that show the specific nature of their movement. Strictly speaking, the Tibetan equivalent (*rlung*) is not a translation of prana but of *vayu*, which means "air" or "wind," the same as the element. This explains why translations from Tibetan often speak of the winds of the subtle body. *Vayu* is probably intended to refer to the actual motion of prana through the nadis, but they are frequently treated as synonyms in Sanskrit. As prana has become quite well known in English, I think it is preferable to continue using it. *Vayu* is also sometimes added to the names of the five energies: there is prana itself, or *pranavayu*, which is called the life-holding energy; then the pervading energy; the ascending energy; the equal energy; and the descending energy.[7] They are not so much different kinds of energy as one energy performing different functions. There are also many other aspects of prana, each fulfilling its own special function, which are identified for the purposes of certain meditations and in medical practice.

Along the length of the central nadi are several focal points or energy centers: the chakras. A *chakra* literally means a "wheel." In certain meditations, they are seen as wheels spinning around, but generally they are pictured as lotuses, each with its own specific number of petals, from which smaller nadis branch out. The two side nadis create knots around the central nadi at these points, constricting it and preventing prana from entering and flowing within it under normal conditions. At death, the knots loosen so that prana enters the central nadi; it can also be made to enter through the power of meditation.

The chakras vary in number according to the purpose for which one is considering them. In relation to *Liberation through Hearing*, there are five main ones, corresponding to the buddhas of the five families, the five aspects of prana, and the five elements, which dissolve at the time of death.

The first chakra, the dwelling of Vairochana, is in the head. There are two important chakras in the head, one at the crown and one in the center of the forehead. In practices that require six or more chakras, these two are clearly distinguished, but in this context, they are both mentioned as the first chakra. It is marked with a mantra, the white syllable OM, and supports the element of space. It is associated with the pervading energy that circulates throughout the body, distributing vital energy and governing movement of the limbs.

The next chakra is situated at the throat and is the seat of Amitabha. It is marked with the red syllable AH and supports the element of fire. It is the origin of the ascending energy that is responsible for speech, tasting, and swallowing. Alternatively, the throat chakra is sometimes said to be the seat of the descending energy, otherwise located in the lowest of the five chakras.

The third chakra is at the level of the heart, the place of Akshobhya. It is marked with the blue syllable HUM. It supports the element of water and the life energy, the original prana that supports and maintains life. It controls the movement of breath and gives clarity to the mind. According to some sources, the life energy is found in the head chakra, while the pervading energy dwells in the heart.

The fourth chakra is at the navel and is the dwelling of Ratnasambhava. It is marked with the yellow syllable SVA. The energy functioning here is the equal energy. It circulates around the internal organs, regulating the digestive system and keeping all the vital functions in balance. It also circulates the inner heat of the body, and an alternative name for it in Tibetan is "firelike," although fire is not its element. Its element is earth, because earth is associated with Ratnasambhava.

Finally, at the base of the spine, at the level of the sexual organs, is the chakra known as the secret place. This is the dwelling of Amoghasiddhi. It is marked with the green syllable HA and supports the element of air. It is the location of the descending energy that flows downward, clearing out waste from the body and regulating urination, defecation, and menstruation. As we have seen, this energy is sometimes said to be located in the throat chakra, changing places with the ascending energy, which then originates in the secret place and rises up from there to the area of the chest and throat.

As shown in chapter 7, the buddhas of the five families embody the transcendent principles of body, speech, mind, quality, and activity. The five chakras are experienced as focal points of these principles: body in the head, speech in the throat, mind in the heart, quality in the navel, and activity in the secret place. By meditating on the chakras as the mandalas of the buddhas, their energies are awakened and transformed into the five buddhas dwelling within us. The meaning of the five chakras, too, is universal; we should not only identify them in ourselves, but also experience them in the environment. As we have already seen, body, speech, and mind refer to the threefold principle of form, energy, and intelligence present throughout the universe. Quality relates to recognizing the qualities of enlightenment in everything around us and to the perception of the whole world as the pure land of a buddha. Activity is meditation in action, a sense of the spontaneous performance of enlightened activities occurring as a natural function of life.

The first three chakras are particularly important from the earliest stages of practice in vajrayana as the focal points of body, speech, and mind. The practitioner meditates on the form of a guru or deity appearing in the sky, with the three syllables shining at the head, throat and heart. At the conclusion of the practice, white rays of light stream out from the OM in the forehead chakra of the guru or deity, red rays of light from the AH in the throat, and blue rays of light from the HUM in the heart. They are absorbed into the practitioner's own three chakras, purifying the ordinary body, speech, and mind and transforming them into vajra body, vajra speech, and vajra mind, the bases of the nirmanakaya, sambhogakaya, and dharmakaya.

It is interesting to consider the implications of mind being located in the heart, whereas body is in the head. This was not through ignorance of the brain in ancient India, where the head was considered to be the most important and honored part of the body and where to touch another person's feet with one's head was the greatest sign of respect. Our sense of individual identity as embodied beings, together with the coarse levels of consciousness that depend on the mental functions of the brain, is felt to be in the head. The head is the focus of our experience of embodiment. As the meditator rests more and more in nonconceptual awareness, without the undercurrent of thoughts, emotional disturbances, and sensory distractions, mind in the sense of awareness and insight is felt increasingly to dwell in the heart chakra, the central point of the subtle body.

The third aspect of the subtle body is bindu, the generative impulse, the quintessence of creative potential. It is polarized into male and female forces, the white and red bindus, which are always seeking to meet and unite. In the natural world, they could be regarded as positive and negative charges. On the outermost level, they correspond to sperm and ovum, and on the innermost level to compassion and emptiness, the male and female principles of enlightenment. Another name for bindu is bodhichitta, the awakened mind, produced from the union of emptiness and compassion, and in the symbolic language of the tantras, the male and female sexual fluids are even called the white and red bodhichittas (red symbolizes menstrual blood).

Mind and bindu are very closely related, with bindu as the basis or instigator of all the different kinds of consciousness. Mind is the creator of everything in samsara and nirvana, but bindu is the creative spark. Trungpa Rinpoche described it as being active, searching, and inquisitive, like a radar system. Mind or consciousness observes, watches what is going on, and responds to it. Bindus pervade the subtle body; they are carried around by prana and they gather in the chakras, where they cause the different modes of consciousness to arise. For instance, bindus of the waking state are concentrated mainly in the head chakra, which corresponds to body and the nirmanakaya, so that during normal waking life, we feel that our identity is centered in the head. Bindus of dream gather at the throat chakra, corresponding to speech and the sambhogakaya. Bindus of dreamless sleep dwell in the heart chakra, which is the place of mind and the dharmakaya.

Chakras, nadis, pranas, and bindus are only visualized to the extent that they are required for the purposes of any specific practice. In the transference of consciousness, for instance, the central nadi may begin at the heart or navel chakra and not extend any lower. In certain meditations, the five buddhas may be placed in different chakras, just as they can change places in the mandala circle. In deity yoga, the visualization of the chakras is often extremely detailed, with different deities and mantras on each petal of the lotuses. All the details of colors, number of petals, syllables, and so on vary from practice to practice, so it is impossible to provide an account of the subtle body that applies to every situation.

The subtle body is the dimension of formlessness emerging into form; its manner of appearance is not fixed and cannot be pinned down. The apparent form it takes is brought to life through our own awareness of it and is transformed through yoga practice. In its perfected state, it becomes the body of the deity: the direct experience of ourselves as the chosen deity whose meditation we are engaged in.

The Very Subtle Level

When we come to the very subtle level, there is even less possibility of description in ordinary language. Nevertheless, it is pictured as two white and red bindus of male and female essence, joined together like a closed round casket, in the center of the heart chakra. This is called the indestructible bindu. Within it is the fundamental life energy, the very subtle prana, supporting the very subtle mind, whose nature is luminosity. Here prana corresponds to body, because it serves as the support and vehicle of mind. The two are identical in essence and are only distinguished by their functions: prana relates to the aspect of movement, whereas mind is the aspect of awareness.

The indestructible bindu is eternal and unchanging. It continues from life to life, without beginning and without end. It is the basic nature of our mind and the essence of life, a continuity of luminous awareness. It is bodhichitta, the awakened heart-mind, and it is tathagatagarbha, the intrinsic buddha-nature, which we all possess but of which we are unaware.

We are unable to recognize it because our mind is always occupied with the coarse, outer level of existence. Ordinary consciousness is incapable of perceiving it; only when the coarser levels cease can the more subtle levels become manifest. To attain this very subtle state means that all the relatively coarse aspects of prana and mind must have entered the central nadi and then dissolved into the bindu at the center of the heart. This happens involuntarily at death, so it is said that the luminosity of death appears to all sentient beings, but if they have not become accustomed to it during life, they do not recognize it. Whenever we go to sleep, we sink down into the very subtle level, sometimes returning again into the subtle world of dreams and sometimes remaining in the luminous state of deep, dreamless sleep. Since we cannot recognize and rest in the luminosity, it seems to us as though we lose consciousness. Even for those who can recognize it, the experience of the luminosity of sleep is not as profound or complete as that of death because not all the prana has dissolved; enough remains circulating through the body to keep it alive and breathing.

It is said that a brief glimpse of luminosity also occurs at orgasm, in fainting, and even in sneezing, but again we do not notice it. The special vajrayana practice of sexual union cultivates this potentiality, using the energy of passion and the experience of bliss to intensify awareness and break through all the obstructions to awakening. By this and other methods belonging to the completion stage of deity yoga, the yogin or yogini can consciously undergo the process that occurs at death, culminating in the recognition of luminosity, without the body actually dying. This is the realization of the dharmakaya, the ultimate source of life and of all appearances. From that state, one can then take on a body of form, arising with the body of a deity in the sambhogakaya or with a physical body in the nirmanakaya. This is how one actually manifests the three kayas on the path.

Chapter Ten

The Great Perfection

LIBERATION THROUGH HEARING comes from the Nyingma tradition, the ancient school, which derives its teachings from those brought
to Tibet by Padmakara and his contemporaries in the eighth century.
The final element in part I is a brief introduction to the distinctive
flavor of this tradition and to some of its special features and terminology.

First of all, instead of the three yanas described in chapter I, the
path is divided into nine yanas.[1] The first two are called the *shravakayana*
(the hearers' way) and *pratyekabuddhayana* (the solitary buddhas' way);
they correspond to the level of hinayana. The third is the *bodhisattvayana*
(the bodhisattvas' way), equivalent to mahayana. The other six fall into
the domain of vajrayana. In both old and new traditions, the tantras are
divided into categories of outer and inner. They share the three classes
of outer or lower tantras, which are known as *kriya* (ritual action), *charya*
(conduct or way of life), and *yoga* (union). In the Nyingma tradition,
these categories of tantra form the next three yanas. In Nyingma terminology, the charya class is also known as *ubhaya* (of both kinds) because
it bridges the other two yanas. The new traditions (Kagyü, Sakya, and
Geluk) have only one category of inner or higher tantra: *anuttarayoga*
(highest yoga); to this class belong the well-known tantras such as

Guhyasamaja, Chakrasamvara, Hevajra, and *Kalachakra.* The Nyingma tradition divides the inner tantra class into its three final yanas: *mahayoga* (great yoga), *anuyoga* (further yoga), and *atiyoga* (transcendent yoga).

Mahayoga is mainly concerned with the stage of creation and anuyoga with the stage of completion, while atiyoga takes the practitioner beyond both. Atiyoga contains the special teaching particularly associated with the Nyingma tradition, generally known by its Tibetan name of dzogchen, meaning "the great perfection." It is arranged in three sections on mind, space, and special instructions,[2] which expound the dzogchen view and the practical means of realizing it.

Unfortunately, no original Sanskrit literature relating to dzogchen has survived, or at least none has yet been discovered, and even the name *dzogchen* is found only in Tibetan.[3] Many texts were later discovered as termas, so they were naturally composed in Tibetan and have no Sanskrit counterparts. These teachings were obviously greatly refined and developed within Tibet, but they probably originated in the far northwestern region of ancient India, now Afghanistan and Pakistan, which was a great stronghold of tantra and the birthplace of Padmakara. This area was a meeting place of many cultures and influences; it was conquered by Muslim invaders several centuries before the rest of northern India, so it is not surprising that much has disappeared.

Dzogchen is a teaching of absolute directness and simplicity, going straight to the heart of the Buddha's message. It is the result of the most subtle and profound insight into the ultimate nature of reality and the mind. Again and again, in journeying along the Buddhist path, we find methods designed to bring about a certain experience, but once that experience has been assimilated, we are reminded that it is not the final stage and we must let go of it in order to progress further. Becoming attached to the accomplishment of any stage is like dwelling in a god realm; it is not complete liberation. Dzogchen relies absolutely on the ever-present reality of buddha-nature. It completely roots out the idea that there is any difference between samsara and nirvana, confusion and wisdom; it cuts through all reference points, destroying the duality of experience and experiencer. This is the principle so vividly expressed by the wild and ferocious energy of the wrathful deities.

The technique used in dzogchen is direct mind-to-mind transmission between guru and disciple, pointing out, or identifying, the true nature of mind. This mind always remains the same, no matter what experiences come and go within it. So if one could rest in that state without distraction, there would be no need for other methods. However, it is not enough just to catch a glimpse of this mind essence; it is much more difficult to maintain it continuously. For this purpose, the practices of the two other inner tantras, mahayoga and anuyoga, are used, based on the preparatory foundation of the preceding yanas. Some dzogchen teachers rely solely on atiyoga, which contains its own unique methods to deepen and stabilize one's realization, but this requires exceptional qualities in both teacher and students, as well as a strong karmic connection with this particular path.

We have seen the word *mind* used in many different ways. In general, it covers all possible states of mind, from the undercurrent of confused chatter through logical thought and reason, emotions and sense perceptions, right up to the awakened state. The awakened state is the fundamental, primordial nature of mind, which is also called "mind itself." But in reality there is only one mind, whether it is deluded or awakened, whether it is coarse or subtle, whether it creates samsara or nirvana. It has been said that the only difference between buddhas and ordinary beings is that ordinary beings do not know they are buddhas. However, the very fact that we think of ourselves as ordinary means that we are in a state of confusion instead of enlightenment. That is why there is a need for dharma, with its many different approaches and methods to suit all kinds of natures and abilities.

A very significant term in dzogchen is *awareness* (Sanskrit *vidya*, Tibetan *rig pa*), the ultimate nature of mind and a synonym for the awakened state. It is knowing as a state of being, a direct personal experience, that gives one complete certainty and confidence. It is unobstructed, meaning that it is omniscient and all-pervading: nothing can obscure it, limit it, or get in its way. It is mind's primordial, intrinsic capacity for recognition, for knowing the real nature of things, before ignorance and confusion ever arise. It is beyond thought, free from thought processes or the distinction between mind and its objects. *Vidya* could be translated in several ways. Trungpa Rinpoche sometimes used "insight," and in the *Tibetan Book of the Dead*, we translated it as "intelligence" or "mind," but "awareness" has now become widely adopted and seems to convey the sense of awakened presence as well as knowing.

In Sanskrit, *vidya* derives from a root meaning "to see" and is one of the many words for knowledge; it covers all the arts and sciences, any branch of learning that has a practical application, and especially the secret, magical knowledge of mantras. Sometimes it refers to the mantra itself: knowledge that becomes word, knowledge that is power, a magic spell in the most genuine sense. Vidya as mantra is a statement of truth that has the inherent power to make itself come true, or rather to reveal the unrecognized true state of things that is always present. This kind of knowledge is not worldly magic, but the spiritual magic of transmuting confusion into wisdom. At the very highest level, we realize that sentient beings have always been awakened, so that no transformation has really been necessary or has actually taken place at all. Magical knowledge or awareness is simply the naked, direct seeing of what is. Although it has gone far beyond the duality of knower and known, vidya as it is used in the language of dzogchen has retained its original sense of practical, firsthand experience.

In *Liberation through Hearing*, this ultimate nature of mind is revealed to be the state of luminosity, which the text describes as inseparable emptiness and clarity. The Buddha himself said that mind is luminous, but it is obscured by defilements that are not intrinsic to it. Its true, fundamental nature is luminosity, the most subtle level of mind, abiding in the indestructible bindu in the heart and continuing from life to life. In the mahayana sutras, emptiness alone is presented as the absolute truth, the highest possible description of reality, while the tantras speak much more frequently of luminosity as the essence of mind and all phenomena. As the *Guhyasamaja Tantra* says, "The nature of all things is luminosity, pure from the very beginning, like space."[4]

Emptiness is the mind's aspect of insubstantiality, nonself, spaciousness, and openness, like the boundless sky. Clarity is mind's power to illuminate its objects, which are really nothing but the display of its own luminous nature. These two aspects are sometimes described as objective and subjective perspectives of luminosity: objective luminosity is the emptiness of inherent existence, and subjective luminosity is the clarity that realizes emptiness. But in dzogchen, no distinction is made between subject and object; rather it is said that emptiness is the essence of luminosity, while clarity is its nature or expression.

The luminosity experienced in meditation is called the path luminosity, simile luminosity, or child luminosity. The true luminosity of our awakened nature is called the basic luminosity or mother luminosity; it dawns at the moment of death, and if it is recognized, the mother and child meet and become one in liberation.

Luminosity is often translated as "clear light," which is a literal rendering of the Tibetan rather than the Sanskrit. Trungpa Rinpoche did not like that term, although he did sometimes use it in his talks, which form the basis of his books, because it is so well known. He felt it had become inextricably associated with such notions as the light at the end of the tunnel in near-death experiences, and that it gave too much of an impression of ordinary, visual light, whereas what is meant is an extremely subtle concept that he thought would be conveyed better by "luminosity." The two terms *luminosity* and *clarity* are frequently not distinguished and are translated by the same word in English, so that we find "clear light," "luminosity," or "clarity" for both.[5] They are certainly very close, since clarity here is not just clear and transparent, but also bright and luminous: the illuminating potential of the mind. In the *Tibetan Book of the Dead*, we used only *luminosity*, but on looking at the text very carefully with this in mind, it is evident that it does distinguish between them, and so it now seems best to do so in the revised passages of translation that follow in part 2.

Luminosity is the ever-present background of *Liberation through Hearing*, out of which the visions of the peaceful and wrathful deities appear. In fact, it is at the heart of the experience of bardo. As Trungpa Rinpoche said, it "comes up as subtle gaps of all kinds" in all six realms of existence.[6] It seems frightening because it offers nothing to grasp at or hang on to; "clear light is the sense of desolation of complete open space."[7] If we can let go into it and merge with it so there is no longer any sense of perceiver and perceived, "when clear light ceases to become an experience, then that itself is space."[8]

Space is another basic concept. This does not refer to the ordinary, physical concept of space, but to the space of mind. Trungpa Rinpoche once said that space is the Buddhist version of God. In his commentary on the *Tibetan Book of the Dead*, he wrote that it is a "Book of Space." Space is not different from mind, but it provides a different perspective; it is the environment of mind, inseparable from mind's awareness. Instead of talking in terms of universal or cosmic mind,

which could easily be interpreted as some kind of vaguely theistic notion, there is vast, limitless, open space that cannot be personified or
deified in any way. One cannot pray to it; one cannot please it or anger
it; one cannot even believe or disbelieve in it. It is simply there, the
primordial basis of everything. Because it is completely open and endless, it is impossible to dwell in it or become fixated on it. This absolute
absence of conceptual thought, fabrication, or effort is the particular
quality of dzogchen or atiyoga. The prefix *ati* means "extreme," "transcendent," "beyond." However far we go, we can never arrive at the
end of space, it is always beyond.

When he talked of space, Trungpa Rinpoche was combining several aspects, for which there are different words in both Sanskrit and
Tibetan. First there is *akasha* (Tibetan *nam mkha'*), the fifth great element,
which also means the "sky." As we saw in chapter 5, even in its most
outward manifestation, space is somewhat apart from the other four
elements. It is the most subtle among them, it is imperceptible, and it
contains and supports them all. In some of the early Buddhist philosophical schools, space was classified as a completely pure, unconditioned dharma, equal with nirvana. According to this understanding,
space transcends the material elements, it has no dimensions, and it lies
entirely outside the usual concepts of space and time.

The *Guhyasamaja Tantra* often mentions space in this way. In one
passage, the supreme buddha Vajrasattva teaches all the buddhas and
bodhisattvas that all phenomena (dharmas) are like a dream, yet they
appear to be real through "vajra illusion" and they exist in "vajra space."
Vajra indicates the pure, brilliant, indestructible nature of the awakened
state. The buddhas and bodhisattvas are astonished by this teaching
and exclaim:

> Although phenomena do not exist in themselves, yet their reality
>   is taught;
> Oh, how wonderful is meditation on space within space!

Vajrasattva then explains that even the vajra body, vajra speech,
and vajra mind of enlightened beings are like this. Everything exists in
space, but since space itself does not exist in any of the three worlds—
the world of desire, the world of form, or the formless world—nothing
has really ever arisen. The tantra continues:

Then all the buddhas asked, "Blessed One, where do all enlightened phenomena exist and where are they born?" He answered, "They exist in your body, speech, and mind and they are born from your body, speech, and mind." They asked, "Where does mind exist?" He answered, "In space." They asked, "Where does space exist?" He answered, "Nowhere." At that all the buddhas and bodhisattvas were filled with wonder and amazement. Contemplating their own mind, the dwelling of the ultimate nature of reality, they remained silent.[9]

Next, there is the word *dhatu* (Tibetan *dbyings*), which in Buddhism has the significance of space as an extension of its primary meaning: a fundamental constituent. Here it conveys the idea of the vast expanse of emptiness, openness, and insubstantiality. It is often combined with other words. *Akashadhatu* implies the infinite nature of space. *Jnanadhatu* is the boundless sphere of primordial knowledge, as well as the inseparable unity of knowledge and space. *Vajradhatu* is the dimension of indestructible vajra nature, where nothing can be destroyed precisely because of its essential emptiness. *Dharmadhatu* is that which contains all dharmas: the realm of all phenomena, all-encompassing space; it can also refer to the mind, which is naturally empty like space, yet is the source of all experience.

Finally, there is the Tibetan word *long* (*klong*), which is characteristically dzogchen. Again, it indicates a vast, open expanse, but here it is space experienced from within, free from the duality of subject and object, "the living space of one's being" as Rigdzin Shikpo puts it. No Sanskrit texts have been found to use an equivalent word in the way *long* is used in dzogchen, nor does there seem to be any suitable English word for it. It can mean a wave, which has the sense of both a flowing current and billowing vastness, and it can also mean the center or interior, the idea of being in the midst of something.[10] We can discover these seemingly disparate meanings combined in the imagery of Tibetan paintings. There the deities and gurus are surrounded by an aureole of rays of light, rippling or gently undulating. They represent the ceaseless waves of compassionate energy emanating from selflessness, or "radiation without a radiator," to use an expression of Trungpa Rinpoche's.

This vibrant space is an image of the *long*, and texts often describe a deity as being surrounded by a *long* of the five colors.

The space of the *long* has no center and no boundary. We are in the midst of the space, and we are the space itself. It is a limitless expanse of openness, ceaselessly giving birth to the dynamic flow of appearances. Different kinds of *long* are described in dzogchen, where it forms the subject of a whole section of teachings. It may be filled with energies appearing vividly as light of the five colors, or it may be totally beyond perception or experience of any kind, beyond even the concept of energy.

Combining these various ways of looking at space in the one English word, Trungpa Rinpoche made it a cornerstone of his teaching. He wrote in the commentary to the *Tibetan Book of the Dead*, "Space contains birth and death; space creates the environment in which to behave, breathe and act, it is the fundamental environment which provides the inspiration for this book."[11]

Space is emptiness and luminosity: luminous emptiness. Because it is empty, nothing exists, yet because it is luminous, everything arises from it. As Trungpa Rinpoche said, the dharmakaya arises unnecessarily out of infinite space. Here there is neither samsara nor nirvana, neither self nor other, neither buddhas nor sentient beings. This state is known as primordial purity because it is not stained or obscured by any hint of confusion or dualistic thought; it is the original, pure nature of all existence, which always remains at the heart of all apparent phenomena.

This is the state of Samantabhadra, the primordial buddha of the Nyingma tradition, whose name means Universal Goodness—absolute goodness before the distinction between good and evil ever existed. He is wakefulness that has never needed to become awakened because it has never fallen asleep; he never departs from nondual awareness.

He is inseparably united with the feminine principle, Samantabhadri. She is the space and emptiness that gives birth to all apparent existence. Because he is one with her, he never departs from this source. She is the supreme form of Prajnaparamita, the wisdom of selflessness, so because Samantabhadra is one with her, he never falls into the illusion of self. All the female deities embody this principle; this is their primary meaning, although they may also express other aspects at the same time. The Tibetan for *dakini*, the embodied feminine principle, is

I. The Wheel of Life.

2. The Buddhas of the Five Families.

3. Samantabhadra and Samantabhadri.

4. The Peaceful and Wrathful Deities of the Bardo.

5. Vidyadhara and Dakini.

6. The Wrathful Deities of the Bardo.

7. The Wrathful Deities of the Bardo.

8. Avalokiteshvara in union with consort in the form of Jinasagara in the center, surrounded by five of his other forms, with Hayagriva on his right, a wrathful red dakini on his left, and a mahasiddha above.

khandroma, which means "she who moves through space." In the mandala of the five families, the central devi is Akashadhatvishvari, the Queen of Space. (Further explanations of the feminine principle and the relationship between the male and female buddhas will be found in chapter 12; details of dakinis are in chapter 13).

In the primordial wakefulness that is Samantabhadra, whatever appears is seen as the dance of energy in space, the play of the mind. Dharmakaya manifests as sambhogakaya. Within this inconceivable, vast expanse, the five lights radiate and transform into magical displays. The five dakinis of the elements dance, each with her own special quality. The Blue Dakini of space encompasses the whole universe with her all-embracing gesture. The Green Dakini flies through space, enlivening every particle with vital energy. The Red Dakini blazes with fierce passion, radiating heat and light in all directions. The White Dakini flows with entrancing grace in rivers and oceans, in rain clouds and torrents of water. The Yellow Dakini dances majestically, forming the solid earth and towering mountains. The five lights of knowledge pervade the whole of existence; nothing lies outside them. The ultimate reality of the dharmadhatu is reflected in the clear mirror; transcendent equalness pervades the unique qualities of each separate thing; love spontaneously arises and enlightened action is automatically accomplished.

The condition of ignorance (*avidya*) instead of awareness (*vidya*) comes about through energy breaking away from its origin and becoming isolated. Trungpa Rinpoche describes this as solidifying space. As the splintered energy speeds up, it seems to become solid and substantial, like the effect of a motion picture created by a spinning reel of film. If energy returns to its source, the openness of space, then it is primordial buddha, but if it continues on into confusion, it becomes sentient beings. The whole process of samsara then develops by means of the five skandhas and the twelve links of dependent arising. At a certain point, that intelligent energy becomes self-conscious and begins to notice that it is separate. The absence of ego, which is the empty aspect of space, becomes frozen into a sense of self, while the luminous aspect that gives rise to appearances is mistakenly perceived as other. It is as though awareness has fallen asleep and woken up to a completely different world of duality, so now it believes this is how it has always been.

There is no reason why all this should happen. It is not regarded as evil or shameful, like some kind of original sin; it is simply how things are. And it is not a story of something that took place only once long ago. The development of ego out of awareness is taking place every moment. After all, it is not really possible to solidify space; the whole elaborate illusion is continuously being created and dissolving away again. The basic space of our nature is always present. As *Liberation through Hearing* reminds us, Samantabhadra and Samantabhadri are the essence of our own mind. The discovery of space is the whole purpose of meditation, from the first stages of calming the restless mind to the final attainment of dzogchen, the great perfection.

Life within samsara consists of the six realms; we are continually circling through them from moment to moment as well as from life to life. But the essence of the six realms is space. They are the various ways in which we try to solidify space, the styles by which we express our confusion. Whatever happens takes place within the environment of space, without which nothing could arise. Space is the nonexistence of everything that exists. So whenever there is a sense of grasping and fixation, there is also the possibility of letting go. Whenever there is a sense of being trapped, there is also the possibility of openness and freedom. Whenever there is a sense of tension and solidity, there is also the possibility of relaxation and dissolving. This relaxation is not a state of passivity and inaction but of clear, precise awareness, free from the interference of the confused mind. Energy arising from that spaciousness is unobstructed, without the preconceptions and limitations that the mind imposes. Action becomes spontaneous, free from hesitation and doubt: Trungpa Rinpoche used to say, "Just do it!" This attitude of simply relaxing and resting in the space of one's basic nature is particularly strong in dzogchen. Trungpa Rinpoche's whole approach to dharma was based on it; whatever kind of practice he was teaching, it was always pervaded by the flavor of dzogchen, or ati, as he usually called it.

The final teachings of dzogchen are found in the instructions section of atiyoga. They consist of two stages called cutting through (*trekchö*) and surpassing (*thögal*).[12] These two stages are the basis of the instructions given in *Liberation through Hearing*. They transcend the stages of creation and completion by dissolving every last subtle trace of clinging to self or conceptual thought, even the concept of enlightenment. This is no longer a path of transformation, but of spontaneous self-liberation resulting from direct recognition of reality.

The first stage, cutting through, is sometimes interpreted to mean cutting through what is hard, through obstacles or solidity, but it can also be cutting hard, directly, and fearlessly. In it, the meditator is taught to identify naked awareness, the very basis of mind, as distinct from the operations of mind or consciousness. Thoughts are self-liberated at the moment of their arising, and one remains continuously in the presence of awareness. One recognizes with complete certainty the original, pure, empty nature of all phenomena, beyond both samsara and nirvana, which is known as primordial purity. This means that all the coarse elements and skandhas are self-liberated in their natural state; it is not a question of their being purified or transmuted into that state, but of being recognized as they really are. The practitioner who has accomplished the practice of cutting through can attain the rainbow body: at death, his or her mind merges with the dharmakaya, while the body simply dissolves away into the five colored lights of the subtle elements.

The final stage, surpassing, means crossing over the top or passing above; it could be thought of as reaching the highest point or even passing beyond the summit of realization. Visionary experiences of light spontaneously manifest from the expanse of primordial purity: dazzling rainbows and rays of light, dancing chains of light, circles of the five colors, and spheres of light in which all the peaceful and wrathful deities appear. This is called spontaneous presence or spontaneous accomplishment. There is no longer any need to meditate; these visions are not objects of meditation, but the natural appearances of reality itself, of our own nature, emerging from within and becoming visible to the eye.

While cutting through is a path of wisdom and emptiness, surpassing is a path of skillful means and compassion. The yogin or yogini who accomplishes it attains complete realization in all three kayas and can manifest in a sambhogakaya or nirmanakaya form at will. His or her body becomes a body of light, appearing simply for the sake of others. He or she remains in the awakened state and does not go through birth and death, in other words, does not experience any of the bardos, even though the body may appear to be born and to die like that of an ordinary person. Guru Rinpoche and a few other exceptional people are said to have achieved this; they remain in the world manifesting in many forms, visionary and material, to those who are able to perceive them.

The descriptions of the bardos and the instructions relating to them contained in *Liberation through Hearing* are really meant for people who have practiced cutting through or surpassing to some extent, or at least have gained some experience in the stages of creation and completion. Yet, because the pure state of awareness is the essence of our mind and all the appearances of the deities that arise from it are the expressions of our own nature, we all possess the inherent potentiality to see and recognize them.

A companion text to *Liberation through Hearing,* discovered by Karma Lingpa in the same terma cycle, beautifully presents the dzogchen view. This text is called *Self-Liberation through Naked Sight Pointing Out Awareness.*[13] It gives instructions on how to recognize and remain in the state of supreme awareness, which it describes in great depth. If a practitioner becomes accustomed to that state during life, then he or she will be able to enter it easily at death. Therefore, besides being an ecstatic poem on the nature of mind, this text provides a teaching on the most profound level in relation to *Liberation through Hearing.* I have translated some short passages from it to give an idea of the dzogchen approach. It begins by stating the fundamental point that confused mind and awakened mind are one and the same in essence, and that all the different paths within Buddhism lead to the same end, the recognition of the true nature of mind:

> Wonderful!
> One mind encompasses the whole of samsara and nirvana.
> It is one's own nature from the very beginning, yet it is not
> recognized.
> Its clarity and awareness flow unceasingly, yet it is not met face-
> to-face.
> Dawning without obstruction everywhere, its reality is not
> grasped.

Just so that this itself may recognize itself,
All the inconceivable eighty-four thousand doors to dharma
Are taught by the buddhas of past, present, and future.
The buddhas have taught nothing at all
Except the realization of this itself.

It is important to remember that in Buddhism "one mind" does not imply any kind of cosmic entity or substance. It simply refers to the illuminating, knowing faculty of mind, which is the same whether it proceeds in accordance with truth, which creates nirvana, or in a distorted fashion, which creates samsara. It cannot accurately be called either individual or universal, either personal or impersonal, because such distinctions do not apply to it. This mind contains the whole spectrum of the awakened state: its essential emptiness, its radiant energy and its unceasing manifestation (see "The Trikaya" in chapter 9).

Within it the trikaya is indivisible and complete in one:
Emptiness where nothing whatever exists is the dharmakaya,
Clarity, the inner radiance of emptiness, is the sambhogakaya,
Dawning everywhere without obstruction is the nirmanakaya,
These three complete in one are its intrinsic nature.

Since our own mind is inherently buddha, all we really need to do is to recognize and rest in our true nature. From this point of view, the awakened state is our own perfectly ordinary mind, our everyday experience. Yet, even after it has been shown to us, we seem unable to retain that realization. Our very attempts to do so get in our way, because they miss the point. We start by making efforts to change ourselves, to find something, or to attain some goal, but these very efforts become counterproductive. In the ultimate sense, there is really nothing to do and nothing to change. Yet we start to have doubts and feel we are unable to achieve anything. We despair at getting nowhere, when really there is nowhere to go. This paradox is highlighted with a series of questions designed to shock us into seeing the absurdity of the whole situation:

When the powerful method of entering into this itself is pointed out,
Your own self-knowledge in the present moment is just this!
Your own uncontrived self-illumination is just this,

So why say you can't realize the nature of mind?
There's nothing at all to meditate on within it,
So why say nothing happens when you meditate?
Your own direct experience of awareness is just this,
So why say you can't find your own mind?
Uninterrupted awareness and clarity are just this,
So why say you can't recognize your mind?
The one who thinks about the mind is the mind itself,
So why say you can't find it even if you look?
There's nothing at all to be done to it,
So why say nothing happens whatever you do?
It only needs to be left naturally in its own place,
So why say it will not stay still?
It only needs to be left at ease, doing nothing,
So why say you cannot do that?
Clarity, awareness, and emptiness inseparable are spontaneously
    present,
So why say your practice is not successful?
Spontaneously self-arisen without cause or condition,
So why say you cannot even if you try?
Thoughts are freed instantaneously as soon as they arise,
So why say antidotes have no power?
Knowing in the present moment is just this,
So why say you do not know it?

This passage is full of typical dzogchen terms such as self-knowledge, self-awareness, self-illumination, and so on. They are ambiguous,
and it is sometimes difficult to decide which aspect to bring out in
translation. The word used here for "self" (Sanskrit *sva*, Tibetan *rang*)
also means "one's own," so in some contexts, it seems appropriate to
emphasize that it is our own mind, our own clarity, our own awareness.
These qualities are not created by anyone, they do not come from
anywhere else, and they do not need to be acquired or improved upon
in any way. That is why we often find translations such as "natural,"
"inherent," or "intrinsic." However, there is more to it than this. In
ordinary usage, self-knowledge implies knowledge of one's inner condition as distinct from knowledge of the external world; but here, what-

ever one knows, perceives, or experiences is recognized as being within the mind and is therefore self-knowledge (*rang shes*). Whatever the mind experiences, it is experiencing itself. The clarity of the mind causes appearances to arise and become visible; this is called self-clarity or self-illumination (*rang gsal*). The phenomena that arise are the mind itself, although they seem to be external; they are known as self-appearance or self-display (*rang snang*). Self-awareness (*rang rig*) in particular refers to the fundamental, innate knowing of reality. It is awareness of the inseparability of emptiness and appearances: the mind being aware of its own creations, of the play between perceiver and perceived, and at the same time being aware of that awareness. Dzogchen also uses the significant term *self-liberation* (*rang grol*), which we discussed in chapter 2. Everything that seems to bind us and delude us comes from our own mistaken perception; mind has constructed its own prison and its own web of deception. So as soon as the true nature of mind is realized, it is seen to have always been essentially free; in that instant, it liberates itself by its own power. The text urges us to look carefully at our own mind and ascertain that this is indeed true:

> It is certain that the nature of mind is empty, without foundation:
> Your mind is nonexistent like empty space.
> Look at your own mind! Is it like that or not?
> It is certain that whatever appears is all self-display:
> Arising of itself as an appearance, like an image in a mirror.
> Look at your own mind! Is it like that or not?
> It is certain that all qualities are spontaneously self-liberated:
> Self-produced and self-liberated like clouds in the sky.
> Look at your own mind! Is it like that or not?

To understand this whole concept, it is not enough just to think or feel that nothing is real or it's all in the mind; it takes a deep and genuine insight into the essence of what mind really is. This is why the teachings on emptiness and nonself are emphasized so strongly before anything else. Fundamental mind itself, the source of all this display, is not "my mind" or "your mind" in the limited, egocentric sense. The entire illusion of self and other takes place within mind, which encompasses them both. But as long as we still believe in a separate self and a world outside, the illusion is certainly real on its own terms. To say that everything is mind from that standpoint would be madness. Dzogchen practitioners are renowned for being extremely practical and down-to-earth. Longchenpa, a great teacher of the fourteenth century, would laugh at people who held idealist philosophical views, saying that of course the external world is real! With the realization of self-awareness, everything is seen to be real in an entirely different way, as the expression of the awakened nature. In between these two views of life, there is the period of transmutation, filled with paradox and ambiguity. We need to establish, through direct personal experience, the different stages of insight that lead to the ultimate state.

Trungpa Rinpoche used to say that the practice of vajrayana is based on abandoning the hope of attaining nirvana and the fear of remaining in samsara. He called this attitude hopelessness, and he described the entire life and teaching of Padmakara as an illustration of hopelessness. For most people, including great saints like Naropa and Milarepa, hopelessness really means the utter despair of losing all hope, hitting rock bottom, before we are able to accept the simple and obvious truth. If what we are seeking is already within us, if our own nature is already awakened, then searching anywhere else can only take us further away from it. The intensity of our hopelessness, its complete-ness and genuineness, determines whether we can make the leap into immediate, direct recognition, or whether we need to follow the more gradual path of transformation. During the creation stage of vajrayana, one practices with the attitude that the result is already accomplished, so that the hope of success and the fear of failure wear themselves out gradually. This conviction is the way to overcome spiritual materialism, the grasping attitude that sees enlightenment as a prize to be won at the end of the journey. With trust and confidence in the ever-present reality of buddha-nature, the path becomes a continual process of redis-covery, an unveiling of what is already fully present, instead of a diffi-cult journey to a far-distant goal.

> How strange that it is unknown, although it is present everywhere!
> How strange to hope for a different fruit, other than this!
> How strange to seek it elsewhere, although it is oneself!
> Wonderful!
> This, aware in the present moment, clear yet insubstantial,

Just this is the summit of all views!
This, without object of thought, all-encompassing yet free
    from all,
Just this is the summit of all meditation!
This, that is called natural, worldly, and relaxed,
Just this is the summit of all conduct!
This, unsought, spontaneously existent from the very beginning,
Just this is the summit of all fruition!

The attainment of enlightenment may seem to be nothing special at all; those who have reached it appear to live in a completely ordinary, worldly way, not even meditating, with no sense of having achieved anything. A dzogchen practitioner's ideal state of being is totally natural; it combines focused awareness with effortless relaxation. From this standpoint, all meditation is contrived and all practices are artificial. Trying to attain liberation by means of them is like a snake winding itself into tighter and tighter knots instead of uncoiling effortlessly into space. One should simply rest naturally and spontaneously in the basic nature of mind. There is a story about a lama called Zurchungpa that illustrates the continuous state of one-pointed awareness this requires. He was being questioned by a student of a different tradition who asked, "In dzogchen, isn't meditation considered the most important thing?" Zurchungpa answered, "What is there to meditate upon?" So the questioner inquired, "Well then, don't you ever meditate?" To which Zurchungpa replied, "What is there that ever distracts me?"

Since there is nothing to meditate upon, not meditating on
    anything at all,
Since there is nothing to be distracted by, stable in undistracted
    mindfulness,
Nakedly look into the state of nonmeditation and nondistraction.
Self-awareness, self-knowing, self-illuminating, clearly shines:
That very dawn is called the awakened mind.

If one has really seen deeply enough into the nature of mind and is able to rest in that state, then it becomes possible to use all the sense perceptions and every experience in life to increase one's realization. Without ever losing sight of the basic emptiness of mind, whatever happens is recognized as the display of its luminous aspect. This is the case during our everyday waking state, during dreams, and also after death during the bardo. It becomes especially important to recognize when the visions of the bardo appear. If we have become accustomed to recognizing whatever arises as an expression of the luminous and empty nature of our own mind, then we will not be taken in by any appearances, however overwhelming or terrifying they may be.

> Awareness of all appearances as mind, without grasping,
> Is awakened, even though seeing and seen arise.
> Appearances are not mistaken, error comes through grasping;
> Knowing the grasping thought as mind, it is self-liberated.

The text continues:

> There is no appearance that is not known to originate from mind,
> Whatever appearance arises is mind itself, unobstructed.
> Although it arises, like water and waves of the ocean,
> Since they are not two, it is freed in the nature of mind.

Our intrinsic essence is a state of the greatest simplicity, yet during the process of unveiling it, we have to work with the complexity and confusion of our minds as they are at present. It may seem that teachings like this one actually encourage us not to meditate or do any formal practice at all. However, the lives of the great dzogchen teachers show that they generally spent many years in retreat and made tremendous efforts before they attained the spontaneous state of natural awareness. In addition, their biographies reveal that they had extraordinary faith and devotion toward their gurus and great respect for all the stages of the path. There may be a few rare people who, as a result of practice in their previous lives, can penetrate straight to the essence in a short time, but the great majority of us need to go through a longer period of preparation. To rest in the state of nonmeditation and nondistraction, we have to practice conventional meditation first, otherwise we just remain under the influence of distraction whether we are aware of it or not. As the text says:

> All beings are in reality the awakened essence,
> But without actually practicing they will not awaken.

Even if we cannot realize that essence at present, simply knowing about it and having faith in it make an enormous difference. These wonderful teachings are like the sun on a cloudy day: we can have complete confidence that the sun is always there behind the clouds. The dzogchen view can subtly permeate the entire path, whatever practice we are engaged in and whatever stage we have reached. The text concludes with this parting advice:

> To see your own awareness nakedly and directly,
> This *Self-Liberation through Naked Sight* is most profound,
> So get to know this itself, your own self-awareness!

Part Two

THE TEXT

Chapter Eleven

Luminosity of Death

ALL THE BASIC IDEAS that lie behind *Liberation through Hearing* were presented in part I, so now we can look at the text in detail in light of these principles. It opens with a verse of praise and devotion to the trikaya, the threefold being of the awakened state.

> Amitabha, infinite light, the dharmakaya;
> Peaceful and wrathful lotus deities, the sambhogakaya;
> Padmakara, incarnate as the protector of beings;
> Homage to the gurus, the three kayas.

This invocation sets the scene for the whole teaching that is to follow. Although this teaching deals with death, the most feared eventuality of our whole existence, with the terrifying apparitions of the period after death, and with the disturbing possibilities of rebirth, it is all completely pervaded by the infinite love and compassion of the awakened state. The Buddha Amitabha, who presides over the Padma (Lotus) family, embodies the principle of compassion, expressed as boundless, radiant light. This is the aspect of enlightenment to which we can most easily connect, especially at times of distress and danger. Because of this, a large number of the practices relating to death developed in the context of devotion to Amitabha. His own pure land is known as

Sukhavati, the Blissful, in Tibetan Dewachen, and is the goal of many mahayana Buddhists after death. Other practices for attaining longevity are centered on Amitabha in the slightly different form of Amitayus, whose name means Infinite Life instead of Infinite Light. Although it is quite legitimate to wish to extend one's human life, the inner meaning of such practices is actually to attain the state of awareness that transcends the very concept of birth and death.

In this verse, Amitabha represents the dharmakaya, even though he usually appears as one of the sambhogakaya buddhas. This is to emphasize the central place of compassion. Sometimes Samantabhadra, who is normally the dharmakaya buddha in the Nyingma tradition, is shown with a red body instead of his usual blue color to indicate his unity with the principle of Amitabha. The dharmakaya is the highest, formless aspect of the guru. Since it is the innermost essence of all beings, it is the universal guru in the ultimate sense, the infinite light dwelling in the heart of all beings.

The sambhogakaya is represented by the mandala of the peaceful and wrathful lotus deities. These are all the various manifestations of enlightenment, male and female, that appear in visionary forms of light during the bardo. Here they are all seen as emanating from Amitabha, radiating the boundless love of the Padma family. The sambhogakaya is the level of communication, inspiration, and transmission, the very nature of the guru principle; it is the divine form of the guru. When the minds of the teacher and the student meet and become one, everything is seen with the eyes of sacred vision; the entire world becomes a mandala of deities arising spontaneously as the expression of the guru's mind. As Trungpa Rinpoche wrote: "The whole of existence is freed and becomes the guru."[1]

Padmakara (Padmasambhava) is the manifestation of Amitabha on the level of the nirmanakaya. Even his name, the Lotus-Born, connects him with Amitabha. He is the perfect exemplar of the guru in human form; that is why he is known as Guru Rinpoche, the Precious Guru. He is the protector of all beings because he possesses the supreme power of dispelling their illusion and awakening them to their own true nature. As the composer and concealer of termas, he is the original human source of *Liberation through Hearing*. By paying homage to him at the start, the reader or listener establishes a direct connection with him.

The last line, "Homage to the gurus, the three kayas," can be taken, as already described, to refer to each of the three kayas in turn as the guru. It could also be taken in a slightly different way to mean homage to all the gurus of the past, present, and future, especially to the great figures of this particular lineage, as well as to one's own spiritual teacher here and now, who are all regarded as manifestations of the complete trikaya. The guru is the embodiment of dharmakaya, sambhogakaya, and nirmanakaya. As we saw in chapter 9, the three kayas are aspects of the path, which is really the whole of daily life. Trungpa Rinpoche described the life and teaching of Padmakara as the living expression of the trikaya: the sense of totality and spaciousness of the dharmakaya, the energy and play of the sambhogakaya, and the practical activity of the nirmanakaya. The trikaya principle also lies at the heart of *Liberation through Hearing*, which we are about to explore.

Liberation through Hearing takes as its subject matter three out of the traditional six bardo states: the bardo of dying, the bardo of dharmata, and the bardo of existence.[2] Its real purpose is guidance during the further stages of the after-death experience; the first section dealing with the bardo of dying is very brief. This section also seems less clear than the rest of the text, as though the reader is expected to be able to fill in the gaps with additional information. There are indeed numerous other teachings relating to the process of dying and to different ways of preparing for death. In particular, a follower of this tradition would be familiar with *Self-Liberation through Signs and Omens of Death,*[3] another text from the same terma cycle.

Literally, the name of this bardo means "the time of death." It is generally taken to include the whole process of dying, beginning at the onset of terminal illness or injury or whatever is the direct cause of death, up to the moment when the most subtle aspect of mind and life force leaves the body. In the case of a long illness, this would refer especially to its final phase, when the dying person undergoes a change in the quality of consciousness. However, some explanations focus only on the final moment, when the mind enters the state of luminosity and has the possibility of complete liberation. This was Trungpa Rinpoche's interpretation, and it is also the main focus of the instructions in

Liberation through Hearing, so in our translation, we called it "the bardo of the moment before death." Here I prefer to take it in its wider sense and call it the bardo of dying.

As we have seen, Buddhism regards the whole of our existence as a succession of births and deaths. On whatever scale we look at it—from life to life, from day to day, or from moment to moment—the conditions of each "life" are determined by the karmic forces set in motion by the previous one. Although innumerable influences are constantly at work within the mindstream, our state of mind during the last moments before death is particularly important in deciding the direction our future will take.

Karmic results are classified into four different degrees of strength. The strongest is called "heavy karma," which can be either negative or positive. Negative heavy karma results from the five extreme actions of murdering one's mother, one's father, or a realized person who is close to enlightenment (technically, an *arhat*); injuring a buddha (a fully awakened person who is beyond birth and death and so cannot truly be killed); and deliberately causing serious dissension within the spiritual community (the *sangha*). These actions are so destructive and so opposed to the basic goodness of our nature that they will come to the fore and dominate the mindstream if they have not been repented and purified during this life. There can also be positive heavy karma resulting from the attainment of certain meditative states, which will exert a powerful influence for good. If there is no heavy karma in the mindstream, then the karma of the period just before death—our final thoughts, words, and deeds—becomes the most significant. Next in importance is the habitual karma of our whole lifetime, and this of course is highly likely to influence the mood of our final moments. Lastly, karma from our previous lives also may have some effect in determining our future rebirth.

If we are fortunate enough to live in a culture where the approach of death is accepted and acknowledged as a great opportunity, or if we have friends with that attitude who will support us, our natural fear can be transformed into a source of inspiration. In Buddhist cultures, it is considered a great blessing to know in advance of our impending death so that we can prepare for it. *Self-Liberation through Signs and Omens of Death* is devoted entirely to this subject; it describes methods of foretelling death months and even years ahead by observing physical symptoms, analyzing dreams, and performing divinations. Another companion text provides methods for what is called cheating death—turning it away, if it is not already inevitable, with practices for purification and longevity. Sooner or later, death is certain, yet it is perfectly right and proper to delay it so that we can make the best use of whatever time we have left. If, after doing such practices, the signs of impending death are still seen to be present, then we are urged to start training in one of the specific practices for dying. Before considering the instructions given in the text, let us look at the actual process of what happens when we die.

Death occurs either when a fatal illness or accident destroys the vital force or when the karmic impetus that determines our natural life span is exhausted. Dying is described as a process of dissolving from the densest and heaviest to the finest and most subtle levels of our being. First, there is the outer dissolution of the four elements that compose the physical body—earth, water, fire, and air—and then the inner dissolution of states of mind. Essentially, what happens at death is that all our vital energy or prana returns to its source: it is reabsorbed into the central nadi and then into the indestructible bindu at the center of the heart. One way of defining death is the separation of the coarse and subtle bodies. As the process of reabsorption takes place, the subtle body is no longer able to maintain the functioning of the coarse physical body. One by one, the five primary and secondary pranas withdraw, the knots of the chakras fall apart, and the elements dissolve; as a result, the bodily functions and the senses begin to fail.

In his commentary, Trungpa Rinpoche explained the dying process in terms of the uncertainty, fear, and confusion we experience as we go through the stages of dissolution. We are leaving behind the real, solid, dualistic world of the living and entering the unreal, shifting, ghostly world of the dead: "the graveyard that exists in the midst of fog." As we would expect, this does not apply only to impending death in the literal sense, but also to the continual occurrence of dissolution in everyday life. Our experience of life is based on duality—self and other, subject and object, good and bad, pleasure and pain; this is the cause of all our confusion. We are programmed in this way by the skandhas, so this mode of experience is what we consider real; it has become the criterion by which we judge reality. When the elements dissolve at death, the whole structure on which our dualistic perception of the world is based begins to crumble away, and our sense of identity is undermined. We shall see examples of how this may happen at each stage of the dissolution process. As the senses deteriorate, the boundary between inside and outside that preserves our identity becomes tenuous, confused, and distorted and ultimately breaks down completely. Even in the echoes of these experiences that occur during life, we can feel equally lost and bewildered; we may begin to doubt our existence and fear that we are losing our sanity.

Yet at the same time, the loss of ego that is forced on us presents us with continual opportunities to let go into clear, open space until we reach the luminosity of our basic nature. The problem does not lie in duality itself; it lies in the fact that we experience duality in an incomplete and biased manner—we identify with one side and reject or grasp at the other. "But if we are completely in touch with these dualistic feelings, that absolute experience of duality is itself the experience of nonduality. Then there is no problem at all, because duality is seen from a perfectly open and clear point of view in which there is no conflict; there is a tremendous encompassing vision of oneness."⁴ Or, as it says in *Self-Liberation through Naked Sight*,

> Appearances are not mistaken, error comes through grasping,
> Knowing the grasping thought as mind, it is self-liberated.

By learning to view the world in such a way, we can experience duality as it really is, fully and completely, so that it is transformed into the all-embracing totality of the awakened state. The practitioner who has stabilized this realization is able to view with equanimity the disintegration of the body and the coarse levels of mind, confident in the natural, innate state of luminosity and emptiness.

This whole process can be observed by outward changes that take place in the body and also by inner sensations experienced by the dying person. As one becomes increasingly disconnected from the external world, awareness of internal states grows stronger. During this period, there are also secret signs in the form of appearances of light within the mind; they are called secret because most people do not even notice them, but they are extremely significant to the trained meditator. They indicate that as the coarser levels of being dissolve, the subtler levels become manifest, until at last the most subtle essence is revealed. These signs are confused glimpses of luminosity, the basic nature of mind, gradually becoming clearer and clearer as the layers of density dissolve away. There are many different signs that may appear both at death and during the yoga that replicates the process of dying; the traditional list of eight signs given here includes only the best known of them.

The series of dissolutions may take place over a relatively long period of time, or it may be extremely quick; in cases of sudden death, it occurs instantaneously, so the different stages cannot be distinguished. In any case, the stages may overlap and the sequence may vary according to people's individual constitutions. There are several traditional descriptions of the whole process, each emphasizing certain aspects and paying less attention to others, and they contain some differences in the details that occur during the sequence of dissolutions. The description that follows is taken from several sources and tries to cover the whole process as coherently as possible, but it can only be a rough guideline. One is not meant to feel that everything must happen in this particular order, but it is very helpful to become accustomed to the general pattern of events so as to prepare oneself and lessen the fear of dying.

First comes the series of outer dissolutions, which affects the physical body and the levels of consciousness associated with it. This does not imply that the body decays immediately, but simply that the vital forces keeping it alive are extinguished. The energy of each element dissolves into the next, more subtle one. As this takes place, the dying person first experiences an intensification of the original element's characteristics, and then, as it dissolves, the qualities of the following element take over and are briefly enhanced. Each of the elements is linked with one of the senses, one of the skandhas, and one of the basic forms of the transcendent knowledge of the five buddhas. Here they are called basic because they exist already within us as our basic nature. Since we do not recognize our ordinary consciousness as transcendent knowledge, we only manifest these aspects in the limited, dualistic manner of samsaric existence. All of them dissolve at the same time as the elements. We should note that in the stages described here the correlation of senses with elements is different from that given in chapter 5, where it was observed that almost any combination can be found in various contexts. Once again, we should remember that these correspondences are not fixed; they are simply patterns in the dance of creation and dissolution that is taking place continuously in mind and body.

The first stage is the dissolution of earth into water. Earth provides the solid structure of the body, our flesh, bones, and muscle. As the process of dissolution begins, the qualities of earth become overpowering; we may feel extremely heavy, as though we are sinking into the ground, or that we are being crushed by its weight. Then, as the earth qualities of solidity and substantiality decrease, our limbs can no longer support us, and we feel weak and exhausted. It is often noticeable in those who are close to death that the body shrinks into itself and becomes smaller. The navel chakra disintegrates, and the equal energy withdraws. The equal energy regulates the digestive system and circulates inner heat, so with its disappearance, these functions slow down. The body can no longer metabolize nourishment, and it begins to lose its internal warmth.

Earth is associated with the skandha of form, which provides the basis for our sense of material existence. As its power declines, everything appears unstable; we begin to lose our ground and our support; our whole world is being swept away from under our feet. Mentally, too, there is a sinking sensation; the dying person feels depressed, bewildered, and overwhelmed with heaviness. It is possible to have a foretaste of this sensation during life; there is a sense of losing touch with reality, as though one is entering into a process that could eventually lead to complete disintegration. As Trungpa Rinpoche put it, "the tangible quality of physical, living logic becomes vague." All the descriptions of what happens at death are relevant to us here and now, if we look carefully into our experience.

As the energy of earth merges into the energy of water, the body begins to feel almost liquid instead of firm and solid. Sometimes we experience this same sensation at moments of fear or anxiety: it is as if our limbs turn to water. The sense of sight, through which we perceive forms, deteriorates, and vision becomes blurred; everything seems to swim before our eyes. Earth is associated with the basic mirror knowledge, which reflects all the objects of the senses and enables us to hold everything clearly in our mind. Without this capacity, the confused mass of people and things surrounding us is too much to take in, as we begin to lose our visual and mental clarity. The mind becomes dull and cloudy like a mirror that has lost its luster. The brightness and glow of the complexion, too, begin to fade away.

The reader may notice an inconsistency here: in chapter 7, we saw that earth is connected with Ratnasambhava, who dwells in the navel chakra, while form and the mirror knowledge belong to Akshobhya, who dwells in the heart. But in this case, the connection comes about through the female buddhas, the devis. The five devis are the essence of the five elements, although the male buddhas also have their own independent associations with the elements. The devi Buddha-Lochana is the essence of earth, and she, as we shall see in the next chapter, is the consort of Akshobhya. Here it is as though she, as the element of earth, takes over certain of her consort's attributes.

The secret sign of this stage, visible to experienced meditators although not to most people, is an appearance like a mirage. Shimmering and unsubstantial, a mirage is a perfect image of the solidity of earth melting into the fluidity of water. Yet this vision is neither earth nor water, but only light: the first gleam of the mind's natural luminosity.

Next, the element of water dissolves into fire, accompanied by the disappearance of the skandha of feeling and the basic equalizing knowledge. The heart chakra disintegrates, and the life energy is reabsorbed. Here again we find a mixture of attributes—in this case, the reverse of the previous situation. Akshobhya dwells in the heart chakra and is connected with water, but the devi Mamaki, who is the essence of water, is the consort of Ratnasambhava, who embodies the equalizing knowledge and the skandha of feeling, so it is Ratnasambhava's attributes that predominate here rather than Akshobhya's.

At first, as the qualities of the element are intensified, the dying person experiences sensations of being saturated with water or carried away by a flood. Fluids may be discharged from the bodily apertures, then, when the energy of water decreases, the liquid constituents of the body begin to dry up and the skin becomes desiccated. The circulatory systems of blood and lymph slow down. The mouth, tongue, and nose dry out, and the dying person feels very thirsty. At this stage, the sense of hearing begins to degenerate; external sounds can no longer be distinguished clearly, and the low, inner humming that is sometimes heard within the ears is no longer present.

The skandha of feeling enables us to react to sense impressions, while our feelings of relative pleasure, pain, and indifference depend upon the basic equalizing knowledge. As their power wanes, we begin to lose this kind of responsiveness. Sensations are dulled and feelings no longer seem so important; we become indifferent, detached from the world outside, and we sink further into our own private, inner world; in Trungpa Rinpoche's words, "you reassure yourself that your mind is still functioning." This stage is sometimes paralleled in ordinary life during periods of aridity and hopelessness, when we feel completely dried up, shriveled and unable to flow with the rhythms and changes of life. At the same time, the dying person may become nervous and irritable, losing the sense of balance bestowed by the equalizing knowledge. With the withdrawal of the life energy, vitality seeps away and the mind becomes unclear, confused, and fearful.

The secret sign appearing to the mind's eye as the energy of water merges into the energy of fire is something like smoke that seems to swirl all around one. This, too, is a partial vision of the luminosity of the mind, still hazy and obscured.

At the third stage, fire dissolves into air, along with the skandha of perception and the basic investigative knowledge. The devi Pandaravasini is the essence of fire and her consort is Amitabha, who dwells in the throat chakra and also embodies fire, so this time there is no discrepancy between the attributes of the male and female buddhas. As the throat chakra disintegrates, the descending energy withdraws. (This sequence follows the less usual scheme, in which the descending energy is stationed at the throat and the ascending energy at the secret place. See chapter 9.)

Initially, the dying person feels hot and feverish and may imagine that the whole environment is burning, but then, as the energy of fire is absorbed, the body loses its warmth and the limbs grow cold. The descending energy regulates urination and excretion, so control over these functions may be lost. The sense of smell starts to deteriorate. Separation from the skandha of perception means that we lose the ability to identify and define the information we receive from the senses.

Without the basic investigative knowledge, we find difficulty in distinguishing the various people and things around us, and eventually we cannot even recognize our loved ones anymore. We try to connect with "the fiery temperature of love and hate," but their flames grow increasingly faint. There is a sense of great confusion, of the mind becoming alternately clear and unclear, and of increasing detachment from this life. The secret sign that fire has dissolved into air is the appearance of sparkling lights all around, like fireflies or red sparks flying up from a fire.

The fourth stage is the dissolution of air, the skandha of conditioning, and the basic action-accomplishing knowledge, along with the disintegration of the secret-place chakra and reabsorption of the ascending energy. Here again, there is no problem of consistency between the devi Tara, the essence of air, and her consort Amoghasiddhi, who dwells in the chakra of the secret place.

The skandha of conditioning is the root of action, the characteristic patterning of concepts and emotions on which our life is based. When it disappears, the dying person loses all motivation and sense of purpose; it is as though one's programming has run down. Without the basic action-accomplishing knowledge, there is no longer any ability to perform actions. The ascending energy enables breathing and swallowing to take place, so these are both affected. Inhalation becomes short and rough, while exhalation is long and sighing, as though all one's breath is returning to the atmosphere from which it came. The sense of taste is lost, and one can no longer eat or drink. There may be sensations of floating and of being blown about in a strong wind; then, as breathing becomes more and more difficult, one may have the feeling of being crushed and suffocated.

In the usual sequence of the five elements, air is followed by space, so we would expect to find that air dissolves into space. Generally, however, it is said that air dissolves into consciousness, the skandha associated with space, and after that consciousness dissolves into space. The secret sign of the dissolution of air is like a candle flame, which in Tibetan texts is always called the flame of a butter lamp. The flame is variously described as guttering on the point of going out, burning low and steadily as though in a windless place, or blazing brightly.

Feelings of extreme dissociation and being disembodied, which are linked with this stage, can be experienced during life, especially under the influence of drugs. They may be felt as the onset of insanity or as its opposite, the entry into mystical experience, the final step before letting go of the self. All these experiences of dissolution, from the first feeling of losing one's ground to the sensation of disembodiment, are part of the inevitable, necessary decay of our ego-centered material nature. At the same time, the secret signs appearing to the mind that is trained to recognize them reveal the ever-closer approach to our luminous spiritual nature. At first, as we go through the stages of dissolution, it appears only as a mirage, shifting and illusory, veiled by our attachment to the physical world. Then it turns into a smoky haze, still vague and indistinct. Next, we start to perceive fiery sparks emerging from the smoke, scintillating points of light that draw us closer, until finally they merge into a single flame.

Now the dying person may have visions of various kinds; whether they are comforting or disturbing depends upon one's previous actions and the thoughts that predominate in the mind. Those who have led violent lives may feel that they are surrounded by frightening, vengeful figures, while those who have led good lives are welcomed by friendly faces. Religious people may see deities, angels, or their spiritual teachers coming to meet them.

When the dissolution of the four outer elements is complete, consciousness begins to dissolve into space, the dimension of unbounded openness and emptiness. The chakra associated with consciousness and space is either the forehead or the crown chakra, the dwelling of Vairochana and Akashadhatvishvari, the Queen of Space. As it disintegrates, the basic all-encompassing knowledge and the sense of touch also disappear. The pervading energy, which is diffused throughout the whole body and causes movement, is reabsorbed, so that the body becomes motionless and rigid. Once the withdrawal of all aspects of prana into the central nadi is completed, respiration ceases with a final exhalation, and externally the dying person now appears to be dead.

There is some ambiguity about the sequence of events at this point, the junction between the inner and outer series of dissolutions. Many accounts include the disappearance of the sense of touch in the previous stage, while according to others, all five senses dissolve together either at the beginning or at the end of the dissolution of the elements. In practice, in cases of natural death, there generally seems to be a gradual closing down of sensory perception. But the whole process is extremely subjective and variable, and it is impossible to pin it down in precise detail.

Now the process of inner dissolution takes place. As individual living beings, we are created from the male and female essences produced by our parents when we were conceived, which remain throughout our lives as white and red bindus held at either end of the central nadi, avadhuti. Now they return to the heart center from which they originated and join together again as they did at the time of conception. At the same time, all the subtle states of mind related to aggression, passion, and delusion cease. These are called the eighty instincts, a collection of primary emotional states arising from the fundamental three poisons.[5] They are not all expressions of aggression, passion, and delusion in any obvious way, but can be described better as the basic energies of rejection, attraction, and indifference, moving from those that are coarser, more dualistic, and require a greater level of energy to those that are subtler, less dualistic, and require less energy. According to some traditions, the eighty instincts all dissolve together at the beginning of the inner process, but according to the Nyingma teachings, they dissolve in three stages. The mind of the dying person is pervaded in turn by a sense of whiteness, redness, and blackness: its own luminosity glimpsed as though through filters tinged by the colors of the three poisons.

First, all the prana that has entered the upper part of avadhuti moves down to the heart, and with it the white bindu received from the father descends from the crown of the head. At the same time, the thirty-three instincts arising from aggression also dissolve. The mind is filled with brilliant white light, like a clear sky flooded with moonlight. Some texts also mention a series of additional signs similar to those that appeared earlier, in this case, a mirage or smoke.

Next, all the prana that has entered the lower part of avadhuti ascends to the heart, along with the red female bindu received from the mother. According to different teachings, the red bindu is said to dwell in the navel chakra, at a point four finger widths below the navel, or in the secret place at the genitals. The forty instincts arising from passion dissolve. The mind is filled with red radiance, like the sky at sunrise or sunset, and there also may be a sign like sparks or fireflies.

It is not completely certain which of the two bindus, with their associated colors of light, will move to the heart chakra first. Sometimes they are reversed, depending on the constitution of the individual. Several accounts have the red first and then the white, but in the yoga practice, it seems to be more usual to experience the white first. Again, some traditions associate passion with the white phase and aggression with the red. Some sources suggest that the outer respiration may not have entirely ceased and the visions of welcoming figures may be seen at this time; others state that even at this late stage it may still be possible for the dying person to revive under exceptional circumstances. Tibetans believe that this is the explanation for certain near-death experiences such as meeting loved ones or seeing a brilliant light, but they are quite definite that it is not possible to return to life after reaching the final state of luminosity itself.

After this, the male and female bindus join together at the heart, enclosing between them the indestructible bindu that dwells there, and the remaining subtle emotional states, the seven instincts relating to delusion, disappear. The mind is overwhelmed with a sense of darkness, the black light. It is described as being like twilight or an eclipse of the sun—a kind of hidden light, a glowing darkness. There also may be a sign like the flame of a lamp obscured in a lantern of clouded glass.

Once the two bindus have united in the heart chakra, there is no longer any possibility of revival. Consciousness dissolves into space, and all the specific mental and emotional characteristics that made up the individual are reabsorbed. For most living beings, the final dissolution of consciousness means the loss of their identity, so they feel that they are being annihilated; the experience of blackness seems like extinction. Then there is a sense of falling into dense, total darkness, and they become unconscious.

Now comes the final stage, the dawning of the luminosity of death. Although the luminosity of death is said to appear to all sentient beings without exception, generally they are unable to recognize or hold it. Just as in deep sleep, when normally we are not aware of being asleep and do not remember it, advanced practitioners are able to rest in that state with an enhanced level of awareness. Within the indestructible bindu at the center of the heart, all the vital energy is now absorbed into the very subtle prana of life energy, the original prana, which supports the very subtle consciousness, the mind of luminosity. The sign that appears to the trained yogin or yogini is compared to a perfectly clear autumn sky at dawn, free from any tinge of moonlight, sunlight or twilight; it is just suffused with its own natural, self-illuminating power.

In his commentary, Trungpa Rinpoche does not mention the series of inner dissolutions, which take place on the subtle level and are imperceptible to most people, but he describes the experience of luminosity as a moment of utter relaxation after abandoning the intense struggle to maintain ego. He compares it to the sensation of being drenched with both icy cold and boiling hot water at the same time, or to simultaneous pleasure and pain that can no longer be distinguished. It is the moment in which duality opens out into oneness. "The dualistic struggle of trying to *be* something is completely confused by the two extreme forces of hope for enlightenment and fear of becoming insane. The two extremes are so concentrated that it allows a certain relaxation; and when you do not struggle any more the luminosity presents itself naturally."[6]

Although the person appears dead externally, there still remains an "inner breath" or "inner pulsation," as the text calls it, until prana finally leaves the body. One remains in a state either of recognition or of unconsciousness for a length of time that depends on the individual and the circumstances. For most people, it may be only a few seconds, while accomplished practitioners are able to rest in the state of luminosity for several days or even weeks. Actual death only occurs when the red and white bindus separate again, releasing the indestructible bindu enclosed between them. They continue traveling to the opposite ends of avadhuti and emerge in the form of a reddish drop of fluid from the nostrils and a whitish drop from the sexual organ. This is the indication that death has finally taken place. The indestructible bindu itself, the entity of indivisible very subtle mind and prana, leaves the body by one of nine or ten possible exit points. If the dying person accomplishes transference to a pure land, it travels straight up avadhuti and emerges through the *brahmarandhra*, the "Brahma aperture," at the crown of the head. But in all other cases, it escapes from avadhuti into one of the two side nadis and finally emerges from the nose, the mouth, the eyes, the ears, the anus, the sexual organ, the navel, or the forehead (two points on the forehead are sometimes distinguished: between the eyebrows and above the hairline). These different exits indicate the realm in which one is destined to be reborn by the force of one's karma.

The entire series of dissolutions, culminating in the experience of luminosity, is the very process that the yogin or yogini undergoes during the completion stage of deity yoga, but without the death of the body.[7] It is accomplished by making prana enter avadhuti, remain there, and dissolve, and by making the red and white bindus unite and move up and down within it. As a result, the meditator experiences increasingly profound realizations of emptiness combined with increasingly intense sensations of bliss. Although this is assisted by certain physical movements, breathing techniques, and imagery, essentially it is a process of letting go on the very deepest level of identification with the physical, emotional, and mental components of one's ordinary state. The practitioner has already been prepared by the yoga of the creation stage, which sets up the appropriate conditions and develops the necessary meditation skills. The creation stage gradually transforms ordinary perception into sacred vision, until everything is experienced as an expression of the deity, the play of awakened mind. During the completion stage, this vision of things as they truly are is actually brought about and becomes a living reality.

The full realization of luminosity is the attainment of dharmakaya. It is paralleled by death and dreamless sleep, in both of which we enter the dharmakaya state without recognition. But for those who can enter it profoundly and retain stability, it is far more than a state of simple peace, clarity, joy, and absence of conceptual thought. It is completely unified with the mind of all the buddhas, all the awakened beings of all time and space; it is the totality of the awakened state. Although the texts say that it appears before us, that it dawns like the rising of the sun, in reality, it was always there: it is more like the sun being revealed as clouds melt away. It is naked awareness, the natural, basic state of mind when all concept of self has completely dissolved.

In *Liberation through Hearing*, it corresponds to the final moment of the bardo of dying.

The dharmakaya is the formless aspect, the source of all phenomena. Just as the sambhogakaya and nirmanakaya, the two aspects of form, arise out of the dharmakaya, so the subtle and coarse bodies reappear from the very subtle, indestructible bindu. After resting in the formless state of luminosity, the meditator experiences the three visions of light and the reappearance of the subtle elements in reverse order. They create a subtle body, known as the illusory body, which has the form of one's chosen deity. This corresponds to the sambhogakaya and can only be perceived by others who have reached the same level of attainment. With an illusory body, one can travel anywhere one wishes, transform oneself, send out emanations, and perform enlightened actions for the sake of others, while remaining in the state of samadhi or profound meditation. This phase is paralleled by dreaming and also by the bardo in its original meaning of the interval between death and rebirth. In dreams we inhabit a whole dream world with a dream body, which is another kind of illusory body, but over which we have no control. Then after death, we have a subtle bardo body, by means of which we go through all the experiences of the bardo. The completion stage practices include methods by which all three kinds of subtle body can be realized as sambhogakaya.

Finally, when the meditator arises from samadhi, he or she returns to everyday life with a physical body that has been purified and transmuted, corresponding to the nirmanakaya. Rebirth and awakening from sleep are analogous to this stage. Here rebirth is equivalent to the final moment of the bardo of existence, when one enters the womb at conception. Working with these three principles during life and gaining accomplishment in them is the means by which one can "manifest the trikaya," as it says in the root verses. During the experiences of death, bardo, and rebirth, we are presented with the opportunity to awaken into the corresponding sphere of enlightenment; that is why it is so important to understand the principle of the trikaya in relation to *Liberation through Hearing*.

The text begins by stating that it is "the means of liberation in the bardo for practitioners of average capacities." First, they should have received the practical, oral instructions on recognizing and resting in the true, ultimate nature of reality. This cannot be learned from books, but must be pointed out directly by the guru to the student in a meeting of minds, a transmission filled with the power of awakened presence. When death comes, practitioners of the highest capacities, who have gained enough depth and stability in their practice, will not need any assistance, but will simply merge their consciousness with the dharma-kaya. The root verse for the bardo of dying describes the best way to die like this:

> Now when the bardo of dying is dawning upon me,
> I will abandon grasping, attachment, and the all-desiring mind,
> Enter undistracted the clear essence of the instructions,
> And transfer into the space of unborn self-awareness.
> As I leave this conditioned body of flesh and blood
> I will know it to be a transitory illusion.

As the verse indicates, the practice to be performed during the bardo of dying is transference, which literally means moving from one place to another, just like moving house.[8] Imprisoned as we are in our perception of three-dimensional space, we naturally think of the mind, spirit, or consciousness as leaving the body at death and reappearing somewhere else. Yet in reality it has no dimension and no location; as the *Guhyasamaja Tantra* says, mind dwells in space and space dwells nowhere.

The six realms of existence are created by the mind. Hard though it may be to accept, we always find ourselves living in circumstances that perfectly conform to the karmic patterns in our mindstream. We create our world with our own projections through our perceptions and thoughts. We do not see this because, on the coarse level, duality is overwhelmingly powerful: we feel that mind and body are separate, self and others are separate, and the individual and his or her environment are separate. But as our awareness of the more subtle levels increases, the unity of mind and body and the interrelationship of the inner and outer worlds become more apparent. On the very subtle level, there is no distinction at all: mind and body are one, and that oneness embraces the whole of existence.

So transference is really the transformation of consciousness into a different type of awareness with new perceptions. In a general sense, all death is a kind of transference, since it is a transformation from one mode of consciousness to another. The difference is that in the practice of transference one deliberately chooses one's new condition of existence; one is in control of the process instead of being controlled by the forces of karma.

There are many different transference practices, as well as different ways of classifying them. They depend on the view of reality the practitioner has been able to reach and maintain during this life. They can lead one to the awakened state in any of its three aspects: dharmakaya, sambhogakaya, or nirmanakaya. Sometimes it seems confusing that there are so many methods, each promising to produce a specific result. All of them are just skillful means, providing supports and structures for the mind. If, when the time comes, we are open enough to recognize the luminosity as our own nature, then we shall become fully awakened, whichever method we have used. If we cannot attain that, then our consciousness will be transformed into whatever level we are capable of maintaining. Although we might aspire to merge with the dharmakaya, if we have never trained the mind to rest in that state during life, we cannot expect to achieve it suddenly at death. Unfortunately, it is not enough just to believe in the ultimate truth and hope that we will be able to recognize it when the time comes. That is why it is always better to choose a method corresponding to the practice we are already used to, which has become second nature. In this way, we enter a higher level of awareness and continue on the path until we are able to recognize the luminosity completely.

The transference that the verse refers to is the supreme method of dharmakaya transference. There is no concept of the mind going anywhere, there is nothing to be transferred and nobody to transfer it, so there is no need for imagery of any sort to assist the practice. The dying person simply relaxes in the primordial nature of mind, just as he or she has been accustomed to do during life. In such cases, the most accomplished practitioners do not even undergo the normal process of dissolution at death. Their bodies can disappear completely, the coarse elements totally dissolving into rainbow light. However, it is said that many great teachers who were capable of this have chosen outwardly to perform a more conventional form of transference in order to demonstrate it to their students, and to leave behind their bodies and the relics that remain after cremation as a source of blessings.

If one has only average capacities, as the text says, one should try to accomplish transference into the dharmakaya when the luminosity appears at the end of the bardo of dying. If that is unsuccessful, there is still a possibility of accomplishing transference into the sambhoga-kaya during the bardo of dharmata or into the nirmanakaya during the bardo of becoming. Pointing out these three opportunities is the main purpose of the instructions in *Liberation through Hearing*.

The six yogas of Naropa also contain transference practices that belong to the completion stage of deity yoga. They require experience in controlling prana, and again they can be effective on different levels, depending on one's previous realization.

A simpler kind of transference is widely taught and is suitable for people who possess strong faith, but who have not had much experience in deity yoga. This practice harnesses the power of devotion to one of the buddhas, especially Amitabha, and its goal is to be reborn in his pure land. Rebirth in a pure land is not yet complete enlightenment. Those who are born there receive teachings directly from the buddhas and bodhisattvas and enjoy the best possible situations for their development on the path. From the ultimate point of view, a pure land is our own pure vision, but in the relative sense, it is a realm created by the aspirations of the buddhas. Many kinds of pure land are described in Buddhist literature, all containing many levels of realization. They may even be here in this world all around us, but ordinarily we cannot perceive them.

Amitabha represents the limitlessness of compassion, the infinite responsiveness of the awakened state to the sufferings of living beings. Before he became a buddha, he vowed to establish conditions where anyone who called upon him would eventually attain enlightenment. His own realm is Sukhavati, and because of his vow, it is the most easily accessible of all the pure lands. Reaching it depends on the strength and sincerity of one's wish more than on the power of one's practice.

In this kind of transference practice, even though one has not learned how to work with the subtle body, one vividly imagines one's entire consciousness and energy concentrated in a single point at the heart, and then makes it shoot up through the crown of the head into the heart of Amitabha. This must be practiced under the guidance of an experienced teacher until one has gained confidence in it and shown some indications of success; at the time of death, it is put into actual effect. The use of imagery and the intense feeling of devotion are powerful aids in transforming our state of mind; we must believe that we can and do actually enter Amitabha's presence through the power of his love. If that thought is strong enough during the last moments before death, it cuts through the karmic chain of cause and effect that would otherwise impel us toward rebirth in one of the six realms of samsara.

For this practice to be successful, one needs to have complete trust and confidence in Amitabha and in one's teacher; it must be genuine and strong enough to keep the mind focused without any trace of doubt or disturbance. This kind of very simple, direct faith actually links up to the dzogchen attitude that everything is already accomplished and perfect. There is absolutely no sense of one's own effort or one's own attainment. However, in this case, there is still a perception of duality; enlightenment is seen as outside oneself in the person of Amitabha, to whom one feels total gratitude and devotion. Yet there is an underlying intuition of oneness and of our own awakened nature. Although we speak of sentient beings needing to be saved and the buddhas as saving them, it is always important to remember that in Buddhism there is no essential difference or distance between the savior and the saved.

Besides the techniques of transference in the usual sense, numerous other methods of focusing the mind at the time of death are taught in all schools of Buddhism. The most important points are letting go of attachment, feeling love and compassion for all beings, remaining mindful and undistracted, and resting in the sense of spaciousness. All the essential teachings of the Buddhist path, whatever one has practiced during one's life, become the means of transforming the mind at death.

If the dying person is unable to perform transference unaided, then the instructions in the first section of *Liberation through Hearing* should be read aloud to help him or her accomplish the dharmakaya transference during the bardo of dying. Only if this is not successful need one continue to read the whole text, with its instructions for the bardos of dharmata and existence. Even the best practitioners may sometimes need this kind of help, because the actual experience of death is so overwhelming. Although one may be experienced in meditation, the mind can be confused by prolonged illness or disturbed by the shock of a sudden accident or violent attack, or the karmic effect of some negative action—especially the breaking of spiritual commitments—may come to fruition unexpectedly. But primarily, this instruction is meant for "all kinds of ordinary people who have received teaching but, although they are intelligent, have not recognized, or who have recognized but did not become accustomed to meditation."

Detailed instructions are given for the reading of the text. If possible, it should be read by the dying person's main guru, otherwise by a dharma brother or sister, meaning those who have shared teachings and empowerments. However, if such a person cannot be found, someone who belongs to the same lineage of transmission may do the reading. If none of these are available, it should at least be done by someone who can read aloud clearly and accurately. The reader should be someone the dying person loved and trusted. At the time of death, when one is naturally confused and frightened, it is particularly important not to arouse negative feelings such as dislike and suspicion. It is also important to have a calm and positive atmosphere, and for this reason, the family should be kept away so that their grief and anxiety do not cause any disturbance. Offerings should be made in a spirit of unbounded generosity, not only in material form, but also by imagining limitless offerings filling the whole universe. This creates the right state of mind for the final letting go of samsaric existence.

The reading can even be done in the absence of the dying or dead person. "If the body is not present, one should sit on the dead person's bed or seat, and proclaiming the power of truth, call on the departed consciousness, imagining that he or she is sitting before one listening, and read aloud."

For an experienced practitioner who is able to reach the subtle levels of mind, distance presents no problem, since mind itself has no physical location. When lamas are requested to attend someone who is dying or has just died, they will start to make a connection with that person's consciousness at once, even if they are far away. They may help the dying person to perform transference by combining both their powers, or if the person is already dead, they may even be able to perform transference on his or her behalf. The idea of transference for another person may be easier to understand if we consider the remarkable effect that certain very accomplished meditators can have on others just by their presence. A kind of transference takes place whenever we allow our minds to be turned away from ordinary concerns and elevated onto another plane of awareness.

Transference must not be attempted too soon, as that would be tantamount to committing suicide. The best time is when respiration is just about to stop, before the final stages of inner dissolution have taken place. But if transference is not accomplished at this stage, the instructions for the bardo of dying should be given. As the text explains, as soon as respiration has stopped, all prana is absorbed into avadhuti and "luminosity free from complexities shines clearly in the consciousness." This is a decisive moment, for it is at this point that most people black out into unconsciousness. Before this occurs, the teacher or friend should prepare the dying person by saying:

> O child of awakened family, now the time has come for you
> to seek the path. As soon as your outer breath stops, the
> basic luminosity of the first bardo, which your guru has al-
> ready pointed out, will dawn upon you. It is the dharmata,
> empty and open as space, a pure, naked awareness, clear and
> empty, without center or circumference. At that moment,
> you yourself should recognize it and rest in that state, and I
> too will point it out to you at the same time.

For those who need more assistance, the whole sequence of the dissolution of the elements should be read aloud so that the dying person understands what is happening. *Liberation through Hearing* gives only a brief indication of this process: "Now the sign of earth dissolving into water is present, water into fire, fire into air, air into consciousness." The reader, who ideally is the dying person's guru, would explain the sequence of events in whatever amount of detail is required or use one of the associated texts.

At every stage of the process of dying, there is the possibility of breaking through into some level of realization, just as there is during every moment of life. Since we are made of the five elements, our essence is the five devis. When the elements dissolve into their pure state, if we have recognized their essence through meditation, we can let go into emptiness instead of identifying with the physical disintegration that is taking place. According to some teachings, the respective colors of the elements each flood the mind in turn.[9] When earth dissolves, everything appears pervaded by a yellow light; by recognizing this as the pure manifestation of Buddha-Lochana, we can instantaneously attain enlightenment in her realm. Similarly, as water dissolves, we can reach the state of Mamaki; as fire dissolves, we can reach the state of Pandaravasini; as air dissolves, we can reach the state of Samaya-Tara; and as consciousness dissolves, we can reach the state of Akasha-dhatvishvari.

When the sequence of dissolutions is almost complete, the dying person is urged to remain fully awake and attentive: "O child of awakened family, do not let your thoughts wander." Then he or she is reminded to arouse the attitude of bodhichitta, the awakened heart and mind, and to meditate in this way:

> I have arrived at the time of death. Now, since I am dying, I will think of nothing but the awakened heart, love, and compassion, and attain perfect enlightenment for the sake of all sentient beings as limitless as space. With this attitude, especially at this time, for the sake of all beings, I will recognize the luminosity of death as dharmakaya. Within that state, I will attain the supreme accomplishment of mahamudra and act for the good of all beings. If I do not succeed, then I will recognize the bardo when I enter it. I will manifest the mahamudra bardo body of inseparable appearance and emptiness, and act for the good of all beings as limitless as space, appearing in whatever way will benefit each of them.

Mahamudra, the great symbol or great seal, is another approach to the nature of reality, which has become particularly associated with the

Kagyü tradition. The name is explained by analogy with a king's seal: whoever carries it represents the king and bears his authority, and whatever is stamped with it is accepted as authentic. The whole of existence is sealed with emptiness; apparent phenomena are recognized as the ambassadors of ultimate truth. Mahamudra can also be seen as a symbol in the sense that everything is a symbol of its own ultimate nature. This is what Trungpa Rinpoche called natural symbolism, expressing the vividness and clarity of things just as they are: "One experiences reality as the great symbol which stands for itself."[10] *Mudra* also means a gesture of the hands in dance or ritual, so mahamudra could be called the great gesture, expressing visually the truth that is beyond words and concepts.

Mahamudra works with form and manifestation: after going through the experience of emptiness, one arrives at the sense of clarity and fullness. Earlier practices focused on emptiness as an antidote to the grasping ego, but mahamudra emphasizes the simultaneity of apparent phenomena and emptiness. It is the sense of the positive that comes after realizing the negative, the fullness of emptiness. Those who have awakened into the formlessness of dharmakaya do not remain there, but manifest through compassion for the sake of others, and this is exactly what the dying person aspires to do. The mahamudra bardo body is a pure illusory body in which appearance and emptiness coexist simultaneously, known as two-in-one.[11] This body can take any form that is appropriate in order to help living beings.

The dying person is then asked to practice whatever kind of meditation he or she is used to, always keeping in mind the attitude of bodhichitta. As soon as it is certain that respiration has stopped, the attendant should help the dying person to lie in the sleeping lion posture—lying stretched out on the right side with the head resting on the right hand. This is the position in which Shakyamuni Buddha passed away:

> At this time, the first bardo, which is called the luminosity of dharmata, the undistorted mind of the dharmakaya, arises in the mindstream of all beings. This is the interval between the ceasing of the outer breath and the inner pulsation, when prana dissolves into avadhuti, so ordinary people call it unconsciousness.

This period lasts for an uncertain length of time. Generally speaking, the greater one's spiritual capacities and training in meditation, the longer it lasts. For some people, it may be no more than a snap of the fingers, while an average period seems to be the time it takes to eat a meal. Experienced meditators may be able to rest in it for several days; these "days" are explained as meaning the length of a meditation session during which one can remain perfectly undistracted, so it could amount to several weeks or even months. To be on the safe side, Tibetans say that, even in the case of ordinary people, the body should be left undisturbed for about three days. In *Liberation through Hearing*, it is recommended that "one should strive to point out the luminosity" for four and a half days.

At the end of that time, the life principle of indivisible prana and mind escapes and leaves the body. Here it is referred to as prana, because the text is talking about its movement, while later on it is called mind or consciousness, addressing its aspect of awareness. In order to accomplish transference, prana must go straight up through the brahmarandhra, so in many practices there are instructions for blocking all the other exits with mantras. Here, the dying person's attendant is instructed to press the "arteries of sleep" in the neck, which will prevent prana from returning into the right and left nadis.

During this period, the actual pointing out of luminosity takes place. For a person of high spiritual attainment, the instruction is brief and unadorned: "Respected one, now the basic luminosity is shining before you. Please recognize it and rest in the practice." But for the majority of people, who need a more detailed introduction, it is pointed out in one of the most beautiful and striking passages in the whole text:

> O child of awakened family, listen! Now the pure luminosity of dharmata is dawning upon you. Recognize it! O child of awakened family, the essence of your knowing awareness at this present moment is pure emptiness, pure emptiness in which there is no essential substance, quality, or color whatsoever: this itself is the dharmata, Samantabhadri. But while your knowing awareness is empty, it is not just blank emptiness; your knowing awareness is unobstructed, sparkling,

pure, and vibrant: this awareness itself is the buddha Saman-tabhadra. These two, your awareness whose essence is empty without any substantiality and your knowing awareness which is clear and vibrant, are indivisible: this itself is the dharmakaya of the buddha. This awareness of yours is a great mass of light, it is inseparable clarity and emptiness, it has no birth or death, therefore it is the buddha of unchanging light. To recognize it is enough. When you recognize the pure essence of your knowing awareness as the buddha, to look into your own awareness is to rest in the intention of the buddha.

This instruction should be repeated three or seven times. By means of it, "first, one is reminded of what the guru has already pointed out; second, one recognizes one's own naked awareness as luminosity; and third, having recognized oneself, one becomes inseparably united with the dharmakaya and is certain to be liberated."

The true nature of mind, "one's own naked awareness," is none other than the primordial state of enlightenment. And this primordial state is the indivisible union of the male and female principles Saman-tabhadra and Samantabhadri—Universal Goodness, without beginning or end. This is the ultimate discovery of our own basic goodness. It is our original awareness, which has never strayed away from the state of wakefulness.

When the luminosity of death is recognized, it is compared to the meeting of mother and child. The mother is the basic, or ground, luminosity that appears before one, the true, fundamental nature of all beings. The child is the personal experience of luminosity, or the luminosity of the path, that one has already attained in meditation. When they come together, it is as though the child runs and leaps into its mother's arms after a long separation.

For an awakened person who has fully understood the meaning of death, it is simply one of the many transformations of limitless life, and for someone who has gained experience and confidence in meditation, it is the supreme opportunity to attain enlightenment. From the absolute point of view, birth, life, and death are the spontaneous play of awareness, continuously arising from and dissolving back into the primordial ground, the space of luminous emptiness. Buddha-nature pervades all time and all existence without any gaps, so there is no bardo within it. Bardos only occur in the samsaric realm of confusion and ignorance, where we identify with the body and the coarse levels of consciousness. Buddha-nature is always present, whether we are waking, sleeping, dreaming, or dying. As we fall asleep or die, the fading of the outer senses and elements means that our inner, subtle awareness manifests, but because we have not become familiar with it, we experience only unconsciousness or death. From the relative viewpoint of our present condition, death is the most devastating event of our whole life, and it is inescapable. So although the goal is to see through the illusion of death, a constant remembrance of its inevitability is one of the most powerful incentives to practice while we are still in this life and following the path.

The "four thoughts that transform the mind" or "four reminders" is a mahayana teaching that is meditated upon again and again for this purpose. The first thought is contemplation of the value of human life. Considering all the possible life forms in the six realms of samsara, it is extremely rare to take birth as a human being, and even more so to be born in a place and time where one has the opportunity to hear and practice the dharma. The second thought is contemplation on impermanence. Everything is ceaselessly changing and passing away; we do not know when death will come, only that it is certain. The third thought is contemplation on karma, the inevitability of cause and effect. Whatever we think, say, or do sets in motion a chain of consequences from which we cannot escape either in this life or the next. The fourth thought is contemplation on the faults of samsara and the suffering inherent in this situation. Looking into the origin of suffering, we recognize that it springs from the greed, hate, and delusion of the ego, clinging to individual existence.

Strange as it may seem, although this grasping ego is really nothing but a cause of grief, it is extremely hard to let go of it. We might expect that, at the moment of death, it would be a tremendous relief to be rid of such a burden and to dissolve into the light of reality. On the contrary, it is a terrifying prospect, because there is still the illusion of someone there hoping to survive. But enlightenment means the death of ego; the person who wants to become enlightened will no longer be there. As Trungpa Rinpoche used to say, "You can't attend your own funeral!" The essence of all the bardo states is related to this paradox, manifesting itself in various situations: the tension between trying to hang on and watch what is happening or letting go completely into the unknowable, the inconceivable.

Since the whole of the Buddha's teaching centers on this predicament, everything it contains is relevant to the time of death. If we have gained no depth or stability in meditation, we shall be unable to remain focused and aware during the process of dying. If we have never understood the truth of impermanence or practiced nonattachment, when death comes, we will cling desperately to our old life. If we have no confidence in the basic goodness of our mind, we shall be unable to let go into open space. If we have not looked beyond the surface of consciousness, we shall not recognize the luminous nature of mind when it is laid bare.

Whatever practice we have done and whatever insight we have gained should therefore be applied at the time of death. Conversely, the views and methods that are taught specifically in relation to death are exactly the same in essence as those that are practiced during life. Falling asleep is the closest analogy to dying in our normal experience. The yoga of sleep and dream trains the practitioner to be aware of the subtle dissolutions and to rest in the luminosity of sleep, which is like a reflection of the luminosity of death, and then to use the subtle dream body as a vehicle for practice.

But there are many other ways in which the whole process of dying is paralleled on several different levels in the experiences of this life. Among the six bardos, the characteristic of the bardo of dying is the dissolution process. It has a particular emotional quality of dread and panic at the disintegration of everything we are and the loss of everything we know. This same feeling can strike whenever we undergo some unexpected shock or receive devastating news; for instance, if we are involved in an accident, if we hear of the sudden death of a loved one, or if we are told that we have a serious illness. It causes a horrible kind of sinking sensation, as though the ground is opening up beneath our feet. As our world falls apart, we may be overcome by weakness, feel sick and faint, gasp for breath as though we are suffocating, or go cold inside, just as it is described during the dissolution of the elements. At all costs, we wish we could go back to the moment before and keep the world just as it used to be. But the tighter we hold on, the worse it gets. Letting go is the only remedy. Here again, the attitudes developed through practice will provide the motivation and the presence of mind to remember and apply whatever we have already learned.

Less dramatically, we also experience the fear of annihilation and loss on a small scale whenever we recognize that a certain period of our life has come to an end. Even in memory, if we look back at the past as we grow older and think, "life will never be like that again," there is a pang of nostalgia, a clinging to what has gone forever, and a fear of the emptiness it leaves behind. It is always painful to let go of something with which we identify. When a project is completed, a consuming interest no longer seems important, or an emotional attachment ends, there can be a real sense of loss. Deep down, we often do not really want to change our habits, our reactions, and our behavior, even if we dislike them and know they cause pain to others. We think, "that's what I am"; they are part of the pattern of our sense of self, and to let go of them is like the dying process.

Yet we cannot avoid letting go, for death occurs at every moment. The process of dissolving from coarse to subtle, followed by the reverse evolution from subtle to coarse, is taking place within us all the time. Occasionally we may be able to catch a fleeting glimpse of it as we fall asleep or awaken from a dream, but normally we are completely unaware of the subtle basis of consciousness and remain totally identified with its superficial manifestations. As each moment of consciousness passes away, it gives birth to the next, so the never-ending flow of samsara goes on and on. But this cycle of birth and death takes place within the openness of space. Underlying all the appearances that arise and pass away is dharmata, the true nature of phenomena, which is "open and empty like space." If we let go into space as each thought, emotion, and experience dies, then the karmic chain reaction is interrupted. There is always a gap—a bardo—between the cessation of one moment and the arising of the next, where luminosity can be recognized and the awakened state is seen to be ever-present and all-pervading.

This letting go is actually the essence of the formless meditation that is taught at the very beginning of the path and that reaches its perfection in dzogchen. When meditation is described as letting go into space, this is not just a fanciful image; it really is like consciousness dissolving into space at death. If we could practice it fully and completely, no other method would be necessary. We would live our life in freedom from the limitations of samsara and die without any fear, like a child running joyfully into its mother's arms.

Chapter Twelve

Invincible Peace

THE GREAT CENTRAL SECTION of *Liberation through Hearing* is a description of the bardo of dharmata, which originates from the visionary experiences that arise during the atiyoga practice of the surpassing stage. *Dharmata* literally means "dharmaness": the essential quality of things as they really are, the true nature of phenomena. It is reality in its pure, original state. It is unconditioned; it is not constructed from or dependent upon anything else, and it cannot be destroyed like the phenomena of samsara. It is unobscured by the veils that distort our vision and uncontaminated by the poisons of passion, aggression, and delusion. When the basic luminosity dawned at the end of the bardo of dying, it was called "the luminosity of dharmata": it is the experience of mind's essential nature, "open and empty like space." Now, from out of that luminosity of dharmata, the appearances of the bardo of dharmata arise—the natural creative energy of mind unfolds in a dynamic play of sound, color, and rays of light. The rainbow colors form the body of the deities; the sounds are the mantra speech of the deities; and the rays of light are primordial knowledge, the mind of the deities. Another way of putting it is that dharmakaya manifests as sambhogakaya.

The mind absorbed in the luminosity of death was identified as dharmakaya, the inseparable union of Samantabhadra and Samantabhadri. This is the state of primordial purity, in which samsara and nirvana, birth and death, or self and other have never existed. Purity has a special meaning in the tantras: it points to the original, essential, inherent nature of everything. It is like a mirror that is never affected by the images it reflects or by the dirt that gathers on its surface. When it is said, for instance, that the purified elements are the devis and the purified skandhas are the buddhas, it means that they have never really been anything else. Seeing things in this way is pure perception or sacred vision.

In the boundless openness of space, which is Samantabhadri, the spontaneous self-display of the awakened state begins to unfold. Nondual awareness, recognizing whatever appears as its own nature, is Samantabhadra, the primordially awakened one. But where there is no recognition, the dualistic consciousness of ordinary sentient beings develops, and experience becomes divided into subject and object. All this takes place in the space of mind itself. In the context of *Liberation through Hearing* this happens to be the mind of someone who has just died, but if we apply it to ourselves here and now, it is taking place within our own mind. Within each of us there is that very subtle essence that remains forever in the primordial state, and simultaneously, there is also the falling away into confusion.

According to the dzogchen teachings, the bardo of dharmata unfolds in a further series of four dissolutions. It is a vision of how appearances continually arise out of the primordial ground. First, space dissolves into luminosity. The opportunity to recognize the basic luminosity has already occurred at the conclusion of the bardo of dying, but for those who did not recognize it, it passed by as though nothing had happened. Now the consciousness of the dead person wakes up again and perceives it as though it were external, manifesting as the subtle energies of light, color, and sound.

Next, the light show of luminosity dissolves into the state of two-in-one. This term, which we discussed in chapter 11, points to the simultaneously empty yet apparent nature of the visions that arise during the bardo of dharmata. The dazzling display of light and color crystallizes into the forms of the deities. All the peaceful and wrathful deities appear before the dead person, as vivid yet insubstantial as rainbows appearing in the sky.

Then all the forms of the deities dissolve into knowledge, the very essence of the buddhas. This knowledge manifests as penetrating rays of light shining out from the hearts of the buddhas into one's own heart and expanding into a brilliant array of sheets and spheres of light—the pure essence of the five ways of knowing reality.

Finally, the rays of knowledge dissolve into the eight gates of spontaneous existence, where all the potentialities of both samsara and nirvana appear simultaneously. Spontaneous existence or spontaneous presence points to the manner in which everything arises from the primordial ground: self-originated, all at once, without effort of any kind.[1] The eight gates present glimpses of all the possible ways of emerging out of the primordial state, from resting in nirvana—through the manifestation of subtle energy and light, the forms of deities, and the pure lands—right down to the cycle of birth and death in the six realms of samsara.

Either one is liberated by recognizing these visions as the manifestations of one's own mind, or one drifts on into the bardo of existence. This series of dissolutions is not described in *Liberation through Hearing*, but it more or less corresponds to the sequence set out in the first part of the bardo of dharmata, with the difference that here the wrathful deities appear at the end.

If the dying person did not recognize the luminosity when it dawned at the end of the bardo of dying, he or she can remain in a state of unconsciousness for anything from a single moment up to four and a half days; on average, it is the time it takes to eat a meal. Then prana escapes from the body and consciousness becomes clear again. Immediately on waking from the unconscious state, the subtle tendencies toward duality and a sense of self are reactivated. In a flash, the dead person experiences the three lights and the reappearance of the subtle elements in reverse order, creating a mental body that can see and hear just as in a dream.

There is some ambiguity here in the text of *Liberation through Hearing*; it describes some of the features of the bardo of existence interspersed with those of the bardo of dharmata. This can perhaps be explained by the fact that the bardo of dharmata, being a dzogchen teaching, is only described in Nyingma texts. It does not appear in the other traditions, such as the six yogas of Naropa. Instead there is the triad of death, bardo, and rebirth, where "bardo" by itself always refers to the bardo of existence. So from the general vajrayana point of view, the dead person enters the bardo of existence as soon as consciousness leaves the body. But from the point of view of dzogchen, the luminous nature of mind from which the bardo of dharmata arises is always present, and with it the potentiality of experiencing the visions of our innate deities. During the bardo of dharmata, consciousness is absorbed in the state of luminosity, but it is constantly on the verge of flickering into the bardo of existence, with its perception of duality and of having a mental body.

Before embarking on the detailed description of the bardo of dharmata, some brief instructions are given first, containing the essence of the advice that will be repeated again and again when the visions appear. The consciousness of the dead person "suddenly becomes clear," unaware of what has happened and not knowing whether it is dead or alive, and "the second luminosity dawns," meaning the luminosity of the bardo of dharmata. Now there is another opportunity to recognize the nature of mind before the consciousness is drawn further into the bardo of existence and overwhelmed by its experiences, so once again the way to liberation is pointed out. "During this time, when the violent hallucinations of karma have not yet appeared and the terrors of the lords of death have not yet arrived, the instruction should be given."

Here the instructions differ for people at different stages on the path. For those who are experienced in the stages of completion or cutting through, only the simple instruction to recognize is repeated, because in these practices, one penetrates directly to the essence of reality with minimal use of imagery. "One should call the dead person's name three times and repeat the previous instruction for pointing out the luminosity."

Those who were practicing the creation stage should be reminded of their particular practice. Here one uses form and imagery to perceive the whole world as a manifestation of sacred being. The description and ritual of one's chosen deity should be read aloud, and one should imagine with total concentration and intensity that one really is the deity and merge with that divine presence. The deity is not visualized with a solid, substantial form, but as made of light, ephemeral and illusory, like the moon reflected in water, the pure expression of luminous emptiness.

Those who were not practicing deity yoga at all are instructed to meditate on Avalokiteshvara, the Lord of Great Compassion. Avalokiteshvara is the bodhisattva emanation of Amitabha; he is the active, living presence of love and compassion in the world. Because of his vows to liberate all sentient beings, he is the natural, universal chosen deity available to everyone; no special empowerment or teachings are needed to meditate upon him and aspire to enter his pure realm.

By these three methods, the dead person has another chance to enter the realms of dharmakaya, sambhogakaya, or nirmanakaya during the bardo of dharmata. "Just as the light of the sun overcomes darkness, so the power of karma is overcome by the luminosity of the path and liberation is attained." As the text repeats again and again, after nearly every instruction, there is no doubt that those who have not recognized previously will do so by being shown in this way, and it is impossible that they will not be liberated. All the same, it points out the necessity of reading aloud the instructions for the sake of those who were not skillful enough in meditation to recognize without help, or who may have become confused by serious illness, or whose minds may be clouded by the karmic effects of broken commitments.

At this point, the text seems to call the bardo of dharmata "the third bardo," following the second bardo, or second luminosity. This is how we translated it in the *Tibetan Book of the Dead*, but I now think it is possible to interpret that particular passage in another way that makes greater sense.[2] Since it mentions "the confused karmic hallucinations of the third bardo," this must refer to the bardo of existence, with its terrifying apparitions of avenging demons and lords of death, not to the pure visions of the deities in the bardo of dharmata. It is a little confusing, but essentially the text is making the point that the instruction should be read right now, before the third bardo takes over:

> In this way one is liberated by recognizing the luminosity of the second bardo, even if one did not recognize the basic luminosity. But if even that does not liberate, then there is said to be the third bardo: after the bardo of dharmata has

appeared, the confused karmic hallucinations of the third
bardo will appear. So, at this time, it is most important that
the great pointing out of the bardo of dharmata is read, for
it is extremely powerful and helpful.

Then the text returns briefly to describing the experiences of entering the bardo of existence. Suddenly awakening from the unconsciousness of death brings with it an enormous sense of confusion,
uncertainty, and fear. At this stage, the very recently departed consciousness still feels a strong link with the old body and environment,
but does not understand what has happened. There is a poignant description of how the dead can see and hear their relatives weeping and
setting about all the tasks that need to be done after a death. The dead
try desperately to make their presence known, but they cannot be seen
or heard, so they go away in despair. Then "sounds, colored lights, and
rays of light" will appear, and they "will grow faint with fear, terror,
and bewilderment." Without the anchor of a physical body and familiar
surroundings, there is a sense of disorientation and instability, as all
kinds of continually changing images arise from the mind like a very
confused dream or a drug-induced hallucination. Nothing is as one
expects it to be; it is as though all one's expectations based on ordinary
experience have been turned upside down. Now the reader should call
on the dead person by name and begin "the great pointing out of the
bardo of dharmata."

The detailed instruction to the dead begins with reassurance, ex-
plaining what has happened already and what is about to take place,
and that they are going through the experience of three out of the six
bardos. Since they did not recognize the luminosity in the bardo of
dying, now they will experience the bardo of dharmata and the bardo
of existence. They are reminded that they are not alone, that death
comes to everyone, and it is impossible to remain in this life however
much they may long to do so. Fear and bewilderment are the predomi-
nant emotions in this bardo, so the most important thing is to convey
a sense of confidence. The root verse for the bardo of dharmata contains the key to confronting it without fear and recognizing whatever
may arise:

Now when the bardo of dharmata dawns upon me,
I will abandon all projections of fear and terror,

Recognize whatever arises as the self-display of awareness,
And know it to be the visionary nature of the bardo.
When the time comes to reach the crucial point
Do not fear the self-display of peaceful and wrathful ones!

The first manifestation of the bardo of dharmata is an overwhelming display of light and sound filling the whole of space. If one is
unprepared, this vibrant energy seems frightening and bewildering, although it is simply the expression of one's own natural qualities. It is
described like this:

> O child of awakened family, when your mind and body sepa-
> rate, the dharmata will appear, pure and clear yet hard to
> discern, luminous and brilliant with terrifying brightness,
> shimmering like a mirage on a plain in spring. Do not be
> afraid of it, do not be bewildered. This is the natural radi-
> ance of your own dharmata, so recognize it.
>
> A great roar of thunder will come from within the light,
> the natural sound of dharmata, like a thousand thunderclaps
> simultaneously. This is the natural sound of your own dhar-
> mata, so do not be afraid or bewildered. You have what is
> called a mental body of karmic imprints, you have no physi-
> cal body of flesh and blood, so whatever sounds, colors, and
> rays of light appear, they cannot hurt you and you cannot
> die. It is enough simply to recognize them as your own self-
> display and know this to be the bardo.
>
> O child of awakened family, if you do not recognize
> them in this way as your self-display and if you have not
> met with this teaching, then in spite of whatever meditation
> practice you have done during your life, the colored lights
> will frighten you, the sounds will bewilder you, and the rays
> of light will terrify you. If you do not understand this essen-
> tial point of the teaching, you will not recognize the sounds,
> lights, and rays, and so you will wander on in samsara.

As Trungpa Rinpoche points out, this kind of hallucinatory experience can occur during our life; although not to such an extreme extent,
"there is a basically desolate quality, loneliness and flickering." It comes
from the fear of emptiness, the fear of losing one's self and becoming

absorbed into the visions of the awakened state: "That sudden glimpse of egolessness brings a kind of shakiness."[3]

The dazzling, kaleidoscopic display of light forms into the rainbowlike images of the bardo deities: appearance and emptiness indivisible. First the peaceful forms of the five buddhas appear, then the passionate vidyadharas, and finally the wrathful herukas. All of them seem overwhelming and frightening to the confused consciousness in the bardo, so the instructions repeat over and over again that we should not fear, but let go and allow ourselves to merge with them.

These phenomena are terrifying because they are so raw and intense. They are not like ordinary sound, light, and color; they are pure energy, expressing the subtle qualities of the five elements. The consciousness in the bardo is no longer protected by the solidity of flesh and bone or limited by the dullness of the physical senses. It is as though one is plunged totally naked into a whirlpool of sensations. It is impossible to tell whether they are coming from within or without. Trungpa Rinpoche discusses the nature of the bardo visions in his commentary, relating it to the meditations of the special bardo retreat practice, which is carried out in total darkness. He says that what occurs is not exactly vision or perception or experience, because that involves a dualistic relationship. Here there is no watcher or experiencer, no way of separating the apparitions from oneself and objectifying them or of looking at one's experience in order to understand it. He points out that this same principle of direct, nondual perception is the key point in understanding the symbolism of tantric art and meditation. We shall return to the subject of symbolism in the next chapter.

Trungpa Rinpoche often spoke of the way we perceive the world as "projection," and we used this word in our translation to suggest the nonduality of the visions and the person who is seeing them. Whatever appears during the bardo is one's own projection. This was simply meant to convey the idea that all the visions come from one's own mind and are the manifestations of one's own nature. However, during the years since the translation was published, I have found that *projection* can sometimes give the wrong impression, especially in connection with the deities. It seems to imply something false and might suggest that the deities themselves are nothing but the projections of our dualistic consciousness. I now prefer to use the term *self-display*. It has a very appropriate sense of ambiguity that helps to sabotage our usual dualistic habit of thought: it suggests at the same time both the appearance of the deities from one's own mind and their own spontaneous, self-existent appearance.

The problem occurs because we tend to think of the ordinary individual ego as the projector. But the deities are the manifestation of our original, awakened nature, which transcends individuality. They are universal realities. When the coarse elements and skandhas dissolve, the innate deities are revealed. They are naturally present, without any effort on our part. This is called spontaneous existence or spontaneous presence. The deities are not just psychological, nor are they created by meditation. They are our true nature, but through countless lives of wandering in samsara we have lost sight of that nature. They are not symbols of abstract ideas, but reality itself. They are the living presence of enlightenment, not ideals of enlightenment. They are what we really are, but they are far more real than we are in our present state.

In describing the experience of the bardo retreat, Trungpa Rinpoche goes on to say: "In order to perceive them properly, the perceiver of these visions cannot have fundamental, centralised ego. Fundamental ego in this case is that which causes one to meditate or perceive something."[4] This refers to the yogin or yogini who is engaged in the retreat and has reached a stable experience of emptiness. But in the bardo, we still grasp at the existence of ego or we would not be there at all, so the deities seem to appear before us as external visions. As soon as we perceive them as separate from ourselves, we react with passion or aggression or fear, and when we turn them into the objects of our emotions, they become our own projections.

Behind all these appearances is the primordial couple, Samantabhadra and Samantabhadri (see plate 3). They do not actually appear until about halfway through the bardo of dharmata, but they have already been identified as the true nature of mind during the bardo of dying. In paintings of the bardo mandala, they are depicted either in the center or at the top. They are shown in the simplest way possible, naked, with no adornments. They are embracing each other in sexual union. His body is the deep blue of space; sometimes he is almost black, the fusion of all colors. She is pure white, symbolizing the purity of the primordial state; it is the closest hue to no color at all, to the transparency of emptiness. The text of *The Hundred Homages* describes them in this way:

> Primordial buddha whose body is changeless light,
> Pure transcendent knowledge, father of all buddhas,
> The color of the sky, seated in meditation posture,
> Homage to Samantabhadra, the dharmakaya.
> Mother who gives birth to all the buddhas of the three times,
> White like the pure, stainless crystal of dharmadhatu,
> Joyfully embracing the father with great bliss,
> Homage to Samantabhadri, the great mother.

It has become the custom in English to call the devis the consorts of the buddhas, but in the original texts, the couple is always referred to as father and mother. This applies to the male and female principles wherever they appear, not only to Samantabhadra and Samantabhadri. They are the parents of enlightenment; together they produce bodhichitta, the awakened mind. Fundamentally, the feminine principle is the creative power that gives birth. She is the space (dhatu), the zero dimension of emptiness (shunyata) from which all phenomena arise. This symbolism of the mother reveals very clearly that emptiness is not negative or passive, but a dynamic state of infinite potentiality. The complementary masculine principle is nondual transcendent knowledge (jnana), spontaneously arising from the openness of space, flowing through it and pervading it. There are many ways of interpreting this union of male and female; for instance, they can symbolize the indivisibility of appearance and emptiness, bliss and emptiness, relative and ultimate truth, knowledge and space, compassion and emptiness, or skillful means and wisdom.

The buddhas of the five families each embody a special aspect of knowledge and quality of wakefulness. Their consorts, the five devis, embody their absence of self, their freedom from limitations, the space and openness of their essential nature. In the context of the bardo visions, Trungpa Rinpoche emphasized the sense of fertility and communication of the feminine principle. She provides the environment through which the male buddha can open out and express the basic quality of his family. She is also the one who inspires him to communi-

cate. Sometimes in the tantras, the buddhas are described as being totally absorbed in the bliss of nirvana, and then it is the devis who arouse
them, requesting them to act and to teach the dharma on behalf of all
beings.

In response to this request, the masculine principle manifests as
compassion, which can only be effective when it is based on the understanding of emptiness. The expression of emptiness is wisdom, the
practical realization of the real meaning of nonself, cutting through
the illusions of solidity, permanence, separateness, and limitation. The
expression of compassion is skillful means, the unhesitating application
of any method that can be used to help living beings in whatever way
possible. So the appearance of the father and mother deities during the
bardo is the self-display of one's own original nature as the union of
these two principles.

The significance of their sexual union is just as important as their
individual meaning. It graphically illustrates the absolute inseparability
and interdependence of the two complementary elements of the awakened state. But above all, it is an ecstatic union that produces bliss. Bliss
is the very essence of enlightenment; it is the waking up of one's whole
being into the transcendent experience of sensitivity. It is called the
great bliss that does not leak away: it is inexhaustible, it is not affected
by any external circumstances, and it never dissipates into the ordinary
emotions of the five poisons. Whether the deities in union are peaceful
or wrathful, the expression on their faces and the attitude of their bodies reveal the bliss that totally pervades them.

The visions that appear during the bardo of dharmata are collectively
known as the hundred peaceful and wrathful deities; the peaceful deities
are common to all the vajrayana traditions, but the wrathful deities are
specifically Nyingma and are not found in quite the same form anywhere else.[5] Many teachers say that untrained people will not see these
visions at all and that only those who are experienced in dzogchen
meditation will see them. On the other hand, they express universal
realities, so it is often stated that they do appear to everyone because
they are the pure manifestation of one's own nature. Just how they will
appear is the question. We may feel totally bewildered by the sounds,

colors, and lights that surround us, but if we are accustomed to meditation, we shall be able to see these chaotic impressions clearly as familiar
deities and merge into their hearts with confidence.

The difference lies in whether we can recognize them or not. Recognition is the key point during the bardo. We may be so dull and
stupefied that we notice nothing at all, in the same way that we are
often unaware of having any dreams at night. Perhaps the next morning
we may just feel that we have had a pleasant dream or a confused and
disturbing nightmare. The analogy with dreams is easy to understand,
but exactly the same principle applies to waking life. The deities are
present here and now, but we do not see them and we completely
misinterpret their messages.

The text tells us that "samsara is reversed and everything appears
as lights and images." Ordinarily, everything within our entire experience is constructed and conditioned by the five elements, the five skandhas, and the five poisons. But during the bardo of dharmata, samsara
is reversed: our ordinary experience is turned back to front, inside out,
and upside down. Instead of perceiving only the coarse, external aspect
of things, we experience their pure, original essence from within. Our
own elements manifest as the devis, our skandhas as the buddhas, and
the five poisons are transformed into the five kinds of awakened knowledge.

Whatever exists, in either the world of samsara or the world of
enlightenment, is produced from the five elemental qualities, appearing
out of basic space as light of the five colors. This brilliant display
pervaded the consciousness when it first awoke in the bardo of dharmata. Now the light of the five elements forms into bindus, spheres of
light within which the visions of the deities crystallize into radiant,
translucent forms, "out of the space of rainbow light."

First, the peaceful deities appear. They are felt as dwelling in one's
heart, the focal point of the principle of mind in the sense of direct,
intuitive intelligence. They embody the fundamental qualities of the
awakened state, peacefully existing just as they are, spontaneously present always and everywhere. They are not at all like the visions of welcoming figures that appeared earlier and that have been reported in
near-death experiences. Nor are they like the reassuring and comforting
divine visions of some religious experiences, producing feelings of bliss

or cosmic unity. Trungpa Rinpoche describes them as irritating and even hostile, especially if one has that kind of expectation. They are beyond anything we could imagine—"a sudden glimpse of another dimension." Their peacefulness is "completely encompassing peace, immovable, invincible peace, the peaceful state that cannot be challenged, that has no age, no end, no beginning."[6] Their sheer presence is so awe-inspiring that it seems threatening. The essence of compassion does not respond to any ego-centered attempts to communicate with it based on hope or fear. They fill the whole of space, the whole of our mind, and the penetrating rays of light from their hearts illuminate every corner of our being so that nothing is left unexposed and there is nowhere to hide.

The deities of the five families appear in their own pure lands or realms, which are the environment or field of the awakened state. Just as the six realms of samsara are produced from the mind, so too are the pure lands. Because of the human tendency to label and categorize in order to understand, we differentiate that infinite, all-pervading field into the pure lands of the different buddhas. We too can perceive them with sacred vision and create them through enlightened activities. But since we do not recognize ourselves and other living beings as deities, we do not recognize the pure lands around us. Instead, we misinterpret our experience of life as the six realms of samsara. Therefore, during the bardo, our tendencies to create the dreamworlds of the six realms also manifest, appearing as beckoning pathways of colored light.

The bardo visions are described as taking place over a sequence of days, but we need not take this too literally. Just as with the pattern of the mandala in terms of space, the human mind needs the support of a familiar structure in order to come to terms with the inconceivable reality that lies behind it, and we inevitably think of time as moving from past to future, one day after another. But this does not mean that events will necessarily follow the order described here, or even that linear time is relevant in the after-death state. In any case, these days are defined as the length of time for which one can remain focused without distraction, so for most of us, they may be as fleeting as a passing thought.

Each of us expresses our energy in characteristic ways, so we each have a special affinity with certain expressions of awakened energy. This

is the meaning of the division into the five families and the reason why
the awakened state manifests in these different forms on different days.
The type of energy that dominates us is the one we are most likely to
notice and respond to in the bardo. Even in ordinary life, we may find
that very strong emotions, such as passion or anger, can arouse us to a
peak of intensity where a gap suddenly opens up. This is the essence of
the bardo experience. The vision of the deities associated with that
particular energy may turn out to be the only one we are able to perceive
during the bardo. It is like the typical problem situation we find ourselves confronting in life, which is the very one that holds the greatest
potentiality for our awakening.

In the naked state of the bardo of dharmata, we are face-to-face
with reality itself; we are confronted with infinite possibilities, beyond
all imagination. These descriptions of successive days are like snapshots
of that total, overwhelming experience taken from different viewpoints;
one or another of them may seem familiar to us in some way so we
find we can make a connection.

Even within the Nyingma tradition there are several slightly different accounts of this bardo. In them, some of the deities may appear
with other colors and attributes, which can be found reflected in paintings of the bardo mandala. (See plate 4, where the peaceful deities are
arranged outside the central circle containing the wrathful deities.) In
addition to the descriptions given in *Liberation through Hearing*, I have
made use of the two texts previously mentioned, *The Hundred Homages*
and *The Dharma Practice*.

The First Day

O child of awakened family, after remaining unconscious for
four and a half days you will move on, and awakening from
your faint you will think, "What has happened to me?" Recognize it to be the bardo. At that time samsara is reversed,
and everything you see appears as lights and images of deities.

The whole of space will shine with a blue light. Then
blessed Vairochana will appear before you from the central

Realm of Expanding Seed. His body is white in color, and he sits on a lion throne, holding an eight-spoked wheel in his hand and embracing the mother, the Queen of Space. The blue light of the skandha of consciousness in its basic purity, the all-encompassing knowledge, clear and bright, sharp and dazzling, will come toward you from the heart of Vairochana in union with his consort, and penetrate you so that your eyes cannot bear it. At the same time, the soft white light of the gods will also penetrate you, both side by side.

The element of space contains all the other elements, so it is the first to manifest as blue light out of the luminous emptiness of the fundamental nature of mind. The family is the Buddha family, appearing within its own pure land at the center of the mandala of the five buddhas. The name of this realm is literally "the expanding bindu": the seed point that contains the whole of existence and spreads out infinitely to pervade and encompass the expanse of space. At the end of this section, it is also called by another name, the Realm of Dense Array. Both these names convey a sense of totality and density: within each atom, there are as many buddhas as there are atoms in the universe.

In this vision on the first day, we find the combination of blue and white that was mentioned previously in connection with the Buddha family. Vairochana, with his radiant white form, is panoramic awareness, the one who sees and knows and illuminates every particle of existence in all directions. He is united with the devi Akashadhatvishvari, the Queen of Space. She is white like him, the color of the moon, while he is the color of a conch shell. They each hold a bell in their left hand. The bell represents the feminine principle of emptiness and wisdom and is always held in the left hand. In their right hands, they each hold a wheel, the symbol of their family. With its eight spokes radiating in the primary and intermediate directions, it represents universality; it is the wheel of dharma, whose eight spokes signify the Buddha's noble eightfold path, and it is also another symbol of sovereignty.

The iconography of these images follows the mahayana ideal in which worldly splendor, beauty, and nobility represent spiritual perfec-

tion. The male and female buddhas are depicted as the king and queen
of their realm, while the bodhisattvas who appear on the following
days are princes and princesses. They wear the "thirteen sambhogakaya
adornments," modeled on the costume of ancient Indian royalty and
consisting of five silk garments and eight items of jewelry.[7] Their clothing is a bodice of white silk embroidered with gold; a lower garment,
like a dhoti, of multicolored silk; a wide, yellow silk sash; a blue silk
shawl; and ribbons in rainbow silk hanging down from a headband.
Their jewelry is of gold and precious gems: earrings, bracelets, anklets,
belt, three necklaces (short, medium, and long), and a crown set with
jewels in the colors of the five families. This list of items may vary
slightly and is not always strictly adhered to in paintings.

The thrones of all five buddhas are formed by lotuses, upon which
is a disk of the moon resting on a sun disk. The lotus is a symbol of
the primordial purity of enlightenment growing out of the muddy
swamp of samsara. It also symbolizes the feminine principle, which
gives birth to all the manifestations of enlightenment. Sitting or standing upon a lotus indicates that the deities have not abandoned samsara
for the peace of nirvana; they enter into the world, but they are not
defiled by it. Since the moon is silver or white, the color of semen, it
represents the masculine principle of compassion and skillful means.
The sun is gold or red, the color of menstrual blood, representing the
feminine principle of wisdom and emptiness. With some exceptions,
peaceful deities are seated on the moon and wrathful deities on the sun.
Generally, both disks are imagined as being present, although only the
uppermost one is actually visible.

Vairochana and the Queen of Space are seated on a throne supported by lions, the king of animals, symbol of sovereignty. In Tibetan
paintings, these are pictured as snow lions, fantastic creatures with
white bodies and turquoise manes and tails. Using an animal as one's
seat or vehicle means that, on the one hand, one has completely overcome and transmuted the negative aspects of its instinctive behavior,
and on the other, one has achieved and integrated its positive characteristics. These animal thrones also represent certain enlightened attributes
possessed by all the buddhas; the lion represents the four kinds of
fearlessness by which the evil forces of the four maras are overcome.

From the heart of the divine couple radiates an intense blue ray
of light; this is the light of all-encompassing knowledge, the knowledge

of the dharmadhatu. It shines out because the skandha of consciousness is "purified in its place," or "in its basis"; that is to say, it is revealed in its own natural, basic purity. In the bardo, we possess all the skandhas in their subtle, purified state, and these skandhas are the five buddhas themselves. The all-encompassing knowledge is the very essence of Vairochana, meaning that our own skandha of consciousness is freed from its dualistic bias and transformed into the all-encompassing non-dual knowledge of total reality.

But the brilliant light of reality is very hard to bear. It is blinding and overpowering as it streams toward us; it pierces the heart like a sharp sword. At the same time, another light flows toward us, invitingly soft and pleasant. This is a white ray of light forming a pathway leading to the realm of the gods. It is created by ignorance and delusion. Ignorance means ignoring and closing off from the clarity and openness of panoramic awareness. Because of the negative effects of past actions, the dead will be terrified by the sharp, penetrating, blue radiance and try to escape from it, but will feel attracted to the pleasant, soothing, white glow of delusion. If they follow that path, they will "wander into the realm of the gods and circle among the six types of existence." The paths leading to the six realms are perceived as softer lights because it is always easier to revert to habitual patterns of behavior than to open out into an entirely new way of being. Trungpa Rinpoche describes this moment of choice as the real meaning of magic: "The point at which we can either extend ourselves further and go towards an unfamiliar brilliance, or return to a familiar and more soothing dimness is the threshold of magic."[8]

There are many possible approaches to enlightenment. If we are unable to recognize the deities and the brilliant light as our own intrinsic nature, we should rely on an attitude of faith, trust, and devotion. We should think of the blue ray of light as Vairochana's compassion, extended like a hook to draw us in to his heart and arouse a feeling of intense longing for it. After the description of the vision on each day, the dead person is reminded of the corresponding verse from the *Aspiration-Prayer for Deliverance from the Dangerous Passage of the Bardo*:

When through intense delusion I wander in samsara,
On the luminous path of all-encompassing knowledge

May blessed Vairochana go before me,
Great mother, the Queen of Space, behind me,
Deliver me from the bardo's dangerous passage
And bring me to the perfect awakened state.

If we surrender ourselves to the brilliant blue ray of knowledge, through either recognition or devotion, we shall "dissolve into rainbow light in the heart of blessed Vairochana in union with his consort and become awakened in the sambhogakaya in the central Realm of Dense Array."

The attitude of devotion is necessary as long as we still feel a sense of separation between the deities and ourselves. Even though we may have understood intellectually, and even experienced to some extent in meditation, that the deities are our own true nature, it is very difficult to integrate and stabilize this realization fully. When we still make a distinction between inside and outside, we must take refuge in the awakened nature that exists beyond ourselves and let go into it without reservation. This does not contradict Trungpa Rinpoche's remarks about the implacability of the peaceful deities. It is true that they cannot be courted or deceived by any kind of self-protective approach, but genuine devotion is the opposite of self-preservation, it is the complete surrender of self.

Those who are experienced in the creation stage of deity yoga or in the surpassing stage of atiyoga will be able to recognize the deities as the display of their own mind and merge with them. Those who cannot recognize directly, but who have enough confidence to let go completely, will also merge with them. Another possibility is for those who have practiced the yoga of illusory body to transform the bardo body into the illusory body and complete their practice in that form. Those who have faith but little experience may be reborn in a lower level of the pure land where they will continue on the path, or at the very least be reborn in this world with excellent connections to dharma. At every point throughout the whole bardo experience, the state we enter depends on the extent to which we give up self-preservation and let go into the visions of reality.

THE SECOND DAY

Because of the karma resulting from ignorance and confusion, we may not have been able to respond to the first vision at all. The five poisons form veils or obscurations, preventing us from seeing clearly, so we continue to wander through the experiences of the bardo. Because the veils of aggression blind us to the presence of the luminosity in which we are immersed, everything in our nature that corresponds to the Vajra family now manifests from our heart to invite and awaken us. In *The Hundred Homages*, the five buddhas are described as not rejecting the five poisons, but embodying their basic purity. Therefore, because we undoubtedly suffer from the five poisons, the five buddhas will inevitably appear as the manifestation of our own intrinsic goodness and wakefulness.

> O child of awakened family, listen without distraction. On the second day, the white light of the purified element of water will shine. Then blessed Vajrasattva-Akshobhya will appear before you from the blue eastern Realm of Manifest Joy. His body is blue in color, and he holds a five-pronged vajra in his hand. He sits on an elephant throne embracing the mother Buddha-Lochana. The two male bodhisattvas, Kshitigarbha and Maitreya, and the two female bodhisattvas, Lasya and Pushpa, surround them. Thus six images of the awakened state will appear. The white light of the skandha of form in its basic purity, the mirror knowledge, dazzling white, clear and bright, will come toward you from the heart of Vajrasattva in union with his consort, and penetrate you so that your eyes cannot bear to look at it. At the same time, the soft smoky light of hell will also penetrate you, side by side with the light of knowledge.

The Vajra family arises out of the sphere of white light of the water element. Akshobhya, the lord of the Vajra family, is here combined with Vajrasattva, the Vajra Being. Vajrasattva is not normally placed within the mandala of the five families but above and beyond it. He is the essence of all the buddhas and contains all the families in himself. He is particularly associated with purification and so is usually white in color, but here he is blue because of his identification with Akshobhya. Again in this family we find the combination of blue and white.

Another unexpected link is provided by his consort, Buddha-Lochana, who is the devi of earth. She too adapts to Akshobhya's color, becoming the blue of lapis lazuli. In relation to the skandhas, earth corresponds to form, and water to feeling, yet in the system of the five families we are using here, Akshobhya goes with both form and water. This crossover of attributes was touched upon in the dissolution of the elements, but it was not discussed in any detail because the union of the male buddhas and the devis had not yet been explained. Now we can see how the combination of water and earth qualities comes about through Akshobhya's union with Lochana. Earth and water need each other. In this case, earth (the devi) provides the environment that supports and contains water (the buddha). As Trungpa Rinpoche pointed out in his commentary, her name means Buddha Eye, so she is the eye of awakening through which the solid, stable characteristics of Akshobhya find an outlet. She "opens out, she provides the exit or activation of the whole thing, the element of communication."

Each of the pair holds a bell in the left hand and a five-pronged vajra in the right. The five prongs at each end of the vajra represent the five male and five female buddhas, so that once again we are reminded of the principle of totality inherent in each of the families.

Akshobhya and Lochana are seated on a throne supported by elephants, suggesting the immovability and strength of the Vajra family. The elephant often symbolizes the mind, wild and dangerous at first, but intelligent and responsive once it is tamed. Here it represents possession of the ten strengths of the buddhas, arising from ten kinds of supernormal and spiritual knowledge.

Around the central couple is their family of bodhisattvas. The bodhisattvas are often called the sons and daughters of the buddhas. In a general sense, all bodhisattvas represent the principle of active engagement for the welfare of others; they are the living manifestation of all the qualities of enlightenment in the world around us. During the bardo visions, sixteen bodhisattvas appear, eight male and eight female, arranged in groups of four in each of the four cardinal directions. They appear because they too are part of our nature.

The eight male bodhisattvas are all well known as independent figures whose stories are told in the mahayana sutras. They also have many different forms apart from those that are found here. Since they embody the male principle of compassionate skillful means, each conveys his own type of compassion. It may be more gentle or more forceful, or it may perform a special function or be directed toward sentient beings in a particular situation. As a group, they represent the natural purification of the eight kinds of consciousness. This means that every experience—without exception—can be enjoyed free from attachment in an awakened way with the attitude of contributing positively to the enlightenment and happiness of the whole of existence.

The eight female bodhisattvas are sometimes known as offering goddesses or puja devis. They represent the transmutation of the objects of the eight kinds of consciousness. This means that everything that arises in the fields of the senses, including the mind, whether it is good or bad, pleasant or unpleasant, happy or sad, is offered to the awakened state and becomes an inspiration to awaken. The feminine always symbolizes emptiness. In their outward form, these eight devis display various kinds of sensory enjoyment, but inwardly they embody their essential emptiness. Without the principle of transmutation, everything we experience simply perpetuates samsara. Food and drink and all the other sensory pleasures only feed our coarse body and mind, so in the end they lead to death. But by offering them to the buddhas, which means enjoying them with awareness from our innate awakened state, they can be transmuted into amrita, the elixir of immortality.

The male and female bodhisattvas are not paired together in corresponding couples, but simply placed in circles of four around the throne of the central couple, according to their individual affinity with the Vajra, Ratna, Padma, and Karma families. They all take on the color of their respective families.

On the right of the throne is Kshitigarbha, Essence of Earth. He represents fertility and growth. He is renowned for his dedication to helping beings in the lower realms, especially in the hells, who are imprisoned within or below the earth. He is the color of a snow mountain. He holds reeds, symbolizing the produce of the earth, in his right hand and a bell in his left hand. He embodies the consciousness of sight, which, as it says in *The Hundred Homages*, should not be rejected as an impure part of samsara but accepted in its natural purity.

On the left side is Maitreya, Friendship. He is the living presence of loving-kindness, the true friend and constant companion of all beings. He is destined to become the buddha of the next age, just as Shakyamuni is the Buddha of the present age. His body is the color of a white cloud. He holds a bell in his left hand. In his right hand is a spray of white "snake-hair" blossom; this is the fragrant Indian *nagchampa* tree, under which it is foretold he will attain full enlightenment as the future buddha. He represents the pure consciousness of hearing.

In front of the central pair of deities is Lasya, Dance. Her name refers to the graceful feminine type of Indian dance, in contrast to the more vigorous masculine style. In Trungpa Rinpoche's words, she "displays the beauty and dignity of the body . . . the majesty and seductiveness of the feminine principle."[9] She represents the basic purity of whatever appears as an object of sight, and she offers this to the eyes of all the buddhas. She is the color of moonstone. She holds a bell in her left hand and in her right is a mirror, the symbol of form.

Behind the central couple is Pushpa, Flower, symbolizing the beauties of nature. She is pearl white and holds a white lotus and bell. The eight female bodhisattvas do not exactly correspond to the eight fields of consciousness, as three of them are said to represent the thoughts of the past, present, and future. It seems that different ideas have been combined in this system. Pushpa purifies all thoughts relating to the past, which could mean memories, regrets, clinging, and so on; it could also mean the concept of past time, which no longer exists yet has such apparent reality and power over our minds.

The brilliant white light of the mirror knowledge, the purified skandha of form, shines out. The skandha of form is the basis of all our assumptions about the nature of material existence. Ordinarily, it is the foundation of our misperception of ourselves and the world as solid and permanent. Now the purified principle of form is transmuted into the great mirror, in which form and emptiness are unified: the mirror is empty, yet forms appear vividly within it. With the awakened eye of Buddha-Lochana, we experience all sense perceptions arising and passing away like a reflection or a dream.

At the same time, a path of softer light, the color of smoke, appears, leading to the realm of hell-beings. The state of hell results from aggression, anger, and hatred, the characteristic negative emotions connected with the Vajra family. The path leading to hell is built from all the aggression accumulated throughout our life. The more accustomed we have become to reacting aggressively, the clearer the smoky path will appear, and the more comforting and inviting it will seem in contrast to the dazzling light of total clarity and self-knowledge. The bardo visions of the deities are really no different from the phenomena of everyday life; they are samsara turned inside out. So if we instinctively respond with aggression to anything we cannot control, the path of our habitual aggressive tendencies will naturally present itself as the easiest way to follow.

The instructions call on the consciousness of the dead person not to look at the path of soft, smoky light. "If you are attracted to it, you will fall down into hell and sink into the muddy swamp of unbearable suffering from which there is never any escape." Instead one should arouse intense devotion toward the brilliant white light. By doing so, one dissolves into the heart of Vajrasattva and attains enlightenment in the sambhogakaya in his Realm of Manifest Joy. The verse for the second day is this:

> When through intense aggression I wander in samsara,
> On the luminous path of the mirror knowledge
> May blessed Vajrasattva go before me,
> Great mother Buddha-Lochana behind me,
> Deliver me from the bardo's dangerous passage
> And bring me to the perfect awakened state.

Now we can see more clearly how these "days" present us with a succession of visions of life in the light of the five families. All the families are complete in themselves, so nothing is left out. It is not that only the Vajra aspects of experience are present on the second day while everything else is cut out of the picture, but more as though at that moment we see our whole world through Vajra spectacles. Everything is suffused with the brilliance, clarity, and precision of the Vajra mode of perception. The objects of the senses, arising from the skandha of form, are crystal clear, sharp, and vivid, appearing as in the new light of dawn. The mind is sharp and clear with the diamondlike intelligence of Vajra. At the same time, there is a sense of firmness and solidity that comes from Akshobhya's nature, enhanced by the earth qualities of Lochana. There is also the compassionate activity of the bodhisattvas and the transmutation of form and vision by the devis. All of these exist inherently within us. They are continually being manifested as the play of our own mind. From moment to moment, we have the choice of either accepting the world in our usual unaware manner, influenced by habitual tendencies toward negativity and aggression, or of waking up and seeing it afresh through the awakened vision of Buddha-Lochana.

The Third Day

If one has not even noticed the vision of the Vajra family or if one was afraid and ran away from it, then the Ratna aspects of one's nature will appear next, in order to transmute the obscuring veils of pride that cause one to continue through the journey of the bardo.

> O child of awakened family, listen without distraction. On the third day, the yellow light of the purified element of earth will shine. Then blessed Ratnasambhava will appear before you from the yellow southern Glorious Realm. His body is yellow in color and he holds a wish-fulfilling jewel in his hand. He sits on a throne of excellent horses, embracing the mother Mamaki. The two male bodhisattvas, Akasha-garbha and Samantabhadra, and the two female bodhisattvas, Mala and Dhupa, surround them. Thus six images of the awakened state will appear out of the space of rainbows, rays, and light. The yellow light of the skandha of feeling in its basic purity, the equalizing knowledge, brilliant yellow, adorned with spheres of light, so clear and bright that the eyes cannot endure it, will come toward you from the heart of Ratnasambhava in union with his consort, and penetrate straight into your heart so that your eyes cannot bear to look at it. At the same time, the soft blue light of the human

realm will also pierce your heart, side by side with the light of knowledge.

Within the yellow sphere of light of the earth element, the deities of the Ratna family appear. Mamaki, the essence of water, is the mother of the family, complementing the earth of Ratnasambhava, the father. She provides the element of fertility that enables earth to be productive. Their bodies are golden, and they each hold a bell and a jewel, the wishing-gem that fulfills all desires.

Their throne is supported by horses. In ancient India, horses were the prized possessions of the ruling and warrior caste, so their presence contributes to the general atmosphere of pride, wealth, and nobility that characterizes the Ratna family. The horse represents attainment of the four bases of miraculous ability, which are like its four legs with their magical speed and endurance.

On the right is Samantabhadra, Universal Goodness. As a bodhisattva, he is distinct from the primordial buddha Samantabhadra. He is topaz yellow; he holds a bell and an ear of corn, symbolizing fruitfulness; and he represents the consciousness of smell. He is renowned for his generosity in making vast offerings to all the buddhas throughout space and time. Here he particularly embodies the goodness of the earth, with its sense of infinite abundance, confidence, and stability.

On the left is Akashagarbha, Essence of Space. He is a rich golden color, holding a bell and a sword. A sword always conveys the action of compassionate wisdom cutting through confusion. His presence suggests the space surrounding the earth in which everything can grow and move; he is the expanse of sky that the earth requires to display its qualities and to balance its own solidity. He represents the consciousness of taste.

In front is Mala, Garland. She is saffron yellow, holding a garland and bell. With graceful gestures, she offers her garlands, woven from the flowers of the earth, as adornments to the buddhas. She represents the concepts of all phenomena, the objects of the mental consciousness.

Behind is Dhupa, Incense. She is the yellow color of the Ratna family's symbolic jewel. She embodies the objects of the sense of smell, and she holds a bowl of incense with which she offers the enjoyment of scent. The fragrance of her incense pervades the atmosphere, filling the whole environment with goodness and freshness.

The equalizing knowledge shines from the heart of Ratnasambhava as a ray of brilliant yellow light. Because Mamaki is the essence of the element of water, the skandha of feeling that goes with water is now associated with the Ratna family. Feeling is the root of all sensations—pleasant, unpleasant, or neutral—which in turn lead to the emotions of attraction, aversion and indifference. When the skandha of feeling is purified, it does not mean that the distinctions between sensations disappear or that we cease to experience emotions, but that we are no longer enslaved by them. The equalizing knowledge of sameness frees us to enjoy the one, essential flavor that lies at the heart of all experience.

The Ratna world is pervaded by an atmosphere of richness, enjoyment, and positivity. Ratnasambhava's pure land is called the Glorious Realm because all the glorious, jewel-like qualities of enlightenment are manifested through it. The equalizing knowledge pierces our heart with its dazzling yellow light ray, arousing us to awaken into that state. The instructions urge us not to be afraid of the brilliant light:

> Rest your awareness upon it, relaxed in the state free from activity, or let yourself be drawn toward it with longing. If you recognize it as the natural radiance of your own awareness, even though you do not feel devotion and longing and do not say the aspiration-prayer, all the rays of light and forms of the deities will dissolve into you inseparably, and you will attain enlightenment.

But the Ratna qualities can be distorted into the poison of pride. Pride is another way of looking at life, another path. It enters our heart as a softer, blue light leading to the human realm:

> That is the inviting path of light of karmic imprints accumulated by your intense pride. If you are attracted to it, you will fall into the human realm and experience birth, old age, death, and suffering, and never escape from the muddy swamp of samsara. It is an obstacle blocking the path of liberation, so do not look at it, but give up pride.

The verse for the third day is as follows:

> When through intense pride I wander in samsara,
> On the luminous path of equalizing knowledge

May blessed Ratnasambhava go before me,
Great mother Mamaki behind me,
Deliver me from the bardo's dangerous passage
And bring me to the perfect awakened state.

By arousing genuine faith and trust in the reality of our awakened nature as expressed through the Ratna characteristics, we can dissolve into the heart of Ratnasambhava and attain enlightenment in his Glorious Realm.

THE FOURTH DAY

The text assures us that liberation is certain when we are shown in this way, yet there may be those who are still unable to recognize because of the harmful effects of their past actions. Next, the Padma family will appear, because desire and passion prevent us from seeing the true nature of our mind.

> O child of awakened family, listen without distraction. On the fourth day, the red light of the purified element of fire will shine. Then blessed Amitabha will appear before you from the red western Blissful Realm. His body is red in color, and he holds a lotus in his hand. He sits on a peacock throne embracing the mother Pandaravasini. The two male bodhisattvas, Avalokiteshvara and Manjushri, and the two female bodhisattvas, Gita and Aloka, surround them. Thus six images of the awakened state will appear out of the space of rainbow light. The red light of the skandha of perception in its basic purity, the investigative knowledge, brilliant red, ornamented with spheres of light, clear and bright, sharp and dazzling, will penetrate straight into your heart from the heart of Amitabha in union with his consort, so that your eyes cannot bear it. Do not be afraid of it. At the same time, the soft yellow light of the hungry ghosts will also shine, side by side with the light of knowledge. Do not take pleasure in it; give up desire and yearning.

Amitabha's Padma family appears from the element of fire. Everything connected with this family expresses the transmutation of passion, the root of samsara, into compassion, the activity of enlightenment. Fire symbolizes them both and is the transmuting force that transforms one into the other. Amitabha is copper-colored, while Pandaravasini is like a fiery crystal. Her white clothing, from which she takes her name, is woven from a material cleansed by fire. They hold bells and red lotuses in their hands. The lotus grows with its roots deep in mud and slime, but its flower rises above the water untainted and unpolluted; it feeds on the rich manure of the poisons and transmutes it into enlightenment.

Amitabha's throne is supported by peacocks, which are reputed to eat poison, consuming and transforming it into the brilliant colors of their tail feathers. They represent possession of the ten powers to perform various miraculous actions. The peacock's tail is a supreme example of beauty and magnificence displayed for seduction and lust, so sitting upon a peacock represents overcoming the negative aspects of the Padma personality. The awakened person uses these great powers of attraction to draw others to the truth, instead of seducing them for selfish ends. Both the lotus and the peacock express the unconditional openness of compassion, its ability to absorb and feed on garbage and poison, welcoming any situation, however negative it may seem.

On the right of the central couple is Avalokiteshvara, the Lord Who Looks Down. Although all bodhisattvas embody compassionate activity, he is the principle of compassion. Wherever we find spontaneous, altruistic love among living beings, that is a manifestation of Avalokiteshvara. He is coral-colored, holding a bell and a red lotus, the flower of compassion. He represents the bodily consciousness, the sense of touch.

On the left is Manjushri, Gentle Glory, who is known as the bodhisattva of wisdom. He embodies the intellectual aspect of compassion, and the intuition of emptiness that alone makes genuine compassion possible: the understanding that helping others and being helped are both illusion, because all beings are already awakened in the sphere of ultimate truth. He is vermilion in color, holding a bell in his left hand. In his right hand, *The Hundred Homages* says that he holds a lotus, while *The Dharma Practice* gives him a sword: this is his usual attribute, the sword of wisdom that cuts through the knots of confusion and doubt, but the two are often combined, as a sword resting upon a lotus. He represents the mental consciousness.

In front is Gita, Song. She is the color of the red hibiscus flower. She is playing a stringed instrument, which originally would probably have been the Indian *vina*, but in Tibetan paintings is more like a guitar. The guitar seems an appropriate image to use in the West. She plays on it to accompany her songs of offering to the buddhas, representing the objects of the sense of hearing.

Behind is Aloka, Light. She is the color of a red lotus, and she holds a brightly shining lamp, offering light to all the buddhas. She purifies the concept of the future and all the thoughts, plans, hopes, and fears relating to it.

The dazzling red light that streams from the heart of Amitabha and Pandaravasini is the light of the skandha of perception transmuted into investigative knowledge. Perception links subject and object together, but in the ordinary state, the dualistic distinction between them always remains and gives rise to emotional reactions. Investigative knowledge transcends duality and sees things as they really are, individual yet undivided. It looks with the eye of love at all living beings and all inanimate objects, distinguishing them and appreciating their different qualities.

In order to dissolve into the radiance of Amitabha's heart, we must let go of grasping and attachment. If we cannot do that, if we find the light too sharp and penetrating, we shall be attracted instead to the soft yellow light. We shall fall back into our habitual ways of wanting, greed, and passion. But samsara is impermanent and unsatisfactory, so we can never really be satisfied and fulfilled within it. If we follow that path, we shall eventually end up in the hungry ghost realm, the world of perpetually frustrated desire. "That is the path of light of karmic imprints accumulated by your intense passion. If you are attracted to it, you will fall into the realm of hungry ghosts and experience unbearable suffering from hunger and thirst."

To avoid falling back into the habit of grasping and to arouse the awakened qualities of the Padma family within us during the bardo, we should remember this verse:

When through intense passion I wander in samsara,
On the luminous path of investigative knowledge
May blessed Amitabha go before me,
Great mother Pandaravasini behind me,
Deliver me from the bardo's dangerous passage
And bring me to the perfect awakened state.

By letting go into the radiant light of Amitabha's presence, we become awakened in Sukhavati, the Blissful Realm, the pure land that he established as the living expression of his vows to liberate all beings. This is the field of experience in which supreme bliss is inseparable from the realization of emptiness. If we cannot attain full enlightenment, we may be reborn there to continue our progress on the path. It is said that to reach the other pure lands, one needs to have strong karmic connections with them or to have performed special practices. But because of Amitabha's compassion, Sukhavati is accessible to all who have faith in him. This implies that the vision of the Padma deities is perhaps the only one that many people will see in the bardo—if indeed they see anything at all. It is an experience of the atmosphere and presence of absolute love, although it may be too intense to bear.

THE FIFTH DAY

If we are unable to respond to the Padma vision, then all our tendencies toward jealousy and envy will come to the fore and we will "wander on downward to the fifth day of the bardo," when the Karma family manifests.

O child of awakened family, listen without distraction. On the fifth day, the green light of the purified element of air will shine. Then blessed Amoghasiddhi, the lord attended by his circle, will appear before you from the green northern Realm of Accumulated Actions. His body is green in color, and he holds a double vajra in his hand. He sits on a throne of *kinnara* birds soaring through the sky, embracing the mother Samaya-Tara. The two male bodhisattvas, Vajrapani

and Sarvanivaranavishkambhin, and the two female bodhisattvas, Gandha and Naivedya, surround them. Thus six images of the awakened state will appear out of the space of
rainbow light. The green light of the skandha of conditioning in its basic purity, the action-accomplishing knowledge,
brilliant green, clear and bright, sharp and terrifying, orna-
mented with spheres of light, will penetrate straight into your
heart from the heart of Amoghasiddhi in union with his
consort, so that your eyes cannot bear to look at it. It is the
natural creative energy of knowledge arising from your own
awareness, so rest without action in the supreme state of
equanimity in which there is neither near nor far, neither love
nor hate, and you will not be afraid of it. At the same time,
the soft red light of the jealous gods, caused by envy, will
also shine upon you, together with the light of knowledge.
Meditate so that you feel neither attraction nor aversion to
it. But if your mind is weak, then simply do not take pleasure
in it.

From the green light of the air element, the Karma family appears
last of the five. The Karma family represents perfect activity; it embodies the energy or skill that accomplishes and puts into action the qualities of all the families. The mother of the family and consort of
Amoghasiddhi is Tara, the most beloved of all the female deities. She
is the feminine embodiment of compassionate action. Primarily she is
the essence of the element of air, yet she has many different forms and
can appear in any of the five families. Here she is specifically named
Samaya-Tara to mark her relationship with the Karma or Samaya family. Amoghasiddhi is turquoise, while Samaya-Tara is the color of an
emerald. They hold bells and double vajras: vajras in the form of a
cross, symbolizing activity that cannot be obstructed in all the four
directions.

Their throne is borne aloft by *kinnaras,* creatures that are half-bird
and half-human. In Indian mythology, kinnaras are celestial musicians,
similar to gandharvas, sometimes appearing as half-bird and sometimes
as half-horse. Here they represent accomplishment of the four indestructible activities and demonstrate the energy and speed of the Karma

family, instantaneously traveling through space. In paintings, they have human faces, bodies, and arms with birds' feet, wings, and tails; two or four of them are placed beneath the throne, playing a variety of musical instruments such as strings, flutes, and cymbals.[10] In his commentary, Trungpa Rinpoche describes this bird, called *shang-shang* in Tibetan, as a type of *garuda*. Amoghasiddhi's throne is also sometimes said to be supported by garudas, although kinnaras are more often seen. Garudas devour serpents and are very fierce-looking, with iron horns, beaks, and talons. They are described in chapter 14, in a mandala in which they support the thrones of the wrathful deities.

On the right of the central couple is Sarvanivaranavishkambhin, Remover of All Obstacles. He is green, holding a bell in his left hand and a book in his right. The book represents the teaching of the dharma, which shows how to overcome all difficulties and hindrances to liberation. He embodies the source consciousness.

On the left is Vajrapani, He Who Holds a Vajra in His Hand. He is emerald-colored, holding a bell and a vajra. As his name suggests, he normally belongs to the Vajra family, and he is more usually found as a wrathful protector deity. Here his vajra symbolizes energy and activity, so he is equally at home in the Karma family. He represents the afflicted mental consciousness or cloudy mind. Even this aspect of consciousness is pure in its natural state and need not be rejected.

In front is Gandha, Fragrance. She is described both as green and as the color of the blue lotus. She holds a conch shell filled with perfume made from precious essences to anoint the bodies of the buddhas. Generally, the offering of perfume symbolizes the sense of touch, because fragrant oils and creams have always been used in India for massage and to soothe the skin in the heat. But here touch is absent from the list, and Gandha is said to purify the thoughts of the present moment.

The last female bodhisattva may be either Naivedya, Food Offering, or Nritya, Dance. Both of them appear frequently in similar lists of eight goddesses. The Tibetan texts available to me have garbled versions of the Sanskrit name, which look closer to Nritya, but iconographically, it is clear that she corresponds to Naivedya.[11] She is sea green and holds a vessel of delicious food containing the elixir of life, offering the objects of the sense of taste to the buddhas. By realizing its essential emptiness, the enjoyment of taste is purified in awareness, and food becomes not just fuel for the perishable body, but nourishment for the awakened mind.

The skandha of conditioning, which leads to all our worldly actions and to the chain of karmic cause and effect, is in its pure nature the action-accomplishing knowledge, which spontaneously performs the work of enlightenment. It shines out from the heart of Amoghasiddhi and Tara as a brilliant green ray. Now that we have reached the fifth day of the bardo, the instructions become even more insistent, reminding us not to fear, not to resist, not to think of the visions as separate from ourselves. Our tendencies toward jealousy, envy, and suspicion will make us feel threatened and draw us to the soothing beam of soft red light. "That is the inviting path of karma accumulated by your intense envy. If you are attracted to it, you will fall into the realm of jealous gods and experience unbearable misery from fighting and quarreling." We should try to reach a state of equanimity where we feel neither fear of the bright light nor attraction to the soft light, but if that is too difficult, we should at least try not to take pleasure in the path of our habitual reactions, and so avoid being sucked into it completely.

This is the verse for the fifth day:

When through intense envy I wander in samsara,
On the luminous path of action-accomplishing knowledge
May blessed Amoghasiddhi go before me,
Great mother Samaya-Tara behind me,
Deliver me from the bardo's dangerous passage
And bring me to the perfect awakened state.

If we are able to respond to the appearance of the Karma deities and dissolve into their hearts, we become awakened on the level of the sambhogakaya in their pure land, here given the alternative name of Realm of Perfected Actions. This is the field in which all the indestructible activities that liberate sentient beings are spontaneously accomplished, where everything is already perfect.

THE SIXTH DAY

If the dead person has not been able to make a connection with any of the five families individually, on the sixth day they will all appear simultaneously.

> O child of awakened family, listen without distraction. Even though the visions of each of the five families were pointed out to you as they appeared until yesterday, you became panic-stricken under the influence of negative karmic imprints, and so you have remained here until now. If you had recognized the inner radiance of the knowledge of those five families as your own self-display, you would have dissolved into rainbow light in the body of one of the five families, and so would have become awakened in the sambhogakaya. But because you did not recognize, you have gone on wandering here until the present. So now watch without distraction. Now the vision of the complete five families and what is called the vision of the four knowledges combined will come to invite you. Recognize them!

The deities of the five families appear exactly as before, each in their own circle of light surrounded by rainbows of the five colors, arranged in one vast mandala. Vairochana and the Queen of Space are in the center, Akshobhya-Vajrasattva with Buddha-Lochana and the other Vajra deities in the east, Ratnasambhava with Mamaki and the Ratna deities in the south, Amitabha with Pandaravasini and the Padma deities in the west, and Amoghasiddhi with Samaya-Tara and the Karma deities in the north. The mandala has four gates, each protected by a pair of male and female guardians. The buddhas of the six realms of samsara also appear, and seated above them all are Samantabhadra and Samantabhadri, the father and mother of all buddhas. This makes up the entire mandala of the forty-two peaceful deities.

Although this is the peaceful mandala, the guardians of the gates appear in wrathful form to carry out their functions. They are there to protect the sacred space of pure vision. They wake us up and guard our awareness from negative influences and from escape into distractions of any kind. They are surrounded by flames, embracing each other in sexual union and trampling upon the corpse of ego.

There are several sets of four that can be symbolically linked to them. In *The Hundred Homages*, the male guardians are described as purifying the four false views. These are not so much philosophical views as instinctive outlooks on life that obstruct our understanding and practice of dharma. First is the belief in permanence, the feeling that we last forever. Second is the opposite belief in extinction, that when we die there is nothing more. Third is the belief in the existence of self as a permanent, independent essence. And fourth is the belief in characteristics by which things can be defined and fixed as permanent and independent. In other systems, these views are sometimes associated with the four female guardians.

Here, according to *The Hundred Homages*, the female guardians embody the four immeasurable states of mind, also known as the four abodes of Brahma. First is compassion, the desire for all beings to be free from suffering. Second is friendship or loving-kindness, the wish for the happiness of all beings. (In meditation practice, these two are usually in reverse order.) Third is joy, unselfish pleasure in the happiness and good qualities of others. And fourth is equanimity, the freedom from any bias toward unbalanced attachment or aversion.

The guardians of the eastern gate are the male Vijaya, Victory, and female Ankusha, Hook. They both have the white color of the Vajra family. Vijaya holds a bell in his left hand and a club in his right. He purifies the view of permanence. Trungpa Rinpoche related the male guardians to the four indestructible enlightened activities, which are four styles of liberation. These were explained in the chapter on the elements and are often also associated with the devis and the female guardians. Vijaya represents the activity of pacifying, which completely overcomes aggression and calms negativities of mind and body. He epitomizes what Trungpa Rinpoche called invincible peace, the irresistible, victorious quality of the peace of the awakened state. Ankusha holds an iron hook to draw us in. In Trungpa Rinpoche's words, the function of her hook is "to catch you like a fish if you try to run away."[12] She represents immeasurable compassion.

Guarding the southern gate are Yamantaka, Destroyer of Death, and Pasha, Noose, both the yellow color of the Ratna family. Yamantaka holds a bell and a staff topped with a skull, and he purifies the view of extinction. He performs the activity of enriching. Yama, the

god of death, literally means "restraint," the ultimate limitation of everything we desire. By putting an end to death, Yamantaka destroys all
limitations and increases both spiritual and worldly wealth. Pasha holds
a noose or rope to tie us up. Trungpa Rinpoche, in his commentary,
paints a wonderful picture of someone trying to escape by puffing
themselves up with pride (the Ratna poison), filling up all the space of
the mandala, so then "the goddess with a lasso ties you from head
to toe leaving you without any chance to expand."[13] She represents
immeasurable kindness.

At the western gate are Hayagriva, Horse-Necked, and Shrinkhala,
Chain, both the red color of the Padma family. Hayagriva holds a bell
and an iron chain and purifies the view of belief in self. The sound of
the bell invites and the chain binds. With his horse's head, he neighs
loudly to wake us up, and he performs the activity of magnetizing,
which attracts and subdues through the energy of passionate compassion. Whatever we need to bring our practice to completion is drawn
to us spontaneously and brought under our control. Shrinkhala also
holds an iron chain to fetter us if we try to run away through passion.
She represents the immeasurable state of sympathetic joy.

Finally, at the northern gate are Amritakundalin, Coil of Amrita,
and Ghanta, Bell. They are both green, belonging to the Karma family.
Amritakundalin holds a bell and the double vajra of unobstructed fulfillment of action. He purifies the view of belief in characteristics. He
performs the activity of destruction, unhesitatingly stamping out negativity when it has gone too far. Amrita is the nectar of immortality that
does not allow us to escape by committing suicide. If we try to destroy
ourselves out of despair or paranoia, Amritakundalin will bring us back
to life. Ghanta holds a bell, which she rings loudly to silence our protes-
tations and screams of fear. She represents the immeasurable state of
equanimity.

Altogether, these eight guardians of the gates show us forcefully
that there is no escape from the true nature of our own mind, our
innate awakened state. The mandala is filled with the principles of the
five families, encompassing the primordial purity of every aspect of our
being. If we are unable to recognize it, and cling to the illusion of ego,
we do not really escape from the brilliant light of knowledge, we just
create a temporary hiding place among the fantasy worlds of the six

realms of samsara. But even there we cannot stay hidden because the buddhas who come to save sentient beings in the six realms are also present in this mandala. In this context, the six buddhas are all regarded as manifestations of Avalokiteshvara, the Lord of Compassion. Wherever we go, the compassion of enlightenment will catch up with us.

In the realm of the gods, Avalokiteshvara appears as Indra Shatakratu, Indra of the Hundred Sacrifices, the leader of the gods in the ancient Vedic pantheon. He is white and purifies the poison of pride. He plays on the stringed instrument, enchanting those who are intoxicated with pleasure and teaching impermanence through the music of the dharma.

In the realm of the jealous gods, he appears as Vemachitra, a hero in shining armor, a great leader bearing weapons of war. He is green in color and purifies envy. He subdues the rampant, paranoid energy and speed of this state of mind by the gentle, invincible strength of the true warrior.

In the human realm, he is born as the Shakyamuni, the historical Buddha. Here on earth, he acts as a homeless wanderer, holding an alms bowl and a beggar's staff, teaching through his example of renunciation. He is yellow in color and purifies passion.

In the animal realm, he has the name Dhruvasimha, Steadfast Lion, since the lion is the king of beasts. He is blue and purifies delusion. He brings with him a book to enlighten the ignorance of the animal mentality.

Among the hungry ghosts, he appears as a powerful and lordly hungry ghost called Jvalamukha, Mouth of Flame. He is red and purifies greed. To satisfy the state of mind of insatiable hunger, he offers divine food in a jeweled dish.

To those who dwell in hell, he is Dharmaraja, the Dharma King. He is black in color and purifies aggression. He bears vessels of cooling water and warming fire to liberate the sentient beings there from the suffering of the hot and cold hells.

Above them all is the principle of universal goodness, Samantabhadra and Samantabhadri in union. The entire display of the awakened state is spread out before us. The instructions remind us once again of its real nature:

The forty-two sambhogakaya deities will emerge again from within your own heart and appear before you. They arise as your own pure self-display, so recognize them. O child of awakened family, those realms do not exist anywhere else, but dwell in the center and four directions of your heart, and now they emerge again from within your heart and appear before you. Nor do those images come from anywhere else, but they too exist from the beginning as the natural creative energy of your awareness, so recognize them in this way.

The culmination of the sixth day is "the vision of the four knowledges combined." The rays of light that stretch from the hearts of the buddhas to our own hearts spread out into luminous cloths of dazzling brilliance, "very fine and clear, like cobwebs of sunbeams joined together." Then, upon this fabric of light, sparkling bindus emerge; they are disks or spheres, resembling jewel bowls turned over to face down toward us from above. This time, the first two colors are reversed. Upon the white cloth of all-encompassing knowledge appear spheres like downward-facing mirrors; upon the blue cloth of the mirror knowledge appear spheres like turquoise bowls facedown; upon the yellow cloth of equalizing knowledge appear spheres like golden bowls; and upon the red cloth of investigative knowledge are spheres like coral bowls. Within each one, there are five similar spheres, five more within each of those, and so on, becoming smaller and smaller, so that it seems as if we are gazing into the infinite depth of space. We are drawn into these pools of light, losing all sense of a reference point, so that there is no center and no boundary.

The appearance of these four lights means that we have the potential to manifest all the qualities of primordial knowledge. But because its manifestation has not yet been fully realized, the green light of action-accomplishing knowledge does not shine along with the others. The fifth aspect of knowledge is the actual accomplishment of the other four. It is called the creative energy of knowledge, implying the potency and skill to express the awakened state fully and completely.

O child of awakened family; these too have arisen from the creative energy of your awareness, they have not come from anywhere else. So do not be attached to them and do not fear them, but stay relaxed in a state free from thought. In that state, all the images and rays of light will dissolve into you and you will become enlightened. O child of awakened family, the green light of action-accomplishing knowledge does not appear because the creative energy of knowledge within your awareness is not perfect.

The experience of these visions is called the inner path or passage-way of Vajrasattva, who is our innermost, indestructible vajra being. This is the final opportunity to merge with the deities in their peaceful form. At this moment, we should try to remember our guru's previous instructions and our earlier experience of the brilliant rays of light, which were pointed out as being our self-display, arising from our own awareness. If we have confidence we shall be able to recognize them—just as in a meeting of old friends or of a mother and child—and dissolve into the light and images to become awakened in the sambho-gakaya.

At the same time, the soft, dull rays of light leading to the six realms of samsara, including that of the animals, which has not ap-peared before, will shine together. These are the white light of the realm of the gods, the red light of the realm of the jealous gods, the blue light of the human realm, the green light of the animal realm, the yellow light of the hungry ghost realm, and the smoky light of the hell realm. If we are attracted to any one of them, we shall take birth there. To prevent this, we should remember the aspiration-prayer:

> When through the five poisons I wander in samsara,
> On the luminous path of the four knowledges combined
> May the victorious ones of the five families go before me,
> The great mothers of the five families behind me,
> Save me from the paths of light to the six impure realms,
> Deliver me from the bardo's dangerous passage
> And bring me to the perfect awakened state.

Through the inspiration of this verse, the best practitioners will recognize their own self-display and merge with the buddhas, those of average abilities will be liberated by the power of intense devotion, and even those of lesser intelligence will attain enlightenment through the passageway of Vajrasattva.

Chapter Thirteen

Crazy Wisdom

AFTER THE PEACEFUL DEITIES have dissolved back into luminous emptiness, they emerge again in a new form: as the five vidyadharas with their consorts, the five dakinis. They are neither really peaceful nor really wrathful, so they are not counted among the hundred peaceful and wrathful deities, and they are not described in the *Hundred Homages*. They are generally depicted in paintings of the complete bardo mandala (see plate 4, where they are shown directly below the central circle), but when the peaceful and wrathful mandalas are painted separately they may appear in either one, be split between them, or even be left out altogether.[1]

The vidyadharas are connected with speech and dwell in the throat, emerging from it to appear before us, just as the peaceful deities emerged from the heart. They are the expressive, communicative energy of the awakened state. As we have been too oblivious or too frightened to respond to the deities in their peaceful manifestations, they now display a different aspect, singing and dancing to attract our attention, inviting and seducing us into waking up. They and their dakini partners are powerful, passionate, and ecstatic, entwined together in union, dancing naked in the sky (see plate 5).

Vidyadhara means a holder of *vidya*, spiritual knowledge, which I have been translating as "awareness." Its meaning is discussed in chapter 10, and all the various implications mentioned there are relevant to the vidyadharas. In Indian mythology, vidyadharas were powerful and magical celestial beings, often depicted as having wings and flying through the air. The term may also refer to highly realized human beings such as great teachers and siddhas: accomplished yogins and yoginis who have attained supernormal powers. They possess the vidya of supreme awareness, the direct experience and presence of the ultimate nature of mind, but they also manifest vidya in its relative sense. They are masters of every kind of learning and skill to the highest degree, which they display as the expression of their realization and as their method of teaching. They are scientists, artists, warriors, and lovers, but above all, they are magicians. Vidya is particularly associated with the knowledge of mantra: sound as the communicative and creative power of the awakened state; the vidyadharas are masters of mantra. Trungpa Rinpoche says in his commentary, "They represent the divine form of the tantric guru, possessing power over the magical aspects of the universe."[2]

Dakini, like devi, is a term that covers the whole spectrum of the feminine principle.[3] It can be used for female buddhas and bodhisattvas as well as for what are called worldly dakinis, such as local deities who still need the guidance of powerful yogins like Guru Rinpoche, who is known as "the tamer of dakinis." It can also refer to advanced women practitioners and spiritual consorts. Using the name dakini rather than devi brings out a special quality of the feminine principle. In Indian mythology, dakinis are witches, whether human or otherworldly; they are wild and often malicious, eaters of raw flesh and drinkers of blood. In vajrayana, their samsaric nature is transformed into an instrument of wisdom and compassion. The fierce, passionate aspect of energy they embody is recognized as a vital element on the path of awakening and as an expression of enlightened realization. The traditional etymology of the word *dakini* derives it from a root meaning "to fly," and the Tibetan translation, *khandro* or *khandroma*, means "sky-going." They dance in the openness of space, exulting in the joy and freedom of the experience of selflessness.

Dakinis carry with them an atmosphere of power, magic, and danger—the magic and power of transmutation, the danger of letting go into space. They embody the whole mystery of *maya*, "illusion," for the feminine principle is the ultimate truth of emptiness, yet it is also the relative truth of the five elements and the fields of the senses. If we are taken in by illusion, the dakinis will appear as tricksters—playful, deceptive, and possibly harmful; but if we see through their façade, they will guide us to enlightenment. They are simultaneously creative and destructive. They are continually bringing us messages, giving us reminders, showing us our mistakes, inspiring us, inviting us to join their dance. They are called the root of the four activities because they are the source of the inspiration and energy necessary for enlightened actions. They are guardians of the secret teachings, whose real meaning is "self-secret," hidden from us until we are ready to understand them through listening to the voice of the dakinis within us.

The vidyadharas and dakinis seem to express in a very special way the spirit of the vajrayana path. They communicate through the language of symbolism, which is so important for understanding *Liberation through Hearing*. There are two aspects of symbolism in vajrayana, the iconography of the deities and the natural symbolism of everyday life, which are intimately linked together. Now that we have explored some of the traditional imagery connected with the peaceful deities, the vision of the vidyadharas gives us a good opportunity to look more closely into the significance and function of this symbolism.

This is not symbolism in its ordinary sense, where one thing stands for something else, usually an abstract concept. Here, as Trungpa Rinpoche said, "the thing itself is its own symbol."[4] He was speaking of the level of realization of mahamudra, which he translated as "the great symbol," but his words apply to the whole of tantric symbolism. It is to do with direct perception, seeing things as they really are. Dharma is not a theory or a system of beliefs imposed on reality, so we do not need symbols to point to something else. Dharma is the discovery of the meaning inherent in the world just as it is; everything already reveals the Buddha's message. According to Trungpa Rinpoche, "The universe is constantly trying to reach us to say something or teach something, but we are rejecting it all the time."[5] We only need to open our eyes and our minds, and the way to do that is through meditation. This does not necessarily mean meditation on the deities, which comes later, but first and foremost, the meditation of letting go, which allows us to experience our world more completely, with greater clarity and precision.

Even without the help of a meditational path, the natural symbolism of everyday life reveals itself spontaneously. Poets and artists have always known it. As William Blake wrote:

> If the doors of perception were cleansed every thing would appear to man as it is: Infinite.
> For man has closed himself up, till he sees all things thro' narrow chinks of his cavern.[6]

Blake claimed that he always saw with "a double vision," perceiving the spiritual nature of things with his inner eye at the same time his outer eye saw their physical appearance. His approach to life was amazingly close to tantra in so many ways, although it seems there remained a sense of dualism in his fundamental view, a conflict between spirit and matter.

The symbolism of vajrayana is based on the ultimate meaning of emptiness, which, as the *Heart Sutra* says, is none other than form. It is a two-way process; form is emptiness and emptiness is form, and there is no opposition between them. This goes back to an understanding of the basic Buddhist principles of impermanence and nonself. We know that everything is impermanent, that life is a continuous process of change. Nothing could exist for a moment if it were really solid and unchanging. So form is constantly revealing its empty essence. Yet emptiness also unceasingly manifests as form, displaying the entire phenomenal universe in its state of natural purity. The awareness of these two elements inseparably linked together is mahamudra, the great symbol, the vision of the deities.

Appreciation of this kind of symbolism depends above all on developing a real sense of the presence of enlightened qualities, which is quite simply what the deities are, and allowing them to awaken within us. It is a process of opening up our vision, not just of developing our imagination and projecting it onto the external world. As we learn to work with the imagery of the creation stage in deity yoga, we gradually come to experience the meaning of the deities directly, without conceptual thought. Instead of "imagining" them, we feel the actual presence of their natures, until eventually they may become so real that we meet them face-to-face.

In our ordinary state, the ego, or watcher, sits at the center of our experience like a spider, paralyzing everything that falls into its web. We project ourselves onto the world; as Trungpa Rinpoche put it, "everything is 'me' all over the place."[7] To use another of his expressions, we solidify space, but once the reference point of ego begins to dissolve, we find that we can experience everything in a different way, within the openness of centerless space. We can perceive directly from our original, empty mind, or "non-reference-point mind," and become one with objects of perception, with sensations and emotions.[8] Then everything becomes much more real, much more alive and vivid. Whatever we see, whatever we hear, whatever we touch, taste, and smell speaks to us of its own inherent nature. "The whole world is symbol— not symbol in the sense of a sign representing something other than itself, but symbol in the sense of the highlights of the vivid qualities of things as they are."[9]

From this point of view, symbolism is closely connected with the mandala principle; it is a bridge between ordinary perception, which creates samsara, and sacred vision, in which everything is seen as the mandala of the awakened state. The whole environment is a pure land, and all the sentient beings within it are deities. But symbolism is not only visual; it includes all the senses. Everything we hear and everything we say is the sound of the deity's mantra, and whatever thoughts and feelings arise within our mind are the expression of the deity's awakened mind. Here symbolism is a tool for transmutation. Yet at the same time, the mandala is already completely present and perfectly accomplished. From that perspective, symbolism is simply a statement of reality and a method of direct recognition.

How can we begin to get a feeling for vajrayana imagery? Already we live in a symbolic world: words are symbols; numbers are symbols; what we do, what we wear, how we move are all symbols; even our thoughts and feelings are symbols. So we are actually quite used to symbolism, although we do not usually think of it in that way. If we learn to appreciate the symbolism of everyday life, we can gradually relate that to the iconographic symbolism of the deities. As Trungpa Rinpoche put it, symbolism does not need to be anything special, it is really very ordinary. "Altogether, it is simply our living situation—life and experience, life and experience—very simple and direct."[10]

Colors are particularly powerful symbols. We often experience emotions in terms of color, and we find that certain colors arouse certain moods. So when we bring colors into the context of vajrayana, they become a very natural and effective means of linking to the awakened state of mind. They are all around us, so they provide continual reminders. For instance, if we are doing the purification practice of white Vajrasattva, any glimpse of white that we see will remind us of the intrinsic purity he represents. We can easily use colors to link to the five families. The principles of the five families are openly displayed in every aspect of life; we only have to look for them.

Events, too, are symbolic. Everything that happens to us carries a message that can be interpreted in terms of the deities. For example, there are various dharma protectors, like the guardians of the gates who appeared earlier. If we have an accident or a sudden shock, it may be a warning from them that we are going off the path in some way. Or we may receive signs to give us confidence that we are on the right track. It is not a question of working it out intellectually, and there is no automatic approach to interpreting such events. Symbolism bypasses the thinking mind. We need to develop sensitivity so that there is an immediate, intuitive recognition of the message. By gradually getting used to their symbolic language, we can learn to trust the innate guidance of the deities.

As our understanding of the deities and our sensitivity to their presence increases through meditation practice, this symbolism takes on ever-deeper meaning. It becomes reality and opens up into magic, which could be called the practical application of symbolism. Here again, the distinguishing feature of tantric magic lies in dissolving the boundaries of ego and letting go into space. It cannot be used for self-interest in any way; it is power over oneself, not power over others. Ordinary power and the ordinary concept of magic are based on passion and aggression, whereas tantric magic is based on transcending them. Its first step is to tame our own mind. Then we need to develop the energy, confidence, and courage of a warrior, to be willing to go beyond our limits and leap into the unknown. This can be very simple and straightforward: making an effort when we feel exhausted, giving up resentment when we feel hurt, showing love and kindness when we feel irritated and annoyed. We always have a choice. As Trungpa Rinpoche said in relation to the bardo visions, the threshold of magic is the point at which we can choose between returning to the comfortable, dim light of samsara or going toward the unfamiliar, awe-inspiring brilliance of awakening.

However much we may be able to appreciate the magical qualities of the universe through its natural symbolism, only the adhishthana of the guru can open the door to the genuine magic of vajrayana. It is the guru who gives us the direct experience of the true nature of mind, which can only be reached through self-surrender. Although the buddha-nature is our own, at some point we have to give up our sense of ego by trusting in someone else. That is when symbolism comes alive and magic takes place. Through this, we learn to dance with the phenomenal world, which becomes a source of inspiration instead of giving rise to identification and grasping. It is a continuous process; the more we open up, the more the magic is revealed. We become one with the energies of the universe, as Trungpa Rinpoche put it. That is why he said that the tantric guru has power over the magical aspects of the universe, and that this is represented by the vidyadharas.

He also sometimes called the vidyadharas "holders of crazy wisdom." His expression "crazy wisdom" has a very profound meaning for understanding the essence of vajrayana and the nature of the tantric guru. It actually refers not to vidya but to jnana, and could equally be called wild knowledge.[11] The differences between knowledge (jnana), wisdom (prajna), and awareness (vidya) are discussed in earlier chapters; it is necessary to distinguish them because they are used as important technical terms, but in practice they overlap and merge. They express different flavors of one reality. Crazy wisdom has the penetrating intelligence of awareness as well as the transcendent, "gone beyond" quality of the perfection of wisdom (prajnaparamita). It is the primordial, awakened knowledge from a tantric perspective, conveying a sense of ecstasy and intoxication, of being drunk with the nectar of knowledge and on fire with the bliss of wakefulness. It is this very quality of wildness and craziness that fuels the most intense energy of compassion, arousing the determination and confidence to do absolutely anything to remove the suffering of existence in the six realms and awaken all life to the glory of its original state. It is traditionally said of Padmakara that he subdues whatever needs to be subdued, he destroys whatever needs to be destroyed, and he cares for whatever needs his care.

This knowledge can be called crazy because it is free of conditioning and transcends conventional concepts; it turns everything upside down. Even the imagery of the vidyadharas is far from the picture of holiness presented by most religions. The lives of human exponents of crazy wisdom, such as Trungpa Rinpoche himself, contradict many of our normal expectations of spiritual behavior. From the conventional point of view, we never know what to expect from the wild, raw energy of the awakened state, totally unfettered and unobstructed. Its spontaneous action sometimes seems outrageous, immoral, or even destructive. It takes a very long-term view, and it sets things in motion that may not bear fruit until another lifetime. It penetrates to the heart of whatever is needed, but we, on the contrary, generally cannot see clearly at all, so the actions of a genuinely awakened person may appear completely incomprehensible. Such behavior is abrupt and totally direct, arising from a state of mind immersed in emptiness and compassion, without strategies or worldly considerations of any kind. Crazy wisdom is fearless, uncompromising, and unhesitating. It clings to no self-image and has gone beyond all reference points, so it no longer cares about comparisons or judgments. It destroys our preconceptions and illusions about the spiritual path and instantly sees through our self-deceptions. It cuts away the ground from under our feet so that we have no choice but to dance in empty space.

The Seventh Day

The vision of the vidyadharas appears to the dead person because he or she did not recognize the peaceful deities during the previous six days and so has not been liberated. The book says that this may happen in the case of people unfortunate enough to have no karmic connections with dharma, either because they were born in uncivilized places where it is not taught or because they had no interest in it or little opportunity to practice. Another situation that would cause people not to recognize is when they have let their samaya commitments degenerate. Samaya is the sacred promise made between guru and disciple on the tantric level that creates an inescapable bond. It is not something that can be undertaken lightly or entered into by mistake. Not fulfilling this commitment means that one is not living up to one's potential for enlightenment. The closer one has come to the magic of vajrayana, the more one hurts oneself by rejecting or abusing it, and therefore one inevitably becomes more and more confused and lost in samsara. Both classes of people— those who have had no contact with dharma and those who have willfully abandoned it, are in danger of being drawn downward toward the animal realm, which is dominated by ignorance and delusion. So now the path of soft green light leading to that realm also appears, along with the vidyadharas and dakinis, the embodiments of total knowledge, wisdom, and awareness.

O child of awakened family, listen without distraction. On the seventh day, the multicolored light of karmic imprints, purified in space, will shine. Then the vidyadhara deities will come from the pure Sky-Farers' Realm to invite you. In the center of a mandala enveloped with rainbow light, he who is called the Fully Matured Vidyadhara, the incomparable Lotus Lord of Dance, will appear. His body is radiant with the five colors and he embraces the mother, the Red Dakini. They dance with hooked knives and skull cups full of blood, gesturing and gazing at the sky.

From the east of the mandala, he who is called the Vidyadhara Established in the Stages will appear. He is white, smiling radiantly, and embracing the mother, the White Dakini. They dance with hooked knives and skull cups full of blood, gesturing and gazing at the sky.

From the south of the mandala, he who is called the Vidyadhara with Power over Life will appear. He is yellow, beautifully proportioned, and he embraces the mother, the Yellow Dakini. They dance with hooked knives and skull cups full of blood, gesturing and gazing at the sky.

From the west of the mandala, he who is called the Mahamudra Vidyadhara will appear. He is red, smiling radiantly, and embracing the mother, the Red Dakini. They dance with hooked knives and skull cups full of blood, gesturing and gazing at the sky.

From the north of the mandala, he who is called the Spontaneously Existent Vidyadhara will appear. He is green, his expression is both angry and smiling, and he embraces the mother, the Green Dakini. They dance with hooked knives and skull cups full of blood, gesturing and gazing at the sky.

The five vidyadharas are given titles that correspond to levels of awakening, rather than proper names. They appear before us because they are the manifestations of our innate potential, calling upon us to recognize them and merge with them. The Vidyadhara Established in the Stages represents the accomplishment of the ten stages of the bodhisattva path in mahayana, while the other four represent levels of accomplishment according to the Nyingma mahayoga system, which also encompass the ten stages from a different perspective.

The five dakinis, too, are unnamed and identified only by their colors. As the feminine principle, they represent the openness and creativity of the awakened state. The attainment of realization is always inseparable from the absence of ego. They are the boundless sky of inspiration in which the miraculous powers and magical activities of the vidyadharas take place. We can also relate them to the five elements, which form the matrix from which all phenomena arise.

In the center of the mandala is the Fully Matured Vidyadhara. Maturing refers to the ripening of the power of adhishthana, and it corresponds to the first of the four levels known as the fruit of mahayoga. However, at this stage, the physical body has not yet been completely permeated by the effects of one's mental realization, so in the case of a living yogin or yogini, the nadis are only partially transformed. Although the central vidyadhara is described here as being of the five colors, embodying all five families, he is usually depicted in paintings as red, as is his dakini consort. There is no blue in this mandala, as it has been displaced by the red of the Padma family. The mandala of the vidyadharas emanates from speech, so it is ruled by Amitabha. The central vidyadhara is also called Lotus Lord of Dance, Padmanarteshvara. This is a name sometimes given to Amitabha or Avalokiteshvara, expressing the essence of the Padma family's compassionate activity. Their dance is the play of appearance and emptiness, which is compared to acting a part in a drama or producing a magical illusion.

In the east of the mandala is the Vidyadhara Established in the Stages, dancing with the White Dakini. In a sense, he represents a combination of the other four, so we might have expected to find him in the center of the mandala. However, since he is white, he is a transformation of Vairochana and belongs to the Buddha family, which is often placed in the east instead of the center. The east is the direction of pacifying and removing suffering, which seems particularly appropriate for the vidyadhara who embodies the spirit of the bodhisattva path.

The ten stages of the bodhisattva path are extremely high levels of attainment, culminating in full and complete enlightenment as a buddha on the eleventh stage. The term *bodhisattva* refers to those great beings who have not yet become buddhas. They work toward full enlightenment by developing their wisdom and compassion through serving all sentient beings. At each of the stages, they attain a greater capacity for understanding and helping others, and through putting these abilities into action, they reach a higher level of awakening.

During the previous visions of the peaceful deities, the great bodhisattvas manifested as the activity of the awakened state. There is no contradiction between these two interpretations when we remember that all beings are inherently buddha from the beginning. One view is looking at them from below, from our standpoint of striving toward enlightenment, while the other is seeing them from above, from the primordial state where everything is the natural expression of enlightenment.

The Vidyadhara with Power over Life represents the second mahayoga level. Here the nadis and elements of the body have been completely transformed so that one has control over one's life span. This power is the first of ten that are attained at this stage; they are power over length of life, over rebirth for the sake of others, over one's mind in entering meditation, over matter so that one can provide necessities for those who need them, over wishes so that one can transform objects into whatever is required, over karma in order to lessen its negative results for others, over aspiration so that one's intention for the welfare of all beings is fulfilled, over miracles in order to convert people, over knowledge of all aspects of dharma, and over dharma itself as skill in teaching.

This vidyadhara is a transformation of Ratnasambhava, appearing in the south of the mandala with his partner, the Yellow Dakini. The Ratna family embodies all enlightened qualities and increases spiritual attainments and realizations. Power over life implies power over death, so there is also a connection with Yamantaka, the Destroyer of Death, who appeared as a guardian of the gate in the south.

The third level is the accomplishment of mahamudra, the great seal or great symbol. Here prana and bindu have been transformed as have the nadis, so that one becomes inwardly identical with the deity, the mahamudra body of indivisible appearance and emptiness. Such a body can appear anywhere, in any form, and emanate countless other forms to carry out enlightened activities. For example, there are many accounts in Indian and Tibetan literature of great teachers manifesting as deities to their students, both from a distance and while they remain present in their ordinary form. The Mahamudra Vidyadhara, appearing in the west, is a transformation of Amitabha. He and the Red Dakini embody the Padma family's communicative power to attract and influence living beings.

In the north of the mandala is the Spontaneously Existent Vidyadhara with the Green Dakini. He represents the fourth level, the attainment of enlightenment. Spontaneity conveys the idea that the awakened state blossoms without effort, all at once, complete and perfect. He is a transformation of Amoghasiddhi, who infallibly accomplishes enlightened activities. It is the culmination of the path, where all the buddha qualities are fulfilled and all concepts of striving and achievement drop away. It is interesting that this vidyadhara is the only one whose expression is described as angry. His anger expresses the active, dynamic energy of the awakened state, which we shall see in its most intense form manifesting as the wrathful deities.

The vidyadharas and dakinis can be either naked or wearing animal-skin wraps around their waists, perhaps with very basic jewelry. Their simplicity and absence of ornaments point to the intuitive quality of direct recognition beyond the complexities of conceptual thought.

Their dancing posture is graceful and dynamic, almost like flight, and the five couples are often shown in different positions, so that we may easily imagine them moving rather than frozen in static poses. They express the state of boundless freedom and ecstatic joy. They perform gestures (mudra) with their hands to accompany special, powerful ways of gazing, which accomplish magical actions.

In their left hands, they hold skull cups filled with blood. The skull cup represents the feminine principle of wisdom, containing the lifeblood of samsara transmuted into elixir, the wild knowledge or crazy wisdom that inspires them with compassionate energy. In their right hands, they each hold a hooked knife, representing the masculine principle of skillful means. This knife is derived from the traditional butcher's knife, its body is crescent-shaped for chopping meat, and it ends in a hook for flaying the skin. With it, they dismember the corpse of ego.

Around the periphery of the mandala is a great throng of lesser deities. These also are not included among the traditional hundred deities and are not normally depicted in bardo paintings:

> Beyond the vidyadharas, countless crowds of dakinis will appear: dakinis of the eight great charnel grounds, dakinis of the four families, dakinis of the three levels, dakinis of the ten directions, dakinis of the twenty-four places of pilgrimage, male and female warriors and servants, and all the male and female protectors of dharma. Wearing the six bone ornaments; carrying drums, thighbone trumpets, skull drums, banners made from the flayed skins of children, canopies and ribbons of human skin, and incense made from human flesh; playing countless different kinds of musical instruments— they fill all the regions of the universe. Crowded close together, rocking and swaying to and fro, they will make all the instruments vibrate with music so as to split one's head. Performing various dances, they will invite those who have kept their samaya commitments and punish those who have let them degenerate.

Just as before, these deities appear in the sky before us, but they can only do so because they are part of our inherent nature. The dwelling places of the various classes of dakinis are external locations, but they also correspond to parts of the body on both coarse and subtle levels. These dakinis, warriors, servants, and protectors are all expressions of our speech and vital energy, our emotional, communicative nature. They are the essence of creative and destructive energy; they do not come to invite us politely, but with wild songs and dances, clamoring urgently to attract our attention. *Warrior*, or *hero*, is another general term for the deities in their passionate or wrathful manifestations and is often used as the male counterpart of dakini, although it has a feminine form as well, and in both forms also refers to human yogins and yoginis. It reminds us that the spiritual path is a continual struggle against delusion and egoism, and that we need courage and energy to follow it. Many of the dharma protectors were originally non-Buddhist deities and local spirits who have been tamed and have vowed to help and protect the teaching and all who follow it. They represent those aspects of our nature that have been turned away from self-interest toward truth and the welfare of others. They can sometimes be fierce and ruthless; they are our true conscience and will use any means necessary to keep us from going astray.

All the things they carry, their musical instruments and the ornaments they wear, are related to the charnel ground, a very important concept in vajrayana symbolism. Charnel, or cremation, grounds correspond to cemeteries in the Western world, although they are much more disturbing and frightening. They would have been even more fearsome many centuries ago when these teachings originated. Then they were desolate places, situated outside inhabited areas, on the edge of a jungle or desert. We can imagine the scene: bones and skulls litter the ground, the smoke and stench of burning flesh fills the air, wild dogs and hyenas roam around snarling and cackling as they scavenge among the dying embers of the funeral pyres, crows peck at the entrails of half-burned corpses, and vultures circle overhead. Tigers, lions, or other wild animals prowl and roar in the nearby forests. The dead bodies of executed criminals hang swaying from the branches of trees, while poisonous snakes slither in and out of holes among the roots. Even more terrifying is the presence of demons who inhabit corpses and ghosts who continue to haunt the remains of their former bodies until they are released by ritual offerings.

Yet these are the places that yogins and yoginis chose to live in for many reasons. They would be isolated and completely abandoned at night, so no one would disturb them. By living there they would come face-to-face with the reality of death and overcome many obstacles to spiritual progress, such as attachment, fear, disgust, pride, and the superiority of caste. They might meet powerful otherworldly beings or great teachers, and especially the dakinis who love to dwell in charnel grounds.

The outer charnel ground has always played a large part in tantric practice, but practitioners do not literally have to go there, for its qualities can be found everywhere once we become attuned to its symbolism. The dismembered corpses, the flesh and blood, the skulls, bones, internal organs, and flayed skin, represent everything that we would rather avoid. They reveal the areas that disgust and revolt us and the secret, sensitive parts that we do not want to look at or expose. Here we find everything that we reject as having nothing to do with our spiritual nature, yet it is the raw source of our energy and must be recognized and accepted. The thought of this terrifying environment, with all its vivid sensory perceptions of sight, sound, and smell, produces an acute awareness of impermanence; of the continual presence of death in life; and of how worldly beauty, pleasure, and perfection can turn into their opposites at any moment. The world is our charnel ground, where everything is continually dying and being reborn. But it is a place of birth as well as a place of death; it is the ground of transmutation.

Sometimes life itself forces this awareness upon us. When we are close to sickness, death, or danger, when we feel suddenly exposed and vulnerable, or when there is too much pain and horror to bear, we enter the charnel ground. It is a state of mind where we can easily become unbalanced; we feel we are living on the edge, and everything crowds in upon us, clamoring with demands. At such times, we may be particularly open to hearing the voices of those enigmatic messengers. But in our state of fear and confusion, we are not sure whether they are helpful or harmful, and we do not know whether to trust them or not. The only solution is to relax, to let go into the dance of life and death that is taking place all the time. The brilliant light of knowledge shines from the hearts of the vidyadharas, inviting us to merge with them, while simultaneously the dull light of ignorance tempts us to retreat into instinctive, automatic behavior, to turn our backs, curl up, and go to sleep.

O child of awakened family, a five-colored light will shine from the hearts of the five vidyadhara lords; it is the light of your karmic imprints purified in space, the knowledge with which you were born. Like strands of color wound together, flashing and shimmering side by side, clear and bright, brilliant and terrifying, it will penetrate straight into your heart so that your eyes cannot bear it. At the same time, a soft green light from the animal realm will also shine together with the light of knowledge. Then, under the influence of karmic imprints that lead you astray, you will become afraid of the five-colored light and run away from it, and instead you will be attracted to the soft light of the animals. So do not fear the bright, radiant light of the five colors when it appears. Do not be afraid, but recognize it as knowledge.

From within the light, the entire spontaneous sound of the dharma will roar like a thousand thunderclaps. It rolls and thunders and reverberates with war cries and the penetrating sound of wrathful mantras. Do not be terrified, do not run away, do not fear. Recognize it as the spontaneously manifesting creative energy of your awareness. Do not be attracted to the soft green light of the animals, do not desire it. If you are attracted to it, you will fall into the animal realm of ignorance and experience the extreme suffering of stupidity, dumbness, and slavery from which there is no escape.

Feel devotion toward the clear, bright light of the five colors and concentrate one-pointedly on the blessed vidyadharas, the divine teachers, thinking: "These vidyadharas, warriors, and dakinis have come to invite me to the pure Sky-Farers' Realm. You give thought to sentient beings like me who have never developed goodness and knowledge. You take pity on those like me who have not been caught, even though until today all the deities of the five families of buddhas of past, present, and future have reached out with their rays of compassion. Now, all you vidyadharas, do not let me go any lower down than this, but grasp hold of me with your hooks of compassion and pull me up quickly to the pure Sky-Farers' Realm." With intense one-pointed concentration say this aspiration-prayer:

> May the divine vidyadharas think of me
> And with their great love lead me on the path.
> When through intense karmic imprints I wander in
> samsara,
> On the luminous path of the knowledge with which I
> was born
> May the vidyadhara warriors go before me
> And the great mother dakinis behind me,
> Deliver me from the bardo's dangerous passage
> And bring me to the pure Sky-Farers' Realm.

The light of the five colors combined is the light of our purified fundamental karmic imprints or tendencies, formed by the effect of past actions, which remain in the source consciousness. They are compared to traces of perfume impregnating the consciousness. These imprints form tendency patterns that predispose us toward a particular environment and specific physical and mental characteristics. Here they are described as "purified in space." Just as the five skandhas were revealed in their naturally pure basic state as the five aspects of knowledge, so the karmic imprints return to their original purity in the space of dharmadhatu. Instead of giving rise to further ignorance, they shine forth as the light of primordial knowledge, which is then called the knowledge born with us, our natural, innate knowledge. It can also be interpreted as the knowledge born together with ignorance or simultaneously born knowledge. The awakened state and the confused state are always present simultaneously within us; we continually give birth to them both together.

But although this knowledge of our true nature always exists within us, we have gone on drifting deeper and deeper into ignorance, during life after life and from moment to moment. In order for our innate knowledge to manifest spontaneously, we need to prepare conditions for it, to develop wisdom and compassion and open up gaps in the thick fog of confusion. This is the whole reason for the practice of dharma. And we are not alone; wakefulness is present everywhere to help us. This is what is meant by the vision of the vidyadharas, the divine teachers, and the dakinis, the principle of inspiration. In the bardo state after death, they appear in the most vivid and compelling form, yet they are all around us here and now. We continually have the choice of falling asleep into ignorance or awakening into knowledge, of opening up to the brilliant light or following the path of the dim light. In Trungpa Rinpoche's words, "This symbolism from the *Tibetan Book of the Dead* is very profound for our actual, everyday life situation. It does not have to refer only to after-death experience. Perhaps the after-death experience just typifies the kind of situation in which choices are most enlightening or stimulating and most immediate."[12]

Chapter Fourteen

Wrathful Compassion

THE VISION OF THE WRATHFUL DEITIES is the culmination of the bardo of dharmata. If the spirit wandering in the bardo has not responded to the invitation of the vidyadharas, the energy of the awakened state manifests in the most powerful and dynamic manner possible, as "the fifty-eight blazing, blood-drinking wrathful ones." Before describing the visions in detail, the text recapitulates the reasons for reading these teachings to the dead person and the vital importance of practicing them during life.

Although the wrathful manifestations are no different in essence from the peaceful buddhas, their appearance can be horrifying to someone who has never contemplated them before. The consciousness of the dead person is also becoming more and more bewildered and exhausted as the experiences of the bardo continue without being recognized. So the sudden fear aroused by these new visions is likely to be devastating unless some sort of previous connection with them exists in the mind; by trying to escape from them in panic, one will fall headlong toward rebirth in samsara. If one reacts with horror or aggression, these negative emotions will propel one in the direction of the lower realms. On the other hand, if there is the slightest glimmer of recognition, the intensity of the situation actually helps to focus the mind. Through

sheer terror, one takes refuge in that glimpse of something familiar
without being distracted, and so one attains at least partial liberation
and reaches a higher state.

At such a crucial time, only previous familiarity with the wrathful
deities will help; otherwise, their ferocious and horrific appearance will
be misunderstood by those who do not know them. Even experienced
practitioners of other traditions, seeing them for the first time, may not
be able to penetrate their true nature under the pressure of fear and
bewilderment.

> Now, if one does not meet with this kind of teaching, even
> an ocean of learning will be no use. In these circumstances,
> even great teachers of philosophy and scholars who have ob-
> served the monastic rule become confused and do not recog-
> nize, so they go on wandering in samsara. It is even more so
> for ordinary people; escaping from their fear, terror, and
> panic, they fall into the lower realms and suffer misery. But
> yogins and yoginis who practiced the secret mantras, even if
> they are the lowest of the low, will recognize these blood-
> drinkers as their own chosen deities as soon as they see them,
> like meeting old friends. So they will trust them and, merging
> inseparably with them, become awakened. The essential
> point is that in the human realm they clearly meditated upon
> these blood-drinking forms, made offerings, and praised
> them, and even if they only looked at their painted or sculp-
> ted images, they will recognize them when they appear here
> and attain liberation.

This statement is not intended to disparage learning or monastic
discipline, but it points to an essential element of vajrayana, the necessity of including every single aspect of life on the path and embracing
wholeheartedly even those things that we would rather avoid. This is
the principle of crazy wisdom and the charnel ground. Monks, nuns,
and scholars who have led pure, virtuous lives devoted to meditation,
study, and religious observances, however excellent they may have been,
will be at a disadvantage at this point, in spite of their good qualities,
if they have not attained liberation at an earlier stage. For now they
find themselves unexpectedly confronted with forces they have pre-

viously rejected and never incorporated within their practice. If the vidyadharas were unconventional, the wrathful deities come as a total shock. This is why even the best practitioners need guidance at such a time, and those who are unprepared are in particular danger:

> While they were alive, they cast abuse at the secret mantra path and could not accommodate it in their minds. They did not know the secret mantra deities during life, so they do not recognize them when they appear in the bardo either. Suddenly seeing something they have never seen before, they think of it as an enemy and feel aggression toward it, and as a result they go down to the lower realms.

The wrathful deities are part of our nature just like the peaceful deities. They are within us, yet they also appear to us externally. They are transpersonal; they do not belong to the individual ego, but to our nondual nature. So we can interpret them and try to understand them from both points of view, within and without.

Regarding them as external, they are expressions of the most intense awakened energy poured forth in response to the ignorance and suffering of sentient beings. Or, to put it another way, this energy is the fundamental, self-existent, compassionate nature of the awakened state, which sentient beings perceive as wrathful because of obscured vision resulting from ignorance and suffering. These deities are expressions of the same awakened state that is present all the time, and in the bardo we are directly exposed to it, like the full, dazzling light of the sun. Since we have not recognized the earlier visions but continued to wander in the bardo, this means that we are drifting further into confusion, we are becoming more involved with ego, and we instinctively react to whatever appears with greater self-protectiveness. The spontaneous display of enlightenment has not changed, but now we perceive it as fiercer and more threatening.

Intensity and passion can often appear threatening even when no harm is intended. We become afraid of our own energy because it so often manifests in the distorted form of the five poisons and so easily turns violent and destructive. But there is no soft and gentle way to contemplate the total power of the awakened state; this is one reason for the awe-inspiring character of the wrathful deities. Another reason is that they forcefully show us the universal coexistence of destruction with creativity. We constantly meet with reminders that dissolution is taking place at every moment, and that without death there can be no birth. The wrathful deities embody the oneness, the equal taste, of life and death within the sphere of wholeness.

Yet they do not merely represent universal principles; they are immediate and personal. There have been some attempts to explain them psychologically as the dark side of our nature, the shadow that we must meet and integrate; but that kind of interpretation, although it may have some validity, misses the essential point. They are indeed the forces of our mind, those same forces that can turn into cruelty, lust, arrogance, and so on. But as the self-display of awareness, they represent that energy in its original, undistorted purity. In relation to the earlier visions, it was said that, simply because we are made of the five skandhas and the five elements, the buddhas and devis will automatically appear. Already in the imagery of the peaceful deities we have seen that their symbolism is concerned with transmutation, but in a manner that reveals the awakened essence as primordially present, simply awaiting recognition. Here the actual process of transmutation is expressed in a much more overt and direct manner. Even the most extreme evil actions of which living beings are capable arise from energy that is pure in its basic nature, and that energy must be liberated; this is what the symbolism of the wrathful deities expresses. So they are not the shadow, but the pure energy that transcends the dualism of light and dark. Spiritual paths that attempt to suppress all negativity or pretend that it does not exist do not allow their followers to experience and recognize this energy, which nevertheless is still latent within them.

The tremendous power of the wrathful deities is completely devoid of ego; it arises from the state of emptiness; it is pure wisdom and compassion. Their entire and only purpose it to wake us up. Their wrath is the fury of those who have awoken directed at the forces that oppose awakening. But in a world of confusion and uncertainty, clinging to our sense of individual existence, it is easy to misinterpret their overpowering presence. They may arouse our deepest fears and anxieties, they may disgust and horrify us so that we feel hatred toward them, or they may seem to be attacking us so that we react with anger and violence.

Trungpa Rinpoche used to speak of how we solidify the experience of luminosity. All phenomena, whether in this world or in the bardo, arise out of luminosity. If we recognize this and let go into openness, we can take part in the play of existence without being taken in by it. But if we start to believe in it, then the whole thing begins to seem solid. We react to the simple presence of the peaceful deities in various ways, trying to ignore them or turning them into objects of fear or attachment. It is just as important not to become attached to them as it is not to be frightened of them. The instructions are to feel intense longing and devotion toward them. These are emotions that open up the heart and allow us to let go; they are not based on the swing between attraction and aversion, which is the reaction of ego. If we are attracted to the peaceful deities and start to believe in them and their environment as externally real, we might imagine we have gone to heaven. Then they turn into wrathful deities to remind us of emptiness and wake us up.

Whatever appears in the bardo is a more dramatic, raw, and naked version of what happens during life. The wrathful deities use shock tactics; the time for gentle persuasion has passed. In ordinary life, it is very difficult for us to accept frightening or distressing situations as opportunities for awakening. It is difficult to maintain awareness under all circumstances, to see the buddha-nature in every living being, to accept things we dislike with equanimity, to react calmly to aggression, and to show compassion to our enemies. These are some of the situations in which we might recognize wrathful deities in a general sense. But whenever we speak of deities, we must remember that they are really our own potential awakened qualities, powers, and functions. We bring them into being as living presences in our lives through receiving adhishthana and through practicing their yoga.

They are called the deities of secret mantra (*secret mantra way* is the normal Tibetan term for vajrayana, corresponding to the Sanskrit mantrayana). Mantras are widely used throughout the Buddhist world, but their secrecy is special to vajrayana because of the importance of adhishthana, through which the guru passes on their power. Of course they are not entirely secret, since they can be read in texts by anyone prepared to go to enough trouble, but they are always self-secret in the sense that they cannot be effective without genuine adhishthana and dedicated practice. The wrathful deities are generally thought of as characteristically tantric and are often chosen as meditational deities by tantric practitioners. Their mantras and practices are kept particularly secret because they are so powerful and can easily be misunderstood; if the energy they release is used for selfish purposes, it only harms the practitioner and others.

The text says that the best tantric yogins and yoginis, those who are above average, will be liberated the moment they stop breathing, while other accomplished practitioners of mahamudra and dzogchen will recognize the luminosity in the bardo of dying. For them, the reading of the text is unnecessary, but for everyone else, it is extremely necessary and helpful. It reawakens the memory of any similar teaching they have received, any practice they have done, or any realization they have attained in the past, so that what is taking place in the bardo becomes familiar and they are able to recognize that whatever appears is simply their own self-display. Or, if they cannot recognize, at least it plants seeds for the future in the consciousness of the dead person, leading to a better rebirth, so that gradually more and more links are established. The seeds that are planted, combined with other circumstances, may ripen unexpectedly, giving the impression of no previous effort or preparation, but there is always a hidden cause in the mindstream. This creation of connections is the secret of the great power of *Liberation through Hearing*, as it explains:

> If they recognize the luminosity during the bardo of dying, they will reach the dharmakaya, and if they recognize during the bardo of dharmata when the peaceful and wrathful deities appear, they will reach the sambhogakaya. If they recognize during the bardo of existence, they will reach the nirmamakaya and be born in a better situation where they will meet with this teaching. Since the results of actions continue into the next life, this *Great Liberation through Hearing* is a teaching that enlightens without meditation, a teaching that liberates just by being heard, a teaching that leads great sinners on the secret path, a teaching that severs ignorance in a single moment, a profound teaching that gives perfect instantaneous enlightenment, so sentient beings whom it has

reached cannot possibly go to lower existences. Both this and the *Liberation through Wearing* should be read aloud, for the two combined are like a golden mandala inlaid with turquoise.[1]

After establishing the importance of the reading, the text continues to point out the successive visions of the bardo. From the eighth to the twelfth days, the male and female principles of the five families appear in the form of the five heruka couples. Heruka is a name referring to any of the wrathful, blood-drinking deities, although it is generally reserved for the chief male deities. The word probably derives from a root meaning "to roar," but its three syllables are interpreted as emptiness, compassion, and their unity. Here they have particular characteristics belonging to the Nyingma tradition. Trungpa Rinpoche observed that, in the Nyingma tantras, the nature of the deities is always more extreme than in the other traditions: the peaceful deities are more peaceful, or invincibly peaceful as he described them, while the wrathful deities are even more wrathful and powerful.

The origin of the herukas is described in the legend of the subjugation of Rudra. Trungpa Rinpoche relates it briefly in his commentary, but different versions exist.[2] Essentially it is an allegory about the perversion of tantric teachings, and in particular the dzogchen approach of spontaneity. Many cosmic ages ago, a certain practitioner of these teachings, which are timeless and appear in every age, misinterpreted them as meaning that he should go and do whatever he pleased. He believed that following a natural, spontaneous way of life, satisfying every desire and impulse, would lead to liberation, but he failed to understand that spontaneity must be based on realization of the true nature of mind. So instead of transmuting the five poisons, he indulged in them, and instead of cutting through the illusion of ego, he strengthened and inflated it. As a result, after his death he suffered for countless ages in the lower realms until he was eventually reborn as a monster, a cannibal rakshasa demon named Rudra. In this form, he amassed enormous power and terrorized the whole universe. After failing to convert him by peaceful means, the buddhas decided that he must be stopped by a forceful method, and they emanated the wrathful manifestation of the herukas in order to defeat him. Through his subjugation, Rudra was liberated and became a protector of dharma as Mahakala, the Great Black One. As a sign of their victory, the herukas assumed his demonic form, complete with all his attributes. Outwardly, this horrific appearance represents the most extreme embodiment of egoism, but inwardly, each aspect of it expresses the transmutation and liberation of ego.

There are many wrathful meditational deities in the Nyingma tradition, and they all share many details of iconography and symbolism, which can be applied here to supplement the descriptions in *Liberation through Hearing* and its related texts. The five herukas that appear during the bardo represent the basic wrathful principles of the mandala of buddhas, so they are simply identified by the names of the five families. Similarly, their consorts, the wrathful aspects of the five devis, are called the wrathful ladies of the five families.

Samantabhadra and Samantabhadri also have their wrathful counterparts, the Great Supreme Heruka and the Wrathful Lady of Space. Although they do not appear in the visions of *Liberation through Hearing*, they are described in both the *Hundred Homages* and the *Dharma Practice*. In paintings, they are placed at the center of the mandala with the Buddha family couple immediately below them. The Great Supreme Heruka[3] is described as being what we translated previously as "wine-colored," but it ranges from dark red to purple, maroon, or brown. The Wrathful Lady of Space[4] is described as dark blue. However, in paintings, they are sometimes both given the same color, either maroon or blue, with the female partner a lighter shade than the male. Several slightly different traditions of bardo teachings exist within the Nyingma tradition, and there are even different descriptions of the deities among the texts in this terma cycle.

The wrathful deities emerge from the brain, the seat of reason and intellect, as opposed to the emotional and intuitive intelligence of the heart. In the five families, the Vajra family is associated with both intellect and aggression. As Trungpa Rinpoche explains, "The intellect here is something aggressive in the vajra sense, something extremely powerful." The wrathful deities express "immense anger, without hatred of course, the most immense anger that the enlightened mind could ever produce, as the most intense form of compassion."[5]

The head chakra, located in the area of the brain, is also connected with the body, the sense of intensely physical, embodied energy of the wrathful deities. It is significant that all the deities are actually described as emanating from the physical organs of the heart, throat, and brain rather than from the chakras associated with them. Those who are in the bardo no longer possess their former bodies, but they are still sentient beings, so they exist on the three levels that we call body, speech, and mind. They experience the sensation of a "mental body" formed from karmic links to the past and the future. Most important, the deities are an inherent part of our physical existence here and now; they are not abstract, not just visions or ideals. Mind and body cannot be separated, and it is only through living as embodied beings that we awaken to enlightenment.

THE EIGHTH DAY

O child of awakened family, listen without distraction. Although the peaceful bardo has already appeared, you did not recognize, so you have wandered on still further to this point. Now, on the eighth day, the blood-drinking wrathful deities will appear. Recognize them without being distracted.

O child of awakened family, he who is called the great glorious Buddha Heruka will emerge from within your own brain and appear before you clearly as he really is. His body is maroon in color, with three heads, six arms, and four legs spread wide apart. His right face is white, his left face red, and his central face maroon. His body blazes like a mountain of light, his nine eyes gaze into yours with a terrifying expression, his eyebrows resemble flashes of lightning, and his teeth gleam like copper. He laughs aloud with shouts of "a-la-la!" and "ha-hee-ee!" and sends forth loud whistling noises of "shoo-oo!" His red-gold hair flies upward blazing, his heads are crowned with dry skulls and with the sun and moon, his body is garlanded with black serpents and freshly severed heads. With his six hands, he holds a wheel in the first on the right, an ax in the middle, and a sword in the last; a bell in the first on the left, a plowshare in the middle, and a skull cup in the last. The mother, the Buddha Wrathful Lady, embraces the father's body. She clasps his neck with her right hand, and with her left she holds a skull cup of blood to his mouth. He makes loud smacking noises with his palate and growling sounds like the roll of thunder. The fire of knowledge flares out from the hairs on his body, which are a mass of fiery vajras. He stands on a throne borne aloft by garudas, with one pair of legs bent and the other pair stretched out.

Do not be afraid of him, do not be terrified, do not be petrified. Recognize him as the form of your own awareness. He is your chosen deity, so do not fear. He is really blessed Vairochana himself in union with the mother, so do not be afraid. Recognition and liberation are simultaneous.

Instead of being surrounded by rainbows, the herukas are enveloped in flames, a firestorm blazing with the force of their wrathful compassion. They are like the incandescent brilliance of the dawning of a hundred thousand suns; they are the nuclear power of enlightenment. They laugh and howl and roar with ear-shattering, thunderous intensity. Their bodies are massive, with swollen, bulging limbs, giving an impression of solidity and unshakable strength. Yet at the same time, they are agile, even graceful, and full of dynamic energy. They are winged, a characteristic that is exclusive to the Nyingma wrathful deities.[6] With their spreading wings and outstretched arms, they look as though they are almost taking flight, yet their heavy, stamping feet remain firmly grounded. But their weight and solidity are metaphors, and they should never be imagined as substantial; their bodies are made entirely of light—they are "empty form."

The herukas of the five families that appear during the bardo each have three heads, six arms, and four legs. In general, whether in peaceful or wrathful deities, the possession of many limbs shows the multiplicity and universality of their powers, while specific symbolic meanings may also apply in each particular case. There are often several different interpretations of which only a few can be given here. These various interpretations do not conflict with each other, but should all be held in the mind at the same time. Together they build up a portrait of the complete transformation of confusion, negativity, and evil into the awakened state.

The three heads of the herukas symbolize the transmuted energy of passion, aggression, and delusion. They show that the herukas are the living expression of the three aspects of wakefulness: dharmakaya, sambhogakaya, and nirmanakaya. They also represent release through the three gateways to liberation: first, through realization of the emptiness and openness of reality; second, through understanding there are no characteristics by which reality can be defined or pinned down; and third, through reaching the point that transcends aspiration and effort, where there is no longer any hope of success or fear of failure.

Their six arms represent the six perfections of generosity, morality, patience, energy, meditation, and wisdom, and also the six kinds of knowledge: the five belonging to the five families plus their unity as the sixth. Alternatively, the six arms demonstrate the liberation of beings from the six realms of existence; in other words, overcoming the negative states of mind that create the six realms.

Their four legs represent the four bases of miraculous ability, which may occasionally be displayed as psychic power but is essentially a process of inner growth and spiritual accomplishment. These bases are defined as renunciation of worldly aims combined with profound concentration in four areas: the wish to awaken, firm intention or will, energy and perseverance, and intellectual inquiry. The four legs also symbolize the four vajra activities of pacifying, enriching, magnetizing, and destroying, and the liberation of beings from the four possible types of birth—from an egg, from a womb, from warmth and moisture, or spontaneously. Their trampling feet demonstrate that the herukas completely vanquish the four maras. The four maras are forces of spiritual and physical death, aspects of the Evil One who always tries to obstruct awakening. They are the mara of the skandhas, the process of building up and maintaining ego; the mara of the afflictions or poisons; the mara of death itself; and the mara called "son of the gods," the attachment to spiritual realization that turns it into another prop for ego.

The herukas have a third eye in their foreheads; their three eyes mean that they see and know everything in the past, present, and future and in the three worlds of desire, form, and formlessness. Their faces are smeared with ointments made of three substances from the charnel ground: ash, blood, and melted fat, symbolizing the three kayas. They bare their four fangs, resembling the crescent moon, with determination to subdue the four maras. They frown menacingly, so that their wrinkled eyebrows ripple like lightning across the dark sky of their foreheads. Their hair streams upward like flames, expressing the unfettered energy of their wrathful nature and the reversal of samsaric tendencies. The moon of skillful means and the sun of wisdom shine in their hair. Their indestructible garuda wings spread wide, symbolizing the fulfillment of all aims.

Like the peaceful buddhas, the herukas wear the fivefold crown, but now it is set with skulls, symbolizing the liberation of the five poisons transformed into the knowledges of the five families. This shows that the poisons need not be abandoned or destroyed, but can be displayed as adornments once their energy is used correctly. They are garlanded with a long, dangling necklace of fifty severed heads. The heads can be interpreted as the fifty characters of the Sanskrit alphabet, the primordial sounds vibrating at the heart of all existence, or as the fifty-one or fifty-two factors in the skandha of conditioning, purified in their natural state. Sometimes a shoulder garland of rotting heads is included in the heruka adornments. The three types of skull—dry, decaying, and fresh—represent the past, present, and future. The long garland may also contain all three and is strung on a rope of intestines, symbolizing the impermanence and insubstantiality of phenomena.

Their clothing consists of three flayed male skins. On top is a cloak of elephant hide stretched out across the shoulders, symbolizing strength and the overcoming of delusion. Below it is an upper garment or shawl of a complete human skin, symbolizing compassion and the transmutation of passion. Around the waist is a loincloth of tiger skin, indicating the taming of the wildness and fierceness of aggression. The tiger skin, with its symmetrical stripes on each side of the spine, also symbolizes transcending the duality of subject and object.

Serpents coil around their limbs, forming five groups of snake ornaments: around the arms and legs, around the neck, around the chest as a sash or garland, through the ears, and binding the hair. These represent the five castes of serpent deities, sometimes said to be of different colors, and they symbolize five levels of passion that have been controlled. Another interpretation connects the elephant skin with the transmutation of delusion, the human skin with passion, the tiger skin with pride, the garland of heads with envy, and the snake ornaments with aggression.

The herukas also wear a set of six bone ornaments: a circular hair ornament, earrings, a necklace, bracelets (counted together with armlets and anklets), a girdle, and ointment made from bone ash. Sometimes the ash is replaced by a chest ornament hung on crossed bands over the torso. They symbolize the six perfections: the hair ornament is meditation, the earrings patience, the necklace generosity, the bracelets morality, the girdle energy, and the ash wisdom. The first five can also correspond to the buddhas of the five families: Akshobhya, Amitabha, Ratnasambhava, Vairochana, and Amoghasiddhi. Not all of these details of clothing and adornment are described in this text or depicted in bardo paintings, but we should certainly imagine the herukas possessing all these qualities.

They stand on thrones of lotus, moon, and sun, with the sun uppermost. Their legs are spread wide apart, with the right legs bent and the left legs stretched out in a heroic dance posture derived from the stance of an archer, trampling on corpses lying beneath their feet. The corpses represent the male and female aspects of Rudra, ego personified, in the forms of various gods and goddesses assigned to each of the five families.

The thrones of the herukas are supported by garudas flying through the air, emphasizing their dynamism and their all-pervading activity of destroying evil. The garuda resembles an eagle with human arms and torso and with talons, beak, and horns of meteoric iron. According to Indian mythology, the original Garuda was a divine bird who hatched from the egg fully grown, his golden body as bright as fire, his wings covering the sky. In both Hinduism and Buddhism, he is a very powerful figure, and particularly in the Nyingma tradition, he became a symbol of the spontaneous accomplishment of awakening. He is courageous and invincible, and he travels instantaneously throughout space. He embodies the energy and determination of the meditator, which carry one to the height of realization on the two indestructible vajra wings of wisdom and skillful means, emptiness and compassion. He is the enemy of serpents, here representing any kind of negativity and poison, and is shown devouring them in his beak. His eyes blaze with light, searching them out in all directions. He is adorned with a wish-fulfilling jewel on his head, which rains down whatever is needed for success in the practice of dharma.

The entire manifestation of the deities is compared to a play in both senses of the word. It is the spontaneous, creative expression of delight, and it is the performance of a drama taking place on the stage of the primordial ground of being. Without ever moving from the tranquillity of their innermost essential nature, they play whatever part is necessary to awaken all beings. In this play, they demonstrate the nine moods or sentiments (*navarasa*) of Indian aesthetics: erotic, heroic, repulsive, humorous, wrathful, fearful, compassionate, wondrous, and peaceful.[7] The Buddhist interpretation differs slightly from the original (which was first formulated for dance), in that the dancer generally acts out the feelings of revulsion, fear, and wonder, while the herukas arouse these reactions in others by their demeanor. Also, in this context, the nine sentiments are grouped into attributes of body, speech, and mind. With their bodies, the herukas are graceful, sensuous, and seductive, expressing the transmutation of passion; they show the energy, power, and courage of warrior heroes, expressing the transmutation of aggression; and they have the repulsive, horrific appearance of rakshasas, with bared fangs, wrathful frowns, and rolling eyes, expressing the transmutation of delusion. With their speech, they laugh aloud with different tones and moods of laughter; they shout violent threats and commands and utter fierce, wrathful mantras; and they make loud, terrifying shrieks, roaring and raging like thunder and lightning. Their state of mind is full of compassion toward all beings; wondrous, extraordinary, and outrageous in order to tame recalcitrant beings; and eternally peaceful, since they never depart from the changeless nature of the dharma-dhatu.

The wrathful ladies have three eyes and ferocious expressions, but in other respects they have a normal physical form. Their single face represents the equality, or single flavor, of all phenomena in ultimate truth. Their two arms symbolize wisdom and skillful means working together in balance and harmony. Their dancing pose, closely entwined around their consort's body, means that wisdom is never separated from skillful means. They leap into the embrace of the herukas with ecstatic abandon, and the whole attitude of both partners radiates the fierce enjoyment of their bliss.

Their appearance is not described in detail in the bardo texts, but generally wrathful female consorts are naked except for a leopard skin skirt, symbolizing fearlessness. They wear the crown of skulls and the bone ornaments without the charnel ground ointment, which symbolizes wisdom, because they themselves are the embodiment of wisdom. They may also have a garland of skulls and other jeweled adornments.

The Buddha Heruka and Buddha Wrathful Lady are transformations of Vairochana and Akashadhatvishvari, who are their fundamental peaceful essence. In this furious form, they symbolize the total transmutation of the energy that lies behind ignorance and self-delusion. This energy in its pure, natural state is the all-encompassing knowledge of reality, liberation into the boundless openness of the dharmadhatu. Because of their wrathful nature, their bodies are not white but the maroon color of the Great Supreme Heruka, who does not appear in the text, but is the origin of the five herukas.

With his main pair of arms, the heruka encircles the wrathful lady's waist, holding the same attributes as his peaceful counterparts: in his right hand, a wheel, the symbol of the Buddha family, and in his left hand, a bell, which rings with the sound of emptiness. In his remaining hands, he carries an ax, a sword, a plowshare, and a skull cup. The ax cuts down the tree of worldly existence and splits asunder the solidity of belief in self, but it is also a battle-ax used as a weapon of war against malignant forces. The plowshare roots out the causes of suffering and prevents the sowing of negative karmic seeds. These two implements are held in opposite hands, and together they represent power over karmic cause and effect. The sword is the universal attribute of a warrior; with its sharp blade, it destroys the five poisons, and it is also a symbol of accomplishing spiritual powers. The particular word used here for the skull cup means a vessel for food, drink, and offerings; it is carried by tantric yogins as a continual reminder of the impermanence of everything in life. In the left hand, it represents wisdom. As an attribute of the herukas, it is filled with the blood of Mara, the lifeblood of samsara, transmuted into the elixir of knowledge.

The wrathful lady is the same color as the heruka, but lighter in shade. She stands on her right leg with her left leg wrapped around his waist. With her right arm, she encircles his neck, and in her right hand, she also holds a wheel, which is hidden behind his head. In her left hand, she holds a skull cup full of human blood, which she holds to her partner's mouth for him to drink. In this context of offering the lifeblood of samsara to the principle of wakefulness, it is known by the coded expression of a red conch shell, because conch shells are often used as containers for offerings.

Several levels of meaning can be identified here. The symbol of the family, held in the right hand, represents the male principle. It stands for that family's particular type of skillful means, the special way in which the buddhas manifest their compassion. The skull cup full of blood is held in the left hand and signifies the female principle of wisdom and emptiness. Considering the skull and its contents individually, the skull represents the male principle, which in this case is bliss; it does so because it is the white color of the male essence, which in the subtle body originates in the crown of the head. The blood contained in the skull is the red of the female essence and represents the female principle of emptiness. So the mother, who symbolizes the objects of experience, presents the unity of bliss and emptiness to the father, who is the experiencing consciousness. Consuming the blood means completely transmuting it and is the activity of compassion, which is only possible in conjunction with the wisdom of emptiness. At the same time, the couple symbolizes the union of these two principles in all their various meanings. In *The Hundred Homages*, the wrathful devis are called the ladies of space of the five families; they are the space, openness, and selflessness in which the unobstructed energy of the herukas flows.

They are the expression of our own true nature, the irresistible explosion of our unrecognized potential for destroying all limitations and cutting through all obstacles to awakening. The instruction is always to recognize them as our chosen deity, who is none other than our buddha-nature, our awakened state of supreme awareness. Anyone who has practiced the yoga of a deity in the Nyingma tradition will be familiar with the appearance of the wrathful herukas and will feel at home with it when they meet it in the bardo. Even if they have meditated only on a peaceful manifestation, if they have really understood the deity's meaning, they will be able to recognize the same essence at the heart of the wrathful aspect. In terms of ordinary life, the more we can deepen and stabilize our awareness in meditation, the greater chance we have of connecting to that awareness in any kind of situation, no matter how disturbing it may be. But if we do not recognize the first heruka and try to run away through fear, another form will immediately appear out of the depth of our own urgent longing for liberation.

The Ninth Day

O child of awakened family, listen without distraction. On the ninth day, the blood-drinking manifestation of the Vajra family, called the blessed Vajra Heruka, will emerge from the eastern quarter of your brain and appear before you. His body is dark blue in color, with three heads, six arms, and four legs spread wide apart. His right face is white, his left face red, and his central face blue. With his six hands, he holds a vajra in the first on the right, a skull cup in the middle, and an ax in the last; a bell in the first on the left, a skull cup in the middle, and a plowshare in the last. The mother, the Vajra Wrathful Lady, embraces the father's body. She clasps his neck with her right hand, and with her left hand she holds a skull cup of blood to his mouth.

Do not be afraid of him, do not be terrified, do not be petrified. Recognize him as the form of your own awareness. He is your own chosen deity, so do not fear. He is really blessed Vajrasattva himself in union with the mother, so feel devotion and longing. Recognition and liberation are simultaneous.

The heruka of the Vajra family represents the transmutation of all ordinary hatred, aggression, and anger into the tremendous wrathful force of the awakened state. Holding a vajra in his right hand, with diamond-sharp clarity he destroys the undercurrents of negativity, irritation, dislike, and resentment that cloud our awareness and reveals the brilliant mirror knowledge, blazing in flames around him. The vajra, besides being the most important symbol in vajrayana, is also a supremely powerful weapon, indestructible and all-destroying. Here it is used with totally ruthless compassion against those forces of denial that prevent us from blossoming into our full potential.

Apart from their colors and the particular implements they hold, the description of the herukas and their consorts who appear in the four directions is the same as that of the central couple, although it is not repeated each time. All the herukas are darker in color than their peaceful counterparts, showing the intensity of their nature. The body and central face of the Vajra Heruka is dark blue, while the Vajra Wrathful Lady is pale blue. She holds a vajra in her right hand as the symbol of the family and a skull cup of blood in her left, just as before. The heruka holds a bell in his primary left hand as before and carries two skull cups, an ax, and a plowshare in his remaining hands, their symbolic meanings being the same as for the Buddha Heruka.

THE TENTH DAY

O child of awakened family, listen without distraction. On the tenth day, the blood-drinking manifestation of the Ratna family, called the blessed Ratna Heruka, will emerge from the southern quarter of your brain and appear before you. His body is dark yellow in color, with three heads, six arms, and four legs spread wide apart. His right face is white, his left face red, and his central face blazing dark yellow. With his six hands, he holds a jewel in the first on the right, a tantric staff in the middle, and a club in the last; a bell in the first on the left, a skull cup in the middle, and a trident in the last. The mother, the Ratna Wrathful Lady, embraces the father's body. She clasps his neck with her right hand, and with her left hand she holds a skull cup of blood to his mouth.

Do not be afraid of him, do not be terrified, do not be petrified. Recognize him as the form of your own awareness. He is your chosen deity, so do not fear. He is really blessed Ratnasambhava himself in union with the mother, so feel devotion to them. Recognition and liberation are simultaneous.

Now the liberated energy of pride and arrogance radiates like the sunburst of a blazing golden jewel, breaking down the barriers that blind us to the equalizing knowledge and the presence of buddhanature in everything around us. The Ratna Heruka is dark golden yellow and the Ratna Wrathful Lady is a paler yellow, the wrathful manifestations of Ratnasambhava and Mamaki. They each hold a wishfulfilling jewel in their right hands and the usual symbols in their opposite left hands. In his other hands, the heruka carries a tantric staff, a club, a skull cup, and a trident.

The trident was a very early Buddhist symbol for the three jewels: the Buddha, the teaching of the dharma, and the community (sangha). Its three prongs can represent any number of the triads that are found in Buddhism. In this context, it is seen particularly as a weapon that destroys the three poisons of passion, aggression, and delusion with a single blow. It also symbolizes the manifestation of the three kayas; the perfection of body, speech, and mind; and the possession of mastery over the flow of prana in the three nadis. The club is a weapon with which to beat, smash, and pulverize harmful and obstructive forces.

The tantric staff, or *khatvanga*, is another very significant emblem in vajrayana. It literally means a "bed leg" and was originally quite short and used as a cudgel. It developed into an ascetic's staff topped by a skull and finally into a long, slender scepterlike staff held by many tantric deities. Its shaft is eight-sided, representing the Buddha's noble eightfold path. Three human heads are impaled upon it; the topmost head is a dry skull symbolizing the dharmakaya, the middle one a decaying head for the sambhogakaya, and the lowest a freshly severed head for the nirmanakaya. Below the heads is a vase filled with the elixir of life, and then a double vajra, symbolizing universal enlightened activity. A scarf is tied below them all, its two ends representing the inseparability of mahayana and vajrayana. It is often topped with a trident, whose prongs represent the three main nadis. The whole staff can also symbolize the central nadi, with the double vajra, vase, and three heads forming the five main chakras. Its possession indicates control of the subtle body. When it is held by a single figure in the crook of the left arm, it represents the consort, whether male or female. Here it is held in the heruka's middle right hand and is a symbol of skillful means, while the opposite left hand holds the skull cup of wisdom.

The Eleventh Day

O child of awakened family, listen without distraction. On the eleventh day, the blood-drinking manifestation of the Padma family, called the blessed Padma Heruka, will emerge from the western quarter of your brain and appear before you. His body is dark red in color, with three heads, six arms, and four legs spread wide apart. His right face is white, his left face blue, and his central face blazing dark red. With his six hands, he holds a lotus in the first on the right, a tantric staff in the middle, and a rod in the last; a bell in the first on the left, a skull cup brimming with blood in the middle, and a small drum in the last. The mother, the Padma Wrathful Lady, embraces the father's body. She clasps his neck with her right hand, and with her left hand she holds a skull cup of blood to his mouth.

Do not be afraid of him, do not be terrified, do not be petrified. Be joyful and recognize him as the form of your own awareness. He is your chosen deity, so do not be afraid or terrified. He is really blessed Amitabha himself in union with the mother, so feel devotion to them. Recognition and liberation are simultaneous.

Amitabha and Pandaravasini manifest in their wrathful aspects like a blazing crimson lotus on fire with the irresistible energy of passion, lust, and greed transformed into the compassion and love of the investigative knowledge. They hold a lotus, the symbol of the Padma family, in their right hands and, as before, a bell or skull cup in their left. Like the Ratna Heruka, the Padma Heruka holds a tantric staff and a skull cup in his middle hands. The skull cups held by the herukas can all be assumed to contain blood, but this time it is specifically described as completely full of blood, perhaps to emphasize the connection of blood with desire—the desire that drives and animates samsara. The small drum is held by a short wooden handle; it resounds with the joyful voice of the dharma. The rod is another type of club or baton;

although the text does not specify this, in paintings of the bardo deities, it always seems to be depicted with a grinning skull on the top, so that it is both a weapon and a symbol of death and transmutation.

THE TWELFTH DAY

On the twelfth and last day of the bardo of dharmata, the heruka and wrathful lady of the Karma family appear, accompanied by a great crowd of various kinds of wrathful dakinis, who represent the dynamic functioning of our inherent awakened consciousness.

> O child of awakened family, listen without distraction. On the twelfth day, the blood-drinking manifestation of the Karma family, called the blessed Karma Heruka, will emerge from the northern quarter of your brain and appear before you. His body is dark green in color, with three heads, six arms, and four legs spread wide apart. His right face is white, his left face red, and his central face majestic dark green. With his six hands, he holds a sword in the first on the right, a tantric staff in the middle, and a rod in the last; a bell in the first on the left, a skull cup in the middle, and a plowshare in the last. The mother, the Karma Wrathful Lady, embraces the father's body. She clasps his neck with her right hand, and with her left hand she holds a skull cup of blood to his mouth.
>
> Do not be afraid of him, do not be terrified, do not be petrified. Recognize him as the form of your own awareness. He is your chosen deity, so do not fear. He is really blessed Amoghasiddhi himself in union with the mother. Feel passionate devotion and longing. Recognition and liberation are simultaneous.

The tremendously active and dynamic energy of the Karma family, with its tendencies toward jealousy, ambition, and paranoia, is transformed into the action-accomplishing knowledge, with the ability to overcome all obstructions and achieve all aims. In his peaceful aspect,

Amoghasiddhi holds a double vajra, but here the heruka wields a sword, the alternative symbol of the Karma family and one that is more appropriate for the wrathful manifestation. With it, he slices through doubts, hindrances, and limitations of all kinds. All the other implements he carries have already been described with their functions. The Karma Wrathful Lady is pale green, and she holds a sword and a skull cup of blood.

The text reminds us that however terrifying the wrathful deities may seem, as soon as their real nature is pointed out, it is easy to recognize them and be liberated. It is just as if we have been terrified by a stuffed lion, thinking it was real, but as soon as someone points out to us that it is only an imitation, all our fear evaporates. When we recognize the herukas as our chosen deity, the personal experience of luminosity we have previously had in meditation merges with the self-existent luminosity of the bardo, like a child running into its mother's arms: "Appearing from itself to itself in order to liberate itself, like meeting old friend, self-illuminating self-awareness is self-liberated."

However, without these instructions, or if the dead person has been unable to hear and respond to them, "even a good person can turn back and wander in samsara." So now a retinue of furious female deities appears from all directions of the mandala, clamoring to arouse and invite us, filling up every corner of space so there is no way to avoid them. They surround the group of all five herukas, so that the entire wrathful mandala reveals itself before us. Some traditions divide these visions into a thirteenth and fourteenth day, making seven days of wrathful visions, corresponding to the seven days of the first part of the bardo of dharmata.

Many of these deities have the heads of wild birds and animals, their bodies are of many colors, and they wear shawls of human skin and leopard or tiger skins around their waists. They are just as vast and overwhelming as the herukas; each of them seems to fill the whole of space. They gesticulate wildly and contort themselves in vigorous dance movements. They carry weapons, emblems of various kinds, and corpses from the charnel ground; they drink blood and eat raw human flesh. Eating and drinking such revolting substances symbolizes accepting all aspects of samsara as fundamentally pure, without making any distinctions, and then completely transmuting them by the act of consuming. The interpretation of the emblems carried by the first three groups is taken from *The Hundred Homages*.

First, eight wrathful dakinis emerge from the eight directions of the brain. In *The Hundred Homages*, they are called mothers (Tibetan *ma mo*), but in *Liberation through Hearing*, they are collectively named the eight gauris after the first of them to appear. Their names, and those of the next group, are listed in Sanskrit transliterated into Tibetan script. In some of the Tibetan blockprints, gauri has been changed to *keuri*, so in some translations they have been called the eight keurimas. Gauri is one of the many names of the feminine principle in Hinduism. It means white, bright, or golden and designates her most peaceful aspect as the beautiful young wife of Shiva. But here she is adopted as a wrathful Buddhist goddess and is accompanied by an equally unexpected collection of ghouls, outcasts, and criminals. They unify all kinds of contradictions within themselves: beauty with horror, purity with impurity, the highest with the lowest, life with death. They demonstrate clearly the paradoxical nature of the dakini principle, using the very things that trap us in samsara to set us free.

As a group, they correspond to the male bodhisattvas of the peaceful mandala, representing the basically pure nature of the eight kinds of consciousness.[8] They have human faces, but are ferocious in appearance: their wild hair streams out like flames, their three eyes roll and stare, and they dance triumphantly upon thrones of human corpses.

In the east is Gauri, the White. She represents the source consciousness. She holds a skull cup of blood in her left hand, and in her right she brandishes a baby's corpse as a club, showing that she subdues the dualistic thoughts of samsara. The lifeless body is a symbol of the original, nondualistic state of mind, and since it is the corpse of a baby, it has never grown up into a world of self and other.

In the south is yellow Chauri, the Thief. She represents the mental consciousness, which grasps and steals whatever comes into its sphere. In the tantras, it is said that we should steal the treasure of enlightenment from the buddhas; she transforms the act of theft so that it leads not to suffering but to awakening. She shoots an arrow from a bow— the bow of wisdom releasing the arrow of skillful means.

In the west is Pramoha, Infatuation. Red with the color of passion, she is the enchantress who ensnares with her arts of illusion. She represents the afflicted mind consciousness where the five poisons operate. She waves a banner made from the skin of a water-monster above her head. The *makara*, or water-monster, is a mythological creature based on the crocodile and combined with features of several other animals. In Hinduism, it is an emblem of Kama, the god of lust, while in Buddhism, it is a symbol of samsara, which is often compared to a river or an ocean. Pramoha raises it on high as a banner of victory to demonstrate that samsara is not abandoned or rejected, but accepted as it really is.

In the north is black Vetali, the Vampire. This is a ghoulish spirit that haunts charnel grounds and enters and animates corpses. She represents the consciousness of body or touch. She gives life to the corpse of existence, which is essentially empty, selfless, and insubstantial. She holds a vajra and a skull cup of blood, symbolizing the indestructible, changeless state of reality, transcending existence and nonexistence.

In the southeast is orange-colored Pukkasi, the Pukkasa Woman, representing the consciousness of smell. Her name indicates that she belongs to one of the many outcaste social groups, generally the result of mixed marriages between castes. She is holding a bunch of entrails in her right hand and stuffing them into her mouth with her left hand. Devouring intestines means that she consumes the poisons just as they are, recognizing their naturally pure state. Eating with the left hand is another sign of impurity in the Indian context, so everything about her defies convention.

In the southwest is dark green Ghasmari, the Voracious, representing the consciousness of taste. She is drinking the blood of samsara from a brimming skull cup held in her left hand. In her right hand, she holds a vajra with which she stirs the blood, bringing pieces of flesh and bone to the surface to be consumed. Blood, bones, and flesh symbolize passion, aggression, and delusion.

In the northwest is pale yellow Chandali, the Chandala Woman, representing the consciousness of sight. Chandalas are the lowest and most despised of the outcaste groups, and their women are particularly praised in tantric literature. She tears the head from the trunk of a corpse, symbolizing separation from false and misleading views. Then holding up the heart, the source of life, in her right hand, she devours the body with her left.

In the northeast is dark blue Shmashani, the Charnel Ground

Dweller, representing the consciousness of hearing. She too is eating a corpse, tearing its head and body apart. This time the action is interpreted as separation from the support of samsaric existence; she tears away the causes that make us wander round and round in the six realms, experiencing the charnel ground of birth and death over and over again.

After the eight mothers, the group of eight pishachis appears.[9] They were originally demonic beings, whose name may be derived either from their flesh-eating habits or from the variegated colors of their heads and bodies. The four in the cardinal directions have the heads of animals and the four in the intermediate directions have the heads of birds. They correspond to the female bodhisattvas in the peaceful mandala, representing the natural purity of the objects of the eight kinds of consciousness.

In the east is Simhamukha, the Lion-Headed. Her body is the same dark maroon or purple as the central heruka, indicating her wrathfulness. She represents the objective field of the source consciousness, the dharmadhatu sphere of reality. Her two arms are crossed over her breast; she carries a corpse in her mouth and tosses her flowing mane, symbolizing her complete domination of samsara.

In the south is Vyaghrimukha, the Tiger-Headed. She is red, with her two arms crossed and pointing downward. She snarls and frowns, and her eyes stare penetratingly in order to pacify samsara. She represents the objects of the mental consciousness.

In the west is black Shrigalamukha, the Jackal-Headed. *Shrigala* primarily means "jackal" in Sanskrit, but the Tibetan text says she has the head of a fox. They are rather similar animals, both to be found scavenging in places such as charnel grounds. She represents the contents of the cloudy or afflicted mind. She brandishes a razor in her right hand, with which she slices out the intestines, heart, and lungs held in her left hand. She eats them and licks up the blood, symbolizing the natural purification of the poisons.

In the north is dark blue Shvanamukha, the Dog-Headed, representing the objects of touch. Again the Tibetan description is slightly at odds with her Sanskrit name, giving her a wolf's head. In any case, it would mean a wild dog, a scavenger of the charnel grounds, very like its wolfish ancestor. She is tearing a corpse apart and holding it up to her mouth with both hands, and her eyes stare piercingly so as to penetrate samsara to its very depth.

In the southeast is pale yellow Gridhramukha, the Vulture-Headed, representing the objects of sight. She carries a human corpse over her shoulder and a skeleton in her hand. The *Hundred Homages* adds that she is pulling out the entrails in order to cut off the three poisons at their root.

In the southwest is dark red Kankamukha, the Heron-Headed, representing the objects of smell. Here the Tibetan says she has the head of a "charnel ground bird," which seems to mean some kind of bird of prey such as a kite or hawk. She throws a flayed human skin over her shoulder to symbolize her acceptance of samsara as pure.

In the northwest is black Kakamukha, the Crow-Headed, representing the objects of taste. She holds a sword in her right hand and a skull cup of blood in her left, and at the same time eats a heart and lungs. Eating the inner organs and drinking the blood symbolize the liberation of the poisons.

In the northeast is dark blue Ulumukha, the Owl-Headed, representing sound, the object of hearing. She holds a vajra in her right hand and a sword in her left, eating at the same time. Alternatively, the *Hundred Homages* describes her as holding a skull cup and an iron hook in order to tear out the false views of samsara.

The deities that have appeared so far compose the inner mandala of our intrinsically pure nature—the skandhas, senses, and consciousness. This mandala is protected by four dakinis who guard the inner gates. They are transformations of the same four female guardians of the gates who appeared earlier, but this time they are even fiercer and have animal heads. In their right hands, they hold their own characteristic implements with which they fulfill their functions, and in their left they hold skull cups of blood to show their wrathful nature.

The *Dharma Practice* says that they shut the doors to the four kinds of birth and open the doors to the four vajra activities. The *Hundred Homages* interprets them as embodying the four immeasurable states of mind. They keep watch at the boundaries of the mandala so that every aspect of relationship with the external world is filled with compassion, kindness, joy for others, and equanimity. These altruistic emotions are the basis of spiritual life; without them, it is impossible to accomplish the four activities or escape from rebirth.

At the eastern gate is the white, horse-headed form of Ankusha, the Devi with a Hook.[10] In her right hand, she holds an iron hook, the hooked elephant-goad, and in her left a skull cup of blood. She represents the boundless compassion that pulls living beings out from the six realms of samsara, and she performs the spiritual work of pacifying suffering and healing the sickness caused by the five poisons.

At the southern gate is the yellow, pig-headed form of Pasha, the Devi with a Noose, holding a noose and a skull cup of blood. She represents infinite loving-kindness, snaring and binding the mistaken views that prevent living beings from realizing the truth. She performs the activity of enriching and increasing all the qualities of enlightenment.

In the western gate is the red, lion-headed form of Shrinkhala, the Devi with a Chain, holding an iron chain and a skull cup of blood. She fetters the poison of ignorance and with unbounded joy rejoices in the awakening of all beings. She performs the spiritual work of magnetizing or attracting everything that is needed and subjugating everything that is harmful.

In the northern gate is the green, serpent-headed form of Ghanta, the Devi with a Bell, holding a bell and a skull cup of blood. She represents boundless equanimity and is impartial toward all beings, and she rings her bell loudly to subdue all thoughts of the five poisons. She frees the imprisoned energy of the poisons by the compassionate activity of destruction.

After these guardians, to complete the entire display, an outer retinue known as the twenty-eight ladies or yoginis gathers around the periphery of the mandala. They represent many different aspects of our characteristics, functions, and activities, ordinarily arising from the poisons, but now bursting forth as spontaneous expressions of awakened energy. No corner of our being is left unillumined and unaroused by the explosion of wrathful compassion. They "arise spontaneously from the creative energy of the self-existent images of the wrathful herukas."

Unlike the previous groups of female deities, the names of these yoginis are given only in Tibetan, but it is possible to identify them in

Sanskrit with a fair amount of certainty.[11] Almost all can be found among similar groups in the main Buddhist tantras, and most of them are also to be found among the sixty-four yoginis of Hindu tradition, whose temples were ecumenical centers of tantric worship.[12] Several of them are the consorts of important Hindu gods, and it is interesting that, although these goddesses are often better known by other names in their own right, here they are identified only by the feminine form of the god's name. This appears to connect them with legends in which they manifest as the active force of the principle represented by the male deity, always for the purpose of defeating some aspect of evil. The best known of these are the "seven mothers," who are also mentioned in the *Guhyasamaja Tantra*, among others, and six of whom appear here. In Hinduism, they are called the *shakti*, the power or energy, of their consorts, and although this term is not generally used in Buddhism, it agrees perfectly with the function of dakinis in this context.

From the point of view of Buddhism, belief in any deity as existing outside ourselves and having power over us is false and misleading. Their worship is spiritual materialism, the desire to gain something from religious activity rather than to understand the nature of mind. However, once we have realized our ultimate empty nature and that of the deities, the principles and forces they represent become transformed into instruments of dharma. In this way, many deities of the orthodox Hindu tradition, as well as lesser-known, local Indian and Tibetan deities, have been assimilated into vajrayana, as appears to be the case with these yoginis.

Some of them hold emblems such as a vajra, wheel, lotus, and vase, symbolizing their enlightened qualities. Some bear weapons like clubs, spears, and razors to destroy the poisons and cut through the dullness of perception. Some drink blood and eat raw flesh to symbolize unbiased acceptance and transmutation. The heads of wild animals show their perfect control of raw energy, their fearlessness and power, uncontrived and unhesitating. The heads of birds of prey show that they seek out with all-seeing eyes the smallest obstacles and evil tendencies in order to devour them. They invite us to experience life completely, without holding back, with total awareness.

They emerge from within one's brain in the four directions. *The Hundred Homages* identifies these four groups with the four vajra activities. It describes all the yoginis as holding the distinctive attribute of their respective families—the vajra, jewel, lotus, or double vajra—as well as the emblems listed below. It also gives a slightly different color scheme: the yoginis have the colors given here on one side of their bodies, while on the other side all those in the east are white, all those in the south yellow, all those in the west red, and all those in the north green (see plate 6). Both color schemes can be found in bardo paintings, or the four groups may be painted in only the basic four colors of white, yellow, red, and green (see plates 4 and 7).

First, the six yoginis of the east appear, performing the activity of pacifying. Rakshasi, the Demoness, is a dark maroon color and has the head of a yak. She holds a vajra or alternatively a skull cup. She embodies bloodthirsty cruelty and violence transmuted into the indestructible awakened mind.

Next comes orange Brahmi (or Brahmani), Consort of Brahma, who represents the universal power of creation. She is better known as Sarasvati, the goddess of wisdom, art, and speech. She has the head of a serpent and holds a lotus, Brahma's emblem of creativity and birth. The serpent rules the waters of existence from which the lotus arises. In Buddhism, Brahma is praised as possessing divine powers of speech, and appropriately the lotus is also connected with speech since it is the emblem of Amitabha, who embodies the speech of the buddhas.

Mahadevi, the Great Goddess, is dark green and has the head of a leopard. All the big cats symbolize fearlessness and fierceness, but the leopard in particular represents feminine energy. Mahadevi is the consort of Shiva Mahadeva, the Great God, the cosmic principle of dissolution and reabsorption. She bears the trident, one of his characteristic emblems, representing the power of yoga and control over the three nadis. It pierces the three poisons of passion, aggression, and delusion.

The next yogini can be identified as Vaishnavi, Consort of Vishnu, who is the all-pervading power of preservation. She is not actually called Vaishnavi in the text, but her identity seems clear. The Tibetan word is unusual and seems to mean greed or desire; it may perhaps refer to the hunger for existence that lies behind the principle of preservation.[13] She has the head of a mongoose, an animal that is often portrayed accompanying the god of wealth and vomiting jewels from its mouth; this may reflect her role as goddess of fortune and prosperity, in which she is better known as Lakshmi. She is blue, the color of Vishnu, and holds a wheel or discus, his miraculous weapon, in her hand. With its razor-sharp edge, it spins into the heart of the enemy hosts and slices them to pieces. In its peaceful form the wheel becomes the symbol of the Buddha's dharma, spreading out in all directions.

Kaumari, the Maiden, is the consort of Kumara, the Youth, the warrior son of Shiva who was born in order to defeat a powerful evil demon. She is red and has the head of a hyena. In Tibetan, the same word may also mean a yellow or snow bear. She wields a short spear, Kumara's weapon, which always hits its target when it is hurled at the enemy and then returns to his hand. It symbolizes piercing through false views with single-pointed insight.

Indrani (or Aindri), Consort of Indra, is white and has the head of a brown bear. Her husband, Indra, is the mighty ruler of the gods. Together they preside over the realm of the gods, with its vast power, gratification of all desires, and illusions of immortality. She dispels these illusions by holding up a noose of entrails, symbolizing the transience of existence.

In the south of the mandala, the six yoginis who perform the activity of enriching appear. Vajra, the Adamantine, embodies everything that the vajra itself represents. She has a pig's head, symbolizing the transmutation of ignorance and delusion into brilliant, indestructible wakefulness. She is yellow in color and holds a razor in her hand. The traditional form of the razor is an extremely sharp curved blade, which cuts away the errors and defilements that obscure the face of our true nature.

Shanti, Peace, is red and holds a vase in her hand. She has the head of a water-monster, showing that she has completely overcome the turbulence of the ocean of samsara and transformed it into tranquillity. The vase contains the water of life and bestows health and longevity.

Amrita, Elixir of Immortality, personifies the most precious treasure of the gods. Its true meaning is the essence of wisdom and knowledge that bestows spiritual life. She has the head of a scorpion, the most poisonous and deadly of creatures, showing that she transmutes death into life. Her color is red, and she holds a lotus in her hand, both suggesting life and transmutation.

Chandra, Moon, is the feminine form of the moon god. The moon is male in Indian tradition and symbolizes the nectar of bliss. The yogini has the head of a hawk or falcon, the sharp-eyed bird of prey that swoops down upon its victims and swiftly destroys negative forces. She is white like the moon, and she holds the vajra of the indestructible awakened mind.

Danda is She Who Bears a Club. In Hindu iconography, the club or rod is particularly associated with Yama, the god of death, so perhaps in this context Danda personifies Yama's instrument of justice. She has the head of a jackal or fox, animals that hunt and scavenge in charnel grounds. She is dark green and brandishes her club in her hand.

Another Rakshasi, Demoness, dark yellow in color, completes the yoginis of the south. She has a tiger's head and holds a skull cup of blood, symbolizing the transmutation of her bloodthirsty, demonic nature.

In the west of the mandala, the six yoginis who perform the activity of magnetizing appear. First comes Bhaksini, the Devourer. She is dark green and carries a club in her hand. She has the head of a vulture, the bird that eats carcasses and hovers over scenes of carnage waiting for death to provide its source of food. With her weapon, she bludgeons malignant forces and then devours them.

Rati, Pleasure, in Hindu tradition is the consort of Kama, the god of love. She is the red of passion and has a horse's head. The horse represents life force and vitality and is also connected with passion, since the wrathful horse-headed deity Hayagriva is a manifestation of Amitabha. She carries the trunk of a human corpse to symbolize the transmutation of ordinary existence based on desire into the experience of great bliss through the realization of emptiness.

Mahabala, She of Great Strength, appears next. She is white and has the head of a garuda, the most powerful of birds. She carries a club or rod to subjugate evil forces.

A third Rakshasi, Demoness, red in color and with a dog's head, follows. As a scavenger the dog was considered an unclean and polluting animal. She holds the vajra of indestructible purity in one hand

and slashes with a razor in the other, cutting away hindrances and defilements.

Kama, Lust, is the feminine form of the name of the god of love. She is red like Rati and has the head of a hoopoe, an elegant, crested bird associated with springtime and the arousal of desire. She shoots an arrow from a bow. This is the typical emblem of Kama, just like Cupid in the West, aiming the arrows of love into the hearts of all living beings. In Buddhism, the bow symbolizes wisdom and emptiness, while the arrows symbolize skillful means and compassion. Here Kama can be seen as combining the two traditions into a beautiful symbol of the transmutation of passion into compassion.

Vasuraksha is the Protectress of Wealth. She is dark green and has the head of a deer. Deer represent gentleness and kindness, and in early Buddhism were used as symbols of dharma because they were present at the Buddha's first teachings. She may be a guardian deity, or she may perhaps be intended as the consort of Kubera, the god of wealth. She holds a treasure vase full of inexhaustible riches.

In the north of the mandala, the six yoginis who perform the activity of destruction appear. Vayavi, Consort of Vayu, the wind-god, appears first. She is blue and has the head of a wolf. She waves a banner in the wind, representing prana, the life force. She is the energy that controls the coming and going of life.

Nari, the Woman, embodies femininity. She is red with the head of a mountain goat or ibex, and she holds a sharp, pointed stake for impaling evil forces.

Varahi, the Sow, is the consort of Varaha, the Boar, one of the ten avatars of Vishnu. She is black and has a pig's head, symbolizing the transmutation of ignorance. She carries a noose of tusks, or one with tusks at each end, to hold tight the minds of living beings in the realm of awareness.

A second Vajra, the Adamantine, appears with the head of a raven or crow. She is red and brandishes the corpse of a child, symbolizing that the sense of self is born anew every moment and is immediately liberated into wakefulness.

Mahanasa, She Who Has a Large Nose, appears with the head of an elephant.[14] The elephant's head represents the taming of the mind's great strength. She is dark green in color. She carries an adult human corpse in her hand, and drinks its blood, symbolizing the liberation of fully developed ego.

Last comes Varuni, Consort of Varuna, the water-god. She is blue, has a serpent's head, and holds a noose of snakes in her hand. The serpent-deities are always associated with water; they control the rivers, oceans, and rainfall and protect the environment. With her noose, she snares and fetters the power of the poisons.

After these twenty-four yoginis of the four directions, the final four yoginis emerge to guard the outer gates of the mandala, bearing the usual emblems of the gatekeepers. In the eastern gate is White Vajra, with the head of a cuckoo, holding an iron hook. In the south is Yellow Vajra, with the head of a goat, holding a noose. In the west is Red Vajra, with the head of a lion, holding an iron chain. In the north is Green Vajra, with the head of a serpent, holding a bell. They protect the outermost boundaries of the experience of the bardo of dharmata, the state in which we see reality face-to-face. By means of the four vajra activities, they liberate us from all the bonds of illusion, and they block the doors to the four kinds of birth so that we do not wander any further toward the bardo of becoming.

Some traditions add two further stages to the bardo of dharmata; they are not included in *Liberation through Hearing*, but they are sometimes illustrated in bardo paintings (see plate 4, lower center). From the navel, the five dakinis of the five families emerge. They are in dancing poses like the vidyadharas, naked, holding curved knives and skull cups of blood in their hands. Since they arise from the navel center, the abode of Ratnasambhava, they represent the enlightened qualities of the five families. Finally, from the secret place comes the great wrathful Heruka Vajrakila (or Vajrakilaya). He embodies the activity of all the buddhas and is one of the most powerful deities of the Nyingma tradition, who overcomes all hindrances to spiritual practice. He is dark blue, embracing his light blue consort, and his appearance is similar to that of the other herukas. With his top pair of hands, he holds a nine-pronged vajra in the right and shoots forth flames from the left. In his lower pair, he holds a five-pronged vajra and a tantric staff. With his main pair of arms, he encircles the body of his partner and rolls between his hands the *kila* after which he is named. This is a three-sided blade, originally a nail or stake, but more suggestive of a dagger, which pierces simultaneously through passion, aggression, and delusion.

All the visions that arise during the bardo of dharmata are the spontaneous, natural expressions of our awakened mind, which is none other than inseparable emptiness and luminosity. As the text explains, our awareness manifests before us; it appears from itself to itself through its own illuminating power, just so that it can recognize itself and be self-liberated. Our state of bondage in samsara is really nothing but nonrecognition; we perpetuate it all the time. The bardo of dharmata is a tremendous opportunity because it presents reality so clearly and nakedly. Liberation is simply seeing things as they really are. As soon as we see the essence of awareness in everything around us, we are instantly freed from all the delusion of samsara. "Recognition and liberation are simultaneous."

But if we are unable to recognize, our confusion and terror will make us perceive these radiant forms of our own mind as demons. Drifting farther and farther away from the original nondual awareness of the ground of being, we begin to feel more and more separate and vulnerable, while they seem ever more external and real.

> O child of awakened family, the dharmakaya arises out of the aspect of emptiness as the peaceful deities. Recognize it. The sambhogakaya arises out of the aspect of clarity as the wrathful deities, so recognize it. When the fifty-eight blood-drinking deities emerge from within your brain and appear before you, if you understand that whatever appears is shining from the intrinsic inner radiance of your awareness, you will immediately awaken, inseparable from the images of the blood-drinking deities. O child of awakened family, if you do not recognize in this way, you will be afraid and flee from them, and so you will return to even greater suffering. If you do not recognize in this way, you will see all the blood-drinking deities as lords of death and you will be afraid of them. You will be petrified and faint with terror. Your hallucinations will turn into demons and you will wander in samsara.

All the wrathful deities will be transformed into the ferocious form of Yama, the Lord of Death, also known as the Dharma King, and all the peaceful deities will be transformed into Mahakala, an extremely powerful protector of dharma. Now we can no longer perceive the visions as awakened beings, but only as demonic, evil, and threatening. We feel that they want to attack us, injure us, or even kill us. We begin to solidify space, crystallizing the appearances of our own mind into projections and then allowing ourselves to believe in them and be completely deceived by them. We move out of the experience of the bardo of dharmata into the bardo of existence.

> O child of awakened family, when visions of this kind appear, do not be afraid. You have a mental body of karmic imprints, so even if you are killed and cut into pieces, you cannot die. You are really the natural form of emptiness, so there is no need to fear any harm. Even the lords of death themselves arise from the intrinsic inner radiance of your awareness; they have no solid substance. Emptiness cannot harm emptiness. Have confidence that the external peaceful and wrathful deities, the blood-drinking herukas, the animal-headed deities, the rainbow lights, and the terrifying forms of the lords of death do not really exist; they only arise from the inherent creative energy of your awareness. If you understand this, all fear is liberated in its natural state, and merging inseparably you will become awakened.

The instruction reminds us again that all these fearful visions are really our chosen deity, our awakened nature. We should call on that deity and on our guru for help in realizing that they are not our enemies and there is nothing to fear. The aspiration-prayer at this stage is much longer than the previous verses. It particularly calls on Avalokiteshvara, the Lord of Great Compassion (see plate 8). The six syllables of his mantra, OM MA NI PAD ME HUM, relate to the six realms of existence. They are visualized in the colors of the buddhas of the six realms, who are the living presence of compassion taking form within each realm, and who appeared earlier among the peaceful visions of the bardo. OM is white and represents the realm of the gods; MA is green and represents the realm of the jealous gods; NI is yellow and represents the human realm; PAD (pronounced *pe* in Tibetan) is blue and represents the animal realm; ME is red and represents the realm of the hungry ghosts; and HUM is black and represents the realm of hell. By meditating on the mantra in this way, we can awaken the power of compassion within ourselves and direct it toward all living beings, while at the same time transmuting the poisons that lead to rebirth in the six realms. Just as the true nature of everything we see is the deity's form, so everything we hear is really the underlying sacred vibration of mantra. The deafening roar of cosmic thunder and the violent, threatening yells of the demons in the bardo all become the liberating sound of the six syllables, transforming our perception so that we recognize the true nature of the visions.

> When through intense karmic imprints I wander in samsara,
> On the luminous path of abandoning projections of fear and
>   terror
> May the blessed ones, peaceful and wrathful, go before me,
> The wrathful ladies of space behind me,
> Help me to cross the bardo's dangerous passage
> And bring me to the perfect awakened state.
> Parted from beloved friends, wandering alone,
> Now when the empty forms of self-display appear
> May the buddhas send out the power of their compassion
> So that the bardo's fear and terror do not arise.
> When the five clear lights of knowledge shine
> Fearlessly may I recognize myself.
> When the forms of the peaceful and wrathful ones appear
> Fearless and confident may I recognize the bardo.
> When I suffer through the power of evil karma
> May my chosen deity remove all suffering.
> When the natural sound of dharmata roars like a thousand
>   thunders
> May it all become the sound of the six syllables.
> When I follow my karma without a refuge
> May the Lord of Great Compassion be my refuge.
> When I suffer the results of karmic imprints
> May the samadhi of bliss and luminosity arise.

May the five elements not rise up as enemies,
May I see the realms of the five buddhas.

This section of the text concludes by repeating once again the vital importance of practice during life and the great benefit even of simply hearing this teaching. It points out that most people are frightened and confused at the time of death, whether they are used to meditating or not, and need the help of this guidance through the bardo. Then, if they practiced while they were alive, those who recognized the nature of mind and attained stability in their realization will be very strong when the luminosity of death appears, and so they will attain liberation. Those who have gained experience in deity yoga will be very strong when the visions of the peaceful and wrathful deities appear, so they too will recognize and be liberated.

It is called *Great Liberation through Hearing* because simply to hear it is enough. Even people who have committed the five deadly sins can be liberated by hearing it, so great is the power of this teaching. By pointing out exactly how to recognize the awakened nature of the visions, it cuts through everything that normally obstructs us and penetrates straight to the essence of our true being, no matter what the circumstances may be. As the final sentence of this section says, "It draws out the essence of all dharma." Whatever practice we have used during life, this teaching goes right to its heart.

In the bardo, we are not constricted by the limitations of the physical body, and it is said that the intelligence is nine times clearer. So even if we have only heard this teaching once, without understanding it at the time, in the bardo it is possible to remember it exactly, word for word, and to grasp its meaning instantly. "Therefore it should be taught to everyone during their life, it should be read at the bedside of all who are sick, it should be read beside the bodies of all the dead, it should be spread far and wide."

But all this depends on the power of connections and adhishthana. We would never even have a chance of hearing it or reading it if we had not previously made some move toward it and established a link. Gradually, over many lives, our understanding and responsiveness grows, so that suddenly a single word may be enough to reawaken our innate knowledge. We must never forget that, along with the harm we undoubtedly do and the negative karmic results we continually create for ourselves, we have also done a vast amount of good during our lives and planted countless seeds of positive potentiality.

To meet with this is great good fortune. It is hard to meet, except for those who have purified the obscuring veils and developed goodness. Even if one meets it, it is difficult to take in. When one hears it, one is liberated simply by not disbelieving; therefore it should be cherished as most precious. It draws out the essence of all dharma.

Chapter Fifteen

At the Womb Door

AFTER FAINTING WITH TERROR at the visions of the wrathful deities, the consciousness of the dead person awakens into existence as a bardo being with a subtle mental body, so this period is called the bardo of existence or bardo of becoming. It lasts until the dead person enters the next life, either through conception or by spontaneous birth. This is the bardo in its original sense, the transition between death and rebirth. It is called the bardo of existence because the sense of self and other, the body and the external world, are all brought into being by the mind through the power of desire and grasping. Existence in Buddhism always implies duality; it is marked by the three characteristics of impermanence, suffering, and nonself.

The bardo of existence corresponds to what most people think of as the after-death state, when our past life is summed up and our future is decided. It is dominated by the law of karma; here the consequences of our thoughts, words, and deeds take form in front of our eyes. It is an extremely volatile and fluid state, described as full of terror and suffering. Our perceptions and the environment around us are continually changing as the effects of past actions come to the surface, like the distorted memories of the previous day's events during a dream. As the text says: "It is your own karma that you are suffering like this, so you cannot blame anyone else."

The instruction for this stage, "the clear reminder of the bardo of existence," should be read aloud from about the tenth day after death. Various periods of time are mentioned in this section and are not entirely consistent, but we should remember that our concept of time does not really apply in the bardo and what happens in it depends entirely on the spiritual state and karma of the dead person. We are told that this bardo generally lasts for twenty-one days, but that it can be anywhere between one week and seven weeks. According to other commentators, it can occasionally continue for many months or even years. Every seven days, one goes very briefly through the experience of death, the visions of the bardo of dharmata, and reawakening into the bardo of existence.

This can be compared to our present life, where the sequence of dissolution, entering a space of infinite potentialities and reemerging, takes place continually in many different timescales. Waking consciousness dissolves when we fall asleep, we spend several hours in what we consider to be unconsciousness, and then we return to the waking state. Within that unconscious period, dreams arise, dissolve, then arise again. In waking life, a dominant mood fades away and leaves a gap of uncertainty before another emotion replaces it. And all the time, fleeting thoughts and feelings come and go; one state of mind dies, there is a moment of openness, then another state of mind is born. If we can accustom ourselves to seeing this whole process as a play of illusion, it will help us to avoid grasping at the chance of rebirth when we are in the bardo of existence.

As consciousness emerges from the state of luminosity we instantaneously experience the three visions of light in reverse order—black, red, and white—and the eighty basic instincts of delusion, passion, and aggression become activated in the mindstream. At the same time, the subtle forms of the elements arise: the energy of air emerges from space, fire from air, water from fire, and earth from water. The reappearance of these subtle phenomena creates the mental body of the bardo determined by the karmic imprints or tendencies in the source consciousness. This bardo being is known as a gandharva, a special kind of hungry ghost. We are not actually in any of the six realms at this point, but if we remain for a very long time without finding a new rebirth, we may become full-fledged hungry ghosts. Gandharvas are known as scent-eaters because they live off the scent of food. But they can only receive sustenance from food that has been dedicated to them, so without it, they feel pangs of hunger just as if they had bodies of flesh and blood. The book describes their nature in greater detail by quoting and commenting on a traditional verse:

Having the physical form of past and future existences,[1]
Complete with all the senses, moving without obstruction,
Possessing miraculous powers resulting from karma,
Seen by the pure divine eye and by those of kindred nature.

The karmic imprints that form the bardo body are impressions left in the source consciousness, which create patterns tending toward certain modes of existence, characteristics, environments, and so on. At first, the memories of the previous life are very strong and the tendencies of that life still prevail, so we feel we still possess our old body. Gradually, the connection fades away and the tendencies that are pulling us toward a new existence take over. As this happens, we begin to feel that we already inhabit the body of our next life. When the verse speaks of a physical form, it is referring to the bodies of our past and future lives, not to the bardo body; the body we experience in the bardo is purely mental and immaterial, but it seems absolutely real, so we are constantly afraid of being hurt or killed.

However, this form does have significant differences from our actual past and future embodiments. It is perfect, like an ideal body of the golden age, and it shines with its own light. Since it is immaterial, it leaves no footprints, casts no shadow, and has no reflection. There is no physical disability, impairment of the senses, or mental deficiency. The intelligence is "nine times clearer," an expression meaning absolutely clear. We have supernormal powers such as clairvoyance, the ability to pass through solid objects, and the ability to arrive instantly wherever we wish just by thinking of it. There are only two places we cannot go. One is our future mother's womb, which would mean that we have entered our next life in samsara. The other is the vajra seat, the place where the Buddha sat in meditation and where he awakened, which symbolizes the attainment of enlightenment and would mean that we have entered nirvana. The supernatural powers we possess are explained as being simply the temporary result of karma, not genuine spiritual attainments accomplished through meditation. We are warned that they are unsuitable and should not distract us, but at the same time, they are useful because they enable us to hear and attend to the instructions.

One of the powers attained at advanced levels of meditation is the pure divine eye, or eye of the gods, which can perceive living beings in all six realms as well as in the bardo. This is how accomplished teachers are able to see and communicate with the dead person, although it is only possible if they concentrate on seeing and if their meditation is not disturbed. The text distinguishes this from the supernatural vision that belongs to the bardo state, by which beings of the same kind who are going to be born in the same realm are able to see each other. All these abilities are signs that one is dead and wandering in the bardo of existence; they are explained in detail so that the dead person will recognize them and understand what is happening.

At first, the dead do not realize that they are dead; they feel that they still have their old bodies and cannot understand why their friends and relatives are ignoring them. They try desperately to communicate, wandering back and forth in frustration and despair. The suffering caused by this rejection is agonizing, "like the pain of a fish rolling in hot sand." All the emotions the dead person goes through are translated into extremely vivid physical experiences:

> O child of awakened family, blown by the restless wind of karma, your mind, without support, helplessly rides the horse of prana like a feather carried on the air, swinging and swaying . . . all the time there will be a gray haze like the pale light of an autumn dawn, neither day nor night . . . the violently whirling hurricane of karma, utterly terrifying and unbearable, will drive you on from behind. Do not be afraid of it; it is your own confused hallucination. Before you is dense darkness, absolutely terrifying and unbearable, curdling your blood with cries of "Strike!" and "Kill!" Do not be afraid of it. Those who have done much evil will see hordes of flesh-eating demons as a result of their karma, brandishing

weapons, yelling war cries, shouting "Kill!" and "Strike!" You will feel that you are being chased by savage wild animals and pursued by armies through snow, rain, storms, and darkness. You will hear sounds of mountains crumbling, of lakes flooding, of wildfire spreading, and of fierce winds springing up. In terror you will flee wherever you can, but you will be cut off by three chasms in front of you—white, red, and black. They are deep and dreadful, and you will be on the point of falling into them. O child of awakened family, they are not really chasms; they are aggression, passion, and delusion. Recognize this now as the bardo of existence and call on the name of the Lord of Great Compassion.

In the previous bardo, our true nature was revealed in its basic state of purity as the self-manifesting forms of the deities, but now our confused nature appears as demonic apparitions arising from karma. As the elements return, they manifest externally in threatening forms, in the words of the verse that was quoted in chapter 5, "as enemies." Earth becomes mountains collapsing upon us, water becomes a great flood that sweeps us away, fire rages all around and scorches us, and air is a violent wind that batters us relentlessly. Passion, aggression, and delusion lie in wait like treacherous abysses opening up beneath our feet. All our inner demons, the karmic results of the harm we have done and the hurt we have caused, pursue us with vengeful fury. These experiences are all the natural self-display of our own mind and we must not be afraid of them, but we are also warned against attachment to the illusory appearances resulting from positive karma and against an attitude of apathy toward neutral appearances:

Those who have developed goodness, were virtuous, and practiced dharma sincerely will be met by every kind of perfect enjoyment and experience every kind of perfect bliss and happiness. Those who were dull and indifferent, who did neither good nor evil, will experience neither pleasure nor pain, but only dullness and apathy will arise. Whatever happens, O child of awakened family, whatever happiness and objects of desire arise in this way, do not be attracted to them or desire them. Offer them to the guru and the three jewels. Give up attachment and longing in your heart. And if the experience of indifference without either pleasure or pain arises, rest your mind in the mahamudra state, free from both meditation and distraction. This is very important.

Since everyone has undoubtedly performed good, bad, and neutral actions, the consciousness of the dead person is tossed around by the wind of karma between these various experiences. Although the disembodied mind has supernormal powers and can go wherever it wishes, it is unable to settle down for any length of time and longs to find shelter and rest. At last, it realizes that it has died. When this realization dawns, "your heart will suddenly grow empty and cold, and you will feel intense, boundless pain."

Then the departed consciousness will wander around everywhere looking for a body; it may even try to return to its former body, but it is too late.

Even if you try over and over again to enter your own corpse, winter will have frozen it or summer made it rot, or your family will have burned it or buried it in a grave or given it to the birds and wild animals, for a long time has passed in the bardo of dharmata, so you will find no spot where you can reenter it. Your heart will sink, and you will feel that you are being squeezed between all the rocks and stony earth. This kind of suffering is the bardo of existence. Even if you look for a body, you will find nothing but suffering, so cut off your longing for a body and rest in the state where nothing need be done, without distraction.

There is still an opportunity to attain liberation at this point, whether it is through the power of faith and devotion, by meditating on the form of one's chosen deity, or by resting in undistracted formless meditation. During this bardo, the habits formed by one's practice during life and the connection with one's guru, the channel of adhishthana, are extremely important. Practitioners of vajrayana who have gained enough experience in their practice of deity yoga will transform the bardo body into the form of their chosen deity and either go to a pure land or take birth as an accomplished yogin or yogini, in order to complete the path and stabilize their recognition of luminosity.

If we do not recognize and continue to be drawn along in the bardo, we must next face the judgment of Yama, the Lord of Death. He is a terrifying, demonic figure, huge and black, sometimes appearing with the head of a ferocious bull or buffalo, attended by his servants who are also called lords of death. He represents the voice of our true conscience, the innermost knowledge of all our secret motives and intentions, even when we have disguised them from ourselves. Our positive and negative aspects are personified as good and bad spirits born within us. They count out heaps of white and black pebbles representing every one of our good and bad actions. Through fear, we make excuses and lie to the Lord of Death, but it is no use; he holds the mirror of karma, in which everything we have done throughout our lives is shown fully and clearly. The instruction reminds us not to be afraid, for even this comes from our own mind. We panic and lie because we believe in the external reality of these events, and when we confront the truth about ourselves in the mirror of karma, our guilt makes us feel that we deserve to be punished.

> Then the Lord of Death will tie a rope around your neck and drag you away; he will cut off your head, tear out your heart, pull out your entrails, lick up your brains, drink your blood, eat your flesh, and gnaw your bones. Yet you cannot die, so even though your body has been cut into pieces, you will recover. Being cut again and again causes extreme pain, so do not be afraid when the white pebbles are counted, do not lie and do not fear the Lord of Death. Since you have a mental body, you cannot die even if you are killed and chopped up. You are really the natural form of emptiness, so there is no need to fear. These lords of death, too, are the natural form of emptiness, your own confused self-display. You are an empty mental body of karmic imprints. Emptiness cannot harm emptiness; that which has no characteristics cannot harm that which has no characteristics. The Lord of Death, the good and bad spirits, the bull-headed demon, and so on have no external reality apart from your confused self-display, so recognize this. At this very moment, recognize everything as the bardo.

Now the text gives a beautiful instruction on simply looking into the nature of things as they really are and resting in that uncontrived state. It is expressed in terms of the three kayas: the empty essence, the luminous expression, and the unobstructed manifestation, united in the fourth, the svabhavikakaya, which is the totality of our essential nature:

> Meditate on the samadhi of mahamudra, the great symbol. If you do not know how to meditate, look closely at the essence of who it is within you that feels fear, and you will see an empty essence where nothing whatever exists. That is the dharmakaya. But this emptiness is not blankness. The empty essence of your fear is a wide-awake, clear awareness. That is the mind of the sambhogakaya. Emptiness and clarity are inseparable from each other: clarity is the essence of emptiness, and emptiness is the essence of clarity. Now the awareness of indivisible clarity and emptiness returns to nakedness and dwells within itself in the uncreated state. That is the svabhavikakaya. And now its inherent creative energy manifests everywhere without obstruction. That is the compassionate nirmanakaya. O child of awakened family, look in this way without distraction. As soon as you recognize, complete awakening in the four kayas is certain. Do not be distracted. This is the boundary where buddhas and sentient beings are separated. It is said of this time:

> > In a single moment, the difference is made,
> > In a single moment, perfect awakening.

The way of recognition is the ultimate view, the highest teaching. There is nothing to change in our nature, nothing to add or take away; recognition is all that is needed. The only difference between buddhas and sentient beings is that sentient beings do not know they are buddhas.

This is the final chance to attain liberation before we begin to be drawn toward rebirth, when it becomes much more difficult to escape from the wheel of samsara. So at this time, "it is very important to make another effort" to help the dead person. Until about the halfway point of the bardo of becoming, we still feel connected with our old bodies and our former homes. With the power of clairvoyance, we are able to see and hear all that is happening and to look into the minds of the people we have left behind. This is a situation of great danger, for emotional reactions are extremely powerful in the bardo. Although our future place of rebirth has already been determined by our karmic tendencies, a sudden outburst of anger or attachment now could dramatically alter our direction.

For instance, we may suddenly feel longing for the wealth and possessions we have been forced to abandon, or we may become resentful at the thought of others enjoying them. Perhaps they are being misused or given to our enemies. Then we are propelled down toward the realms of hell through anger, or toward the hungry ghost realm through attachment. To prevent this from happening, we should let go of all possessive thoughts and mentally make an offering of everything that was once ours.

During the time when we are wandering in the bardo, our friends and family are conducting funeral rites for us. They may be performing unsuitable rituals that are not helpful in creating a good atmosphere. In some societies, animal sacrifices may be offered; this will make us feel violent and angry, either through revulsion or through emotional participation in the act of killing. Even when the correct rituals are performed by qualified people, we are extremely sensitive to any mistakes that are made. We can read the minds of the participants and see their inattention, their doubts, their thoughts about us, and their hidden motives for being present. This will make us feel cheated and deceived, and we will despair and lose faith. To counteract these feelings, we must remember that everything we see is our own distorted perception, "like seeing the faults of my own face reflected in a mirror." We must try to arouse sacred vision, knowing that in their pure essential nature, our friends are the community of the sangha, their words are the holy dharma, and their thoughts are the wisdom of the Buddha. Seeing things in this way actually transforms ordinary, fallible, human actions into pure actions that will be of great benefit to us.

Even if we have caused a lot of harm during our lifetimes and are heading for the lower realms, if we see that our teachers and spiritual friends are performing rituals for us with genuine faith and devotion, the joy and gratitude we feel will cause us to go to a higher realm. So again the principle of sacred vision is extremely important. The dead person is instructed to repeat part of the prayer that concluded the bardo of dharmata. It should be repeated many times, with absolute conviction that it is true and not false:

> Parted from beloved friends, wandering alone,
> Now when the empty forms of self-display appear
> May the buddhas send out the power of their compassion
> So that the bardo's fear and terror do not arise.
> When I suffer through the power of evil karma
> May my chosen deity remove all suffering.
> When the natural sound of dharmata roars like a thousand
>   thunders
> May it all become the sound of the six syllables.
> When I follow my karma without a refuge
> May the Lord of Great Compassion be my refuge.
> When I suffer the results of karmic imprints
> May the samadhi of bliss and luminosity arise.

About halfway through the bardo of existence, or after four and a half days according to the text, the connection to our previous life fades away and we feel increasingly drawn toward the next life. The colors of the six realms will shine, soft and inviting: the white light of the realm of the gods, the red light of the realm of the jealous gods, the blue light of the human realm, the green light of the animal realm, the yellow light of the hungry ghost realm, and the smoky light of the realm of hell. The light of the realm in which we are going to be reborn shines the most brightly.

The most important thing now is to avoid being attracted to any of the six realms. There is still a chance of awakening into what is called a pure nirmanakaya realm, a higher level of existence where we continue to progress along the final stages of the path. The colored lights represent the mental states that create the realms of samsara. They appear before us from within our own mind. They lure us with all the force of our karmic tendencies, our habitual responses, and our instinctive urge to return to our old way of life. We can feel this mag-

netic attraction when we are pulled in a certain direction by our emotions, yet at the same time sense the possibility of resting in a state of
equanimity and openness instead of being led by habit. Even in meditation we may suddenly feel nostalgic for old attitudes, and a perverse
longing can arise to go back to being ordinary and to seeing things in
an ordinary way. This is like the shining of these illusory lights in our
mind.

The instruction given at this point is about transforming our perception of the six realms through the practice of sacred vision. If we
have previously practiced the yoga of a deity, we should meditate on
the colored lights as being that deity or, if we have no specific practice,
as Avalokiteshvara. We imagine intensely, with our whole being, that
whatever we see is nothing but the compassionate presence of the deity.
And the essence of the deity is emptiness: emptiness and appearance are
indivisible, ceaselessly flowing into each other, emerging and dissolving—until we transcend the distinction between real and unreal and the
concept of a separate self becomes meaningless.

O child of awakened family, at this time the instruction is
absolutely essential: whatever light shines, meditate on it as
the Lord of Great Compassion. Meditate on the thought
that when the light arises, it is the Lord of Great Compassion. This is the most profound, essential point; it is very
important and will prevent birth.

Meditate for a long time on whichever is your chosen
deity as a vision without any real nature of its own, like an
illusion. This is called the pure illusory body. Then let the
deity disappear from the edges inward and rest for a while
in the state of emptiness and clarity where there is no grasping and nothing whatever exists. Meditate again on the deity,
then again on the luminosity. Meditate like this alternately,
then let even your awareness disappear from its outer limits
inward. Wherever there is space, there is awareness; and
wherever there is awareness, there is dharmakaya. Rest qui-
etly in the selflessness and simplicity of dharmakaya. From
that state, birth will be prevented and you will awaken.

Here simplicity refers to the absence of any mental manifestation;
it literally means without expansion or elaboration, what Trungpa

Rinpoche referred to as "the complexities of samsara and nirvana." It is a concept based on the understanding that phenomena have no independent existence but arise from mind as spontaneous self-display. Dharmakaya is the state of nondual omniscience, in which luminous awareness knows everything as itself by its own light. There is no grasping by the self as subject and no phenomena existing separately as object. If we are able to rest in that state with some degree of stability, we can awaken into a pure land instead of returning to samsara. Similarly, in everyday experience, if we can rest in openness and equanimity even for a short time, it will prevent us from drifting straight into the next negative emotional reaction that beckons us.

With the sensation of possessing a mental body, the gandharva or bardo consciousness feels extremely vulnerable and disoriented, so it desperately searches for any place of refuge. It is ceaselessly buffeted by the wind of karma and continues to endure the experience of being pursued through darkness, whirlwinds, snow, and hail. In trying to escape, those who have led evil lives feel they are fleeing into even greater misery, while those who have led good lives feel they are traveling toward a place of happiness. Finally, visions of men and women in sexual union appear. If a gandharva with the right connections to these future parents is present, it now has the opportunity to slip in between the sperm and ovum as they unite, and so "enter a womb."

The book explains that there are two principal methods that can be applied to avoid rebirth: "stopping the person who is entering, and closing the womb door that is about to be entered." The first method is similar to the instruction that has just been given, emphasizing again that if one does not have the empowerment of any specific deity, one should meditate on Avalokiteshvara. The person in the bardo simply merges with the luminous emptiness of the deity's essence and does not proceed any further toward rebirth. But if that does not work, there are five different ways of shutting the womb door so that one cannot enter. The root verse for the bardo of existence contains the essence of the instructions:

Now when the bardo of existence dawns upon me,
I will hold my aspiration one-pointedly in mind
And strive to prolong the course of good karma.

I will close the womb door and remember resistance.
This is a time for strength of mind and pure vision,
Abandon jealousy and meditate on the guru as father and mother!

Concentrating on our aspiration toward awakening is extremely important at this stage because of the unprecedented power of the mind in the bardo, so that whatever we think of is immediately fulfilled. Even a fleeting thought of fear can completely unbalance us, or a moment of nostalgia can send us hurtling toward rebirth. Equally, we can be liberated by an instant of recognition. The effect of applying single-minded concentration at this time is comparable to controlling a horse with a bridle or using a catapult to fire a missile.

Prolonging the course of good karma means continuously reinforcing the chain reaction created by positive thoughts and actions by extending it instead of deviating from it into fear, anger, attachment, or other negative emotions. The fundamental nature of all sentient beings is basic goodness, the state of Samantabhadra, but through ignorance we have cut off our connection to our source. So hearing these instructions in the bardo is like mending a broken water main by inserting a pipe. With its help, the vital link is reestablished; the current of positive cause and effect will flow along steadily without dispersing in other directions and lead us back to our own natural perfection.

The verse says that we must "abandon jealousy." Since we are going to be born as either male or female, we already possess the polarity of our future gender; when we see a man and woman, our potential parents, making love, jealousy immediately arises within us. It is produced from the fundamental opposing emotions of attraction and aversion. We feel attraction, lust, and passion toward the parent of the opposite sex and aversion, hatred and aggression toward the parent of the same sex. This is what propels the gandharva into the womb, entering in between the male and female essences of the parents, the white and red bindus. It is as though a door has opened for us, inviting us to enter.

Closing the womb door really means cutting off the mental conditions required for entering a womb by transforming our perception and attitude toward it. So the first instruction is to imagine the couple as the embodiment of the guru in male and female form. Instead of an ordinary man and woman driven by lust, we see our guru immersed in the samadhi of supreme bliss with his or her spiritual consort. This pure perception completely changes our attitude; we feel intense devotion and ask them for teachings. As a result, we merge with the spaciousness of their awakened mind instead of being enticed into the web of samsara.

If that does not succeed, we should meditate on the couple as our chosen deity, or as Avalokiteshvara in union with his consort. The male and female principles embody the inseparable union of appearance and emptiness, showing us directly the illusory nature of everything we see. We should mentally make offerings to them and ask them to grant us spiritual realizations. This will have the same effect as the first method.

Both these methods relate to the practice in daily life of trying to perceive whatever arises as the expression of the guru or the deity. With this kind of sacred vision, we do not need to become entangled in each new situation that arises. Every experience is recognized as an expression of the awakened state. It means that we are continually freeing the mind into openness, letting go of the egoistic agenda that normally influences all our thoughts, words, and actions.

But if we still find ourselves at the very threshold of a womb, the third instruction is on "turning away passion and aggression" by contemplating the dreadful consequences of entering under their influence. As the gandharva penetrates the union of the two essences, it experiences a moment of bliss, then it loses consciousness; this is the death of the gandharva state. From that moment on, the next life begins. There are many sources describing the evolution of the embryo in the womb, derived from ancient Indian medical theory.[2] In turn the various pranas, nadis, and chakras appear, spreading out from the heart, which forms at the place where consciousness originally entered between the red and white bindus. Depending on the subtle body, the physical body of the fetus gradually develops, resembling first a fish and then a sequence of various mammals as it grows. The whole process is said to cause great discomfort; existence in the womb is like being in a prison, and birth is extremely painful.

Here the text mentions being reborn in the animal realm as a very real possibility. At this stage, experienced practitioners will already have been liberated, so these instructions are addressed to all kinds of people in the bardo, even those who have sunk very low, and this reminder of the suffering of samsara is a powerful warning against giving in to passion and aggression.

> You will open your eyes and find you have come back as a puppy. Previously you were human, but now you have become a dog, so you will suffer in a kennel, or else in a pigsty, an anthill, or a wormhole; or perhaps you may be born as a young bull or goat or lamb. You cannot return here; you will endure all kinds of misery in a state of great delusion and stupidity. Circling like this around the six realms of the hell-beings, the hungry ghosts, and so on, you will be tormented by endless suffering. There is nothing more powerful or terrifying than this.

Many people who believe in reincarnation think it is impossible to revert from the human state to a lower one, but the traditional Buddhist view is that we circle around the six realms again and again over immense periods of time. To be born in a different realm requires a complete transformation of our whole outlook. An animal body can only manifest as the natural expression of an animal mind, and the same is true for all the other realms. So to say that one suddenly awakens in the body of a puppy does not mean that one would have a human consciousness. All the same, from a human point of view, it is still a vivid warning. Above all, the warning is relevant during this life, for even now we seldom notice when we are slipping into the states of mind of the lower realms. The instruction here is to meditate on this resolution:

> Alas, for a sentient being of evil karma, such as I! Although I have circled around samsara many times before, I am still wandering about like this as a result of passion and aggression. If I go on feeling passion and aggression in this way, I shall wander endlessly in samsara and be in danger of sinking down into the ocean of suffering for a long time, so now I shall feel absolutely no passion or aggression. Alas, alas!

Concentrating on this powerful resolve will destroy the precondition for entering a womb, so the door will be shut.

If that method is not successful, the fourth technique is to meditate on the unreality of all our experiences. Both the terrors of the bardo
and the apparent refuge offered by our future parents arise from our
own mind, and that mind itself is essentially illusory and nonexistent.
We take what is not real to be real and what does not exist to exist,
which is why we are trapped in samsara. The text quotes the traditional
analogies that apply to every aspect of life: "Now they are all like
dreams, like magic, like echoes, like castles in the air, like mirages, like
reflections, like optical illusions, like the moon in water. They are not
real even for a moment. Certainly they are not true, but false." This
meditation is extremely powerful because it directly undermines belief
in duality and self; the entrance to rebirth is automatically closed, because there is no longer any sense of an individual to be reborn.

The final method of closing the womb door is essentially a dzogchen meditation on the luminosity and emptiness of mind, the simplest
of all teachings.

> O child of awakened family, if even after doing that the
> womb door is not closed, now it should be closed by the
> fifth method, meditation on luminosity. The meditation
> should be done in this way: "Everything that exists is my
> own mind, and this mind is emptiness, unborn and unob-
> structed." As you contemplate this thought, let your mind
> rest naturally and easily within itself in its own way, like
> water poured into water, self-contained, loose, open, and re-
> laxed, so that your mind is not spoiled by anything artificial.
> This will definitely close the womb door to all four kinds of
> birth; it is quite certain. Meditate like this again and again
> until it is closed.

In providing all these different instructions, just as during the bardo of
dharmata, the text is pointing out the multitude of possibilities continually present all around us as potential gateways to awakening. In life,
just as in the after-death state, not all opportunities are available to
everybody, and we are not always able to respond to them. We cannot
stay in the bardo of existence forever, so if we have neither attained

liberation nor entered a womb, there comes a time when we have to embark on a new existence. The final instructions are concerned with choosing the best possible rebirth. The point of giving all the details that follow is to make sense of the bewildering experience the dead person goes through, to provide some kind of map for this journey into unknown territory, where we are driven by karma toward the ripening of the seeds we have sown.

Within the colored lights of the six realms, features of their landscapes begin to appear as we approach them. Perhaps we are drawn very strongly toward one realm and so we perceive only that, or perhaps we see glimpses of other realms as different aspects of our karma come to the fore. All the time, we are desperately searching for somewhere to hide, so whatever we see will appear as a place of refuge. This is when we should "think of resistance," as the verse says. The book describes the signs and characteristics of each of the realms, so that if we are about to be born in them we can recognize the indications and resist the lure of entering a womb.

In choosing a new place of birth, the most important thing to consider is the opportunities it provides for practicing dharma. From this point of view, the human realm is regarded as the very best, even better than the higher realms of the gods and jealous gods. The human realm consists of four regions or continents in the four directions around Mount Meru, the axis of our world system, but they are not all equally suitable. If we are going to be born in the eastern continent we shall see a lake on which geese are swimming. The sign of the western continent is a lake where horses are grazing, and the sign of the northern continent is a lake surrounded by trees and cattle. They are all places of wealth and happiness, but they are too materialistic and "dharma does not flourish there," so they should be avoided. Only the southern continent, corresponding to our world, has conditions that support dharma. If we have the karmic qualifications to be born there, we shall see many luxurious houses, and we should enter them to find our future parents.

We may also see visions of the other realms. If we are going to be born in the realm of the gods, we see heavenly palaces, many stories high and fashioned entirely of jewels. Although the life of the gods is considered to be altogether too easy and pleasant for the serious pursuit of dharma, it does possess many excellent qualities, so we should enter it if we can.

The jealous gods are violent and aggressive, although they share the nature of the gods, so we should try hard not to be drawn into their realm. As we approach it, we see delightful forest groves and revolving wheels of fire, magic weapons that spit forth flames as they spin toward their targets.

If we are going to be born as animals, everything will appear "as if through a mist." We dimly perceive the habitations of various kinds of creatures: caves in rocks, holes in the ground, and flimsy shelters of straw. We should definitely not go into them.

The realm of the hungry ghosts appears dark and shadowy. Ghosts can dwell in all kinds of strange places, for instance, inside trees or beneath the earth. So the black mouths of pits in the ground, or blasted tree stumps, or any black protuberance or patch of earth may seem to offer shelter. We should persevere in resisting any thought of entering there.

Lastly, the signs of the realm of hell are described. It will seem as if we are traveling along a black road where there are black and red dwellings, black pits, and islands of dense, gloomy darkness. We may have to enter helplessly, against our will, lured by the songs of those with evil karma, so we should be extremely careful and resist as strongly as possible.

All the time, we are being pursued by the illusory manifestations of karma, the demons, murderers and avengers, savage beasts, darkness, hurricanes, and storms of snow and hail. The whole atmosphere is terrifying, so if we see a grove of trees, we quickly hide among them, or if there is a house, we rush inside it; we may even creep down a hole in the ground or curl up inside the cup of a flower. Then we become attached to our hiding place and are too frightened to come out, so we end up taking a body in that realm. "That is a sign that demons and evil forces are obstructing you now. At this time there is a profound instruction, so listen and understand."

The instruction is to call on the help of the wrathful deities for protection. Even though we were afraid of them when they appeared earlier on, now that we are in such desperate straits, we have another opportunity to understand their profound meaning as the embodiments of the most powerful energy of our own awakened nature. If we have previously meditated on a wrathful form, it is best to visualize that one. Otherwise we can call on the Great Supreme Heruka or on Hayagriva or Vajrapani, wrathful manifestations of the Padma and Vajra families, whose images would be well known to anyone familiar with vajrayana. It does not really matter which deity is chosen; the point is that we should be able to call it to mind immediately and vividly in an emergency. The deity should be imagined "with a huge body and bulging limbs, standing in a terrifying attitude of wrath that crushes all evil forces into dust. Separated from the avengers by his adhishthana and compassion, you will have the power to choose a womb door. This is the true, profound secret of the instruction, so understand it well."

This meditation removes the immediate, overwhelming sense of fear and danger, so that we can pause and give thought to our next life. Of the four different ways of being born, birth from a womb and birth from an egg are similar in resulting from the union of two parents. Insects and other primitive organisms were believed to be spontaneously produced from warmth and moisture, for instance, inside a dung heap, which attracts the gandharva by its smell. Other sentient beings with immaterial, mental bodies, like gods, hungry ghosts, evil spirits, and hell-beings, are miraculously born without any outside agency. Gods of the formless realm arise from the attainment of samadhi. In the volatile state of the bardo, it is possible to enter lower kinds of existence through a sudden transformation in our mental attitude, so we should guard against this happening. The best protection is mahamudra meditation on the emptiness of whatever appears, but if we cannot rest in that realization, we should simply try to understand the illusory nature of everything and watch it all unfold without being drawn in. As a last resort, we should at least avoid feeling attracted to anything and meditate on Avalokiteshvara.

Even at this late stage, it is still possible to perform transference to a pure land to complete our progress on the path. Depending on previous connections, this might be the realm of one of the five buddhas, or of Guru Rinpoche or the future Buddha Maitreya, but the ideal of many Buddhists is to go to Amitabha's Realm of Bliss. Transference is achieved by intense concentration on the resolve to escape samsara and the longing to go to that particular pure land. As soon as we think of our chosen pure land with complete faith, we shall instantly find ourselves there.

If transference is not successful, then the only course left is to choose a suitable womb to enter, even though it is "an impure, samsaric womb door." It is important not to be deceived by our own preconceptions under the influence of karma. If we have karmic tendencies toward birth in a revolting dung heap, it will seem sweet-smelling and attractive. Just as in life, it is very easy to think that a certain course of action will bring us happiness when everyone else can plainly see that it will be disastrous, or to reject a more difficult choice that is really for the best. "Even if a womb door seems good, do not trust it, and even if it seems bad, do not dislike it. The true, profound, essential secret is to enter into the supreme state of equilibrium in which there is no good or bad, acceptance or rejection, passion or aggression."

We should make a firm resolve to be born in a situation where we can practice dharma and be of benefit to all living beings. This might mean being born into a position of power and influence, either worldly or spiritual, or simply as the child of a religious family whose practice is pure and genuine. Then, when we find suitable parents, we should think of the mother's womb as a divine palace and enter it requesting all the buddhas and bodhisattvas for their adhishthana. Even if we cannot manage that, at the very least we should enter a womb with faith and confidence:

> O child of awakened family, if you do not know how to choose a womb door and cannot part from passion and aggression, whatever of these experiences may arise, call on the three jewels and take refuge in them. Supplicate the Lord of Great Compassion. Go on with your head held high. Give up attachment and longing for the friends and family, sons and daughters, you have left behind; they cannot help you. Enter now into the blue light of the human realm or the white light of the realm of the gods; enter the jeweled palaces and the pleasure gardens.

This is the final instruction of *Liberation through Hearing*. It ends by emphasizing once again the great value and usefulness of reading it aloud to those who have died. With so many different instructions pointing out the nature of the bardo experiences, "like the steps of a ladder," people of all levels of understanding will recognize at one stage or another, or else achieve a good rebirth where they will meet a true spiritual friend and teacher. It is easy to reach and influence the consciousness of the dead, because they have mental and not physical bodies. They have supernatural perception, extremely clear intelligence, and the power to travel instantly wherever they wish, so however far away they have wandered, they will come when they are called and listen to the teachings. This responsiveness of the mind in the bardo is compared to floating a huge tree trunk in water in order to transport it easily, while on dry land even a hundred men would not be able to move it.

Not only should *Liberation through Hearing* be read aloud to the dead but everyone should read it for themselves, make sure they really understand its meaning, and learn the important points by heart, especially when death is near. "This teaching does not need any practice; it is a profound instruction that liberates just by being seen or heard or read." Now we can appreciate the meaning of this statement, which has been repeated so often. It does not mean that we need do no practice of any kind during this life, but that this teaching, because of its special nature, needs no specific preliminary training to be effective. The instructions point out the nature of the mind so clearly and directly that they easily link to whatever we have previously practiced or realized. In addition, they are imbued with the power of adhishthana flowing to us through a long lineage of awakened beings: from the primordial buddha mind itself, through Shakyamuni Buddha, the Precious Guru Padmakara, the discoverer Karma Lingpa, right down to the great masters of our own time, such as Trungpa Rinpoche, who transmit them in a way that speaks to our hearts. As the closing words say: "Even if the buddhas of the past, present, and future were to search, they would not find a better teaching than this."

In relation to everyday life, the bardo of existence represents each new moment just as it is about to arise: every thought, every action, and every form of expression we make. It is conditioned by the past and in turn shapes the future. But the chain of cause and effect is not unalterable; it can be interrupted and transformed by recognizing its illusory nature and by tapping into the inconceivable energy of our natural awakened state.

We can most easily catch the moment of coming into existence when an emotional mood or frame of mind is starting to develop. We are not yet committed to the emerging feeling of anger, jealousy, or desire, whatever it may be, and we can see that if it is allowed to manifest, it will cause suffering. It may still be possible at this stage to avert it and make a direct connection with our basic sanity and goodness. One of the most effective ways of doing this is to remember our deity or spiritual guide, whatever tradition we follow. Often the stronger the emotion, the greater opportunity there is for a sudden glimpse of clarity. The intense energy of the poisons is transmuted into a powerful feeling of the presence of the wrathful protecting deities, forcefully cutting off the flow of negative karma. Sacred vision is the all-important practice, seeing the whole environment as a pure land and ourselves and all the other beings in it as deities.

We may wish we could stop the future's unfolding and go back to the past. But at every moment, the past dies and we cannot return to it, just as we cannot reenter our old bodies after death. The sense of ego depends on clinging to the past. By seeing this clearly and letting go, we can prevent our past mistakes from repeating themselves over and over.

If positive patterns emerge in our mindstream, we may feel full of joy and hope, waking up in a cheerful mood, and looking forward to the next phase in our lives. Then we should try not to enter it blindly and selfishly, but make use of it to increase our understanding and to benefit others and mentally share our happiness with all sentient beings. If we have no choice but to enter a painful situation, we can make an aspiration to take the suffering of all beings into our own pain.

As Trungpa Rinpoche put it, the essential quality of this bardo is the threshold between grasping with hunger and giving up hope. Hunger means grasping at solidity, permanence, a form that will define us and make us real; the ego continually wants to reinforce its existence, to recreate itself and fulfill itself. Giving up means relaxing into the openness of being where the magical play of forms takes place, as in a dance.

The three kinds of bardo experience that we encounter when we die reveal the three dimensions of the awakened state. At the final moment of the bardo of dying, we come face-to-face with the luminous emptiness of dharmakaya, our essential nature. In the bardo of dharmata, we experience the visions of our innate deities, the expressive energy of the sambhogakaya. At the end of the bardo of existence, we take on a bodily form, the manifestation of nirmanakaya. According to our degree of recognition at any stage, we can reach a corresponding level of awakening, until we are finally able to recognize the basic luminosity, like the meeting of a long-separated mother and child.

Everything that is not the awakened state is bardo; we are always in a bardo state, just as the three kayas are always present in our lives. As the past dissolves, the mind merges with the nonexistence of everything that exists, the omnipresent openness of space, the totality from which all phenomena arise and to which they return: the dharmakaya. In the gap between the disappearance of one thought and the arising of the next, the mind rests in the state of clarity, luminous awareness vibrant with the magical display of energy: the sambhogakaya. As each new moment of consciousness arises, it gives form to the mind's natural awakened qualities and brings them to life in this world as the continual manifestation of body, speech, and mind: the nirmanakaya.

Recognition is the keynote of this whole teaching, but we cannot recognize what we have never met. So its message to us during this life is to get to know all these manifestations of mind while there is still time. All meditation is about getting to know the mind: first, our individual minds, and then the essence of mind itself. There is no bardo outside the mind, no gods or demons outside the mind, no existence or awakening outside the mind. If we learn to know our mind during this life, we shall understand that the same mind continues after death, and that whatever occurs after death also happens here and now.

After the verse for the bardo of existence, the *Root Verses of the Six Bardos* ends with a final stanza, admonishing us not to keep returning to samsara time after time with nothing to show for it:

Heedless mind without a thought of death's approach,
Now that the meaningless business of life is accomplished,
To come back empty again this time is utterly deluded!
Recognition is the sacred, divine dharma that you need,

So why not practice divine dharma at this very moment?
Thus have the great siddhas spoken:
If you do not keep your guru's teaching in your heart
Will you not be a traitor to yourself?

Without the practice that makes recognition possible, it is doubtful that we shall actually see any of the appearances that are described in such detail. These descriptions are meant for people who are able to retain some level of awareness through death, to clarify what is taking place and remind them of their previous experience. Others may perhaps be aware of dazzling light and flashing colors, or tremendous waves of sound. They will probably feel buffeted by rapidly changing emotions without understanding their cause. There will be feelings of intense awe, of attraction and desire in one direction, and hatred and terror in another, but above all of complete bewilderment. Everything the text describes will be present since it is naturally within the mind: the luminosity of our essential nature is there, our innate deities are there, the six realms are there, and the karmic effects of our past actions are there, but we shall not perceive them clearly or know them for what they are.

The events of the three bardos are expressed here entirely in terms of Buddhist doctrine and to a great extent in specifically dzogchen terms. People of other traditions who are able to maintain some awareness at this time may not necessarily experience everything in the same way. That it is why it is so important to try to understand the inner meaning of the imagery presented here. But, just as we cannot discard the use of language, we cannot discard these symbolic forms. Until we have fully accomplished the ultimate formless realization, naked reality must remain clothed with imagery. Thus the inconceivable awakened state ceaselessly plays through the magical phenomena of life, death, and the bardos and transparently reveals itself to the eye of sacred vision.

Aspiration

The limitless expanse of emptiness
Is luminous with all-pervading light,
In clear mind sky, free from complexities,
The rainbow of phenomena shines forth.

Where neither confusion nor freedom has ever existed,
The father and mother of all, Universal Goodness,
Dwell in the secret great bliss beyond thought
Yet reveal the miracles of love's unceasing play.

Whatever the eye sees is sacred vision,
Whatever the ear hears, the voice of truth,
Whatever thought arises in the mind,
Its own self-liberated self-awareness.

May all awaken to that great perfection!

Notes

Chapter 1. A Book of the Living

1. Translations currently available are: W. Y. Evans-Wentz, *The Tibetan Book of the Dead*, London, Oxford University Press, 1927; Francesca Fremantle and Chögyam Trungpa, *The Tibetan Book of the Dead*, Berkeley, Shambhala Publications, 1975; Robert A. F. Thurman, *The Tibetan Book of the Dead*, Bantam (USA) and Aquarian/ Thorsons (UK), 1994; Stephen Hodge with Martin Boord, *The Illustrated Tibetan Book of the Dead*, London, Thorsons, 1999.

2. This is addressed by Trungpa Rinpoche at the end of his commentary to our translation *The Tibetan Book of the Dead*, pp. 27–29, and in Chögyam Trungpa, *The Heart of the Buddha*, Boston, Shambhala, 1991, Chapter 9 "Acknowleging Death." Sogyal Rinpoche, *The Tibetan Book of Living and Dying*, London, Rider and Harper San Francisco, 1992, covers all aspects of Buddhist practice in life and death, with particular reference to the bardos and *The Tibetan Book of the Dead*. See also Bokar Rinpoche, *Death and the Art of Dying in Tibetan Buddhism*, San Francisco, Clear-Point Press, 1993.

3. *The Tibetan Book of the Dead*, p. 1.

4. *Guhyasamaja Tantra*, Chapter 5. Adapted from my unpublished doctoral thesis, SOAS, University of London, 1971.

5. *Hevajra Tantra* I. ix. 19. Adapted from the translation by David Snellgrove, *The Hevajra Tantra*, London, Oxford University Press, 1959.

6. Chögyam Trungpa, *Journey Without Goal,* Boulder, Prajna Press, 1981, p. 5.

7. For the history of Tibet, see David Snellgrove and Hugh Richardson, *A Cultural History of Tibet,* London, Weidenfeld and Nicholson, 1968. For Buddhism with particular reference to Tibet, see David Snellgrove, *Indo-Tibetan Buddhism,* London, Serindia, 1987; and John Powers, *Tibetan Buddhism,* Ithaca, Snow Lion, 1995.

8. For translations of his traditional biography, see Yeshe Tsogyal, *The Life and Liberation of Padmasambhava,* Berkeley, Dharma Publishing, 1978; Yeshe Tsogyal, *The Lotus-Born,* Boston, Shambhala, 1993; and W. Y. Evans-Wentz, *The Tibetan Book of the Great Liberation,* London, Oxford University Press, 1954. For Trungpa Rinpoche's teachings on the life of Padmasambhava, see Chögyam Trungpa, *Crazy Wisdom,* Boston, Shambhala, 1991.

9. See Dudjom Rinpoche, *The Nyingma School of Tibetan Buddhism,* Boston, Wisdom Publications, 1991; and Eva M. Dargyay, *The Rise of Esoteric Buddhism in Tibet,* Delhi, Motilal Banarsidass, 1977.

10. Chögyam Trungpa, *Transcending Madness,* Boston, Shambhala, 1992, p. 10.

11. Tenga Rinpoche, *Transition and Liberation,* Osterby, Khampa Buchverlag, 1996, p. 30.

12. Information about these texts and others relating to death can be found in Detlef Ingo Lauf, *Secret Doctrines of the Tibetan Books of the Dead,* Boulder, Shambhala, 1977.

13. In Tibetan, *zab chos zhi khro dgongs pa rang grol* and *kar gling zhi khro.*

14. In Tibetan, *chos nyid bar do'i gsol 'debs thos grol chen mo* and *srid pa'i bar do ngo sprod gsol 'debs thos grol chen mo.*

15. In Tibetan, *bar do thos grol, thos grol chen mo,* and *thos grol.*

Chapter 2. Liberation: Uncoiling in Space

1. I am treating karma as a naturalized English word because it is so well known; Sanskrit words are normally quoted in their uninflected form, which in this case is *karman.*

2. Chögyam Trungpa, *First Thought Best Thought,* Boulder, Shambhala, 1983, p. 1.

Chapter 3. Hearing: The Power of Transmission

1. A very interesting discussion can be found in *Sleeping, Dreaming and Dying,* Dalai Lama, Wisdom Publications, Boston, 1997. See especially pp. 165–170.

2. *The Tibetan Book of the Dead,* p. xi.

Chapter 4. Bardo: The Experience of Nowness

1. This information is taken from an article in the *Sunday Times*, London, January 31, 1999, which included a short extract from the thirty-line poem, "Crow in the Bardo." The papers of the late Ted Hughes are held by Emory University, Atlanta, Georgia. Another poem that shows his interest in the *Tibetan Book of the Dead* is "Examination at the Womb-door," published in Ted Hughes, *Crow*, Faber and Faber, London, 1970.

2. *Transcending Madness*, p. 132.

3. *Transcending Madness*, p. 3.

4. Padmasambhava, *Natural Liberation*, Somerville, Wisdom Publications, 1998. The text is translated by B. Alan Wallace, with a commentary by Gyatrul Rinpoche.

5. See Herbert V. Guenther, *The Life and Teaching of Naropa*, London, Oxford University Press, 1963; Glenn H. Mullin, *Tsongkhapa's Six Yogas of Naropa*, Ithaca, Snow Lion, 1996; and Glenn H. Mullin, *Readings on the Six Yogas of Naropa*, Ithaca, Snow Lion, 1997. For a Nyingma approach to the six yogas related to the bardos, see the final chapter of Thinley Norbu, *White Sail*, Boston, Shambhala, 1992.

6. In Tibetan, *bar do drug gi rtsa tshig*.

7. *Transcending Madness*, p. 62.

8. The life of Naropa is related in Guenther, *The Life and Teaching of Naropa*, and Chögyam Trungpa, *Illusion's Game*, Boston, Shambhala, 1994.

9. *Transcending Madness*, p. 187.

Chapter 5. The Rainbow of Elements

1. Thinley Norbu, *Magic Dance*, New York, Jewel, 1981, is a celebration of the nature of the five dakinis as well as other topics from the point of view of a Nyingmapa yogin.

2. Chögyam Trungpa, *The Sadhana of Mahamudra*. Not commercially available.

3. In Tibetan, *bar do 'phrang sgrol kyi smon lam*.

Chapter 6. The Five-Step Process of Ego

1. See Shenpen Hookham, *The Buddha Within*, Albany, SUNY, 1991.

2. Chögyam Trungpa, *Glimpses of Abhidharma*, Boston, Shambhala, 1975.

Chapter 7. The Display of the Awakened State

1. Chögyam Trungpa, *Orderly Chaos*, Boston, Shambhala, 1991, deals particularly with the mandala principle. Teachings on both the mandala principle and the five families are found in many of his books.

2. See "Five Styles of Creative Expression" in Chögyam Trungpa, *Dharma Art*, Boston, Shambhala, 1996, p. 82.

Chapter 8. Six Styles of Imprisonment

1. There are many excellent books on Hindu mythology, which is too vast and diverse to be contained in any single volume. One of the best works of reference is Alain Daniélou, *The Myths and Gods of India*, Vermont, Inner Traditions International, 1991 (originally published as *Hindu Polytheism*, New York, Bollingen Foundation, 1964). For inspired retellings and interpretations of some of the myths, see Heinrich Zimmer's *Myths and Symbols in Indian Art and Civilization*, New York, Bollingen Foundation, 1946, and *The King and the Corpse*, New York, Bollingen Foundation, 1948. An enjoyable recent adaptation of a selection of stories is Roberto Calasso, *Ka*, London, Jonathan Cape, 1998. I would also recommend any of the books by Wendy Doniger O'Flaherty.

2. Traditional descriptions of the six realms can be found in Gampopa, *The Jewel Ornament of Liberation*, translated by H. V. Guenther, Berkeley, Shambhala, 1971, Chapter 5, and Patrul Rinpoche, *The Words of My Perfect Teacher*, London, Harper Collins, 1994, Chapter 3. Both these books also cover many other aspects of Buddhism.

3. John Milton, *Paradise Lost*, Book I.

4. See especially Chögyam Trungpa, *The Myth of Freedom*, Boulder, Shambhala, 1976. Other chapters on and references to the six realms can be found in many of his books.

5. See Sarat Chandra Das, *A Tibetan-English Dictionary*, p. 1132.

6. These are *vetalas*, about which there is a marvelous collection of stories in Sanskrit. Some of these appear in *The King and the Corpse* (see note 1), and they are translated in full in Sivadasa, *The Five-and-Twenty Tales of the Genie*, New Delhi, Penguin, 1995.

7. An excellent source of information is Terry Clifford, *Tibetan Buddhist Medicine and Psychiatry*, Wellingborough, Aquarian Press, 1984.

8. In Tibetan, *brgya phyag sdig sgrib rang grol zhes bya ba bar do thos grol gyi cha lag* and *chos spyod bag chags zhes bya ba bar do thos grol gyi cha lag*, respectively.

9. See *Transcending Madness*, pp. 244 and 253.

10. *Natural Liberation*, p. 150.

11. *Transcending Madness*, p. 295.

12. *The Tibetan Book of the Dead*, p. 10.

13. *Transcending Madness*, p. 60.

14. *The Myth of Freedom*, p. 26.

Chapter 9. The Threefold Pattern of the Path

1. Trungpa Rinpoche's teachings on the trikaya as the path, exemplified in the life of Padmasambhava, can be found in Chögyam Trungpa, *Crazy Wisdom*, Boston, Shambhala, 1991.

2. William Blake, *The Marriage of Heaven and Hell.*

3. *Journey Without Goal*, p. 72.

4. *Journey Without Goal*, p. 75.

5. In Tibetan, *rtsa, rlung,* and *thig le,* respectively.

6. The Tibetan names for the main nadis are *dbu ma* (madhyama), *kun 'dar ma* (avadhuti), *rkyang ma* (lalana), and *ro ma* (rasana).

7. In Sanskrit and Tibetan, these are *pranavayu* (*srog 'dzin rlung*), *vyanavayu* (*khyab byed rlung*), *udanavayu* (*gyen rgyu rlung*), *samanavayu* (*mnyam rgyu rlung*), and *apanavayu* (*thur sel rlung*).

Chapter 10. The Great Perfection

1. For Trungpa Rinpoche's teachings on the nine yanas, see Chögyam Trungpa, *The Lion's Roar*, Boston, Shambhala, 1992. For Nyingma and dzogchen in general, see Dudjom Rinpoche, *The Nyingma School of Tibetan Buddhism*; Patrul Rinpoche, *The Words of My Perfect Teacher*; and Longchen Rabjam, *The Practice of Dzogchen*, translated by Tulku Thondup, Ithaca, Snow Lion, 1989.

2. In Tibetan, *sems sde, klong sde,* and *man ngag sde,* respectively.

3. Some Tibetan texts give the term *mahasanti* in the Sanskrit version of their titles, and the great Nyingmapa scholar Rongzom Pandita (eleventh to twelfth centuries) proposed that this should read *mahasandhi,* meaning "great union." Namkhai Norbu suggests that *mahasanti* is a Prakrit, or dialect, form and need not be amended. In that case, it would mean "great peace." One would expect to find *mahasampanna,* which is given as the Sanskrit equivalent in Sarat Chandra Das's *Tibetan-English Dictionary,* but without quoting a source. For further information, see John Myrdhin Reynolds, *The Golden Letters*, Ithaca, Snow Lion, 1996, pp. 264–265. This book contains excellent sections on the origins, view, and practice of dzogchen, as well as translations of some of its most important basic texts.

4. *Guhyasamaja Tantra,* Chapter 2.

5. Luminosity is *'od gsal* in Tibetan and *prabhasvara* in Sanskrit; clarity is *gsal ba* in Tibetan and *svaccha* (with other possible alternatives) in Sanskrit. There is a potential problem in translation from Tibetan alone, because theoretically both words can be abbreviated in certain circumstances to *gsal.* However, it seems to me that they are generally distinguished, and certainly so in *Liberation through Hearing.* When I was working on this text with Trungpa Rinpoche, I did not appreciate the

distinction and so did not ask him about it; he used only "luminosity" at that time. By contrast, Rigdzin Shikpo prefers to use only "clarity" and tells me that Trungpa Rinpoche also preferred it when they were working together in the 1960s.

6. *Transcending Madness*, p. 290.

7. *Transcending Madness*, p. 254.

8. *Transcending Madness*, p. 299.

9. *Guhyasamaja Tantra*, Chapter 15.

10. In dictionaries, the Sanskrit is generally given as *urmi*, "wave." In Tulku Thondup Rinpoche, *Hidden Teachings of Tibet*, London, Wisdom Publications, 1986, p. 268, it is given in the glossary as *abhyantara*, "interior," but elsewhere translated as "great expanse."

11. *The Tibetan Book of the Dead*, p. 1.

12. In Tibetan spelling, *khregs chod* and *thod rgal*, respectively.

13. In Tibetan, *rig pa ngo sprod gcer mthong rang grol*. A full translation of it is included in Thurman, *The Tibetan Book of the Dead* and in Evans-Wentz, *The Tibetan Book of the Great Liberation*. John Myrdhin Reynolds, *Self-Liberation through Seeing with Naked Awareness*, New York, Station Hill Press, 1989, presents the Tibetan text, translation, and commentary. I have very gratefully made use of this text for my own translated excerpts, as it is not included in any of the collections of the *kar gling zhi khro* to which I have access.

Chapter 11. Luminosity of Death

1. Trungpa Rinpoche, *The Sadhana of Mahamudra*.

2. Apart from Trungpa Rinpoche's *Transcending Madness* and his commentary to the *Tibetan Book of the Dead*, extensive information on these three bardos can be found in the following books: Tsele Natsok Rangdrol, *The Mirror of Mindfulness*, Boston, Shambhala, 1989, and its commentary, Chökyi Nyima Rinpoche, *The Bardo Guidebook*, Hong Kong and Kathmandu, Rangjung Yeshe Publications, 1991; Lama Lodö, *Bardo Teachings*, Ithaca, Snow Lion, 1982; Bokar Rinpoche, *Death and the Art of Dying*, San Francisco, ClearPoint Press, 1983; Tenga Rinpoche, *Transition and Liberation*; D. I. Lauf, *Secret Doctines of the Tibetan Books of the Dead*. Chapters on the three bardos are also included in Sogyal Rinpoche, *The Tibetan Book of Living and Dying*; Tulku Urgyan Rinpoche, *Repeating the Words of the Buddha*, Kathmandu, Rangjung Yeshe Publications, 1991, and *Rainbow Painting*, Rangjung Yeshe Publications, 1995; Kalu Rinpoche, *The Dharma*, Albany, SUNY, 1986, *Secret Buddhism*, San Francisco, ClearPoint Press, 1995, and *Luminous Mind*, Boston, Wisdom, 1997; Thinley Norbu, *The Small Golden Key*, 1997, and *White Sail*, Boston, Shambhala, 1992; Tulku Thondup, *Enlightened Journey*, Boston, Shambhala, 1995.

3. In Tibetan, *'chi ltas mtshan ma rang grol*. Glenn Mullin has translated this text with eight others relating to the subject of death. See Glenn H. Mullin, *Death and Dying: The Tibetan Tradition*, Boston, Arkana, 1986.

4. *The Tibetan Book of the Dead*, p. 3.

5. In Sanskrit, *prakriti*, meaning "natural, original, primary"; in Tibetan, *rang bzhin rtog pa* or *rang bzhin kun rtog*, meaning "natural thought or concept."

6. *The Tibetan Book of the Dead*, pp. 4–5.

7. Further details of the yoga practices and their relationship to the bardos can be found in Daniel Cozort, *Highest Yoga Tantra*, Ithaca, Snow Lion, 1986; Lati Rinbochay and Jeffrey Hopkins, *Death, Intermediate State and Rebirth in Tibetan Buddhism*, London, Rider, 1979; Geshe Ngawang Dhargyey, *Kalachakra Tantra*, Dharamsala, Library of Tibetan Works and Archives, 1994.

8. Often known by its Tibetan name, *powa* (*'pho ba*); the Sanskrit is *samkranti*. For Nyingma teachings on transference, see Patrul Rinpoche, *The Words of My Perfect Teacher*, Part Three, and Thinley Norbu, *White Sail*.

9. Lama Lodö, *Bardo Teachings*, and Bokar Rinpoche, *Death and the Art of Dying*.

10. Chögyam Trungpa, *The Heart of the Buddha*, Boston, Shambhala, 1991, p. 168. Many of Trungpa Rinpoche's books contain references to mahamudra, but see especially *Illusion's Game*.

11. In Sanskrit, *yuganaddha*; in Tibetan, *zung 'jug*. This very important term is often translated as "union" or "unity," which I feel are too general and can be used for many other words. "Conjunction" might be acceptable, especially bearing in mind its alchemical significance. Other helpful translations include "unitive Being" (Guenther), "integration" (Thurman), "coalescence" (Dorje and Kapstein), and "both-at-once" (Hookham), but I prefer Snellgrove's "two-in-one." The Sanskrit term literally means "joined in a pair." It implies the simultaneous coexistence of two distinct and equal elements, rather than their merging or dissolving. As well as referring to appearance and emptiness, it is frequently used for the experience of bliss and emptiness or for the realization that the relative and absolute truths are not separate.

Chapter 12. Invincible Peace

1. In Sanskrit, *anabhoga*; in Tibetan, *lhun grub*.

2. This refers to p. 39, paragraph 3, in our translation. The other current translations in English are fairly similar.

3. *The Tibetan Book of the Dead*, p. 15.

4. *The Tibetan Book of the Dead*, p. 12.

5. The mandala of the hundred peaceful and wrathful deities originates in the

Mayajala (*Net of Magical Illusion*) cycle of Nyingma tantras, whose basic text is the *Guhyagarbha Tantra* (*Secret Essence Tantra*). This has been translated with commentaries by Gyurme Dorje in his unpublished doctoral thesis: *A Critical Edition of the Guhyagarbha-tantra*, SOAS, University of London, 1988. While the most important deities are the same, some of the details of their iconography and the lesser figures in the mandala differ from those in *Liberation through Hearing* and its associated texts. See also, Herbert Guenther, *Matrix of Mystery*, Boulder, Shambhala, 1984.

6. *The Tibetan Book of the Dead*, p. 13.

7. For a comprehensive and beautifully illustrated book on iconography and its meanings, including many attributes of the peaceful and wrathful deities, see Robert Beer, *The Encyclopedia of Tibetan Symbols and Motifs*, London, Serindia Publications, 1999.

8. *Journey Without Goal*, p. 111.

9. *The Tibetan Book of the Dead*, p. 18.

10. These strange creatures can clearly be seen in many older Tibetan paintings. For instance, see Steven M. Kossak and Jane Casey Singer, *Sacred Visions*, New York, The Metropolitan Museum of Art, 1998, plates 4, 23c, 25, and 36c, the last of which also shows a garuda above Amoghasiddhi's head.

11. In the associated terma text of *Liberation through Wearing*, she is referred to as *zhal zas ma*, the Tibetan form of Naivedya, although her mantra contains *nritye*.

12. *The Tibetan Book of the Dead*, p. 23.

13. *The Tibetan Book of the Dead*, p. 23.

Chapter 13. Crazy Wisdom

1. For a matching pair of thangkas showing the peaceful and wrathful deities, in which the vidyadharas are split between them, see W. Essen and T. Thingo, *Die Götter des Himalaya*, Munich, Prestel-Verlag, 1989, Vol. I, plates 119 and 120. For an example where they are included among the wrathful deities, see Detlef Ingo Lauf, *Tibetan Sacred Art*, Berkeley, Shambhala, 1976, plate 6.

2. *The Tibetan Book of the Dead*, p. 24.

3. An excellent book on the dakini principle is Judith Simmer-Brown's *Dakini's Warm Breath*, Boston, Shambhala, 2001.

4. *Illusion's Game*, p. 116.

5. *Dharma Art*, p. 35.

6. William Blake, *The Marriage of Heaven and Hell*.

7. *Dharma Art*, p. 47.

8. *Dharma Art*, p. 43.

9. *The Myth of Freedom*, p. 156.

10. *Dharma Art*, p. 36.

11. In Tibetan, *ye shes 'chol ba*, an expression used particularly in dzogchen.

12. *Glimpses of Abhidharma*, pp. 101–102.

Chapter 14. Wrathful Compassion

1. This refers to another text in the same terma cycle: *Liberation through Wearing, the Self-Liberation of the Skandhas*. In Tibetan, *btags grol phung po rang grol*. It consists mainly of the mantras of the hundred peaceful and wrathful deities.

2. The earliest form of this legend occurs in the *Sarvatathagatatattvasamgraha* and is given in Snellgrove, *Indo-Tibetan Buddhism*, pp. 134–141. A later form can be found in Yeshe Tsogyal, *The Life and Liberation of Padmasambhava*, Cantos 5 and 6.

Rudra, meaning "howler" or "roarer," was a name applied in the Vedas to many deities and principles, such as the winds and breath. It was also the earliest name of the deity who later developed into Shiva, the Auspicious, one of the most important gods of later Hinduism. Belief in such a deity as a real external being goes directly against the central idea of Buddhism, so as Mahadeva, the Great God, he was regarded as the personification of mistaken views that prevent awakening. To be fair, this is more the Buddhist perception of Hindu belief than genuine Hinduism, especially with regard to tantra. At the same time, he had another, quite different, image. From the earliest days, Rudra-Shiva was an outsider among the orthodox pantheon, the most spiritual of all, who penetrated most deeply beyond the samsaric nature of the gods. He represents the principle of dissolution, which outwardly is seen as destruction, but inwardly is the return of consciousness to its primordial state of true knowledge. He is the Lord of Yoga, the prototype of the tantric yogin, and he came to represent the liberated consciousness. Therefore, as a symbolic figure, he may have been perceived as the greatest rival and threat to vajrayana at a time when the two tantric traditions were developing in close relationship to each other. However, the Buddhist legend bears absolutely no resemblance to any of the Hindu legends of Rudra or Shiva. He does share some iconographic features with the herukas—the moon in his hair, the skull garland, the tiger skin round his waist, the ash smeared on his body, and the serpents coiled around his limbs—but he does not have wings or the ugly form of a rakshasa.

3. In Sanskrit, *mahottara heruka*; in Tibetan, *che mchog heruka*.

4. In Sanskrit, *krodhadhatvishvari*; in Tibetan, *khro mo dbyings phyug*.

5. *The Lion's Roar*, p. 202.

6. Except for one attested form of Mahakala as "Lord of the Tent"; see Nebesky-

Wojkowitz, *Oracles and Demons of Tibet*, Graz, Akademische Druck-u. Verlagsanstalt, 1975, p. 51. This may also be a Nyingma image.

7. As the nine sentiments are so important in the arts of India, it may be helpful to list them in Sanskrit with their Tibetan equivalents (*nyams dgu*): erotic (*shringara, sgeg pa*); heroic (*vira, dpa' ba*); revulsion/repulsive (*bibhatsa, mi sdug pa*); humorous (*hasya, dgod pa*); wrathful (*raudra, drag shul*); fearful/frightening (*bhayanaka, 'jigs su rung ba*, alternatively sometimes given as *gshe ba*, abusive); compassionate (*karuna, snying rje*); wonder/wonderful (*adbhuta, rngams pa*); and peaceful (*shanta, zhi ba*). In other tantric contexts, they may be interpreted differently; for instance, see Alex Wayman, *Yoga of the Guhyasamajatantra*, Delhi, Motilal Benarsidass, 1977, pp. 327–328. For source references, see Herbert V. Guenther, *Matrix of Mystery*, Boulder, Shambhala, 1984, p. 271, notes 16 and 17.

8. The correspondence of the eight gauris and eight pishachis to the consciousnesses and their fields is taken from Tulku Thondup, *Enlightened Living*, Boston, Shambhala, 1990, pp. 134–135, notes 16 and 17.

9. In Tibetan, *phra men ma*, pronounced *tramenma*. Although I have not found it in dictionaries, I was told by the late Khunu Rinpoche in 1975 that *pishachi* is the Sanskrit equivalent. Khunu Rinpoche was not only a great yogin, but also a renowned Sanskrit scholar.

10. Some versions call her "tiger-headed," which we followed in the *Tibetan Book of the Dead*. However, the majority of blockprints appear to have "horse-headed." It is easy to confuse them in Tibetan (*rta gdong* and *stag gdong*), both in written and spoken form.

11. The list of twenty-eight yoginis in the *Guhyagarbha Tantra* does not entirely agree with the list given here. It, too, gives the names only in Tibetan; half are the same, while a few more appear under alternative names, but the rest cannot definitely be said to correspond. In his translation, Gyurme Dorje gives their names in Sanskrit, obtained from their mantras. The commentary describes all of them as the consorts of various major and minor Hindu gods. However, many of these identifications seem rather questionable and do not accord with Hindu sources, so I have not made use of them here.

12. See H. C. Das, *Tantricism: A Study of the Yogini Cult*, New Delhi, Sterling, 1981.

13. In the *Tibetan Book of the Dead*, we named her Lobha, but Trungpa Rinpoche was not sure of her identity. The Tibetan is *gtogs 'dod*, an unusual word, which he translated as "greed." Evans-Wentz calls her the Goddess of Inquisitiveness, evidently from a variant Tibetan reading of *rtogs 'dod*. In the *Guhyagarbha Tantra*, she is listed as *'jug sred mo* (Vaishnavi), while in the commentary she is called *rtogs 'dod*. Lauf (*Secret Doctrines*, p. 151) lists her as Vaishnavi, although I am not clear which text he is using as a basis for this.

14. In the *Tibetan Book of the Dead*, we called her Mahahastini, Great Elephant, but she is more likely to be Mahanasa (a literal translation of her Tibetan name), listed among the dakinis of the *Chakrasamvara Tantra*. In the *Guhyagarbha Tantra*, Gyurme Dorje gives her the Sanskrit name of Bhujana, which again means "elephant."

Chapter 15. At the Womb Door

1. This line can be translated and interpreted in several ways; I have translated it in accordance with the explanation that follows in the text. A different traditional interpretation can be found in Lati and Hopkins, *Death, Intermediate State and Rebirth*, p. 55.

2. Accounts of the development of the embryo can be found, for example, in Clifford, *Tibetan Buddhist Medicine and Psychiatry*; Dhargyey, *Kalachakra Tantra*; Lati and Hopkins, *Death, Intermediate State and Rebirth*.

Illustration Credits

1. The Wheel of Life; painting by Gonkar Gyatso, acrylic on canvas.
2. The Buddhas of the Five Families; painting by Gonkar Gyatso, acrylic on canvas.
3. Samantabhadra and Samantabhadri; painting by Francesca Fremantle, oil on canvas.
4. The Peaceful and Wrathful Deities of the Bardo; Tibetan thangka painting, nineteenth century, artist unknown.
5. Vidyadhara and Dakini; painting by Gonkar Gyatso, watercolor on paper.
6. The Wrathful Deities of the Bardo; Tibetan thangka painting, nineteenth century, artist unknown.
7. The Wrathful Deities of the Bardo; Tibetan thangka painting, eighteenth century, artist unknown.
8. Avalokiteshvara; Tibetan thangka painting, nineteenth century, artist unknown.

All illustrations are from the author's collection. Photography by Alan Tabor.

Index

as light, 111–12
preceded by precipitating experience, 68
awareness
as aspect of crazy wisdom,
295–96
as ultimate nature of mind,
197–98

bardo(s). *See also* dharmata, bardo of;
dying, bardo of; existence,
bardo of; this life, bardo of
concept of, 53–54
of dream, 58, 62–64
experiences of, 366–67
illusory body as, 162
implications of, 54–55
of meditation, 57, 58–62, 172
pervasiveness of, 367
practice within, 55
related to six realms, 67–68, 145
the self in, 46
six states of, 55
as word, 53
bardo visions. *See* visions
Bhaksini (the Devourer), 337
bindu(s)
expanding, realm of, 263
indestructible, 192–93, 230–32
subtle body and, 186, 191–92
when dying, 229–32
birth
four ways of, 363
link in chain of cause and effect,
24–25
Blake, William, 60, 177, 292
bliss, nature of, 259
Blissful Realm, 278. *See also* Sukhavati
blue, qualities of, 86

Blue Dakini, 203
bodhi, as term, 21
bodhichitta, 35
bodhisattva(s)
eight male and eight female, 108,
269, 270
manifesting in bardo of dharmata,
268–70, 273, 276–77, 280–
81, 299
as term, 13, 299
body
coarse level of, 185
corresponding to nirmanakaya,
180–82
identified with head, 191
as part of fivefold division, 117,
190
subtle level of, 186–87, 191–92
body, speech, mind. *See also individual
components*; levels of density
concept of, 180–82
transforming, 183, 184
Brahma
giving birth to pretas, 150
ruler of worlds of form/formless-
ness, 170
brahmarandhra (Brahma aperature),
231, 242
Brahmi (Consort of Brahma), 335
breath, air element and, 83–84
buddha families. *See* families of buddhas
Buddha family, 140, 159, 263. *See also*
Vairochana
element/skandha of, 134, 136
and gods realm, 170–71
poison of, 135
positive/negative attributes of,
134–36
time/season/color of, 136–37

Buddha Heruka, iconography of,
315–16, 321–22
Buddha-Lochana. *See* Lochana
buddha-nature, concept of, 35
Buddha Shakyamuni, 168, 241
enlightenment of, 171–72
in human realm, 285
manifestations in the six realms,
148–49, 155, 159, 162–63,
166–67, 172
as teacher, 8–9
tempted by Mara, 117–18
buddhas of the five families, 111. *See
also* families of buddhas; *individual buddhas*
during bardo of dharmata, 95, 116
as masculine principle, 258–59
Buddha Wrathful Lady, iconography
of, 316, 321–22
Buddhism. *See also* Tibetan Buddhism
development/yanas of, 9–11
as religion, 9
three indispensable aspects of,
56–57

candle flame, as secret sign, 227
chain of cause and effect, twelve links
of, 24–28
chakras
forehead/crown, 228
head, 189, 190
heart, 189–90, 225
as meditative focal points, 190–91
navel, 190, 224
secret place, 190, 227
subtle level and, 188–91
throat, 189, 226
Chandali (the Chandala Woman),
330

Chandra (Moon), 337
charnel ground, significance of,
302–4
Chauri (the Thief), 329
Chögyam Trungpa Rinpoche, 41
on bardo, 54, 55
bardo visions and, 256, 257
on Buddha-Lochana, 88
on Buddha Mamaki, 88
on clear light, 199
and crazy wisdom, 295–96
experience of luminosity, 231
and hopelessness, 210
on intellect, 314
on liberation, 48
on magic, 265
on natural symbolism, 241, 291,
293–94
on space, 202
on symbolism of *Tibetan Book of the
Dead*, 306
use of *transmission* and, 48
on vajra mind, 184
on vajrayana, 15
and vidyadharas, 290
yanas and, 12
clarity, luminosity and, 198–99
coarse level, 71, 185–86
cold hells, 147
color. *See also individual colors*
symbolism and, 294
compassion, emptiness and, 39–40
completion stage, 60–61, 232–33
instruction during bardo of dharmata, 252
concentration, as conditioning factor,
103
conditioning
factors of, 101–4

samaya commitments, abandoning,
297
Samaya-Tara, 227, 240
in bardo of dharmata, 278–79,
281, 282
devi of air, 89
sambhogakaya (body of enjoyment),
174, 175–76
corresponding to speech, 182–83
deity yoga and, 233
manifested in Amitabha, 218
nature of, 177–79
as subtle level, 186
samsara. *See also* realms of existence/
samsara; wheel of life
contemplation on, 244
deities of, 59, 89–90
described, 22–23
reversed, 260
stages of cause and effect, 23–28
three characteristics of, 30–35
samskara, as word, 100–101
Sarasvati, 335
Sarvanivaranavishkambhin (Remover
of All Obstacles), in bardo of
dharmata, 279, 280
sarvastivada, 10
second day, during bardo of dharmata, 267–72
secret essence, 72. *See also* very subtle
level
secret place chakra, 190
when dying, 227
secret signs, 225, 226, 227, 228
associated with dying, 222–23
progression of, 228
self. *See also* ego
allied with karma, 45–46
arising of sense of, 203–4

in the bardo, 46
and great self, 35–36
as illusion of skandhas, 93–94
modern/psychological concept of,
36–37
and nonself, 33–35
self-absorption, and gods realm,
170–71
self-awareness, as dzogchen term, 209
self-knowledge, as dzogchen term,
208–9
self-liberation, as dzogchen term, 209
Self-Liberation through Naked Sight, 222
on trikaya, 174–75
on true nature of mind, 206–13
*Self-Liberation through Signs and Omens of
Death*, 219, 220–21
sensation, link in chain of cause and
effect, 26
senses. *See also individual senses*
dharmas of, 92, 96
dissolution of, 228–29
relationship to elements, 72–73,
79, 82, 85
senses, six. *See also individual senses*
link in chain of cause and effect,
26
sentiments, nine, 320
seventh day, during bardo of dharmata, 296–306
sexual organs. *See* secret place
Shakyamuni. *See* Buddha Shakyamuni
Shanti (Peace), 336
Shatakratu, in gods realm, 172, 285
Shiva Mahadeva (the Great God),
335
Shmashani (the Charnel Ground
Dweller), 330–31
Shrigalamukha (the Jackal-Headed),
331